Solidarity and Power

Religion in the Modern World

Series Editors

Kwok Pui-lan, Episcopal Divinity School
Joerg Rieger, Vanderbilt University

This series explores how various religious traditions wrestle with the dynamic and changing role of religion in the modern world and examines how past changes reflect on today's critical issues. Accessibly and engagingly written, books in this series will look at secularization, global society, gender, race, class, sexuality and their relation to religious life and religious movements.

Titles in the Series:

Solidarity and Power

Feminist Approaches to Religious Ethics

Edited by

Rosemary Kellison and Shannon Dunn

BLOOMSBURY ACADEMIC

NEW YORK • LONDON • OXFORD • NEW DELHI • SYDNEY

BLOOMSBURY ACADEMIC
Bloomsbury Publishing Inc, 1385 Broadway, New York, NY 10018, USA
Bloomsbury Publishing Plc, 50 Bedford Square, London, WC1B 3DP, UK
Bloomsbury Publishing Ireland, 29 Earlsfort Terrace, Dublin 2, D02 AY28, Ireland

BLOOMSBURY, BLOOMSBURY ACADEMIC and the Diana logo are trademarks of
Bloomsbury Publishing Plc

First published in the United States of America 2025

Cover designer: Diana Nuhn
Cover image © Raymond Boyd, Getty Images

Library of Congress Cataloging-in-Publication Data Available

ISBN: HB: 978-1-5381-8757-9
PB: 978-1-5381-8758-6
ePDF: 979-8-7651-5490-8
eBook: 978-1-5381-8759-3

Typeset by Deanta Global Publishing Services, Chennai, India
Printed and bound in the United States of America

For product safety related questions contact productsafety@bloomsbury.com.

To find out more about our authors and books visit www.bloomsbury.com and
sign up for our newsletters.

Contents

Section 4 Challenging Exclusionary Forms of Solidarity

Introduction

Rosemary Kellison and Shannon Dunn

It is perhaps unsurprising that Americans are increasingly appealing to the concept of solidarity in a time characterized by what can feel like an all-out assault on human rights and our ability to build and sustain community. In just the past few years we have experienced the loss of reproductive rights, a coordinated campaign against the rights of trans children and adults to seek medical care and even to openly exist, attempts to ideologically shape the history and culture children learn by rewriting curricula and banning books, widespread refusal to promote public health via vaccination and masking during the COVID pandemic, waves of racist hostility to migrants and refugees, open attacks on our democratic way of life, and more. The prevalence of cell phone cameras has increased our ability to witness violence we otherwise might not have seen, such as police violence against Black Americans and the mass killings of Palestinian civilians. Such events often leave us feeling profoundly disconnected and uncertain of how to relate to one another. Solidarity beckons to us, not only as a means for coming together to challenge these injustices but also as an end: a community, forged across differences, organized around something other than the will to power that characterizes these assaults.

Activists working on all these issues have regularly invoked solidarity in their work. So too have scholars; solidarity has been a recurrent theme of recent work in our field of religious ethics.[1] The authors whose work is collected here share the hope that motivates these appeals to solidarity. Yet, as feminist ethicists, we are also keenly aware of the challenges that can inhibit both the building of solidarity and its efficacy. Feminist approaches to the study of ethics are distinguished by their attention to the relationship between power and morality, the importance of particularity and difference, and the ways that morality is lived in embodied practice. Attempts to build solidarity that ignore these issues are likely to result in movements that are exclusionary and even oppressive, in addition to being less capable of withstanding the powerful forces that protect the status quo.

For a few weeks in the spring of 2024, American colleges and universities—the workplaces and communities of the authors whose work is collected here—dominated the news. In one sense, the story was a hopeful and inspiring one. Following the horrific kidnappings and murders of Jewish Israeli civilians perpetrated by Hamas on October 7, 2023, the Israeli military responded by invading Gaza with overwhelming force. As scenes of devastation and death inflicted on Palestinian civilians during the US-supported war filled the news and their social media feeds, many students reacted by engaging in public shows of solidarity with the Palestinian people. They employed protest tactics that have a long history on American college campuses, engaging in peaceful (though sometimes rule-breaking) acts including holding marches, building encampments, and occupying university buildings. In some cases, their objective was primarily to draw attention to the situation; in others, student protesters made specific demands of their institutions, including most commonly divestment from companies seen to support or benefit from the war in some way.[2] When asked about their reasons for protesting, the students regularly made clear that they were informed not only by their instinctive reactions to the news they were seeing out of Gaza but also by what they had learned in their college courses.

But the reaction to these protests was swift and crushing. Demonstrators were accused of antisemitism. Several US Congressional Representatives and Senators alleged that the students were "pro-Hamas" and thus supporters of terrorism; university presidents who struck deals with protesters were called before Congress to explain themselves.[3] Other university presidents called on police departments to quell the protests;[4] student demonstrators and their faculty supporters were met with violence, arrests, and lengthy bans from campuses across the nation.[5] As we write this introduction a few months later, many of the protests have fizzled out and the war rages on. As Palestinian human rights lawyer Raja Shehadeh, who described the hope he felt in response to the American students' protests, said in June 2024, "With all this solidarity, and with all this vociferous support, nothing has changed."[6]

This story feels somewhat familiar. Just four years ago, following a police officer's murder of George Floyd, an unarmed Black man, the largest protests in American history swept across the nation. Demonstrators decried racism and police brutality while marching in solidarity with the Black Lives Matter movement. In response, legislators and executives promised new conversations about police reform. In several states, monuments celebrating the Confederacy were removed and institutions bearing the names of figures associated with slavery or Jim Crow were renamed. But today there is a widespread sense that any momentum generated by the protests has faded. As political theorist Mie Inouye writes in a recent reflection on solidarity,

> Even though we recently experienced one of the most remarkable displays of interracial solidarity in our country's history, interracial solidarity—and solidarity across any form of difference, for that matter—seems less plausible now than it did before 2020. There are many enduring legacies of the George Floyd rebellions, but I think we can say that a sustained multiracial movement against policing and mass incarceration is not among them.[7]

The question of solidarity's efficacy—and more fundamentally, its very possibility—is clearly raised by these contemporary cases. Though the stakes feel especially high in the present moment, however, the questions themselves have been asked at many times and in many places; solidarity is a significant concept in many moral traditions and communities.

In the chapters that follow, feminist and womanist scholars of religious ethics consider an array of cases of solidarity-building in a wide variety of religious and national contexts and in response to a range of issues. In different ways, each speaks to both the challenges and the hope for solidarity in the present moment, with careful attention to how power, particularity, and practice shape solidarity's possibilities. The volume opens with a section, "Foundations," devoted to narrating the present landscape of academic work on religious ethics, feminism, solidarity, and decoloniality, giving a sense of the conversation as it stands and highlighting the new directions in which the contributions to this volume will take us. In chapter 1, Rosemary Kellison offers a brief overview of the concept of solidarity in feminist work, focusing in particular on the ways that feminists have addressed the apparent tension between solidarity and identity (or universality and particularity). She argues that religious ethicists might learn from feminists' approach to this problem in carrying out the normative aspects of their work. In chapter 2, Shannon Dunn attends to the mode of relating appropriate for solidarity in a decolonial or postcolonial context, using primarily the work of Sylvia Wynter and Wynter's fundamental rejection of the subject/object binary. She argues that to further undo this binary, practices of nonviolence and a commitment to rituals of apology are necessary.

Hearing the word *solidarity*, particularly in a political context, may bring to mind extraordinary heroic acts or mass movements for justice. But enacting a shared commitment to justice can also take other, more mundane forms. Indeed, for many, it is an essential part of their practices of solidarity that such commitments are not confined to a particular moment or space, but rather permeate one's life and form one's existence as an individual in addition to shaping one's relationships with others. In section 2, "Living Solidarity," three scholars consider examples of solidarity as lived in more ordinary ways, in both religious and domestic contexts.

Drawing on her time observing a pilgrimage–ordination ceremony in Bodhgaya, India, as well as interviews with leaders of supporting Buddhist organizations, in chapter 3 Darcie Price-Wallace offers a rich ethnographic account of how solidarity is forged both among Buddhist *bhikkunis* (nuns) undergoing ordination and between those *bhikkunis* and the larger Buddhist community. Price-Wallace's account illuminates the productive role that ritual can play in building solidary bonds, as well as in enacting resistance to traditional exclusionary norms.

In chapter 4, Rima Vesely-Flad examines the life and writings of Audre Lorde to narrate how Lorde enacted and encouraged solidarity with other women in various aspects of her life, from her writing to her activism to her own experience of cancer. Vesely-Flad argues that reading Lorde through the lens of Buddhist ethics brings to light important themes we might not otherwise notice in her work: suffering, impermanence, and compassion. By demonstrating how these particular concepts relate to Lorde's practice of solidarity, Vesely-Flad challenges the notion that Buddhist teachings are intrinsically nonpolitical.

Drawing on the work of womanist theologians as well as the story of her mother, in chapter 5 Nikia Smith Robert argues for solidarity with Black mothers who are criminalized by our current economic and legal structures. Robert describes how indigent Black mothers who make the choices necessary to survive and protect their families are deemed deviant and worthy of punishment. In response, she develops a theology of Abolition Womanism that recognizes and celebrates the virtues enacted by these mothers.

In their recent study of solidarity, Leah Hunt-Hendrix and Astra Taylor draw on the work of Émile Durkheim in emphasizing the role of ritual and shared practices in the development of solidarity.[8] Section 3, "Organizing, Activism, and Protest as Solidarity," focuses on political movements that foster and express solidarity against injustice. The authors examine organizing and activism for a range of causes and from within a variety of religious and nonreligious contexts. Together, their contributions reveal the central importance of solidarity in building and maintaining grassroots political movements that challenge oppression and violence.

In chapter 6, Candace Jordan explores how developing relationships of solidarity can overcome the alienation a marginalized person might experience from oneself, similar others, or a larger community as a result of stigmatization and other harmful social practices. In contrast to analyses of anger that presume it would likely contribute to alienation and pose a barrier to solidarity, Jordan argues that anger can be a powerful tool of solidarity, particularly when it is evoked and expressed in community rituals. Moreover, insofar as the successful expression of anger can serve one's emotional needs and facilitate self-construction of one's identity, the anger channeled in such rituals is a potentially significant means of overcoming alienation.

Focusing on examples of activism and protest that involve the practice of rituals, Molly Farneth analyzes the potential of ritual to bring about or prefigure actual change in the world in chapter 7. She describes how, in building and deepening solidarity, ritual can generate connections and mutual obligations among participants in a social movement while also orienting those participants toward a shared political goal. At the same time, however, insofar as the goals of some movements, such as the reproductive justice movement, emphasize a principle of individual autonomy, some may question whether solidarity is a helpful tool. Farneth argues that conceiving autonomy as relational reveals the potential value of solidarity (and solidarity-building rituals) for this movement.

In chapter 8, drawing on interviews with American Muslim activists advocating for reproductive rights, Maria Tedesco offers an in-depth analysis of the reasoning, scriptural and otherwise, employed by Muslims in defense of the right to abortion. Tedesco emphasizes the activists' embrace of feminist and secularist values that enable them to work in solidarity with reproductive justice organizations representing other religious and nonreligious communities. Moreover, as she demonstrates, these values become part of the substantive argument for the right to abortion as an element of both Muslims' bodily autonomy and their religious freedom.

Chapter 9 illuminates how organizing for justice facilitates not only the development of solidary bonds among diverse participants in particular movements but also across social movements and among activists working on a large variety of causes. Juliane Hammer's chapter highlights points of existing and potential solidarity between two such movements: advocates for the liberation of Palestine and Muslim women's organizations fighting against sexual violence. Hammer outlines similar challenges facing both movements, including the pressure to be silent and the requirement that victims be "perfect." Based on ethnographic work with a Muslim women's organization, she outlines an ethic of care that could confront these challenges and enable solidarity across movements for justice.

In his work on solidarity, religious ethicist Richard B. Miller argues that "we can distinguish between good and bad solidarity."[9] Miller proposes to base this distinction on the moral values and vision to which solidarity is committed; specifically, good solidarity is "ruled by substantive egalitarian principles" and commits coalition participants to "working for a society of political and social equality."[10] The chapters in section 4, "Challenging Exclusionary Forms of Solidarity," also address this question, highlighting both activist movements and theological interpretations that promote more inclusive and egalitarian forms of solidarity over nonfeminist or exclusionary forms. As these authors show, the achievement of genuine solidarity is often a work in progress, and inclusive coalitions are the result of intentional practices of both learning and unlearning.

Through an analysis of American and Israeli Jewish movements against the occupation of Palestine, Atalia Omer shows in chapter 10 that answering the ancient Rabbi Hillel's questions, "If I am not for myself, who will be for me? If I am only for myself, who am I? And if not now, when?" requires a relational solidarity that involves an intentional unlearning and remaking of oneself. Drawing on feminist, queer, and decolonial theory, Omer argues that activists must reject exclusionary forms of solidarity that focus on the liberation of one group at the cost of ignoring or contributing to the oppression of others.

Emma McDonald Kennedy's analysis of solidarity in the Catholic tradition in chapter 11 begins with a study of how the Church has advocated for the heterosexual nuclear family as a place to develop solidarity that can then radiate out toward others. Using interviews with Catholic women experiencing infertility along with other sources, Kennedy shows that the exclusion of diverse family structures can generate only an exclusionary form of solidarity. She highlights some Catholic practices and organizations that offer an alternative, more inclusive understanding of both family and solidarity.

In chapter 12, Kori Pacyniak critiques trans-exclusionary conceptions of feminist solidarity. Focusing on Catholic feminist spaces, Pacyniak shows that the exclusion of trans people is directly contrary to feminist commitments. Moreover, as they emphasize, such exclusion is likely to perpetuate the significant dangers faced by trans people in our communities. Pacyniak argues in favor of an inclusive solidarity that builds coalitions out of difference.

Though the movements we describe and the conclusions we draw are quite diverse, some common themes recur in the contributions collected here. We highlight forms of solidarity that not only include but are strengthened by differences. We focus on examples of solidarity that are lived in actual practices. We consider how the reality of power imbalances—both within solidary coalitions and between those coalitions and those whose unjust practices they target—can inhibit the development and success of solidarity movements. We consider how lived solidarity that depends on difference and that successfully counters unjust power differentials requires not only listening to and reaching out to others but reflexively critical self-transformation. As Matilde Moros wrote, "Our decolonizing work must begin with our own anti-racist work, our anti-anti-blackness work, our anti-sexist work."[11] Before her untimely death, Mati had planned to contribute to this volume. We hope that this project is a worthy response to both her challenge and her belief in the transformative potential of heeding that call.

Acknowledgments

We extend our sincere thanks to the many people who have helped us bring this volume to fruition. First and foremost, we are grateful for the contributors who have shared their work here and for their collaborative spirit along the way—and to the many colleagues who helped us bring this group together. We are so appreciative of our editor, Richard Brown, for his excitement about and guidance of this project; thanks too to Victoria Shi at Bloomsbury. Finally, we want to acknowledge the support and encouragement of a trio of dear teachers and mentors, Aline Kalbian, Martin Kavka, and John Kelsay, who have been formative influences on our understandings of religious ethics and of feminism. Our own academic collaboration began under and was shaped by their guidance. With gratitude, we dedicate this volume to them.

Notes

1 Solidarity is a major theme in several recent books by religious ethicists, including Nichole M. Flores, *The Aesthetics of Solidarity: Our Lady of Guadalupe and American Democracy* (Washington: Georgetown University Press, 2021); Leah Hunt-Hendrix and Astra Taylor, *Solidarity: The Past, Present, and Future of a World-Changing Idea* (New York: Pantheon, 2024); Atalia Omer, *Days of Awe: Reimagining Jewishness in Solidarity with Palestinians* (Chicago: University of Chicago Press, 2019); and Traci C. West, *Solidarity and Defiant Spirituality: Africana Lessons of Religion, Racism, and Ending Gender Violence* (New York: New York University Press, 2019). The concept of solidarity also plays a significant role in several recent articles in the field's leading journal, the *Journal of Religious Ethics*. See Andrew Beauchamp and Jason A. Heron, "Solidarity in a Technocratic Age: Commercialization, Catholic Social Teaching, and

Moral Formation," *Journal of Religious Ethics* 47, no. 2 (2019): 356–76; Gerald J. Beyer, "Advocating Worker Justice: A Catholic Ethicist's 'Toolkit,'" *Journal of Religious Ethics* 45, no. 2 (2017): 230–54; Kenneth R. Himes, "Catholic Social Teaching, Economic Inequality, and American Society," *Journal of Religious Ethics* 47, no. 2 (2019): 283–310; Sam Houston, "Organizing Muslim Virtue: Community Organizing, Comparative Religious Ethics, and the South African Muslim Struggle against Apartheid," *Journal of Religious Ethics* 51, no. 1 (2023): 143–69; Megan K. McCabe, "A Feminist Catholic Response to the Social Sin of Rape Culture," *Journal of Religious Ethics* 46, no. 4 (2018): 635–57; Cristina L. H. Traina, "Between a Rock and a Hard Place: Unwanted Pregnancy, Mercy, and Solidarity," *Journal of Religious Ethics* 46, no. 4 (2018): 658–81; and Paul Weithman, "Solidarity and the New Inequality," *Journal of Religious Ethics* 47, no. 2 (2019): 311–36. Together, these works address a range of issues including migration, economic inequality, sexual violence, abortion rights, and racism, among others.

2 Collin Binkley, Steve LeBlanc, and Bianca Vázquez Toness, "Students Protesting on Campuses across US Ask Colleges to Cut Investments Supporting Israel," *Associated Press*, April 24, 2024, https://apnews.com/article/college-protests-israel -divestment-palestinians-3f37f96f7be8e1124f266842d9caa627.

3 Annie Ma and Collin Binkley, "Rutgers, Northwestern Defend Deals with Student Protesters: 'We Had to Get the Encampment Down,'" *Associated Press*, May 23, 2024, https://apnews.com/article/congress-antisemitism-northwestern-ucla -rutgers-41cd2b843999523bccc927004b13d5e0.

4 The letter the Columbia University president, Shafik Minouche, who later stepped down, sent to the New York Police Department requesting help in removing protestors from campus can be read at https://publicsafety.columbia.edu/content/ letter-nypd (accessed August 12, 2024).

5 Laura Meckler and Hannah Natanson, "Massive Pro-Palestinian College Protests Bring Rare Surge in Discipline," *Washington Post*, May 6, 2024, https://www .washingtonpost.com/education/2024/05/06/college-protests-suspensions -expulsion-arrests.

6 Claire Armitstead, "Interview: Palestinian Author Raja Shehadeh: 'All This Solidarity from the World—Yet Nothing Has Changed,'" *The Guardian*, June 8, 2024, https://www.theguardian.com/books/article/2024/jun/08/palestinian -author-raja-shehadeh-all-this-solidarity-from-the-world-yet-nothing-has -changed.

7 Mie Inouye, "Solidarity Now," *Boston Review*, September 19, 2023, 9–32, 18.

8 Hunt-Hendrix and Taylor, *Solidarity*, 282–83, 292–95.

9 Richard B. Miller, *Friends and Other Strangers: Studies in Religion, Ethics, and Culture* (New York: Columbia University Press, 2016), 141.

10 Miller, *Friends and Other Strangers*, 141.

11 Matilde Moros, "Inversion and Diasporas: Decolonizing Racialized Sexuality Transnationally," in *Decolonial Christianities: Latinx and Latin American Perspectives*, ed. Raimundo Barreto and Roberto Sirvent (New York: Palgrave Macmillan, 2019), 183–202.

References

Armitstead, Claire. "Interview: Palestinian Author Raja Shehadeh: 'All This Solidarity from the World—Yet Nothing Has Changed.'" *The Guardian*, June 8, 2024. https://www.theguardian.com/books/article/2024/jun/08/palestinian-author-raja-shehadeh-all-this-solidarity-from-the-world-yet-nothing-has-changed.

Beauchamp, Andrew, and Jason A. Heron. "Solidarity in a Technocratic Age: Commercialization, Catholic Social Teaching, and Moral Formation." *Journal of Religious Ethics* 47, no. 2 (2019): 356–76.

Beyer, Gerald J. "Advocating Worker Justice: A Catholic Ethicist's 'Toolkit.'" *Journal of Religious Ethics* 45, no. 2 (2017): 230–54.

Binkley, Collin, Steve LeBlanc, and Bianca Vázquez Toness. "Students Protesting on Campuses across US Ask Colleges to Cut Investments Supporting Israel." *Associated Press*, April 24, 2024, https://apnews.com/article/college-protests-israel-divestment-palestinians-3f37f96f7be8e1124f266842d9caa627.

Flores, Nichole M. *The Aesthetics of Solidarity: Our Lady of Guadalupe and American Democracy.* Washington: Georgetown University Press, 2021.

Himes, Kenneth R. "Catholic Social Teaching, Economic Inequality, and American Society." *Journal of Religious Ethics* 47, no. 2 (2019): 283–310.

Houston, Sam. "Organizing Muslim Virtue: Community Organizing, Comparative Religious Ethics, and the South African Muslim Struggle Against Apartheid." *Journal of Religious Ethics* 51, no. 1 (2023): 143–69.

Hunt-Hendrix, Leah, and Astra Taylor. *Solidarity: The Past, Present, and Future of a World-Changing Idea.* New York: Pantheon, 2024.

Inouye, Mie. "Solidarity Now." *Boston Review*, September 19, 2023, 9–32.

Ma, Annie, and Collin Binkley. "Rutgers, Northwestern Defend Deals with Student Protesters: 'We Had to Get the Encampment Down.'" *Associated Press*, May 23, 2024. https://apnews.com/article/congress-antisemitism-northwestern-ucla-rutgers-41cd2b843999523bccc927004b13d5e0. Accessed August 12, 2024.

McCabe, Megan K. "A Feminist Catholic Response to the Social Sin of Rape Culture." *Journal of Religious Ethics* 46, no. 4 (2018): 635–57.

Meckler, Laura, and Hannah Natanson. "Massive Pro-Palestinian College Protests Bring Rare Surge in Discipline." *Washington Post*, May 6, 2024. https://www.washingtonpost.com/education/2024/05/06/college-protests-suspensions-expulsion-arrests.

Miller, Richard B. *Friends and Other Strangers: Studies in Religion, Ethics, and Culture.* New York: Columbia University Press, 2016.

Moros, Matilde. "Inversion and Diasporas: Decolonizing Racialized Sexuality Transnationally," in *Decolonial Christianities: Latinx and Latin American Perspectives*, edited by Raimundo Barreto and Roberto Sirvent, pp. 183–202. New York: Palgrave Macmillan, 2019.

Omer, Atalia. *Days of Awe: Reimagining Jewishness in Solidarity with Palestinians.* Chicago: University of Chicago Press, 2019.

Shafik, Minouche. "Letter to NYPD," April 18, 2024. https://publicsafety.columbia.edu/content/letter-nypd. Accessed August 12, 2024.

Traina, Cristina L. H. "Between a Rock and a Hard Place: Unwanted Pregnancy, Mercy, and Solidarity." *Journal of Religious Ethics* 46, no. 4 (2018): 658–81.

Weithman, Paul. "Solidarity and the New Inequality." *Journal of Religious Ethics* 47, no. 2 (2019): 311–36.

West, Traci C. *Solidarity and Defiant Spirituality: Africana Lessons of Religion, Racism, and Ending Gender Violence.* New York: New York University Press, 2019.

Section 1

Foundations

1

Solidarity and Feminist Religious Ethics

Rosemary Kellison

Religious ethicists and feminist scholars share an interest in communities, and by extension, in how communities and their social norms are constituted by their members and others. Solidarity, defined loosely as having to do with the relationships that bind members of a community to one another, is thus an obvious area of inquiry for a study of feminist religious ethics. In this volume, we hope it will become clear that it is also a particularly productive topic because it enables critical analysis of some of the most significant and challenging questions facing both feminists and religious ethicists today, including issues related to cross-cultural inquiry and coalition-building; diversity between and among groups; the varying impacts of power, privilege, and oppression (and oppressive systems including patriarchy, white supremacy, and heteronormativity) on the life experiences of members of various communities; and, ultimately, the purpose of academic studies in both areas. While the chapters that follow will explore various aspects of and responses to these persistent questions, here I will focus on offering a more detailed explanation of some of the key terms and basic conditions framing these conversations.

In this chapter, I will argue that among the many scholarly challenges to which feminist writing on solidarity might help us respond is the contemporary debate in religious studies regarding the place of the normative work often produced by scholars of religious ethics. In their analysis of solidarity, feminists have confronted and addressed many of the same problems that are said to accompany normative religious ethics scholarship. Within the field of religious ethics, however, explicitly feminist writing has all too often been respected for its contributions on the specific issues of sex and gender, but not directly responded to by other religious ethicists addressing these more theoretical and methodological questions. As Fannie Bialek puts this point, "feminist projects are easily *included* in the field of religious ethics as part of a simply different ethical tradition, to which other traditions are not accountable. Inclusion can become a mechanism to escape critique where it defines difference without requiring engagement."[1] One area in which engagement with and accountability to feminist work would greatly benefit religious ethics is discussions of the appropriateness and positive value of projects in which a normative commitment to justice is central.

Our goal in this volume is not to offer a final definition of solidarity itself; as will become evident, that concept itself is a contested one that may be employed by communities in a wide variety of ways depending on their particular experiences and objectives. Indeed, one value of this book, we hope, will lie in the diverse perspectives it offers on the definition and value of solidarity itself. Moreover, as explained by feminist philosopher Sally Scholz, there are different forms of solidarity. Scholz argues that in all its forms, solidarity involves some kind of mediation between individuals and the community, some kind of unity among group members that connects them and makes the group recognizable to outsiders, and some set of moral obligations to which community members are committed by virtue of their membership.[2] Scholz identifies three types of solidarity: social solidarity between members of a particular group or culture who share an obligation to observe certain customs or mores, civic solidarity between citizens of a particular state who share obligations to that state and one another (and vice versa), and political solidarity.[3]

This volume will focus on the latter, which Scholz describes as solidarity that "arises in response to a situation of injustice or oppression" and is based not on shared identity or interests but on "shared commitment to a cause."[4] Scholz notes that this cause can be defined quite broadly, such that the solidary group may accommodate a large diversity of participants. What sets political solidarity apart from the other two forms of solidarity, according to Scholz, are two key characteristics. First, political solidarity is essentially oppositional, insofar as it is based on shared opposition to some unjust or oppressive situation. Second, political solidarity begins not from some shared identity or experience but rather from shared duties and obligations to other members of the group and to the furtherance of the shared political vision.[5]

As I will explain in greater detail, for most feminist authors and activists, feminism is by definition a normative project and one that requires what Scholz calls political solidarity between those committed to its achievement. That said, both the content of that goal and the membership of that community have been the topic of intense contestation among feminists, some of whom have also questioned both the desirability and the possibility of feminist solidarity. Historically, the solidary group of feminism was often described (particularly in the works of second-wave white feminists) as consisting fairly self-evidently of *women*. In other words, the predominant assumption was that by virtue of their shared experience of patriarchal oppression and their shared desire to end patriarchy, women naturally share a solidarity that brings them together to form a coherent and united community fighting for feminist aims. These assumptions have now been thoroughly debunked by a wide range of intersectional, womanist, and decolonial thinkers. Importantly, each of these schools of thought first emerged among women of color, who have made the most significant theoretical contributions to feminist thought in recent decades. It is their collective contributions, along with those of queer theorists, that have most effectively posed the challenges that this volume is dedicated to exploring.[6]

Feminists on Solidarity and Identity

Nearly fifty years ago, the Black women of the Combahee River Collective outlined some of these issues in their famous 1977 statement.[7] In the statement's introduction, they presented what would become one of the basic theses of intersectional feminism: "the major systems of oppression are interlocking." As a result, they declared that their movement was dedicated to fighting not only racism and sexism but also heterosexism and classism.[8] The text's authors identified as Black feminist lesbians and contended that "the most profound and potentially most radical politics come directly out of our own identity."[9] At the same time, however, they emphasized the need to build solidarity with people of other identities; indeed, they explicitly rejected separatism as a strategy both because it excludes people and because it encourages a focus on only one form of oppression rather than confronting the reality of interlocking forms. As the authors noted, that kind of myopic focus had the effect of enabling racism to continue within the white feminist movement. One of the most important tasks in building feminist solidarity, then, was for white feminists to address their own racism and for Black feminists to demand this accountability from them.[10]

A second foundational text on this topic is Bernice Reagon's 1981 speech on "coalition politics." Reagon emphasized the importance of building community with people who share one's identity and who can engage together in the collective work of building that shared identity. Such spaces, she argued, are like a nurturing home. Yet those spaces will not survive if they exist only in isolation, and so one must at times emerge to do the difficult and even dangerous work of building coalitions.[11] Coalitions, Reagon argued, allow people with different identities, coming from different "homes," to work together for mutual survival in their resistance to various forms of oppression.[12] Arriving at this kind of solidarity will not be easy, nor will it be comfortable, but it is necessary. Only through coalition can we recognize the possibility that others who are threatening to us also share with us the desire and need to resist oppression. As Reagon put it, "It must become necessary for all of us to feel that this is our world"—the "our" here including "everybody you have to include in order for you to survive."[13]

What both of these texts make clear, first of all, is that different levels of community are essential to resistance projects. On the one hand, identity groups in which one feels at home are significant insofar as they provide a nurturing and safe place in addition to grounding the narratives by which we can most forcefully and radically articulate our social critiques. On the other, the ability to forge connections between these groups, to build solidarity through larger and more diverse coalitions, is a powerful and necessary tool in the process of resisting and deconstructing the interlocking oppressive social systems that impact members of each of these groups in similar but also quite different ways. Second, both emphasize the inherent danger of such coalition-building. Because of our widespread refusal to recognize and grapple with the intersectionality of oppression and its resulting differential impacts, even our liberation movements themselves are frequently implicated in the perpetuation of the oppression of their own participants. This is part of why the preservation of diverse identities is so important to both arguments; the kind of solidarity suggested by the Combahee River Collective and Bernice Reagon is one that includes and even is deepened by differences (as opposed to a solidarity that smooths over or erases them).

Over the past couple of decades, feminists have continued to grapple with what this sort of solidarity might look like. Some, like Naomi Zack, have worried that the recognition of difference that accompanies intersectional analysis renders feminist solidarity impossible; Zack doubts that genuine solidarity can be achieved without some shared definition of *woman*—a shared identity that would underlie the empathy she regards as necessary for feminist solidarity.[14] Others, like Judith Butler in early writings, have expressed a fear that solidarity may be an "exclusionary norm," at least to the degree that solidarity requires some kind of unity among group members.[15] Both of these objections rest on a sense that identity and solidarity are intrinsically opposed to one another. By contrast, the Combahee River Collective's and Bernice Reagon's descriptions of feminist coalitions suggest the possibility of some sort of balance between identity and solidarity; many recent feminist works have focused on theorizing how such a balance might be achieved.

One influential line of thought addressing these issues has focused on the problem of speaking for others. Part of what makes solidary coalitions so potentially powerful is that they enable people with quite diverse identities and interests to speak in a shared voice. But this raises important questions about who will be empowered to speak on behalf of the coalition and the degree to which that party will be able to accurately represent the interests and needs of their diverse fellow coalition members. In response to this challenge, Linda Alcoff builds on Gayatri Chakravorty Spivak's contention that while speaking for someone else is problematic, so too is assuming that individuals have ultimate authority in interpreting their own experiences. Alcoff endorses Spivak's suggestion that rather than speaking for others or remaining silent, it is most productive to speak *to* others, remaining open to hearing their responses.[16] Alcoff describes this practice as involving what might be seen as a form of the virtue of humility: not only is the speaker in this instance receptive to hearing from those to whom she speaks that her representation of their interests is mistaken in some way, but she is also sufficiently committed to the solidary cause that she is willing to risk making these mistakes in her effort to pursue justice.[17]

On Jodi Dean's account, it is this sort of inclusive communication that makes *reflective solidarity* possible. In coalitions characterized by reflective solidarity, the debates and mutual critique that emerge from group members' diversity create a communicative bond among the participants carrying on these difficult conversations.[18] The fact that participants are simultaneously insiders and outsiders to the solidary coalition, able to draw on their experiences both as members of the coalition and members of what Reagon called their "home" groups, means that they are well positioned to offer productive critique.[19] Drawing on examples from groups made up of nonwhite feminists, Dean describes how through communicative practices including questioning and disagreement, coalition members begin to collaboratively construct a "we" that connects them without requiring the kind of sameness that might exclude potential participants.[20] Allison Weir offers a similar account, arguing that solidarity requires moving beyond a notion of identity as a stable category. Instead, Weir focuses on what she calls "identification with," which involves a purposive choice to identify with particular values and a particular community. The "we" of a solidary coalition involves multiple relational identities constructed by the participants who commit to the group and to the values they collectively choose to endorse.[21] Far from signifying a politics based on siloed, static, discrete groups, Weir argues, "*identity politics is about an active historical, political process of identification with, shaping and creating a 'we.'*"[22]

This understanding of solidary communities as diverse coalitions consisting of many relational (and thus ever-changing) individual and group identities is not merely a normative goal for activists but is also more descriptively accurate. Anna Carastathis notes that if we take the arguments of intersectional feminists seriously, the notion of stable group identities is quickly revealed to rest on an illusion. Even the smaller groups that we think of when we envision the "home" communities described by Reagon are not in fact groups of individuals who share the same identity. On the contrary, intersectional analysis reveals that all groups are internally diverse and shaped by power relations.[23] Carastathis argues that the groups who join together in political solidarity are thus already themselves coalitions and already possess diverse resources that will enable the construction of larger coalitional "we"s.[24]

According to Weir, the creation of a "we" ultimately involves not only the construction of a collective but also the transformation of its individual members.[25] The idea that human relationships shape the individuals who participate in them is consistent with Butler's more recent work arguing that it is impossible to tell the story of some "I" without also telling the story of the social relations and norms in which that "I" has come to be—and without recognizing the importance of the other who has asked the "I" to tell its story in the first place.[26] One's "I," one's identity, they argue, does not simply exist, nor does the person narrating that "I" have the ability to freely write their own story in a manner unaffected by their relationship to other people and to social and moral norms. While this reality means that one's identity is constrained in various ways, it also means that one's identity is changeable, in flux, and responsive to relationships—opening opportunities for the reconstruction of identity in ways that support political solidarity projects.

For many feminists today, this kind of cooperative construction of identity is a central moral imperative of participation in a feminist movement. As Cressida Heyes writes in an essay on gender and sexuality diversity within feminist solidarity, "feminism entails not only organizing for change but also changing oneself."[27] Such changes occur not in isolation but in solidarity with others. For Weir, engagement and identification with the solidarity coalition enable the self-critical transformation of one's own identity in part because this process of engagement allows one to more clearly see one's own position within larger webs of asymmetrical relationships.[28] For those who come to the coalition from a relatively more privileged social position, this clarity may lead to, first, a recognition of the ways in which one's identity presupposes one's participation in and benefits from systems of unjust domination, and second, a resultant commitment to transforming one's identity in solidarity with those who have been harmed by those systems and thus by my participation in them.[29] In her study of Jewish solidarity with Palestinians, Atalia Omer describes this process as an "unlearning" and remaking of identity that facilitates a shift from "exclusionary" forms of solidarity to more inclusive and equitable ones.[30]

Ann Ferguson describes the possibility of building "bridge identities" based on a more self-reflexive understanding of one's own positionality as well as empathy with others.[31] Bridge identities span the gap that exists between the self-interests of relatively more and less privileged members of solidarity coalitions; as relatively more privileged individuals transform their identity in solidarity with others, Ferguson argues, their own interests expand to include the collective interests of the larger coalition—and therefore the dismantling of the systems by which they have been unjustly privileged.[32] Thus, according to Ferguson, coalitions that achieve the kind of solidarity that results from the development of bridge identities are likely to be committed to anticapitalist and antiglobalization causes. The better feminists understand the intersectional relationships between capitalism and other oppressive systems (including patriarchy and white supremacy), the more likely they are to describe their aims in anticapitalist terms.[33] Responding to what she sees as the incorrect characterization of her position as implying opposition to the goal of transnational feminist solidarity, Chandra Talpade Mohanty similarly suggests that such solidarity is possible but will require opposition to global capitalism, given that "capital as it functions now depends on and exacerbates racist, patriarchal, and heterosexist relations of rule."[34]

Mohanty's and Ferguson's attention to the interlocking forms of oppression that participation in feminist coalitions will ideally make evident is indicative of the widely shared view among contemporary feminists that far from preventing solidarity, recognition of intersectionality is in fact absolutely necessary to the construction of genuine solidarity. Of course, recognizing the importance of intersectionality in the abstract is far different from successfully building the communicative connections needed to not only learn about the way real people are impacted by intersecting oppressions but then incorporate that knowledge in the self-critical and cooperative construction of a "we" identity that involves a commitment to radical change in oppressive systems that benefit some coalition members.[35] These challenges are evident even in the simple fact that so many of the arguments I've recounted here implicitly take the perspective of more privileged participants in feminist coalitions, focusing on how they can and ought to reform their identities in solidarity with less privileged co-participants. There is, then, always the peril of losing sight of what Reagon called the danger of coalition-building—dangers that pertain primarily to those participants who are relatively more oppressed or marginalized.

The foregoing review has focused primarily on feminist philosophers and political theorists and has been framed in terms of a conversation regarding the challenges of establishing solidarity—understood in part as a shared foundation for normative political and moral projects—despite (or through) the realities of diversity and the differential impacts of intersectional oppressive systems on those who might participate in such projects. As this volume will demonstrate, this same conversation is taking place among religious ethicists (and much like in philosophy and political theory, it is especially vibrant among feminists and intersectional thinkers). However, in contrast to these other disciplines, it is not taken for granted in religious studies that it is desirable or appropriate to identify foundations for normative projects, particularly those related to social justice. Thus, to more fully contextualize the particularities of this debate within religious ethics, it is important to consider the state of the disciplinary conversation regarding normativity and the ways in which this discourse does and does not parallel that described above.

Normativity and Religious Ethics

Over the past several decades, a growing number of religion scholars have explicitly argued against the inclusion of normative moral claims as part of academic work.[36] Notably, these scholars' concerns share significant similarities with those of feminists worried about the ability to promote feminist aims without some form of solidarity as well as those who fear that claims of solidarity may mask the exclusion of various groups. Their reasons for rejecting normative arguments often begin with a specific rejection of theological arguments in the academic study of religion and are followed by the assertion that normative claims regarding justice, peace, solidarity, and human rights are not substantively different from theological claims regarding metaphysical realities. In both cases, the argument goes, these claims are either (1) put forward without any justification, (2) supported by "grounds" that are inaccessible to and incontestable by outsiders to the speaker's tradition or community, or (3) supported by reasoning that claims to be universal but actually reflects the particular interests of one individual or party (and therefore may mask what is in reality the legitimation of violence or domination in the interests of some particular group as universal moral reasoning). Based on these characterizations of normative moral claims, influential scholars such as Russell McCutcheon have concluded that it is inappropriate for scholars of religion to make evaluative judgments of the material they study or to employ their scholarship in support of normative aims such as the promotion of justice.[37]

A second kind of rejection of normative arguments is sometimes implicit in the writings of scholars, often strongly influenced by Foucault and often engaged in anthropological work, whose work emphasizes the embeddedness of human beings within hierarchical power relationships and the extent to which powerful institutions and social norms shape each person's moral self and sense of moral values—rendering scholars and religious subjects alike unable to achieve a position from which to advance a normative proposal that might somehow escape those power relations. Insofar as this line of thinking highlights the fact that the concepts used by many ethics scholars emerge from a Western-dominated colonial discourse, this concern raises the issue of solidarity in a particularly clear way, as it leads naturally to the question of whether the enterprise of just relationship across differences is inherently fraught or even impossible. As a result, scholars who emphasize these concerns may consciously limit themselves to critique—exposing the mechanisms and impacts of these workings of power—without then going on to present normative claims based on that critical analysis.[38]

Nearly all of these critics of normativity have come from outside the subfield of religious ethics (i.e., the subfield most obviously engaged with normative argumentation), putting religious ethicists on the defensive with respect to the importance and legitimacy of their work. Assuming this defensive stance or moving away from normative work altogether does not have merely academic or theoretical effects. Rather, doing so has profound practical and political implications. In particular, it limits the impact of the valuable contributions of feminist and womanist scholars who have made normative claims (and consequent action) regarding such issues as oppression, injustice, violence, white supremacy, patriarchy, and the violation of human and civil rights a central purpose of their scholarship. In other words, given the inherently political nature of feminist work, the rejection of normativity becomes just one more way to suggest the inferiority and/or the interested particularity of feminist scholarship. It may also inhibit the building of solidarity among coalitions of individuals and groups interested in pursuing action to achieve normative aims.

In response, many religious ethicists have put forward arguments defending the place of evaluative and normative work within the academic study of religion. Five strands of thought stand out here. First is a more recent iteration of a classic approach to religious ethics that views religious traditions as a source of ethical knowledge (and especially seeks to identify knowledge shared across traditions). William Schweiker and David Clairmont suggest that religious traditions are troves of moral knowledge that we would be foolish to discard as resources for constructing our own moral judgments and worldviews.[39] Second is the liberal argument. Scholars like Richard Miller argue that it is essential that we preserve the ability to advance liberal values by criticizing cultural or religious values that result in violations of basic human rights.[40]

There is a significant overlap between the final three approaches. Third is the pragmatist argument, most famously advanced by Jeffrey Stout, according to which ethicists can concede that there is no infallible or transcendent position from which to make normative pronouncements but rather can focus their evaluative judgments on the extent to which stated norms do or do not match up with the norms implicit in social practices, as well as on whether individuals or communities are justified in making certain claims given their particular epistemic resources.[41] Fourth is an argument that draws on philosophy of religion. Scholars like Thomas Lewis and Kevin Schilbrack argue that the proper criterion for what counts as "academic" argumentation is whether contestable reasons are offered in support of a given claim— not the content of the claim itself. Thus, they argue that it is illegitimate to altogether exclude theological claims from academic discourse given that many such claims are supported by reasons.[42] Finally, some scholars of ethics and religion (such as James Laidlaw, Jason Springs, and representatives of the "third wave" of comparative religious ethics) have appealed to various sorts of anthropological approaches in stressing the degree to which self-formation and the development of moral autonomy are possible not only within power relations but at least in part through those relations.[43]

Normativity in Feminist Religious Ethics

Importantly, though their voices have not dominated the discussions focused explicitly on methodology and theoretical approaches in the study of religious ethics, various feminist religious ethicists have worked from each of these paradigms. However, the potential contribution of feminist work for analyzing the question of normativity and how normative work might address the critiques mentioned above has not been fully realized. Though in their work on solidarity, among other topics, feminists have long been producing scholarship that directly tackles the questions addressed by these five approaches, they have not always been directly engaged by those promoting these paradigms. This lack of engagement is especially noteworthy given that feminist ethicists were discussing these issues years before anyone else in religious studies was. In the work of nonwhite feminist and womanist theologians in particular, we find a long tradition of scholars making the case that normativity is unavoidable in scholarship that takes power and injustice seriously.[44] Moreover, as will become clear, many of the strategies and arguments feminist religious ethicists employ in their normative work are similar to those used by feminists attempting to forge solidarity in a world shaped by differences in power and identity.

For most feminists, feminism is by definition a normative approach, insofar as the entire point of feminist scholarship and activism is to challenge patriarchy and other forms of oppression and domination. As Lisa Cahill put it in a 2015 *Journal of Religious Ethics* focus issue on feminist ethics: "[F]eminist ethics is by definition committed to the improvement of the human condition—especially the condition of women—within whatever opportunities the political realities provide in specific times and places."[45] Unsurprisingly, then, the vast majority of feminist essays published in the *Journal of Religious Ethics* and of ethics-related essays published in the *Journal of Feminist Studies in Religion* have included significant normative elements if not a central normative argument. Thus, the important questions and issues raised by the critics and defenders of normative work in the academic study of religion have always been a central part of feminist scholarly conversation. Religious ethicists, then, ought to deeply engage with feminist scholarship as a tradition to which they are mutually accountable. Not only will doing so entail critically confronting how religious ethics has implicitly or explicitly upheld inequitable power relations, but it will also enable religious ethicists to provide even stronger justifications for their normative projects.[46]

A few themes have been central to feminist arguments regarding normative scholarship in religion; here I will focus on three in particular. While different scholars may emphasize one or more of them, these three themes are intertwined and together represent a fairly cohesive feminist approach to ethics and normative argumentation—one that is reflected in much of the work collected in this volume. Moreover, in a manner that demonstrates the analogous nature of debates about normativity to debates about solidarity, these themes echo significant aspects of feminist conversations about how to build solidarity not despite difference but through it.

First, feminist religion scholars have argued that an exclusive focus on rational arguments as the sole acceptable basis for normative claims is problematic. Rather, they argue, nonrational and embodied experiences, affects, and reactions also provide a significant foundation for persuasive normative claims.[47] Here we might be reminded of the Combahee River Collective's assertion that it was their identity as Black lesbian feminists that generated the heart of their political critique. Feminist and womanist scholars of religion have emphasized how ethnographic approaches that highlight the experiences of actual people and communities add a necessary complement to more abstract forms of ethical study.[48] For example, Monique Moultrie builds on Thelathia "Nikki" Young's work in Black queer ethics by privileging the lived experiences of Black Christian childfree women in her womanist ethical study of nonnormative forms of family creation; Moultrie notes that this approach enables the imagination of disruptive new futures.[49] Laura McTighe argues that when scholars "epistemologically privilege . . . the everyday knowledge that people most affected produce about the interlocking systems of violence governing their lives," they transform the people they study from objects into partners in both the creation of theory and the development of projects oriented toward justice and change.[50] Failing to consider nonrational sources as grounds for normative arguments often means a failure to consider the perspectives of women or marginalized groups.

Privileging people's own understandings of their lived experiences sometimes requires engagement with theological sources on which they may base those understandings. Thus, this argument leads many feminist religious ethicists to agree with proponents of the religious–knowledge argument described earlier that religious traditions themselves may also include valuable resources for feminist projects. Many projects in feminist religious ethics take the form of critical rereadings of traditionally authoritative religious resources. These rereadings often involve a new focus on the role of gender in the text or a commitment to reading the text with women and women's experiences in mind.[51] Take for instance Zahra Ayubi's careful reading of Islamic juristic rulings on issues related to women's health. Ayubi finds that in many fatwas, "preservation of patriarchy is the ruling ethos while medical knowledge is perhaps secondary or informative and women's experiential knowledge is inconsequential"; this critique grounds her recommendation that alternative epistemological approaches would better serve "Islamic moral imperatives" regarding respect for women.[52] Some feminists argue that religious resources can be applied to address contemporary issues related to sex and gender.[53] Margaret Kamitsuka, for example, has identified concepts and stories from Christian tradition (including the story of Mary as well as eschatological teachings) that might be deployed in support of abortion rights.[54] Others employ a feminist theoretical lens in critical rereadings of traditional sources, intending to produce liberatory reinterpretations of the texts.[55] In her study of motherhood in Buddhist texts, Karen Derris employs a justice-oriented feminist hermeneutic that enables her to question entrenched assumptions about the relationship between motherhood and Buddhist soteriology, and in so doing "to explore a different interpretive possibility that might support gender justice."[56]

Excluding arguments seen as nonrational or overly particular also often leads to the enforcement of certain dominant forms of argument-making that by definition exclude the powerless and render them less able to effectively critique those in power.[57] Attention to these nonrational grounds allows for a point of agreement with defenders of the pragmatist view described earlier, insofar as practical experiences and affective reactions are often indicative of the kinds of gaps between stated and implicit norms in which pragmatists are interested. It also provides a corrective to the philosophy-of-religion argument's focus on the provision of supporting *reasons* as a necessity for an argument to be considered academically legitimate; that is, while these scholars have offered convincing cases for including arguments that are based on theological reasoning within academic debate, they have often simultaneously privileged disembodied and abstract modes of reasoning.

The feminist commitment to recognizing various sources of knowledge, including experience and emotion, as authoritative makes for a more inclusive and therefore critical contribution to scholarship in ethics. Keri Day, citing Katie Cannon's notion of "metalogue" or critical reflection on dialogue, argues that womanist traditions in particular challenge dominant epistemological frameworks in religious ethics to expand our notion of whose voices and experiences are constitutive of ethical knowledge.[58] Additionally, feminists and womanists embrace (rather than run from) the role that identity can play in reasonable deliberation and debate. Feminists thus have much to contribute in response to some of the significant open questions related to these issues. These include the degree to which personal experience is open to critique and questioning from others, and whether such openness is indeed a necessary quality of academic argumentation, as well as how democratic virtues can be upheld and even strengthened via appeals to experience, emotion, or identity. Such are some of the questions that will be addressed by contributors to this volume.

Second, feminists argue that normative approaches must resist the liberal urge to privilege universals (or so-called universals) over the particular. While the quest for universals has had many implications in ethical work, perhaps its most striking consequence is the way that it has for centuries resulted in ethicists' willfully ignoring such vastly important concepts as gender, race, sexual identity, and the various systems and structures by which such concepts are often violently regulated and enforced. This outcome brings to mind the danger, described by Bernice Reagon and the Combahee River Collective, that the desire for a shared foundation of solidarity may, when inattentive to difference and intersectionality, lead to the exclusion of many people. Feminists respond directly to the concern articulated by critics of normativity that normativity necessarily involves the smuggling-in of particular interests presented as universal values, showing to the contrary that it is possible to build solidarity and put forward normative arguments without neglecting particularity.[59] As explained in the discussion of feminist solidarity, some of the strategies for doing so include privileging the standpoints, experiences, and speech of the most marginalized and the most vulnerable; reimagining one's own identity in response to empathetic encounters with members of marginalized communities; expanding one's own interests to include a commitment to radical change in oppressive systems—even when that change might cost one's own unearned privilege by benefiting others; and actively avoiding the tendency to pit struggles for gender freedom against struggles for the freedom of particular oppressed groups.[60]

For many feminists, this attention to the particular is necessary not only because of concerns about how pretensions to universalism often end up marginalizing members of particular communities but also because morality is by definition embedded in particular contexts from which it cannot be extracted.[61] Moreover, historically, some of the most acute tensions among feminists have had to do with how dominant forms of white feminist thought in particular have themselves claimed a kind of false universalism. This presumption that the experiences and perspectives of mostly middle-class cis white women represent those of feminists in general has been roundly criticized, especially by those promoting more intersectional approaches to feminist activism and scholarship. These critiques continue to drive discussion and what many would consider to be significant progress within the feminist movement, yet some also worry that these tensions may threaten to undermine feminist inquiry more generally. Some of the important related questions that will be taken up in this volume include whether solidarity is most effectively grounded in shared experiences of oppression that transcend identity and/or in experiences that follow more directly from one's individual or group identities, the degree to which (if at all) appeals to liberal values are a necessary or useful tool in feminist scholarship, and how attempts to build solidarity across cultural and/or national borders can avoid the all-too-common tendency to fall back on colonizing discourses and practices.

The third important theme in feminist normativity in religious studies is the view that normative work must take account of the role of human relationality—meaning the inevitable disparities of power that shape our interrelations and thus our moral norms and moral experiences. This emphasis on relationality and power is evident above in feminist descriptions of solidarity as involving reflexive communication between differently positioned people and groups alongside the work of unlearning and rebuilding the identities of relatively more privileged coalition members in solidarity with others.

For feminists, analyses of morality cannot take place absent analyses of power. Indeed, as Margaret Urban Walker summarizes the point: "Feminist ethics is inevitably, and fundamentally, a discourse about morality and power."[62] Here, feminists find much overlap with advocates of the fifth argument outlined above (and offer a needed corrective to the third [pragmatist] argument, which sometimes elides attention to power in its focus on reasoned debate). Feminists emphasize the profound impact of humans' basic interrelationality and resulting dependency, vulnerability, precarity, and responsibility on morality.[63] They note that these states of being are not distributed equally within relationships and that attention to how they are distributed reveals much about the distribution of power within any community. Thus, careful study of these distributions and their practical impacts is perhaps the most important starting point for feminist normative arguments.

This grounding for normative claims is, notably, particular, contextualized, and open to public scrutiny by others; it also enables solidarity between people and groups possessing a wide range of identities and moral values. Moreover, because our interrelationality means that we find ourselves already within normative relations of responsibility and vulnerability, it is this human condition that provides the means by which we can form moral selves and advance moral arguments.[64] Here too feminists have engaged (and will continue to engage in this volume) in productive debates that sharpen ethicists' ability to respond to rejections of normative work. Along these lines, feminists have offered varied assessments of the degree to which human beings can effectively resist powerful gender norms and the institutions that enforce them, as well as of the degree to which agency ought to be defined by acts of independence or resistance. Many of the chapters here will address related issues.

Conclusion

As evidenced in both feminist activists' and scholars' writings on solidarity and feminist religion scholars' work on normativity, feminists have much to contribute to ongoing debates within religious studies concerning the status and appropriateness of normative work. Feminists offer a long history of diverse arguments that might help religious ethicists more effectively respond to rejections of their normative arguments—criticisms that echo many of the concerns raised about solidarity. Feminists also add many more dimensions to this conversation. For one, feminist arguments offer a powerful statement of *why* normative work is needed. For many feminists, not only is a commitment to the promotion of justice inextricable from their academic work but to abandon normativity is to, in Atalia Omer's words, "condemn" scholarship to "utter irrelevance and isolation" from real human life.[65]

Additionally, unlike nonfeminist religious ethicists who assume a defensive stance against these rejections of normativity, feminist ethicists (often led by those writing from the margins) start from a stronger position of assuming its relevance and necessity. Indeed, one of the feminist thinkers' primary concerns regarding normativity has been whether certain approaches might foreclose the possibility of effective normative political argumentation and action. To put this point another way, it is striking that while within religious studies, scholars have felt pressed to defend their normative approaches, within feminist circles, scholars have to the contrary felt pressed to prove that their work still allows for a normative ethical stance.[66] Feminists have also offered strong arguments against those who argue scholars must stop at critique, suggesting that critique is coherent only when it rests on some kind of evaluative judgment about the sorts of power structures that are bad.[67] In all of these ways and more, as this volume will demonstrate, the resources and approaches of feminist religious ethics form a necessary and neglected tradition within religious ethics specifically and within broader conversations about justice and solidarity more generally.

Acknowledgments

My sincere thanks to Alana Dickey, Shannon Dunn, Aline Kalbian, Ross Moret, several anonymous reviewers, and participants in Florida State University's Religion, Ethics, and Philosophy Colloquium for very helpful feedback on earlier drafts of this chapter.

Notes

1 Fannie Bialek, "The Problem of Inclusion: Feminist Critique in Religious Ethics," *Journal of Religious Ethics* 51, no. 2 (2023): 213–24, 214.

2 Sally J. Scholz, *Political Solidarity* (University Park, PA: Penn State University Press, 2008), 18.

3 Scholz, *Political Solidarity*, 21–22, 27.

4 Scholz, *Political Solidarity*, 34.

5 Scholz, *Political Solidarity*, 35–36.

6 Anna Carastathis argues convincingly that to fail to emphasize the specific origins of intersectional feminist in Black feminist thought is to lose some of its distinctive and helpful contributions. See Anna Carastathis, "The Concept of Intersectionality in Feminist Theory," *Philosophy Compass* 9, no. 5 (2014): 304–14.

7 For more on the history of this organization, see Keeanga-Yamahtta Taylor, "Until Black Women Are Free, None of Us Will Be Free," *The New Yorker*, July 20, 2020, https://www.newyorker.com/news/our-columnists/until-black-women-are-free -none-of-us-will-be-free.

8 Combahee River Collective, "Combahee River Collective Statement," 1977, accessed July 15, 2024, https://www.loc.gov/item/lcwaN0028151.

9   Combahee River Collective, "Statement," 2.

10   Combahee River Collective, "Statement," 4.

11   Bernice J. Reagon, "Coalition Politics: Turning the Century," in *Home Girls: A Black Feminist Anthology*, ed. Barbara Smith (New Brunswick, NJ: Rutgers University Press, [1981] 2000), 343–56, 345–46.

12   Reagon, "Coalition Politics," 352.

13   Reagon, "Coalition Politics," 352.

14   Naomi Zack, *Inclusive Feminism: A Third Wave Theory of Women's Commonality* (Lanham, MD: Rowman & Littlefield, 2005).

15   Judith Butler, *Gender Trouble: Feminism and the Subversion of Identity* (New York: Routledge, [1990] 2006), 20–21.

16   Linda Alcoff, "The Problem of Speaking for Others," *Cultural Critique*, no. 20 (Winter 1991–1992): 23. On this problem, see also Elena Ruíz and Kristie Dotson, who emphasize the fact that the epistemic and discursive resources at the disposal of less privileged participants in feminist coalitions who seek to share their experiences with others are themselves products of colonial and otherwise oppressive systems (Elena Ruíz and Kristie Dotson, "On the Politics of Coalition," *Feminist Philosophy Quarterly* 3, no. 2, article 4 [2017]: 12–13).

17   Alcoff, "The Problem of Speaking for Others," 22–23.

18   Jodi Dean, *Solidarity of Strangers: Feminism after Identity Politics* (Berkeley: University of California Press, 1996), 29, 31–32.

19   Dean, *Solidarity of Strangers*, 33.

20   Dean, *Solidarity of Strangers*, 31–32.

21   Allison Weir, "Global Feminism and Transformative Identity Politics," *Hypatia* 23, no. 4 (2008): 115–18.

22   Weir, "Global Feminism and Transformative Identity Politics," 119 (italics in original).

23   Anna Carastathis, "Identity Categories as Potential Coalitions," *Signs: Journal of Women in Culture and Society* 38, no. 4 (2013): 942.

24   Carastathis, "Identity Categories as Potential Coalitions," 945.

25   Weir, "Global Feminism and Transformative Identity Politics," 126.

26   Judith Butler, *Giving an Account of Oneself* (New York: Fordham University Press, 2005), 8, 11.

27   Cressida J. Heyes, "Feminist Solidarity after Queer Theory: The Case of Transgender," *Signs: Journal of Women in Culture and Society* 28, no. 4 (2003): 1094.

28 As Weir writes, "once I recognize that I am in a relation of power with you, I need to re-identify—re-cognize—myself to accommodate that recognition" (Weir, "Global Feminism and Transformative Identity Politics," 126).

29 Ann Ferguson emphasizes the first step here does not necessarily lead to the second. Ann Ferguson, "How Is Global Gender Solidarity Possible?" in *Sexuality, Gender and Power: Intersectional and Transnational Perspectives*, ed. Anna Jónasdóttir, Valerie Bryson, and Kathleen B. Jones (New York: Routledge, 2011), 245.

30 Atalia Omer, *Days of Awe: Reimagining Jewishness in Solidarity with Palestinians* (Chicago: University of Chicago Press, 2019). Omer emphasizes that this process requires adopting an "epistemology from the margins" (Atalia Omer, "Friends on the Margins," *Journal of Religious Ethics* 47, no. 1 [2019]: 200).

31 On the other hand, some feminists, such as Alison Bailey, argue against the model of empathy insofar as it may unintentionally reify asymmetrical relationships by prioritizing the feelings of the relatively more privileged person. Bailey suggests that feminists instead focus on listening to and learning from others in the coalition, expanding one's knowledge in ways that enable self-transformation. Alison Bailey, "On Intersectionality, Empathy, and Feminist Solidarity: A Reply to Naomi Zack," *Journal for Peace and Justice Studies* 19, no. 1 (2009): 30–31. This approach is consistent with decolonial commitments to critically analyzing who is empowered to speak on behalf of whom; see, for example, Gayatri Chakravorty Spivak, "Can the Subaltern Speak?" in *Colonial Discourse and Post-Colonial Theory: A Reader*, ed. Patrick Williams and Laura Chrisman (London: Routledge, [1994] 2015).

32 Ann Ferguson, "Feminist Paradigms of Solidarity and Justice," *Philosophical Topics* 37, no. 2 (2009): 173.

33 Ferguson, "Feminist Paradigms of Solidarity and Justice," 171.

34 Chandra Talpade Mohanty, "'Under Western Eyes' Revisited: Feminist Solidarity Through Anticapitalist Struggles," *Signs: Journal of Women in Culture and Society* 28, no. 2 (2003): 510.

35 Linda Zerilli notes that while feminists largely agree on the importance of particularity, there is still significant work to be done in articulating what, precisely, that means; from her perspective, one significant implication is the importance of moral imagination and attention to the perspectives of marginalized people. Linda M. G. Zerilli, *Feminism and the Abyss of Freedom* (Chicago: University of Chicago Press, 2005).

36 In this regard, religion scholars might be contextualized within a broader trend throughout the humanities, narrated by Rita Felski, to see critique as the single appropriate mood or approach to scholarly interpretation. Rita Felski, *The Limits of Critique* (Chicago: University of Chicago Press, 2015).

37 Russell McCutcheon, *The Discipline of Religion: Structure, Meaning, Rhetoric* (London: Routledge, 2003); Russell McCutcheon, "A Direct Question Deserves a Direct Answer: A Response to Atalia Omer's 'Can a Critic Be a Caretaker Too?'" *Journal of the American Academy of Religion* 80, no. 4 (2012): 1077–82.

38 Two exemplars of this approach are Talal Asad and Saba Mahmood. See, for example, Talal Asad, *On Suicide Bombing* (New York: Columbia University Press, 2007); Talal Asad, "Thinking about Terrorism and Just War," *Cambridge Review of International Affairs* 23, no. 1 (2010): 3–24; Saba Mahmood, *Politics of Piety: The Islamic Revival and the Feminist Subject* (Princeton, NJ: Princeton University Press, 2005); Saba Mahmood, "Religious Reason and Secular Affect: An Incommensurable Divide?" *Critical Inquiry* 35, no. 4 (2009): 836–62.

39 William Schweiker and David A. Clairmont, *Religious Ethics: Meaning and Method* (Hoboken, NJ: Wiley, 2019).

40 Richard B. Miller, *Terror, Religion, and Liberal Thought* (New York: Columbia University Press, 2010); Richard B. Miller, *Friends and Other Strangers: Studies in Religion, Ethics, and Culture* (New York: Columbia University Press, 2016).

41 Jeffrey Stout, *Democracy and Tradition* (Princeton, NJ: Princeton University Press, 2004).

42 Thomas A. Lewis, *Why Philosophy Matters for the Study of Religion and Vice Versa* (New York: Oxford University Press, 2015), 55–58; Kevin Schilbrack, *Philosophy and the Study of Religions: A Manifesto* (Hoboken, NJ: Wiley-Blackwell, 2014), 197. Note that these scholars also offer a second response to anti-normative arguments made by critics within religious studies: the claim that these critics, too, are engaged in normative work insofar as they are committed to certain norms regarding what makes scholarship appropriately "academic." While not unimportant, this response fails to engage with the more central question of this project, which has to do specifically with normative arguments concerning justice, solidarity, freedom, and the like.

43 James Laidlaw, *The Subject of Virtue: An Anthropology of Ethics and Freedom* (Cambridge: Cambridge University Press, 2014); Jason A. Springs, *Healthy Conflict in Contemporary American Society: From Enemy to Adversary* (New York: Cambridge University Press, 2018). On the "third wave" of comparative religious

ethics and the suggestion that the construction of theory in religious ethics may be a more modest and appropriate normative aim, see Elizabeth M. Bucar, "Methodological Invention as a Constructive Project: Exploring the Production of Ethical Knowledge through the Interaction of Discursive Logics," *Journal of Religious Ethics* 36, no. 3 (2008): 355–73. In a recent article, Eunyoung Hwang makes explicit the normative commitments of several postcolonial scholars who have historically been accused of eschewing or even rejecting normativity. Eunyoung Hwang, "The Normative Project of Postcolonial Approaches: Taylor, Asad, and Bhabha on the Subaltern Religions of Ethnic-Religious Minorities, Secularity, and Liberal Democracy," *Journal of Religious Ethics* 49, no. 1 (2021): 112–37.

44 Womanist ethicist Keri Day traces the history by which increasing demographic diversity within the field of religious ethics has been accompanied by a turn toward activism and dissent that challenges unjust power relations inside and outside the academy. Keri Day, "Religious Ethics and the Spirit of Undomesticated Dissent," *Journal of Religious Ethics* 51, no. 1 (2023): 44–65.

45 Lisa Sowle Cahill, "Renegotiating Aquinas: Catholic Feminist Ethics, Postmodernism, Realism, and Faith," *Journal of Religious Ethics* 43, no. 2 (2015): 193–217, 213.

46 Zahra Ayubi offers a similar defense of the value of a feminist orientation for moving beyond old debates about the role of normativity in Islamic studies. Zahra Ayubi, *Gendered Morality: Classical Islamic Ethics of the Self, Family, and Society* (New York: Columbia University Press, 2019), 246.

47 Again, this argument has a long history within feminist and womanist traditions. Consider, for example, Audre Lorde's and bell hooks's explorations of how anger and rage can ground resistance to white supremacy and sexism, or Iris Marion Young's observation that it is feeling or hearing a "cry of suffering or distress" that often becomes the foundation for discourses of criticism of one's own community. bell hooks, *Killing Rage: Ending Racism* (New York: Owl Books, 1995); Audre Lorde, "The Uses of Anger: Women Responding to Racism," *Sister Outsider: Essays and Speeches* (Berkeley, CA: Crossing Press, [1984] 2007); Iris Marion Young, *Justice and the Politics of Difference* (Princeton, NJ: Princeton University Press, 1990), 5.

48 On ethnography and feminist religious ethics, see Elizabeth Gish, "'Are You a "Trashable" Styrofoam Cup?' Harm and Damage Rhetoric in the Contemporary American Sexual Purity Movement," *Journal of Feminist Studies in Religion* 34, no.

2 (2018): 5–22; Nina Hoel and Saʿdiyya Shaikh, "Sex as *Ibadah*: Religion, Gender, and Subjectivity Among South African Muslim Women," *Journal of Feminist Studies in Religion* 29, no. 1 (2013): 69–91; Rebecca Todd Peters, "Listening to Women: Examining the Moral Wisdom of Women Who End Pregnancies," *Journal of Religious Ethics* 49, no. 2 (2021): 290–313; Thelathia Young and Shannon Miller, "*Asé* and Amen, Sister! Black Feminist Scholars Engage in Interdisciplinary, Dialogical, Transformative Ethical Practice," *Journal of Religious Ethics* 43, no. 2 (2015): 289–316.

49 Monique Moultrie, "'Making Myself': An Exploratory Study of Black Christian Childfree Women's Concepts of Family," *Journal of Religious Ethics* 49, no. 2 (2021): 314–36, 318.

50 Laura McTighe, with Women With A Vision (WWAV), "Theory on the Ground: Ethnography, Religio-Racial Study, and the Spiritual Work of Building Otherwise," *Journal of the American Academy of Religion* 88, no. 2 (2020): 407–39, 411, 432.

51 See for example Elizabeth L. Antus, "'Was It Good for You?' Recasting Catholic Sexual Ethics in Light of Women's Sexual Pain Disorders," *Journal of Religious Ethics* 46, no. 4 (2018): 611–34; Nichole M. Flores, "'Our Sister, Mother Earth': Solidarity and Familial Ecology in *Laudato Si*'," *Journal of Religious Ethics* 46, no. 3 (2018): 463–78; Gail Labovitz, "More Slave Women, More Lewdness: Freedom and Honor in Rabbinic Constructions of Female Sexuality," *Journal of Feminist Studies in Religion* 28, no. 2 (2012): 69–87; and Susanne Scholz, "Dismantling the Phallic Economy with a Hermeneutics of Reproductive Justice: A Reconsideration of the Sotah in Numbers 5:11–31," *Journal of Religious Ethics* 49, no. 2 (2021): 270–89.

52 Zahra Ayubi, "Authority and Epistemology in Islamic Medical Ethics of Women's Reproductive Health," *Journal of Religious Ethics* 49, no. 2 (2021): 245–69, 258, 266.

53 See for example Rebecca J. Epstein-Levi, "Person-Shaped Holes: Childfree Jews, Jewish Ethics, and Communal Continuity," *Journal of Religious Ethics* 49, no. 2 (2021): 226–44; Megan McCabe, "A Feminist Catholic Response to the Social Sin of Rape Culture," *Journal of Religious Ethics* 46, no. 4 (2018): 635–57; Shadaab Rahemtulla and Sara Ababneh, "Reclaiming Khadija's and Muhammad's Marriage as an Islamic Paradigm: Toward a New History of the Muslim Present," *Journal of Feminist Studies in Religion* 37, no. 2 (2021): 83–102; and Michelle Wolff, "Companion Sex Robots: Racialized Household Economics," *Journal of*

Feminist Studies in Religion 37, no. 2 (2021): 43–64. Such reinterpretations may also be used to support new approaches to contemporary moral problems that may not be explicitly framed in terms of gender; see for example Arminta Fox, "Decentering Paul, Contextualizing Crimes: Reading in Light of the Imprisoned," *Journal of Feminist Studies in Religion* 33, no. 2 (2017): 37–54.

54 Margaret Kamitsuka, "Unwanted Pregnancy, Abortion, and Maternal Authority: A Prochoice Theological Argument," *Journal of Feminist Studies in Religion* 34, no. 2 (2018): 41–57; Margaret Kamitsuka, "Disabled Bodies on Earth and in Heaven: Eschatology and the Ethics of Selective Abortion," *Journal of Religious Ethics* 49, no. 2 (2021): 358–80.

55 Some examples include Julia Watts Belser, "Improv and the Angel: Disability Dance, Embodied Ethics, and Jewish Biblical Narrative," *Journal of Religious Ethics* 47, no. 3 (2019): 443–69, and Catherine R. Osborne, "Migrant Domestic Careworkers: Between the Public and the Private in Catholic Social Teaching," *Journal of Religious Ethics* 40, no. 1 (2012): 1–25.

56 Karen Derris, "Interpreting Buddhist Representations of Motherhood and Mothering," *Journal of Feminist Studies in Religion* 30, no. 2 (2014): 61–79, 63, 65, 69.

57 As several feminist ethicists have noted, we clearly see this enforcement at work in calls for "civility" in democratic protest. See Iris Marion Young, *Inclusion and Democracy* (Princeton, NJ: Princeton University Press, 2000); Linda M. G. Zerilli, "Against Civility: A Feminist Perspective," in *Civility, Legality, and Justice in America*, ed. Austin Sarat (New York: Cambridge University Press, 2014), 107–31.

58 Day, "Religious Ethics and the Spirit of Undomesticated Dissent," 59, 62.

59 This is not to say that feminists have always succeeded in this goal; indeed, they have often been susceptible to criticism from other feminists on this point. In 1995, Judith Butler urged feminists to be more self-critical about how their construction of categories like "feminism" and "woman" has been enabled by exclusion; in 2005, Butler noted that uncritical claims of universality can do violence. Judith Butler, "Contingent Foundations," in *Feminist Contentions: A Philosophical Exchange*, ed. Seyla Benhabib, Judith Butler, Drucilla Cornell, and Nancy Fraser (New York: Routledge, 1995), 35–58; Butler, *Giving an Account of Oneself*, 7. For a discussion of this topic representing a variety of views from feminist religious ethics, see Elizabeth M. Bucar, Grace Y. Kao, and Irene Oh, "Sexing Comparative Ethics: Bringing Forth Feminist and Gendered Perspectives," *Journal of Religious Ethics* 38, no. 4 (2010): 654–59, as well as Grace

Y. Kao, "The Universal Versus the Particular in Ecofeminist Ethics," *Journal of Religious Ethics* 38, no. 4 (2010): 616–37.

60 On the last point, Judith Butler describes the danger that arises "when women's sexual freedom or the freedom of expression and association for lesbian and gay people is invoked instrumentally to wage a cultural assault on Islam that reaffirms U.S. sovereignty and violence" (Judith Butler, *Frames of War: When Is Life Grievable?* [London: Verso, 2010], 104–5). As an example of the sort of feminist argument Butler is criticizing here, we might think of religious ethicist Jean Bethke Elshtain's book *Just War against Terror* (New York: Basic Books, 2003).

61 Margaret Urban Walker's book *Moral Contexts* (Lanham, MD: Rowman & Littlefield, 2003) offers a strong presentation of the feminist argument that ethics is and must be embedded within particular contexts.

62 Walker, *Moral Contexts*, 104. Walker goes on to argue that it is this critical attention to power that makes an ethical approach feminist (rather than a focus on women as such).

63 On this point, see Judith Butler, *Precarious Life: The Powers of Mourning and Violence* (London: Verso, 2006); Butler, *Frames of War*; Margaret Urban Walker, *Moral Understandings: A Feminist Study in Ethics*, 2nd ed. (Oxford: Oxford University Press, 2007).

64 See Butler, *Giving an Account of Oneself.*

65 Atalia Omer, "Rejoinder: On Professor McCutcheon's (Un)Critical Caretaking," *Journal of the American Academy of Religion* 80, no. 4 (2012): 1083–97, 1094.

66 Amy Allen, for example, pressed this critique of Judith Butler. Amy Allen, *The Power of Feminist Theory: Domination, Resistance, Solidarity* (Boulder, CO: Westview Press, 1999); Amy Allen, *The Politics of Our Selves: Power, Autonomy, and Gender in Contemporary Critical Theory* (New York: Columbia University Press, 2008). Shannon Dunn has offered a similar critique of Saba Mahmood. Shannon Dunn, "Ethnography and Subjectivity in Comparative Religious Ethics," *Journal of Religious Ethics* 45, no. 4 (2017): 623–41.

67 Allen made an argument along these lines in Amy Allen, *The End of Progress: Decolonizing the Normative Foundations of Critical Theory* (New York: Columbia University Press, 2016). Butler even has seemingly adopted some elements of this point of view; Butler suggests that, for example, Asad's critique of the differential ways in which liberals discuss the killings of innocent people when they are caused by states engaged in "just wars" versus when they are caused by militant groups engaged in "terrorism" makes sense only when undergirded by a tacit

normative commitment to the idea that all such violence ought to be minimized. Judith Butler, "The Sensibility of Critique: Response to Asad and Mahmood," in *Is Critique Secular? Blasphemy, Injury, and Free Speech*, ed. Talal Asad, Wendy Brown, Judith Butler, and Saba Mahmood (Berkeley: University of California Press, 2009), 101–36.

References

Alcoff, Linda. "The Problem of Speaking for Others." *Cultural Critique*, no. 20 (Winter 1991–1992): 5–32.

Allen, Amy. *The End of Progress: Decolonizing the Normative Foundations of Critical Theory.* New York: Columbia University Press, 2016.

———. *The Politics of Our Selves: Power, Autonomy, and Gender in Contemporary Critical Theory.* New York: Columbia University Press, 2008.

———. *The Power of Feminist Theory: Domination, Resistance, Solidarity.* Boulder, CO: Westview Press, 1999.

Antus, Elizabeth L. "'Was It Good for You?' Recasting Catholic Sexual Ethics in Light of Women's Sexual Pain Disorders." *Journal of Religious Ethics* 46, no. 4 (2018): 611–34.

Asad, Talal. *On Suicide Bombing.* New York: Columbia University Press, 2007.

———. "Thinking about Terrorism and Just War." *Cambridge Review of International Affairs* 23, no. 1 (2010): 3–24.

Ayubi, Zahra. "Authority and Epistemology in Islamic Medical Ethics of Women's Reproductive Health." *Journal of Religious Ethics* 49, no. 2 (2021): 245–69.

———. *Gendered Morality: Classical Islamic Ethics of the Self, Family, and Society.* New York: Columbia University Press, 2019.

Bailey, Alison. "On Intersectionality, Empathy, and Feminist Solidarity: A Reply to Naomi Zack." *Journal for Peace and Justice Studies* 19, no. 1 (2009): 14–36.

Belser, Julia Watts. "Improv and the Angel: Disability Dance, Embodied Ethics, and Jewish Biblical Narrative." *Journal of Religious Ethics* 47, no. 3 (2019): 443–69.

Bialek, Fannie. "The Problem of Inclusion: Feminist Critique in Religious Ethics." *Journal of Religious Ethics* 51, no. 2 (2023): 213–24.

Bucar, Elizabeth M. "Methodological Invention as a Constructive Project: Exploring the Production of Ethical Knowledge through the Interaction of Discursive Logics." *Journal of Religious Ethics* 36, no. 3 (2008): 355–73.

Bucar, Elizabeth M., Grace Y. Kao, and Irene Oh. "Sexing Comparative Ethics: Bringing Forth Feminist and Gendered Perspectives." *Journal of Religious Ethics* 38, no. 4 (2010): 654–59.

Butler, Judith. "Contingent Foundations." In *Feminist Contentions: A Philosophical Exchange*, edited by Seyla Benhabib, Judith Butler, Drucilla Cornell, and Nancy Fraser, pp. 35–58. New York: Routledge, 1995.

———. *Frames of War: When Is Life Grievable?* London: Verso, 2010.

———. *Gender Trouble: Feminism and the Subversion of Identity.* New York: Routledge, (1990) 2006.

———. *Giving an Account of Oneself.* New York: Fordham University Press, 2005.

———. *Precarious Life: The Powers of Mourning and Violence.* London: Verso, 2006.

———. "The Sensibility of Critique: Response to Asad and Mahmood." In *Is Critique Secular? Blasphemy, Injury, and Free Speech*, edited by Talal Asad, Wendy Brown, Judith Butler, and Saba Mahmood, pp. 101–36. Berkeley: University of California Press, 2009.

Cahill, Lisa Sowle. "Renegotiating Aquinas: Catholic Feminist Ethics, Postmodernism, Realism, and Faith." *Journal of Religious Ethics* 43, no. 2 (2015): 193–217.

Carastathis, Anna. "The Concept of Intersectionality in Feminist Theory." *Philosophy Compass* 9, no. 5 (2014): 304–14.

———. "Identity Categories as Potential Coalitions." *Signs: Journal of Women in Culture and Society* 38, no. 4 (2013): 941–65.

Combahee River Collective. "Combahee River Collective Statement." 1977. Accessed July 15, 2024, https://www.loc.gov/item/lcwaN0028151.

Day, Keri. "Religious Ethics and the Spirit of Undomesticated Dissent." *Journal of Religious Ethics* 51, no. 1 (2023): 44–65.

Dean, Jodi. *Solidarity of Strangers: Feminism After Identity Politics.* Berkeley: University of California Press, 1996.

Derris, Karen. "Interpreting Buddhist Representations of Motherhood and Mothering." *Journal of Feminist Studies in Religion* 30, no. 2 (2014): 61–79.

Dunn, Shannon. "Ethnography and Subjectivity in Comparative Religious Ethics." *Journal of Religious Ethics* 45, no. 4 (2017): 623–41.

Elshtain, Jean Bethke. *Just War against Terror.* New York: Basic Books, 2003.

Epstein-Levi, Rebecca J. "Person-Shaped Holes: Childfree Jews, Jewish Ethics, and Communal Continuity." *Journal of Religious Ethics* 49, no. 2 (2021): 226–44.

Felski, Rita. *The Limits of Critique.* Chicago: University of Chicago Press, 2015.

Ferguson, Ann. "Feminist Paradigms of Solidarity and Justice." *Philosophical Topics* 37, no. 2 (2009): 161–77.

———. "How Is Global Gender Solidarity Possible?" In *Sexuality, Gender and Power: Intersectional and Transnational Perspectives*, edited by Anna Jónasdóttir, Valerie Bryson, and Kathleen B. Jones, pp. 243–58. New York: Routledge, 2011.

Flores, Nichole M. "'Our Sister, Mother Earth': Solidarity and Familial Ecology in *Laudato Si'*." *Journal of Religious Ethics* 46, no. 3 (2018): 463–78.

Fox, Arminta. "Decentering Paul, Contextualizing Crimes: Reading in Light of the Imprisoned." *Journal of Feminist Studies in Religion* 33, no. 2 (2017): 37–54.

Gish, Elizabeth. "'Are You a "Trashable" Styrofoam Cup?' Harm and Damage Rhetoric in the Contemporary American Sexual Purity Movement." *Journal of Feminist Studies in Religion* 34, no. 2 (2018): 5–22.

Heyes, Cressida J. "Feminist Solidarity after Queer Theory: The Case of Transgender." *Signs: Journal of Women in Culture and Society* 28, no. 4 (2003): 1093–120.

Hoel, Nina, and Sa'diyya Shaikh. "Sex as *Ibadah*: Religion, Gender, and Subjectivity among South African Muslim Women." *Journal of Feminist Studies in Religion* 29, no. 1 (2013): 69–91.

hooks, bell. *Killing Rage: Ending Racism.* New York: Owl Books, 1995.

Hwang, Eunyoung. "The Normative Project of Postcolonial Approaches: Taylor, Asad, and Bhabha on the Subaltern Religions of Ethnic-Religious Minorities, Secularity, and Liberal Democracy." *Journal of Religious Ethics* 49, no. 1 (2021): 112–37.

Kamitsuka, Margaret. "Disabled Bodies on Earth and in Heaven: Eschatology and the Ethics of Selective Abortion." *Journal of Religious Ethics* 49, no. 2 (2021): 358–80.

———. "Unwanted Pregnancy, Abortion, and Maternal Authority: A Prochoice Theological Argument." *Journal of Feminist Studies in Religion* 34, no. 2 (2018): 41–57.

Kao, Grace Y. "The Universal Versus the Particular in Ecofeminist Ethics." *Journal of Religious Ethics* 38, no. 4 (2010): 616–37.

Labovitz, Gail. "More Slave Women, More Lewdness: Freedom and Honor in Rabbinic Constructions of Female Sexuality." *Journal of Feminist Studies in Religion* 28, no. 2 (2012): 69–87.

Laidlaw, James. *The Subject of Virtue: An Anthropology of Ethics and Freedom.* Cambridge: Cambridge University Press, 2014.

Lewis, Thomas A. *Why Philosophy Matters for the Study of Religion and Vice Versa.* New York: Oxford University Press, 2015.

Lorde, Audre. "The Uses of Anger: Women Responding to Racism." *Sister Outsider: Essays and Speeches.* Berkeley, CA: Crossing Press, (1984) 2007.

Mahmood, Saba. *Politics of Piety: The Islamic Revival and the Feminist Subject.* Princeton, NJ: Princeton University Press, 2005.

———. "Religious Reason and Secular Affect: An Incommensurable Divide?" *Critical Inquiry* 35, no. 4 (2009): 836–62.

McCabe, Megan. "A Feminist Catholic Response to the Social Sin of Rape Culture." *Journal of Religious Ethics* 46, no. 4 (2018): 635–57.

McCutcheon, Russell. "A Direct Question Deserves a Direct Answer: A Response to Atalia Omer's 'Can a Critic Be a Caretaker Too?'" *Journal of the American Academy of Religion* 80, no. 4 (2012): 1077–82.

———. *The Discipline of Religion: Structure, Meaning, Rhetoric.* London: Routledge, 2003.

McTighe, Laura, with Women With A Vision (WWAV). "Theory on the Ground: Ethnography, Religio-Racial Study, and the Spiritual Work of Building Otherwise." *Journal of the American Academy of Religion* 88, no. 2 (2020): 407–39.

Miller, Richard B. *Friends and Other Strangers: Studies in Religion, Ethics, and Culture.* New York: Columbia University Press, 2016.

———. *Terror, Religion, and Liberal Thought.* New York: Columbia University Press, 2010.

Mohanty, Chandra Talpade. "'Under Western Eyes' Revisited: Feminist Solidarity through Anticapitalist Struggles." *Signs: Journal of Women in Culture and Society* 28, no. 2 (2003): 499–535.

Moultrie, Monique. "'Making Myself': An Exploratory Study of Black Christian Childfree Women's Concepts of Family." *Journal of Religious Ethics* 49, no. 2 (2021): 314–36.

Omer, Atalia. *Days of Awe: Reimagining Jewishness in Solidarity with Palestinians.* Chicago: University of Chicago Press, 2019.

———. "Friends on the Margins." *Journal of Religious Ethics* 47, no. 1 (2019): 192–202.

———. "Rejoinder: On Professor McCutcheon's (Un)Critical Caretaking." *Journal of the American Academy of Religion* 80, no. 4 (2012): 1083–97.

Osborne, Catherine R. "Migrant Domestic Careworkers: Between the Public and the Private in Catholic Social Teaching." *Journal of Religious Ethics* 40, no. 1 (2012): 1–25.

Peters, Rebecca Todd. "Listening to Women: Examining the Moral Wisdom of Women Who End Pregnancies." *Journal of Religious Ethics* 49, no. 2 (2021): 290–313.

Rahemtulla, Shadaab, and Sara Ababneh. "Reclaiming Khadija's and Muhammad's Marriage as an Islamic Paradigm: Toward a New History of the Muslim Present." *Journal of Feminist Studies in Religion* 37, no. 2 (2021): 83–102.

Reagon, Bernice J. "Coalition Politics: Turning the Century." In *Home Girls: A Black Feminist Anthology*, edited by Barbara Smith, pp. 343–56. New Brunswick, NJ: Rutgers University Press, (1981) 2000.

Ruíz, Elena, and Kristie Dotson. "On the Politics of Coalition." *Feminist Philosophy Quarterly* 3, no. 2 (2017): 1–15, article 4.

Schilbrack, Kevin. *Philosophy and the Study of Religions: A Manifesto*. Hoboken, NJ: Wiley-Blackwell, 2014.

Scholz, Sally J. *Political Solidarity*. University Park, PA: Penn State University Press, 2008.

Scholz, Susanne. "Dismantling the Phallic Economy with a Hermeneutics of Reproductive Justice: A Reconsideration of the Sotah in Numbers 5:11–31." *Journal of Religious Ethics* 49, no. 2 (2021): 270–89.

Schweiker, William, and David A. Clairmont. *Religious Ethics: Meaning and Method*. Hoboken, NJ: Wiley, 2019.

Spivak, Gayatri Chakravorty. "Can the Subaltern Speak?" In *Colonial Discourse and Post-Colonial Theory: A Reader*, edited by Patrick Williams and Laura Chrisman. London: Routledge, (1994) 2015.

Springs, Jason A. *Healthy Conflict in Contemporary American Society: From Enemy to Adversary*. New York: Cambridge University Press, 2018.

Stout, Jeffrey. *Democracy and Tradition*. Princeton, NJ: Princeton University Press, 2004.

Taylor, Keeanga-Yamahtta. "Until Black Women Are Free, None of Us Will Be Free." *The New Yorker*, July 20, 2020. Accessed July 15, 2024, https://www.newyorker.com/news/our-columnists/until-black-women-are-free-none-of-us-will-be-free.

Walker, Margaret Urban. *Moral Contexts*. Lanham, MD: Rowman & Littlefield, 2003.

———. *Moral Understandings: A Feminist Study in Ethics*, 2nd ed. Oxford: Oxford University Press, 2007.

Weir, Allison. "Global Feminism and Transformative Identity Politics." *Hypatia* 23, no. 4 (2008): 110–33.

Wolff, Michelle. "Companion Sex Robots: Racialized Household Economics." *Journal of Feminist Studies in Religion* 37, no. 2 (2021): 43–64.

Young, Iris Marion. *Inclusion and Democracy*. Princeton, NJ: Princeton University Press, 2000.

———. *Justice and the Politics of Difference*. Princeton, NJ: Princeton University Press, 1990.

Young, Thelathia, and Shannon Miller. "*Asé* and Amen, Sister! Black Feminist Scholars Engage in Interdisciplinary, Dialogical, Transformative Ethical Practice." *Journal of Religious Ethics* 43, no. 2 (2015): 289–316.

Zack, Naomi. *Inclusive Feminism: A Third Wave Theory of Women's Commonality.* Lanham, MD: Rowman & Littlefield, 2005.

Zerilli, Linda M. G. "Against Civility: A Feminist Perspective." In *Civility, Legality, and Justice in America*, edited by Austin Sarat, pp. 107–31. New York: Cambridge University Press, 2014.

———. *Feminism and the Abyss of Freedom.* Chicago: University of Chicago Press, 2005.

2

Interrogating the Symbolic Order, Working for Transformation

A Proposal for Decolonial Feminist Religious Ethics

Shannon Dunn

What does it mean to decolonize the field of religious ethics, among other fields of study? There are numerous calls to "decolonize the curriculum" and even decolonize our individual thinking in ways that overlap with anti-racism initiatives in the classroom and workplace. Decolonizing has become a progressive political mantra for changing lives and reforming political systems, viewed as a necessary step in righting history and signaling a recognition of how past injustices contribute to structural injustices in the present.

In such calls to decolonize, however, there is uncertainty about to what extent decolonizing allows for the meaningful transformation of relationships and systems of power. If decolonizing is primarily seen as a means of clearing one's conscience through rhetorical overtures, people are not actually doing the ethical-political work necessary for justice. As Tyler Austin Harper explains in his objection to some anti-racism rhetoric, it "offers little more than a Marie Kondo-ism for the white soul, promising to declutter racial baggage and clear a way to white fulfillment without doing anything meaningful to combat structural racism."[1]

Solidarity in feminist religious ethics is not possible without decolonizing the field.[2] Yet if we are to avoid the error that Harper describes—including what he names as the "political sterility" of such therapeutics—the effort of decolonizing must be framed by a political ethic of responsibility for others. Solidarity will remain elusive if the more powerful party engages in decolonial rhetoric for the sake of simply feeling better about itself. Ultimately, decolonizing must aim for a better mode of relating to others in society.

In the first part of the chapter, I discuss the decolonial critique of modernity, identifying a historical-ideological global paradigm shift for human relationships that began with the rise of European hegemony in the sixteenth century. This modern colonial paradigm is responsible for the creation of the subject/object binary in which groups of people were deemed "good" based on their identification with, or proximity to, Western culture. The scholarship of Sylvia Wynter is critical for comprehending the reach of colonial thinking, as she identifies the symbolic order of colonialism and calls for a code switch.

In the second part of the chapter, I address how the interrogation of colonial categories and the dissolution of the subject/object binary is necessary for the constitution of a new ethic. Specifically, I argue that solidarity requires practices and ways of conceptualizing the world that hold in tension past injustices and the goal of justice for present and future relationships, without erasing history. I continue to draw upon Wynter's work and identify how Judith Butler's work on nonviolence and Danielle Celermajer's work on the ritual of apology describe practices capable of breaking the cycle of colonial violence and introducing or expanding norms. Butler describes the imperfect ethical subject who must exercise prudence in a social world conditioned by violence.[3] Celermajer argues that recognition of the Other's experience in a shared framework of norms (like human rights) means acknowledging the limitations and violence of the system, an unacceptable status quo.[4] Ethical case studies reveal an aporia between the rhetoric of human rights, for example, and the systematic denial or unattainability of those rights to certain groups.

In the final section, I highlight what feminist religious ethicists can both learn from, and add to, the conversation on decolonial work. I examine the possibility of ethical, spiritual, or social transformation that may figure as a central part of decolonial thinking and imagine such transformation as both a precursor to and an ongoing practice alongside solidarity. Specifically, I suggest that decolonial feminist thought calls into question a rigid distinction between the fields of religious studies and theology regarding the appropriateness of normative work.

Decolonial Thinking

A decolonial framework begins by identifying a turning point for human history in the sixteenth century: the conquest of the Americas and its influence on modern epistemology and ethics.[5] The Age of Discovery was elemental to the modern categories of race and religion.[6] Afro-Caribbean scholar Sylvia Wynter's cultural and literary analysis is particularly attuned to these dynamics. Wynter maintains that sixteenth-century arguments and actions by Spanish conquistadors and the Spanish crown are emblematic of a broader phenomenon wherein European consciousness and reasoning shifted from religious to secular, alongside the categorical dehumanizing of non-European peoples. This change coincided with the move from a feudal or agrarian society in Europe to a system of modern industrialized capitalism, with disastrous consequences for humanity's relationship with nature.

According to Wynter, ideologically central to the economic and social dominance of the West in the past five hundred years is the invention of Western Man, the idealized European white subject who has come to stand in for the human being-in-general. The powerful fiction of Western Man, however, depends on the absolute negation of non-Western others, effectively rendering them as nonhuman. This overrepresentation of Western Man thus requires an "unsettling" of its colonial origins (and its very being) and an inquiry into the modern rational and secular forms of politics that have aided and abetted its ideological success.[7]

By abandoning a theocentric framework, Wynter claims, Western Man elevated "reason" and assumed some of God's powers for himself. For Wynter, theocentrism is a symbolic order in which people are fundamentally equal to and answerable for one another, and before God. Secular reason, stripped of the forms of human equality and relationality that Wynter imagines to be a part of the theocentric paradigm, does not prevent people from mistaking their power as divine power. As Wynter explains, "While reason is not a god, it partakes of some of God's function in that it is intended to rule over a 'lower order of reality.'"[8] This elevation of Western Man above all other peoples and cultural representations resulted in the development of human institutions, with corresponding modalities of ethics and epistemology, that have caused untold harm.

In this analysis, the form of slavery that had existed in the medieval world—often through taking prisoners of war—is qualitatively distinct from the large-scale agricultural slavery that began with the colonization of the Americas. Medieval Europeans had argued that slavery was a byproduct of original sin and that practice had been incorporated into a just war framework that regulated its use according to a moral code. In contrast, the enslavement of Native Americans and the initiation of the transatlantic slave trade in the service of European imperial expansion represents a marked change in terms of how slavery was rationalized. European and American colonizers and slaveholders defined non-Europeans as fundamentally irrational and thus disposable beings. Wynter describes the violence that ensued when entire groups of people were defined as nonhuman. "For the first time in human history a small group of peoples now had at their disposal the rest of the peoples and the resources of the earth."[9] Racism assumed the ideological form of this control, and European culture was itself transformed into a weapon of domination. Crucially, Western-dominated economic and political structures created and maintained the binary between Western Man and everyone else. They consigned Indigenous peoples to landlessness and rightlessness and permitted the exploitation of their labor and eventually the introduction of plantation slavery.

Wynter offers insight into how the sixteenth-century Spanish conquistadors attempted to justify violence against the native peoples. She recounts a signal argument at Valladolid between Bartolomé de Las Casas and Juan Gines de Sepúlveda wherein Las Casas thought in terms of a Christian evangelizing imperative and Sepúlveda thought in the terms of the instrumental reason of the Spanish empire.[10] Las Casas argued for an ethic of reciprocity with the native peoples; Sepúlveda, in contrast, argued for European superiority and dominance. There was also a crucial metaphysical difference between them: Las Casas postulated that natives had a soul and religion, while Sepúlveda did not share the same assumption. As Nelson Maldonado-Torres explains, "The absence of religion indicates the possible absence of a soul—as the perceived primary constituent of humanity that serves for establishing a relation between human being and the divine."[11] The then-novel imperial position broke with the medieval scholastic classification division between Christians, infidels, and idolaters, maintaining a new distinction between religious/nonreligious that could then become the basis for "justified" violence and genocide.

The imperial argument ultimately prevailed throughout the colonial period and beyond, and Wynter argues that Las Casas was simultaneously "behind and ahead" of his time—looking backward in his harkening to a scholastic-theocentric model of humanity, but also ahead in pointing the way toward a new type of universalism—a science of human systems. Wynter characterizes this debate in terms of religious versus secular orientations, with the secular one advancing an instrumentalist, dehumanizing argument regarding the status of the natives.[12] A Christian ethic, Wynter argues, was effectively replaced by an ethic of the state.[13] Conceptually both the state and the new political subject of the citizen were founded on erroneous assumptions about the humanity of Western Man as standing in for all others and the norm of human relations as (European) dominance and hierarchy.

The binary of Western Man versus Other underwrites the logic and defines the form of modern politics, and thus it is the central subject of decolonial critique. Decolonial theorists collectively reject the liberal-political conception of the subject as an autonomous individual and call for new forms of sociality. They highlight the tenacious grip of white European hegemony and its related capitalist ideology that produces not only radical material inequality but also what Frantz Fanon names the existential "zone of non-being."[14] Some lives are deemed worthy/visible and others are unworthy/invisible, a pattern which continues despite the reality that historical colonialism has ended.[15]

The field of religious ethics has, for much of its history, reflected an orientation toward Western Man. Historically, scholars of religious ethics often uncritically reinforce the binary rather than question it or seek to dissolve it. Not only have scholars in religious and theological ethics privileged Christian paradigms for ethics—revealing an entrenched hierarchy in the academy— but they have privileged white Christian male experiences disproportionately as standing in for the human perspective.[16] Feminist ethical critique has interrogated this positioning, and womanist critiques have identified the limits of both white feminism and Black patriarchal modes of thought in religious ethics.[17] Scholars in the field must address the persistence and the harm of the binary as it continues to shape the types of inquiry we pursue, and whose voices and experiences we privilege. As Wynter explains, our modern systems of representation are in continual need of reorientation. Because humans have evolved to be a "symbolic and self-representing species," we rely on social norms to understand and make sense of our place in the world.[18] Scholarship is one prominent place where symbolic representation occurs, and thus it is necessary for us to identify both deficiencies of representation as well as overrepresentation.

Wynter's later work addresses how, in addition to the harm wrought by the colonial binary that undergirds our political conceptions, modern science as a system has failed to provide human beings with sufficient guidance about how to live ethically. She writes that the natural sciences "remain incapable of giving us any knowledge of our uniquely human domain and have nothing to say of the urgent problems that beleaguer mankind [sic]."[19] Wynter highlights the way that modern ethics and epistemology have negatively altered the way that human beings relate to one another and to nature.

Solidarity

What is required to effectively transform the relationship between the subjects who have been appositionally framed by the colonial binary? In posing this question, it is appropriate to note that in fundamental respects, this is a question that individual communities with particular histories must work out together. Yet if we are to do the work of decolonizing or anti-racism, we must begin the theoretical task of envisioning a new political ethic, in which the binary is dissolved, and solidarity is possible. There are two components involved: interrogation of dominant ethical norms, and interruption of related normative practices. What follows interrogation and interruption is the potential transformation of the relationship.

First, decolonial work interrogates the malformation of ethical subjects. To undo this poor formation, we must first question the symbolic order we have inherited and its normative influence. The dis-orientation of the modern world, based on a subject/object binary, means that the ethical system of Western Man has been based on erroneous ideals. According to the logic of late capitalist modernity, people act out of a sense of scarcity, self-interest, and fear. This is not merely posited as a description of human motivation, but rather a normative Hobbesian state of affairs.[20] For Western Man, the enshrined norm of individual autonomy, alienated from long-standing ethical traditions and communities, is revered above all else. This "ethical" orientation is in fact not ethical at all, and it leads to a pattern of violence, destruction, and ultimately annihilation of all life forms. Our ethical formation, in many respects, has been a long process of malformation. If modernity operates through a death ethic of war, in which "altruism and solidarity are fundamentally skewed,"[21] what options do we have?

Louiza Odysseos highlights the relationship between social coding and the possibility of ethical relationships in Wynter's work.[22] Odysseos describes this relationship in the following way: "The harms of modernity-coloniality . . . extend beyond their material and sociogenic aspects to distort the realm of ethical relationality through the continuing restriction of the 'common universe of obligation.'"[23] In modernity those with the most power (on account of their identification with Western Man) fundamentally lack, or are deprived of, comprehension and imagination about to whom they have ethical obligations. This idea resonates with Judith Butler's argument that our modern institutions mediate reality for us, framing some lives as valuable (grievable) and others as not-valued (not-grievable).[24] These frames actively work to allow us to apprehend some lives, but not others, as having worth.

Wynter argues for a symbolic order in which oppressed people recognize their humanity and do not participate in the domination of others, as domination is the normative practice according to the logic of late capitalism. *Sociopoesis* is the mechanism by which oppressed peoples reclaim dignity and engender a new community. In speaking about the Black experience in the Americas, Wynter explains that Black popular culture became the way that Blacks "reinvented themselves as a *We* that needed no *Other* to constitute their *Being*; that laid down the cultural parameters of a concretely universal *ethnos*."[25] She argues that poetry allows resistance to dehumanization in the modern world system of racist capitalist exploitation, as poetry is "the inventor/guarantor of the concretely human."[26]

Philip McReynolds observes that for Wynter, hidden social codes shape our world. These codes are a product of, and yet also reinforce, a symbolic boundary between the West and all Others. He notes that Wynter calls for a poetics of humanization, in which the first step "involves a critical phase of identifying the cultural codes that give dominance to the object and result in Man's alienation from the human."[27] The code of life inscripted by the Color Line must be understood and then dismantled. For Wynter, ethical subjects are not merely passive recipients of codes, images, and ideology. Rather we are social creatures with co-creative capacity—we accept, reject, and modify the social norms in which we are immersed and with which our social institutions provide us. Wynter paraphrases Paul Ricoeur when she argues that "It is not man, but his systems of representations that should be accused."[28] Our systems of representation impact our sense of who we are, collectively, and our understanding of to whom we have ethical responsibilities.

By first comprehending the logic of the binary, and its influence on making invisible or incomprehensible both the true scope and the nature of ethical relationships, space is created to envision different modalities of relationship. Interrogations of the status quo lead to an expanded understanding of our human capacity for social transformation. For Wynter, people exist in community, and the goal is a new symbolic order, removed from the scourge of white supremacy and instead grounded in ecumenical kinship.

Following this interrogation, decolonial work seeks to interrupt the social practices and beliefs that perpetuate the myth of Western superiority and reinforce the subject/object binary. Wynter's work focuses on how the negated Other (who is the inhabitant of the zone of nonbeing) positively inhabits subjectivity—"a counter-invention of the self"—in light of this binary, by drawing on Black culture.[29] María Lugones explains, "In our colonized, racially gendered, oppressed experiences we are also other than what the hegemon makes us to be."[30] Reflection on encounter with the Other-as-Western-Man entails a Hegelian confrontation with one's image as mirrored by the Other. As Wynter explains, for members of historically oppressed groups, regaining a sense of their inherent value through participation in cultural rituals and connecting with the transcendent is a primary goal.

For people whose identity and ethical subjectivity more closely align with the ideal of Western Man, the conditions necessitate a somewhat different approach—while also requiring a fundamental re-valuing of the self and a connection with the transcendent—through reflection on encounter with the Other. In what follows, I will identify two examples in recent philosophical literature—practices that correlate with inner dispositions—that can effectively interrupt the logic of the binary, which may make possible the practice of solidarity.

The first interruptive practice is nonviolence, which is critical given the inherent violence of the binary and the colonial ideological edifice upon which it rests. I will refer specifically to Judith Butler's definition of nonviolence, as their mode of conceptualizing social norms through frames make them a natural conversation partner with decolonial scholarship. I draw upon two books, *Frames of War* (2016) and *The Force of Nonviolence* (2020), texts through which they develop and advance an argument about the importance of nonviolence. In decolonial parlance, nonviolence allows moral subjects to resist participation in the death ethic of modernity.

In *Frames of War*, Butler acknowledges that our social norms of violence shape us as moral agents, and that it is "precisely because one is mired in violence that the struggle exists and the possibility of nonviolence emerges."[31] Butler rejects an understanding of nonviolence as a stance of righteous purity. Instead, they argue for a mixed subject (good/bad) who seeks to limit the injury she causes. It requires a type of ascetic orientation involving self-restraint at the core. Nonviolence derives from "an understanding of the possibilities of one's own violent actions in relation to those lives to which one is bound, including those whom one never chose and never knew."[32] While grounded in the present moment of relationship, this description applies to debates on critical race theory in the United States and elsewhere, and the ongoing anxiety about how to make sense of past oppression and legalized violence toward minority ethnic and religious groups. When my animating question becomes, "how do I limit my own sense of rage and frustration so that I do not harm others?" I signal an awareness of the social conditions of violence as well as my own subjective freedom.

If the overriding ethic of modernity is a war ethic, nonviolence grounds a distinctly different modality of ethical subjectivity. Liberalism's construction of the idealized rational subject fails to adequately account for the affective dispositions involved in conflict, and how these inform human deliberation and action. In describing nonviolence, Butler emphasizes the necessity of prudent restraint and self-understanding, which hold salience for those who hold disproportionate social capital and power. In refusing to perpetuate a cycle of violence—and thus effectively rejecting the subject/object binary—we acknowledge that we *as a collective* are constituted by a wound, and that we have power to address it. For Butler, the ethical subject acts freely insofar as she assumes responsibility "for living a life that contests the determining power" of the [social] production of violence.[33] Butler argues that nonviolence is an iterable practice and realizes the possibility of doing something different than what the past has determined.

In *The Force of Nonviolence*, Butler argues that the ethics of nonviolence cannot be grounded in individualism or an ethic of individual action. The self is implicated in social relations in a way that individualism, and for example, the rhetoric of self-defense, deeply obscures. In examining the world around us—with its inequality in terms of whose lives are grievable on account of systemic racism—we come to learn that "violence operates as an intensification of social inequality."[34] Like Wynter, Butler argues for a new sociopolitical imaginary funded by a radical equality of persons in relation to one another.[35] It involves imagining a world that does not yet exist and in which relationships are transformed through commitment to the equality and grievability of all lives.

Related to nonviolence, both as practice and as disposition, is the discrete action of apology. In terms of a political ethical practice, apology also has the potential to elicit transformation of the binary relationship (oppressor/oppressed). Danielle Celermajer focuses on the agent who oppresses or has been a member of a historically oppressing group. In *The Sins of the Nation and the Ritual of Apologies*, Celermajer argues for the necessity of examining the identity of the dominant party. In her case study, the focus is on the nation of

Australia's reckoning with its unjust treatment of its indigenous peoples. She discusses the process and justificatory moves that the Australian government made in attempting to atone for its colonial past. Following Hannah Arendt, she maintains that "forgiveness opens up the possibility of breaking the absolute determinism of the past."[36] Of course, neither Arendt nor Celermajer imagines forgiveness to be a simple process, but they understand its capacity to interrupt a pattern of violence and injustice.

In Australia the disenfranchisement of Aboriginal peoples was justified by the European imperial doctrine of *terra nullis.* When the link between the ideological justification of the doctrine and the constitution of the nation was legally established through the *Mabo* (1992) Supreme Court decision, the white settler population of Australia was confronted with the choice to address it through an apology. Engaging in the process of apology entailed undergoing a transformation through encounters both with the history of the nation and those Aboriginal peoples alive today. Celermajer traces this complex encounter, including the impact of historical wrongs on the present, and argues for the necessity of apology as a relational expression of shame, an admission that wrongful actions have occurred that can no longer continue with legitimacy. Apology is both past-condemning and forward-looking.

Critically, for Celermajer apology is a collective action initiated by a group due to historical injustice, for which that group bears some responsibility. Identifying this dynamic is central to our inquiry since the actions of a collectivity have made possible the scale and scope of social and legal oppression. A key part of this process is the recognition that the collectivity or majority group has not been true to its own norms. The ritual of apology makes explicit the commitment to a future in which those norms are interpreted more inclusively and more expansively. Apology is thus an action undertaken with the intent of transforming the fundamental relationship between persons and groups. This form of apology is qualitatively different from the superficial "conscience-cleansing" apology discussed at the beginning of the chapter and requires concrete political remediations such as financial reparations, legal changes, and changes to symbolic representations of the nation. Moreover, the practice of apology related to colonial trauma and injustice is not a one-and-done event. Turning to Jill Stauffer's argument in *Ethical Loneliness,* most political reconciliations are fragile, incomplete, and in need of renewal.[37] Thus the interruptive practice of apology is necessarily repetitive and attentive to the moral contexts of the injured parties.

The work of Jewish philosopher Emmanuel Levinas figures prominently for Butler, Celermajer, and Stauffer in theorizing the obligation of the self-to-Other as a means of establishing the primacy of human relationship in ethics.[38] If the modern colonial ethic has effectively obfuscated this primary ethical encounter and suspended it in a binary of subject/object, a decolonial ethic requires a return to this encounter *and* simultaneously a recognition and rejection of the violent conditions imposed by modern epistemology and ontology. Ethical subjects must locate themselves within, and assume some responsibility for, their participation in contemporary political systems. There is indeed complexity involved in terms of taking responsibility for the ethical actions that belong to us individually and those that belong to society more generally, whether in the form of historical misdeeds by ancestors and/or whether such actions are sanctioned by prevailing unjust social norms. The concept of liberal individualism, with its focus on individual culpability, falls short in terms of comprehending this reality. By assuming a neat divide between individual/collective, and public/private, the binary has once again come up short in terms of explanatory power. A more complex rendering of responsibility is necessary.

Returning to the specific question of how feminist religious ethicists ought to conceptualize and engage in the work of solidarity, we can identify several interrelated points. Following Wynter, we recognize that our comprehension of both the breadth and depth of ethical obligation has been stymied by the subject/object binary and observe that a new symbolic and ethical order is needed. Butler and Celermajer name particular modes of ethical engagement that may effectively interrogate, interrupt, and possibly transform the normative ethical world that had been previously imagined along the binary of Western Man/Other. Significantly, the dissolution of the binary should not involve historical amnesia. Rather, there is a necessary confrontation with the violence of the past and present, and an acknowledgment of one's capacity to do violence to the Other, that must precede and accompany social transformation. Historical and geographical power asymmetries imply that those who have more power have special responsibilities to acknowledge wrongdoing and lead the process of moral repair.

Feminist religious ethicists approach the question of solidarity from different positions of power within society and the academy. Following decolonial analysis, the question of solidarity hinges on an acknowledgment of a "first estrangement" based on colonial histories of violence and rupture and the related construction of white/European women's identity in relation to the identities of colonized women and slaves.[39] In this subject/object binary, women occupy a gender-differentiated category within each side, which requires its own deconstruction—something along the lines of Lugones's work on the coloniality of gender.[40] To state it another way, as Kwok Pui-Lan argues, a postcolonial perspective "must insist that not all women are included in the pronoun 'our,' [and] the boundaries of patriarchy's space are not the same."[41]

For Kwok, Lugones, and Wynter, the work does not end with the deconstruction of colonial categories, however. There is a common understanding that binary thinking is powerful and seductive in our modern context, and that deconstruction alone cannot summon the resources to resist and challenge this pervasive model of categorization. Lugones names the coalitional work necessary for transcending coloniality. She argues that feminists need to "learn about each other as resisters to the coloniality of gender" and "without necessarily being an insider to the worlds of meaning from which resistance to coloniality arises."[42] Since all people alive today have inherited and share the fractured world system of ethics and meaning, all are invited to dwell in the histories of resistance to colonial difference.

Transformation

In the final part of the chapter, I will consider what feminist religious ethicists may learn from decolonial scholarship, and how ethical discourses might participate in interruptive and transformative practices that have the power to constructively shape the direction of religious ethics as a field of inquiry. I also discuss the necessity of co-striving for emancipatory politics as a part of solidarity.

My first point pertains to the inadequate conceptualization of the relationship between religious studies and theological studies, specifically in the field of ethics. Although many scholars presume a strong division between theology and religious studies as two distinct approaches to knowledge in ethics, with the idea that the former field is grounded in metaphysics or other unverifiable or unshared claims, decolonial feminist scholarship necessitates that we revisit this distinction. A decolonial analysis reveals the strict division between a secular and a theological worldview to be a product of Western hegemony and yet one more example of the subject/object binary. The reality of living in a postcolonial world demands a more nuanced understanding of the relationship between religious studies, theology, and how modern epistemological and ethical frameworks have obscured the human dignity of those on the margins.[43]

Since our global shared symbolic field is dominated by the market value of things (capitalism) and the stubborn pervasiveness of the subject/object binary, there needs to be a symbolic intervention and an inclusive one at that. Some conservative Christian theological critics argue for an intervention but they also largely fail to acknowledge the reality of religious pluralism, racism, and the inequalities faced by women and sexual minorities in our world system.[44] In their respective uses of the term "tradition," these scholars ground an alternative response to the nihilism of modernity, but they unfortunately neglect the question of Otherness that forms the dividing logic of modern thought.

Drawing on various theological arguments to make wide appeals for solidarity in feminist religious ethics does not entail uncritical acceptance of a theo-political paradigm which is inherently exclusionary, nor does it involve privileging a theocentric ethical framework over a non-theocentric one. Rather, we must be more thoughtful about how we articulate and imagine the relationship between politics and religion. For example, the civil religious possibilities to which Wynter and Celermajer speak involve a fundamental reorientation to the Other in a pluralistic social context. For Wynter, the "degodding" which occurred in tandem with European colonialism provides an instructive lesson about the danger of social-political hierarchies. This particular expression of secularism resulted in a hierarchical system in which

Western Man resided at the apex, "in the place of angels."[45] This act of idolatry created a distorted ethical system based on the subject/object binary.

In an essay on Rastafarianism, Wynter explains that the quest to locate one's identity in divinity is both a necessary part of liberation from oppression of the binary, and yet also it is important to distinguish this as a *symbolic* act apart from the project of secular modern politics.[46] The Rastafarian view recognizes the inherent danger of political configurations in which one group/identity resides "in the place of angels"—a phenomenon bequeathed by modern colonialism—which Wynter makes explicit. Since the subject/object binary has left the Other bereft of understanding of their divine birthright/belonging, the quest for the transcendent or divine is critical to their self-recovery. To implement Rastafarianism as a political program would necessarily entail corruption, however, as the rational world of modernity inevitably would betray the emancipatory telos of the movement.[47]

Wynter's contribution to the specific question of solidarity in feminist ethics has a distinctly religious orientation—striving to see Others as created in the divine image, in defiance of the subject/object binary. Importantly, she does not advocate for the political implementation of a particular religious tradition. Rather, the act of striving for emancipation, as well as kinship and solidarity, requires a recognition of reciprocity or an effort to see Others as created in that divine image.

Celermajer also argues for the retrieval of religious concepts and symbols, but this time in the service of concrete political goals. She persuasively draws upon Jewish theological understandings of repentance (*teshuvah*) and covenant, which are based on an understanding of a community with moral obligations to one another and God. While noting that Australia is a secular state, Celermajer maintains that these religious teachings offer guidance for how to best conceptualize the ethical challenges of collective life, noting its continual re-creation and return to normative principles. Emmanuel Levinas's work is central to her interpretation of the tradition, as she explains: "what drives ethical progress is the recognition of the claim of the other, the one who had been excluded from the conversation through which the law is interpreted."[48] If citizens can productively engage in this work, they can hold the tension between the past, present, and future moment—acknowledging the inalterability of the past, but committing to a more just future. Some examples of action are formal apologies (like Australia's to its indigenous peoples) and the creation and support of ballot initiatives to remove Confederate statues in the United States. Decolonial scholarship in the service of a political ethic might aim for a civil religious "re-covenanting" in which citizens encounter the perspectives of marginalized and disenfranchised others as they interact with the dominant and often exclusionary ethical and political norms of the nation. Ultimately, re-covenanting signifies a transformation in the relationship between self and other, allowing for "the development of existing norms beyond their historical expression."[49]

Re-covenanting depends on a formal acknowledgment that the state legal system has marginalized, and/or been complicit in violence toward, the formerly colonized Others within the system. Both marginalization and oppression have detrimental impacts on the representation of these Others within law and within society more generally (recall Wynter's emphasis on the symbolic order). A deficient legal system thus makes it difficult, if not impossible, for citizens to recognize these people as fellow citizens deserving of equal rights and ethical recognition. Reciprocity remains unrealized.

The act of re-covenanting entails redress for the systemic legal wrongs visited upon formerly colonized groups within the state. Re-covenanting is distinct from a kind of re-contracting that invokes a secular liberal model of coexistence. For Celermajer, re-covenanting invokes that absolute obligation to the Other based on their inviolability and my duty to not harm them based on their createdness in the divine image. We might extrapolate from this that the possibility of solidarity in feminist ethics resides in a recognition of mutual vulnerability as well as a recognition of responsibility for one another.

As for what reciprocity entails, it does not mean that both sides of the binary have equal responsibility for righting the wrongs of the past. (It avoids whataboutisms.) Instead, we should think of reciprocity in terms of a shared commitment to restoring moral equivalence through truth-seeking, nonviolence, and apology. In Jill Stauffer's work on Jean Améry and the Holocaust, she explains Améry's wish that "Everyone, all victims and perpetrators, should be joined in wishing the past were otherwise, asserting that what happened should not have happened."[50] She describes this as Améry's desire to restore moral equivalence in the world, which fundamentally pertains to a sense of safety and trust. One cannot meaningfully practice solidarity without trust—without meaningful assurances and commitments that the terror inflicted was unnecessary, unjust, and morally unacceptable. Collective statements, apologies, and other actions that recognize harm, "effect a revision of an injurious past and grants to those most harmed by that past the liberty in the present moment to imagine a future not determined by past harm."[51] Such actions may increase the ethical freedom of those who have suffered harm as a result of entrenched legal representations of the subject/object binary, enabling the work of striving for collective emancipation to continue.

To conclude, feminist religious ethicists have an obligation within the wider field of religious ethics to dismantle the subject/object binary and to pursue social transformation. The social transformation that Wynter envisions and for which other decolonial scholars hope, is something that can spark our imagination in difficult times. Our communities experience a continued need for collective processes of liberation from the injustice of colonialism and other forms of oppression. The settled patterns of relationality described in a classical liberal system, in which autonomous individuals act primarily in self-interest, are inadequate both in terms of what they describe and prescribe for social life. They fail to acknowledge the fundamental interdependence of all beings. Liberation cannot be achieved by individuals alone. Change is dependent on the transformation of our social symbols, particularly the ones that condition how we think of ourselves in relation to others, and the cultivation of practices that interrupt the status quo of violence and harm. For some scholars, theological language performs the work of reminding people of their fundamental relationality and responsibility; in such cases, a theocentric ethic can be a useful tool for the decolonial imaginary. For those persons not interested in a theocentric paradigm, the act of envisioning radical equality still requires a symbolic re-ordering away from individualism and a re-orientation toward reciprocity and mutuality. Fundamentally, a decolonial feminist ethic requires that we envision, establish, and live out a symbolic order capable of strengthening a commitment to nonviolence and making possible the ability to offer apology or forgiveness.

Notes

1 Austin Harper, "The Problem with 'Centering Blackness' in Everyday Conversations: On Good and Bad Color-Blindness," *The Atlantic*, August 14, 2023.

2 The use of the term "decolonize" as a verb in relation to solidarity resonates with Kwok Pui-Lan's discussion of the postcolonial imagination in *Postcolonial Imagination and Feminist Theology*. According to Kwok, both colonizer and colonized are interdependent, and must reckon with the injustice that is inherent in that relationship. See Kwok, *Postcolonial Imagination and Feminist Theology* (Louisville, KY: Westminster John Knox Press, 2005).

3 Judith Butler, *The Force of Nonviolence: An Ethico-Political Bind* (New York: Verso, 2020).

4 Danielle Celermajer, *The Sins of the Nation and the Ritual of Apologies*, Vol. 72 (New York: Cambridge University Press, 2009).

5 Decolonial methodology is distinct in its geographic and historical turning point, which distinguishes it from postcolonial thought focused on the Middle East and Asia. Yet it shares in the critique of European hegemony and the related construction of racism as having inimical and durable impacts on modern epistemology and ethics. See Kwok, 2005.

6 Maldonado-Torres, "Race, Religion, and Ethics in the Modern/Colonial World," *Journal of Religious Ethics*, 42, no. 4 (2014): 691–711.

7 Sylvia Wynter, "Unsettling the Coloniality of Being/Power/Truth/Freedom: Towards the Human, after Man, Its Overrepresentation—An Argument." *CR: The New Centennial Review*, 3, no. 3 (2003): 257–337.

8 Wynter, "Unsettling the Coloniality of Being/Power/Truth/Freedom," 287.

9 Sylvia Wynter, "Ethno or Socio-Poetics," *We Must Learn to Sit Down Together and Talk about a Little Culture: Decolonizing Essays*, 1967–1984, ed. and with an introduction by Demetrius L. Eudell (London: Peepal Tree Press, 2022), 428.

10 Wynter, "Unsettling the Coloniality of Being/Power/Truth/Freedom."

11 Maldonado-Torres, "Race, Religion, and Ethics in the Modern/Colonial World," 699.

12 Ashley J. Bohrer argues that while Sepúlveda and others exploited the natives through an ideological program of explicit dehumanization, Vitoria used a natural law paradigm that maintained the natives' humanity. Vitoria did so, however, in such a way that defined as "natural" practices that gave economic

advantage to the Spanish settlers and explorers, paving the way for genocide. Bohrer describes this as a "devastating" application of natural law theory (29), lending more nuance to Wynter's argument but supports the overall point that the Spanish were mainly interested in defending their practices of domination. See Bohrer, "Just Wars of Accumulation: The Salamanca School, Race, and Colonial Capitalism," *Race and Class* 59, no. 3 (2018): 20–37.

13 Wynter, "Unsettling the Coloniality of Being/Power/Truth/Freedom," 289. Wynter's rendering of a Christian ethic against a secular ethic at times appears overly simplistic. When we attend to the emancipatory telos of her Christian ethic—its inclusiveness as well as its radical equality of beings—her reasoning behind this juxtaposition becomes clearer. For Wynter, secularism is tainted by its association with capitalism, naked greed, and it produces an alienated moral subject. The "reason" that supposedly justifies secularism and promises liberation instead is used to oppress.

14 Frantz Fanon, *Black Skin, White Masks* (New York: Grove Press, 2008).

15 For those living in this zone of nonbeing, or more broadly, the borders or margins of political communities, Walter Mignolo, and others have argued for the need to delink from the hegemonic epistemology of colonialism. See, for example, Mignolo, "The Logic of the In-Visible: Decolonial Reflections on the Change of Epoch," *Theory, Culture, and Society* 37, no. 7–8 (2020): 205–18. Anibal Quijano coined the term "coloniality of power" to refer to the totalizing effects of colonialism on the production of knowledge, including the systematic degradation of non-European forms of knowledge. See Anibal Quijano, "Coloniality of Power, Eurocentrism, and Social Classification," *Coloniality at Large: Latin America and the Postcolonial Debate* 192 (2008).

16 Notably there are scholars of religious ethics that seek to understand and address the implications of the Christian orientation of the field. For example, see Jung H. Lee, "The Legacy of Christian Ethics in Comparative Religious Ethics," *Journal of Religious Ethics* 47, no. 4 (2019): 754–58.

17 See Delores S. Williams's critique of James Cone in *Sisters in the Wilderness: The Challenge of Womanist God-Talk* (Maryknoll, NY: Orbis Books, 2013).

18 Wynter, "Unsettling the Coloniality of Being/Power/Truth/Freedom," 326.

19 Wynter, "Unsettling the Coloniality of Being/Power/Truth/Freedom," 328.

20 Wynter (2003) and Butler (2020) each fault Hobbes and his interpreters for the outsize focus on individualism in Western political conceptions of subjectivity. According to Butler, the idea that ethical subjects should be prepared to wage war

with anyone who is not like them is fundamentally Hobbesian. See Butler, *The Force of Nonviolence*, p. 39.

21 Maldonado-Torres, "Race, Religion, and Ethics in the Modern/Colonial World," 702.

22 Louiza Odysseos, "After Rights, after Man? Sylvia Wynter, Sociopoetic Struggle and the 'Undared Shape,'" *The International Journal of Human Rights* (2023): 1–28.

23 Odysseos, "After Rights, after Man? Sylvia Wynter, Sociopoetic Struggle and the 'Undared Shape,'" 7.

24 Judith Butler, *Frames of War: When Is Life Grievable?* (New York: Verso Books, 2016).

25 Wynter, "Ethno or Socio-Poetics," 431.

26 Wynter, "Ethno or Socio-Poetics," 434. Poetry, art, music, and other forms of creative expression all serve to connect people in community and to their humanity.

27 Philip McReynolds, "Dewey, Wynter, and Cesaire," in *Decolonizing American Philosophy*, ed. McCall and McReynolds (New York: State University of New York Press, 2021), 63–79.

28 Sylvia Wynter, "New Seville and the Conversion Experience of Bartolomé de Las Casas, Parts 1 and 2," in *We Must Learn to Sit Down Together and Talk about a Little Culture: Decolonizing Essays*, 1967–1984, ed. and with an introduction by Demetrius L. Eudell (London: Peepal Tree Press, 2022), 580.

29 Sylvia Wynter, "We Know Where We are from: The Politics of Black Culture from Myal to Marley," in *We Must Learn to Sit Down Together and Talk about a Little Culture: Decolonizing Essays*, 1967–1984, ed. and with an introduction by Demetrius L. Eudell (London: Peepal Tree Press, 2022), 484.

30 María Lugones, "Toward a Decolonial Feminism," *Hypatia*, 25, no. 4 (2010): 746.

31 Butler, *Frames of War: When Is Life Grievable?* 171.

32 Butler, *Frames of War: When Is Life Grievable?* 179.

33 Butler, *Frames of War: When Is Life Grievable?* 170.

34 Butler, *The Force of Nonviolence: An Ethico-Political Bind*, 142.

35 Butler, *The Force of Nonviolence: An Ethico-Political Bind*, 62.

36 Celermajer, *The Sins of the Nation and the Ritual of Apologies*, 104.

37 Jill Stauffer, *Ethical Loneliness: The Injustice of Not Being Heard* (New York: Columbia University Press, 2015), 168.

38 See Emmanuel Levinas, *Totality and Infinity: An Essay on Exteriority*, trans. Alphonso Lingis (Pittsburgh: Duquesne University Press, 1969).

39 A good example is found in the work of Ann Laura Stoler, *Carnal Knowledge and Imperial Power: Race and the Intimate in Colonial Rule* (Berkeley: University of California Press, 2010). The construction of the white/European citizen is an unstable entity when compared across colonial contexts. It is important to recall that fundamentally, whiteness is a social construction that is dependent on configurations of power. For example, historically Jewish European women have been Othered in modern political configurations of citizenship. Laura Levitt traces how Jews in modernity remained outsiders within the European state in ways that are distinct from, and yet have parallels to, colonial subjects outside of Europe. See Levitt, "Letting Go of Liberalism: Feminism and the Emancipation of the Jews," in *Postcolonialism, Feminism and Religious Discourse* (New York: Routledge, 2015), 161–79.

40 Lugones, "Toward a Decolonial Feminism."

41 Kwok, *Postcolonial Imagination and Feminist Theology*, 59.

42 Lugones, "Toward a Decolonial Feminism," 753.

43 The work of Muslim feminists, broadly construed, illustrates the porous boundaries between religious studies and theological studies. The emancipatory projects undertaken by Muslim feminists involve deconstructing patriarchy as well as Orientalism, hegemonic secularism, and sometimes racist discrimination. See, for example, Aysha Hidayatullah, *Feminist Edges of the Qur'an* (New York: Oxford University Press, 2014).

44 The work of Alasdair MacIntyre is particularly representative of this stance. See MacIntyre. *After Virtue* (London: A&C Black, 2013).

45 Wynter, "Ethno or Socio-Poetics," 431.

46 Wynter, "We Know Where We Are From," 456–599.

47 Wynter, "We Know Where We Are From," 456–599.

48 Celermajer, *The Sins of the Nation and the Ritual of Apologies*, 104.

49 Celermajer, *The Sins of the Nation and the Ritual of Apologies*, 209.

50 Stauffer, *Ethical Loneliness: The Injustice of Not Being Heard*, 123.

51 Stauffer, *Ethical Loneliness: The Injustice of Not Being Heard*, 137.

References

Bohrer, Ashley. "Just Wars of Accumulation: The Salamanca School, Race, and Colonial Capitalism." *Race & Class* 59, no. 3 (2018): 20–37.

Butler, Judith. *Frames of War: When Is Life Grievable?* New York: Verso Books, 2016.

———. *The Force of Nonviolence: An Ethico-Political Bind.* New York: Verso Books, 2020.

Celermajer, Danielle. *The Sins of the Nation and the Ritual of Apologies.* Vol. 72. New York: Cambridge University Press, 2009.

Fanon, Frantz. *Black Skin, White Masks.* New York: Grove Press, 2008.

Harper, Austin Tyler. "The Problem with 'Centering Blackness' in Everyday Conversations: On Good and Bad Color-Blindness." *The Atlantic*, August 14, 2023.

Hidayatullah, Aysha. *Feminist Edges of the Qur'an.* New York: Oxford University Press, 2014.

Kwok, Pui-Lan. *Postcolonial Imagination and Feminist Theology.* Louisville, KY: Westminster John Knox Press, 2005.

Lee, Jung H. "The Legacy of Christian Ethics in Comparative Religious Ethics." *Journal of Religious Ethics* 47, no. 4 (2019): 754–58.

Levinas, Emmanuel. *Totality and Infinity: An Essay on Exteriority.* Translated by Alphonso Lingis. Pittsburgh: Duquesne University Press, 1969.

Levitt, Laura. "Letting Go of Liberalism: Feminism and the Emancipation of the Jews." In *Postcolonialism, Feminism and Religious Discourse.* New York: Routledge, 2015.

Lugones, María. "Toward a Decolonial Feminism." *Hypatia* 25, no. 4 (2010): 746.

MacIntyre, Alasdair. *After Virtue.* London: A&C Black, 2013.

Maldonado-Torres, Nelson. "Race, Religion, and Ethics in the Modern/Colonial World." *Journal of Religious Ethics* 42, no. 4 (2014): 691–711.

McReynolds, Philip. "Dewey, Wynter, and Cesaire." In *Decolonizing American Philosophy*, edited by McCall and McReynolds, pp. 63–79. New York: State University of New York Press, 2021.

Mignolo, Walter. "The Logic of the In-Visible: Decolonial Reflections on the Change of Epoch." *Theory, Culture, and Society* 37, no. 7–8 (2020): 205–18.

Odysseos, Louiza. "After Rights, after Man? Sylvia Wynter, Sociopoetic Struggle and the 'Undared Shape.'" *The International Journal of Human Rights* (2023): 1–28.

Quijano, Anibal. "Coloniality of Power, Eurocentrism, and Social Classification." *Coloniality at Large: Latin America and the Postcolonial Debate*, 192 (2008).

Stauffer, Jill. *Ethical Loneliness: The Injustice of Not Being Heard.* New York: Columbia University Press, 2015.

Stoler, Ann Laura. *Carnal Knowledge and Imperial Power: Race and the Intimate in Colonial Rule.* Berkeley: University of California Press, 2010.

Williams, Delores S. *Sisters in the Wilderness: The Challenge of Womanist God-Talk.* Maryknoll, NY: Orbis Books, 2013.

Wynter, Sylvia. "Ethno or Socio-Poetics." In *We Must Learn to Sit Down Together and Talk about a Little Culture: Decolonizing Essays*, 1967–1984, edited and with an introduction by Demetrius L. Eudell, pp. 421–44. London: Peepal Tree Press, 2022.

———. "New Seville and the Conversion Experience of Bartolomé de Las Casas, Parts 1 and 2." In *We Must Learn to Sit Down Together and Talk about a Little Culture: Decolonizing Essays*, 1967–1984, edited and with an introduction by Demetrius L. Eudell, pp. 554–84. London: Peepal Tree Press, 2022.

———. "Unsettling the Coloniality of Being/Power/Truth/Freedom: Towards the Human, after Man, Its Overrepresentation—An Argument." *CR: The New Centennial Review* 3, no. 3 (2003): 257–337.

———. "We Know Where We Are From: The Politics of Black Culture from Myal to Marley." In *We Must Learn to Sit Down Together and Talk about a Little Culture: Decolonizing Essays*, 1967–1984, edited and with an introduction by Demetrius L. Eudell, pp. 456–599. London: Peepal Tree Press, 2022.

Section 2

Living Solidarity

3

On Pilgrimage in Bodhgaya, India

Buddhist Nuns' Ordination and Solidarity

Darcie Price-Wallace

"We can break separate sticks, but we cannot break a bundle of sticks. So, sticking together, solidarity, being united is our strength of the saṅgha."
—Bhikkhunī Viditadhammā Mahātherī

Preparing for *Bhikkhunī* Ordination

Adorned in their different robes like autumn leaves in shades of burgundy, mustard, and saffron, the senior *bhikkhunīs* (fully ordained nuns) instructed the *bhikkhunīs*-to-be on the ritual details for their upcoming ordination (figure 3.1).

They began with a familiar practice. Resting their knees and shins on small square fabrics, palms together above their heads, they bowed to the golden image of the Buddha at the front of the Mahā Bodhi Society's temple in Bodhgaya, India. Their actual ceremony would take place in a few days at a nearby Laotian temple. Such an event would have been impossible for Buddhist women in the Theravāda tradition just a few decades ago.

Theravāda *Bhikkhunīs'* Solidarity

For over twenty-five years, Buddhist women and their advocates have chosen Bodhgaya as a site for transforming a narrative that many Buddhist communities share: the extinction of the fully ordained nuns' orders for women of the

Figure 3.1. Ordination Rehearsal, Bodhgaya, 2022. Photo by Darcie Price-Wallace

Theravāda and Tibetan Buddhist traditions. When journalist Raymond Lam reported on the international *bhikkhunī* ordination in Bodhgaya in November 2022, he wrote, "The old narrative of the 'extinction' of the Bhikkhunī Order, and ongoing 'attempts' to 'revive' it, is outdated in multiple respects."[1] His article points to the on-the-ground extraordinary re-establishment of an order of fully ordained women in the Theravāda Buddhist tradition over the past twenty-eight years through *bhikkhunī* ordinations performed in Bodhgaya and other pilgrimage sites. This transformation depends on pilgrimage, ceremony, and the double-vision of these *bhikkhunīs*, aspiring *bhikkhunīs*, and *bhikkhunī*-supporters.

Two Buddhist organizations, the United Theravada Bhikkhunī Saṅgha International (UTBSI) and the Mahā Bodhi Society of India (MBSI), make *bhikkhunī* ordination happen against the grain of traditional narratives and lineages.[2] Their solidarity is necessary for continued *bhikkhunī* ordinations and is achieved through the union of UTBSI and MBSI who purposefully include transnational practitioners of diverse backgrounds in ordination rituals, encourage monastic training, and collaboration among Buddhist women. UTBSI and MBSI sustain their communities with *bhikkhunī* ordinations and the first *bhikkhunī* training center in India. These ordinations replicate what they seek to transform, the Buddhist *saṅgha* (community of Buddhist practitioners).[3] They ensure that the Buddha's vision of the fourfold *saṅgha*, consisting of the *bhikkhu* (monk), *bhikkhunī* (nun), *upāsaka* (male laity), *upāsikā* (female laity), continues. Presently, senior *bhikkhunī*s educate, train, and give ordinations with supportive *bhikkhu*s to aspiring *bhikkhunī*s in the face of twenty-eight or more years of incredulity from other *saṅgha* members who insist that full ordination for women is unacceptable because the lineage was discontinued centuries ago.[4] UTBSI and MBSI transform the *saṅgha* through solidarity created during in-person rituals at a pilgrimage site, maintaining these connections in online gatherings that feature monastic training, celebrations of *bhikkhunī*s, and international scholarship.

UTBSI and MBSI's collaboration serves as an example of how solidarity is forged within the fourfold *saṅgha*. These organizations share the common cause of supporting monastic women by providing conditions for connecting, training, and holding rituals. They share a religious identity, yet their ethical endeavor manifests through the collaborative effort to include differences rather than smoothing over them. Some of these differences include language, cultural nuances, and their own local communities' receptivity to full ordination. They model "power-with," the capacity to work together for a common cause.[5] MBSI, UTBSI, and their affiliated *bhikkhunī*s, aspiring *bhikkhunī*s, and/or *bhikkhunī*-supporters reshape the *bhikkhunī saṅgha* in Theravāda Buddhism with ordinations enabled through pilgrimage and ceremony.

Their solidarity, I argue, is supported by a passage from collected verses of women's experiences from the *Therīgāthā*: "you are welcome here; this is where you belong."[6] It reflects a double-vision shaped by pilgrimage, which facilitates a type of "co-seeing" of the mundane and the fantastic,[7] a double-vision which, I argue, facilitates Buddhist women's solidarity. The *bhikkhunīs* at the center of my case study embody such solidarity in their vision for an inclusive *saṅgha*, a vision which is essential for the ongoing transformation of diverse orders of Buddhist monastic women.

Historical Background and Supporting Organizations

Across Buddhist worlds, there are three main codes of monastic regulations (*vinayas*) still in use for giving monastic ordination. Today, these are differentiated mainly by the locations where these traditions took root outside of India and continued. They can be roughly paired up as follows: the Pali Vinaya predominantly upheld in Southeast Asia (associated with Theravāda), the Dharmaguptaka Vinaya in East Asia (associated with Mahāyāna), and the Mūlasarvāstivāda Vinaya in Tibet (associated with Vajrayāna). There are also different types and levels of ordination in Buddhism, the highest being full ordination for men (*bhikkhu*) and women (*bhikkhunī*). *Bhikkhunī* ordinations ideally require a quorum of both the *bhikkhu* and *bhikkhunī saṅgha*.[8]

When the *bhikkhunī saṅgha* ceased in Sri Lanka in the eleventh century after a period of foreign invasions, the order went defunct for Theravāda *bhikkhunī*s. It continued only in Vinaya traditions in East Asia. Without Theravāda *bhikkhunī*s, the lineage could not be restarted. However, in 1996 and 1998, *bhikkhunī*s from the Dharmaguptaka Vinaya tradition came together with Theravāda women, even though they use different versions of monastic regulations, to restart the *bhikkhunī saṅgha*. Bias against these *bhikkhunī* ordinations persists due to concerns about scriptural validity among the *saṅgha*.[9] The Sri Lankan government and male monastic heads did not unanimously accept this ordination because the new Theravāda *bhikkhunī*s received their vows from Mahāyāna *bhikṣuṇī*s, who follow a different Vinaya. Proponents of these ordinations argue that all Vinayas stem from the earliest Buddhist schools. Following the 1998 ordination, the new Theravāda *bhikkhunī*s received a second ordination administered by Sri Lankan Theravāda *bhikkhu*s in accordance with their own Vinaya.[10] UTBSI and MBSI skillfully navigate such bias by developing sustainable alternatives that draw upon earlier precedents and now rely upon Theravāda *bhikkhunīs* and *bhikkhus*, making them valid alternatives.

Sri Lankan involvement in revitalizing *bhikkhunī* ordination has several precedents, but one that is most relevant for this project is that MBSI's founder, Anagārika Dharmapāla, wrote about his aspiration for revitalization of the nuns' order in his own diaries.[11] While Dharmapāla never restarted the *bhikkhunī sangha*, he established MBSI in 1891 with the mission to sustain and renew the teachings of the Buddha amid British colonialism in Sri Lanka and India. In 1996, MBSI was integral in the revival of the Theravāda *bhikkhunī sangha*.[12] In fact, the 1996 ordination demonstrates a longer genealogy of inclusiveness and intentional collaboration between transnational organizations across groups of Theravāda, Mahāyāna, and Vajrayāna Buddhists, such as alliance with Fo Guang Shan monastics from Taiwan and conferences organized by ecumenical Buddhist women's advocacy organizations like Sakyadhita International Association of Buddhist Women.[13]

Central interlocutors in this project, like senior UTBSI members, Bhikkhunī Viditadhammā Mahātherī of Vietnam and Bhikkhunī Dhammananda Mahātherī of Thailand, both ordained in Sri Lanka in the early 2000s. Since then, they have conducted ordinations in Bodhgaya in 2019 and 2022. Ordinations in the 1990s set precedents for ordinations at pilgrimage sites, but those in 2019 and 2022 were distinct since they relied solely on the Theravāda *sangha*. In my interview with MBSI's current General Secretary Venerable Pelawatte Seewalee Thero, he explained that MBSI has been invested in the revival of nuns, mirroring the aspirations of its founder Dharmapāla, since 1996.[14] He added that "Anyone who defies re-establishing it goes against the word of the Buddha, who saw the *sangha* as a group who relied and cared for each other."[15] Since 1998, the Sri Lankan community has continued to hold *bhikkhunī* ordinations with quorums of Theravāda *bhikkhunīs* and *bhikkhus* in Sri Lanka.[16] Increasingly, the laity are crucial supporters of *bhikkhunī* ordination due to their strong affective ties with their local *bhikkhunīs*.[17]

This recent collaboration between MBSI and the *sangha* of international Theravāda *bhikkhunīs* first occurred in Bodhgaya in 2019 when twenty-four women from several countries received vows and were accepted as *bhikkhunīs* by the dual sangha of Theravāda *bhikkhus* and *bhikkhunīs*.[18] Bhikkhunī

Tathālokā Mahātherī (hereafter Tathālokā Therī) describes how UTBSI took root.

> The idea was proposed that the gathered bhikkhunī preceptors, teachers, and leaders of ten countries form a World Theravada Bhikkhunī Council in order to support the harmonious collaboration and cooperation of the growing transnational Bhikkhunī Sangha, to guide training and ordinations of samaneris [novices] and bhikkhunīs, and to altogether support the renaissance of the Bhikkhunī Sangha in its homeland of India as well as around the world.[19]

Formally established in November 2021, UTBSI aims to educate, ordain, support, and train women. UTBSI's mission statement asserts: "Working together for the solidarity and harmony of the Buddhist Bhikkhu and Bhikkhunī Sanghas."[20] The 2022 ordination relies on these precedents but stands apart in its intentional dedication and determination to provide consistent ordinations in Bodhgaya, with training both online and in person at the seat of the Buddha's awakening.

Pilgrimage Facilitating Co-Seeing

Catherine Hartmann uses the idea of "co-seeing" to describe the experience of the pilgrim. In her exploration of pilgrimage travel guides, she highlights how pilgrimage directs the pilgrim's ordinary perception to the extraordinary, facilitating "a state of seeing the place in two ways at once . . . which creates the conditions for the possibility of the transformation of perception."[21] Co-seeing offers a way of thinking about how pilgrimage boosts Buddhist women's solidarity in multidirectional ways and transforms individual and institutional perceptions.

UTBSI and MBSI's collaboration provides a lens into one type of Buddhist women's solidarity, an endeavor to strive for a shared common cause with a sense of obligation towards a similar vision. When these transnational communities come together under shared identities, they share a vision for the continuation, support, and maintenance of the fourfold *sangha*, suturing together the social fabric of Buddhist institutions as they don robes. These women are part of a community of Buddhist women who are (re)claiming a lineage and place in a tradition that some have denied them.[22] They co-see the fantastic, inspiration from the Buddha's awakening in Bodhgaya, alongside the mundane: the contestation of their legitimacy as *bhikkhunīs* within their local communities. They have this double vision and change perceptions of earlier ideas of who religious women are as they become and train *bhikkhunīs*. They gather under the auspices of the mundane reality—their aspirations for ordination are not universally supported due to persistent gender asymmetries on the ground. These ceremonies reinforce their solidarity because the act of pilgrimage supports their shared perception of obligation and devotion to the Three Jewels.

Shared Obligation and Devotion for the Three Jewels on Pilgrimage

Among national and international pilgrims, solidarity coalesces around devotion to the Buddha. These attitudes are born out of devotees' collective knowledge of the Buddha's life stories and ultimate awakening.[23] In their ethnography of Buddhist rituals, David Geary and Kiran Shinde note, "As places of memory, the Buddhist pilgrimage sites provide a ritual environment that helps reinforce and internalize the truths of the Dhamma because they help bring to life the stories of the Buddha in the holy land in ways that are morally transformative."[24] A shared understanding of taking refuge in the Three Jewels—Buddha, Dhamma, and Saṅgha—solidifies the varied expressions of Buddhism that manifest more particularly, often locally or regionally. Pilgrims demonstrate mutual commitments to nationality through practices specific to their own regions that they import into Bodhgaya.

Bodhgaya contains multiple celebrated sites correlating with the life story of the Buddha, particularly the site of his awakening, the *vajrāsana*, enshrined at the Mahābodhi Temple in the center of the town.[25] UTBSI and MBSI members intentionally travel to the celebrated site of the Buddha's awakening for acts of devotion and ordination, a decisive commitment to practice on the path set forth by the teachings of the Buddha. Members of UTBSI and MBSI are pilgrims (i.e., co-seers) on a shared pilgrimage in Bodhgaya where they perform ordinations and establish a training center for monastic women. These actions mirror their broader aspiration of harmony among the *saṅgha*.[26]

The solidarity forged between UTBSI and MBSI depends upon their active re-establishment of the fourfold *saṅgha* and support for training. They purposefully build solidarity due to shared values and identities as Buddhists, even when their practices and beliefs may be quite distinct. The canonical sanctioning of pilgrimage appears in the Pali version of *Mahāparinibbāna Sutta* when the Buddha gives final instructions to his foremost disciple, saying, "Ānanda, there are four places that are apt to cause emotion and ought to be seen by a faithful follower."[27] The Buddha lists the sites of his birth, supreme awakening, where he first taught the *Dhamma*, his *parinibbāna*, and adds, "Ānanda, faithful monks, nuns, laymen and laywomen should visit these places. And those who pass away while going with faith on pilgrimage to these shrines will be reborn, at the break-up of their body after death, in a good realm, a heaven." The Buddha's response to Ānanda is a way for devotees to be reborn in heaven and "a solution to the Buddha's absence—a way for them to continue to 'see' and venerate him after his passing."[28] Pilgrimage facilitates encountering the Buddha by directly seeing him.[29] This experience arouses religious emotion in the pilgrim who is moved by his absence as they recall the stories of his life at these respected sites.[30]

In my case study, stories shared among members of UTBSI and MBSI on pilgrimage serve to recall the Buddha and foster solidarity through shared affinity for the Dhamma amid the suppleness of different culturally sanctioned practices. When I interviewed Venerable Karma Lekshe Tsomo, one of the founders of Sakyadhita, she explained that "pilgrimage entails learning."[31] She described the act of pilgrimage as an ethical pursuit that facilitates a key practice: a willingness to transform oneself through discipline, meditation, and wisdom.[32] The pilgrim may experience new perceptions through practice and the process and journey of attending to the Buddha's presence at these sites. Similarly, John Strong argues that "pilgrimage to these sites was fundamentally soteriological, resulting in either a favorable rebirth or in escape from *saṃsāra*."[33] Encounters with sacred places, either physically or even mentally, incite an inward transformation. The pilgrim is inspired by the Buddha's qualities, both in the moment and on the return journey. In this regard, pilgrimage has the potential to compel knowledge.

Bhikkhunī Viditadhammā noted that UTBSI chose Bodhgaya for the ordination and training center because the *vajrāsana*, the seat of the Buddha's enlightenment, is a powerful draw for practitioners.[34] She added that "Bodhgaya is the most sacred place in India, and it's usually the first place Buddhists want to go."[35] She continued, "Everyone wants to stay in Bodhgaya for a long time, and the Mahā Bodhi Society offered this space for us" (see figure 3.2).[36] Her response highlights both the fantastic and the mundane; this site is sacred and acts as a site of solidarity. MBSI provided the facilities for the members of UTBSI during the inauguration of the training center and the ordination, a more practical reason for holding the ordination there.

Other Buddhist organizations such as Sakyadhita build solidarity among Buddhist women, centering their meetings at pilgrimage sites or ensuring that pilgrimage is an aspect of their meetings. Akin to Bhikkhunī Viditadhammā's explanation, Karma Lekshe Tsomo offered similar reasoning for holding the inaugural Sakyadhita meeting in 1987 in Bodhgaya. She notes,

> We chose Bodhgaya because it's a central location that Buddhists frequent. It was difficult to hold in Dharamsala where some of the community perceived Buddhist women as threatening. Bodhgaya is also a meeting place that is inspiring and gives insight into the Indian Buddhist world. It is a blessed place and any virtuous deed performed there accrues one-hundred thousand times the merit.[37]

Her explanation speaks to the fantastic and mundane. Regarding the fantastic, performing virtuous acts in a pilgrimage site like Bodhgaya accumulates more merit; in terms of the pragmatic, Bodhgaya had a sizable space for the inaugural conference, and a conference of women was more accepted within this space.

In Bodhgaya, there is also a sense of solidarity among pilgrims in general. Pilgrims reside in vibrant *vihāras*, monastic centers with temples, guestrooms, gardens, and other amenities for Buddhist devotees. These beautifully adorned *vihāras* often reflect the regional architecture, Buddhist imagery, symbols, and ethical commitments associated with their host countries, underlining the commitments of the pilgrims who sponsor and donate to them and the resident

Figure 3.2. Ordination Rehearsal at the Mahā Bodhi Society, 2022. Photo by Darcie Price-Wallace

monastics who sustain these religious residences. Presently, there are *vihāras* associated with Bangladesh, Bhutan, Cambodia, China, Japan, Korea, Laos, Myanmar, Nepal, Sri Lanka, Taiwan, Thailand, Tibet, Vietnam, and specific states in India such as Arunachal Pradesh, Ladakh, Sikkim, and others.

UTBSI, founded in November 2021, and Sakyadhita, founded in 1987, share many similarities when it comes to thinking about Buddhist women's solidarity. UTBSI and Sakyadhita share the aim to create solidarity among the *sangha* with regard for respective nationalities, languages, and cultures. Sakyadhita meetings, which occur every two years and are organized in different countries, emphasize celebrating, encountering, and participating in Buddhist practices in the respective host country while facilitating a sense of unity among attendees.[38] Conference attendees also have the option of going on pilgrimage in the respective host country to experience the key Buddhist sites together.

Members of UTBSI come from Australia, Cambodia, Germany, India, Laos, Malaysia, Myanmar, Sri Lanka, Thailand, the United States, Vietnam, and other countries. Throughout the training program, the *bhikkhunīs* and *bhikkhunīs*-to-be are one collective group, but they are often unified and connected more intimately through their own national heritage and the different supports and resistances they endure within their local communities. Marlai Ouch, a dedicated lay member who co-founded the Cambodian Bhikkhunī Sangha Initiative in alliance with Dhammadharini Monastery, fundraises and builds awareness about Cambodian women seeking ordination and the resistance they have experienced at home. She explains,

> I support these women to dispel the current structure of Buddhist institutions, create access for women to gain knowledge and agency, and provide opportunities and support for women who wish to become *bhikkhunīs*. By establishing the Cambodian Bhikkhunī Sangha Initiative, I work to introduce the Buddha's teaching on *bhikkhunīs* and share scholarly research on the history of the *bhikkhunī* lineage of Theravada *bhikkhunīs* in the Cambodian community.[39]

Ouch directly presents Cambodian *bhikkhus* with textual evidence for the necessity of the *bhikkhunī saṅgha*, but she has been censored by *bhikkhus* who oppose ordaining *bhikkhunīs*.[40]

Ouch sponsored the first four Cambodian *bhikkhunīs* because her initiative "completes the fourfold assembly."[41] She explains that "[t]he aim of my sponsorship was to provide a first-hand experience of Theravāda ordination at the international level for these brave women who have paved the way for future Cambodian *samaneris* and *bhikkhunīs*."[42] Her efforts build solidarity among the *sangha* through working with UTBSI and MBSI.[43] She comments,

"When bhikkhunīs learn and practice the Buddha's teachings and teach others to do the same, they are seeking awakening for themselves and others. To be awakened today means to make the Buddha's teaching accessible and available to everyone to learn and practice."[44] Ouch's vision for Cambodian monastics extends to welcoming any practitioner who wants to study the Dhamma.

When UTBSI and MBSI host ceremonies, the act of being in a pilgrimage site transforms ordinands' perceptions of themselves—their ordinations may be contested in their respective local cultures but are recontextualized when performed in this international site of wonder. A change of perception occurs because of the solidarity forged through the ceremonial rites of ordination. The preference for giving these vows at sites deeply embedded with the Buddha's presence illustrates how pilgrimage not only serves to provide a second layer of legitimization to these women's contested vows but also becomes a place of acceptance and toleration of differences.[45] Such a collaboration is an energetic compromise between structure and the emergence of a Buddhist solidarity that cuts through biases against new modalities of full ordination rituals.

Ordination, Pilgrimage, and Solidarity

The solidarity between MBSI and UTBSI has precedents in previous ordinations held in pilgrimage sites, such as the ordinations in 1996 in Sarnath and in 1998 and 2019 in Bodhgaya.[46] These full ordinations required extensive collaboration around their shared obligation of sustaining the fourfold *saṅgha* harmoniously. These ordinations, however, also depended upon the presence and establishment of organizations like MBSI and others such as Bo Miyun Sa Temple in South Korea in 1996, the Fo Guang Shan monastics in Taiwan in 1998, Sakyadhita, and the *bhikkhunīs* who now are members of UTBSI.[47]

When Dharmapāla established MBSI in 1891, he sought to free the Mahābodhi temple from the Saivite Mahant, restore it to its stature, and revive Buddhism in India.[48] His investment in resuscitating Buddhism in the land of its birth also meant reforming Buddhism in Sri Lanka.[49] Dharmapāla's writings are a mirror of the complex debates on this topic. Perspectives range from soteriological inclusiveness, the implication that the path to awakening is free from the constraints of sex and gender, to reinforcing contemporary standards of the ascetic misogyny that institutionally subordinate women and deny the validity of giving *bhikkhunī* vows after the decline of the lineage.[50] Tessa Bartholomeusz suggests that Dharmapāla's interest in the re-establishment of *bhikkhunī* order aligns with his sense of elevating Buddhism in Sri Lanka, whereas his establishment of MBSI and its vision include broader implications for sustaining Buddhism and resisting colonialism.[51]

MBSI has supported *bhikkhunī* ordinations in India since 1996 when Sri Lankan *bhikkhunīs* received their vows in Sarnath, the pilgrimage site where the Buddha first turned the wheel of *Dhamma*, expounding the four truths—suffering, its cause, cessation, and path to its cessation.[52] Bhikkhunī Kusuma, one of the most eminent among women to receive these vows, described her own experience in a *Sakyadhita Newsletter*:

> On December 8, 1996, the premises of the Mahabodhi Society in Sarnath was a site of unimaginable splendor. The ordination candidates and preceptors were taken in procession, complete with caparisoned elephants and horses. Large crowds of Sri Lankan pilgrims and nuns carried Buddhist flags. *Bhikkhus, bhikkhunīs,* and laypeople had arrived from Sri Lanka, Thailand, and many other countries to witness the ceremony. Bhikkhunī Karma Lekshe Tsomo, president of Sakyadhita, was among them. The venue was the very spot where the Buddha preached the first sermon. . . . Both *bhikkhus* and *bhikkhunīs* of the Korean Sangha participated in the ceremony, with an interpreter to translate from Korean to English. . . . The ceremony took eight hours and the discipline and formality were so austere that my knees ached and were bleeding from all the kneeling. . . . I felt confident of my Dhamma path, in accordance with the Theravada Pali tradition and the two years of training that I received. . . . As the Sri Lankan monks recognized the ordination, we were offered Sri Lankan robes. Because I was the first to be ordained, I was considered the first of the ten *bhikkhunīs*. On this path of renunciation, I am forever grateful to everyone who extended their kind help to establish the *bhikkhunī* order in Sri Lanka after a lapse of almost a thousand years.[53]

In addition to her awe, joy, and gratitude, Bhikkhunī Kusuma describes multiple collaborations including the role of MBSI, Sakyadhita, the monks from Bo Miyun Sa Temple in South Korea, and others.[54] Her ordination set a precedent for the *bhikkhunī* ordinations that follow and map a vision for continued ordinations. Bhikkhunī Kusuma's descriptions offer us a way to see collaborations in support of *bhikkhunī* ordination as multidirectional in thought and activism and as possibly creating new interests and identities.[55] She expresses her personal transformation in her new identity as a *bhikkhunī* that occurred at the pilgrimage site. She actively envisioned, strived, and became part of the continued revisioning of *bhikkhunī* ordinations one thousand years after the decline of the order in Sri Lanka.

The continuity of subsequent ordinations is not a given. Seewalee Thero of MBSI and UTBSI noted that the 2022 ordination and establishment of the training center in Bodhgaya were examples of "how we must continue what she [Bhikkhunī Kusuma] fought for. It is a tribute to her when we give these vows again."[56] His respect and reverence for Bhikkhunī Kusuma came across not only in his description of her as "like a mother to all of us," but also in his continued support of subsequent ordinations in 2019 and 2022.

Similarly, in 1998, MBSI was one of several organizations supporting the ordination of *bhikkhunīs* in Bodhgaya. Xingyun, the founder of the Fo Guan Shan Order, expressed that these ordinations demonstrate the possibility of international cooperation, which furthers monastic continuity.[57] Yuchen Li's ethnography of the 1998 Bodhgaya ordination highlights that all the monk supporters "come from different countries and wear different style robes, but their mission to revitalize Buddhism in the place of its birth has joined them in a long term cooperation."[58] Bodhgaya acted as a starting point for these ordinations, and the *bhikkhus* active in the Bodhgaya Buddhist community also joined in collaboration.[59] These local supporters shared Xingyun's concern that "to exclude women from bhikṣuṇī ordination was to waste half of the Buddhists' potential energy worldwide."[60] He saw *bhikkhunī* ordination as necessary for Buddhism's longevity.[61]

Since 1998, *bhikkhunī* ordinations have continued in Sri Lanka, where they form their own transnational networks, making full ordination viable for anyone who aspires to it.[62] In her work on theology and pilgrimage, Holly Hillgardner uses "faith-with-legs" as shorthand for how pilgrimage gets us places, metaphorically and physically.[63] Hillgardner adds, "Rather than being any kind of ableist reference, 'legs' here describes a comparative theological practice where people can travel into worlds that are different without fear of one's own faith being diminished."[64] The Sri Lankan *bhikkhunī* community exemplifies faith-with-legs. From the early ordinations in the pilgrimage sites of Sarnath and Bodhgaya, they have mobilized subsequent ordinations in Sri Lanka.

Susanne Mrozik's ethnographic work on *bhikkhunī* ordination highlights the profoundly complex views on *bhikkhunī* ordination among the Sri Lankan *sangha*. Some believe that the *bhikkhunīs* are part of the Mahāyāna order and not entitled to membership in the Sri Lankan Theravāda *sangha*.[65] Ordination proponents maintain that the Dharmaguptaka Vinaya, the monastic code relied upon by Mahāyāna monastics, is essentially a northern counterpart to the Pali Vinaya in Theravāda. Further justification is that after the *bhikkhunīs* received their vows in the international ceremony, they received the monastic regulations from Sri Lankan *bhikkhus*. The *bhikkhunī sangha* is not unanimously recognized, but it endures because of the support of the laity, progressive *bhikkhus* and because of the *bhikkhunīs'* pious agency, social service, and moral restoration.[66] Presently, there are approximately two thousand members of the *bhikkhunī sangha* in Sri Lanka.[67] When it comes to *bhikkhunī* ordination, it is not only faith-with-legs or pilgrimage-with-legs but also solidarity-with-legs.

This solidarity-with-legs came full circle on January 28–29, 2019, when MBSI supported the first international all-Theravāda Bhikkhunī ordination in Bodhgaya. Twenty-four women from several countries received their vows and were fully accepted as *bhikkhunīs* by the dual *sangha* of Theravāda *bhikkhus* and *bhikkhunīs*.[68] Following the ordination, new *sangha* members joined the "Global Conference on Buddhism and Women's Liberation."[69] The culmination of these pivotal events exemplifies solidarity manifesting on pilgrimage. Participants came together as they progressed to the *vajrāsana* and concluded the gathering with virtuous activities under the bodhi tree. Tathaloka Theri adds:

On the last day of the conference, in the chilly winter's dawn, the new Theravada bhikkhunīs, led by senior bhikkhunī teachers, walked in a long line barefoot and bareheaded for *pindapata* (almsround, *pindacariya*) through the town of Bodhgaya, coming finally to the Mahābodhi Temple, and then taking their almsmeal, offering flowers, and meditating together at the roots of the Jaya Sri Maha Bodhi Tree together, as the daughters of the Buddha.[70]

These daughters of the Buddha foster solidarity-with-legs as they commemorate the Buddha and welcome new *bhikkhunīs* to sustain the *sangha*.

Seewalee Thero described the inspiration and collaboration that came out of this 2019 ordination including an International Bhikkhunī Day celebration and the twenty-fifth-year anniversary of the *bhikkhunīs* revival in the Theravāda tradition in Sarnath.[71] MBSI and the members of the soon-to-be UTBSI organized a Theravāda Bhikkhunī Webinar on International Bhikkhunī Day entitled, "The Significance and Challenges of the *Bhikkhunī Sangha*: Past, Present, and Future," on September 20, 2021, to commemorate the 2,605th anniversary of the foundation of the *bhikkhunī sangha*. Talks celebrated the Buddha granting women ordination, offered explanations of the expansion and decline of the women's *sangha* in the tenth and eleventh centuries, and explored continued efforts for sustaining the *bhikkhunī sangha*. Bhikkhunī Viditadhammā emphasized that all ordinations depended upon Mahāpajāpatī and all the early *bhikkhunīs* who "struggled and sacrificed their lives for the equal religious rights of women in the Buddha *sāsana*."[72]

The *bhikkhunīs*, aspiring *bhikkhunīs*, and *bhikkhunī*-supporters of UTBSI build solidarity through their diverse coalition of *bhikkhunī* networks in numerous countries, by restructuring "the interlocking oppressive social systems that impact members of each of these groups in similar but also quite different ways."[73] The collaboration between MBSI and UTBSI culminated with a twenty-fifth-year celebration of the first *bhikkhunī* ordination in Sarnath.[74] Held as a three-day webinar titled, "Theravāda Bhikkhunī Sangha: Past, Present, and Future," this online event included international monastic and nonmonastic speakers who spoke about the collaboration required for supporting the longevity of the *sāsana*. Speakers celebrated Bhikkhunī Kusuma's role in receiving the full *bhikkhunī* vows and her close collaboration with Sakyadhita, especially its local branch in Sri Lanka, and the ongoing *bhikkhunī* ordinations that continue.[75]

This and other online events that followed range from celebrating Bhikkhunī Mahāpajāpatī Gotamī, the first nun, to Sanghamitta, the *bhikkhunī* who brought the lineage to Sri Lanka in the third century BCE, to global Vesak events, which celebrate the Buddha's birth, enlightenment, and *parinibbāna*. These two organizations also collaborate in online training for *bhikkhunīs* to strengthen solidarity and bridge the transnational worlds of *bhikkhunīs*.

An International *Bhikkhunī* Training Center and Ordination

UTBSI and MSBI's joint inauguration of the first International Bhikkhunī Training Center in India, followed by an ordination event in November 2022, illustrates their double vision in terms of solidarity. The ordination relied on the vision of earlier ordinations but was unique because of its purposeful focus on bringing together a more diverse group of ordinands across Theravāda worlds. The implication of having the ordination in Bodhgaya, overseen by these two organizations, requires the co-seeing of bringing together practitioners of diverse national backgrounds, which in turn facilitates solidarity among ordinands. Earlier ordinations were primarily conducted for the benefit of Sri Lankan *bhikkhunīs* by their Mahāyāna preceptors, but these newer ordinations are intentionally international and collaborative. With the blessings of Seewalee Thero, I joined as a participant observer in some of these events between November 6–14, 2022.

Leading up to these events were two full days of training on *bhikkhunī* vows and history. Then after the morning of training, on the full moon day of November 8, 2022, all the *bhikkhunīs*, *bhikkhunīs*-to-be, *bhikkhunī* supporters, novices (*samaneris*), members of MBSI, UTBSI, reporters, international pilgrims, and local leaders departed from the early morning teaching and training at the Mahā Bodhi Society. Twenty-five or so rickshaws lined up within the gates of the Mahā Bodhi Society, snaking outward to the front of the building and waiting as everyone crowded into them. As attendees squeezed into seats, the drivers waited until all the rickshaws were filled before they proceeded in a long winding procession through the heart of Bodhgaya to the opening ceremony. Arriving directly behind what is locally known as the Big Buddha, attendees unloaded from the rickshaws, trickled into the gates, and encircled the front entrance to the first International Bhikkhunī Training Center in India.

After opening prayers, flanked by *bhikkhunīs* from UTBSI, Seewalee Thero stood at the center under the awning and explained that this center used to be a school but had closed during COVID-19 (see figure 3.3). The effects of the pandemic were still visible, with nearly half of the crowd in masks. He explained how UTBSI was established over a year ago; during this time they realized the utmost necessity for having a centralized training center where monastic women could come to study and practice together in Bodhgaya. This building, he explained, had been donated exactly for this purpose.

Bhikkhunī Viditadhammā provided background on the necessity of this training center. She explained to the saffron-robed crowd, dotted with members of the laity donning white, that the Indian *bhikkhunīs* from Nagpur had come to train in Vietnam for three months. They had expressed a wish for more training, specifically a need for a center where they could practice and

Figure 3.3. Inauguration of the International Bhikkhunī Training Center. Photo by Darcie Price-Wallace

train together under the guidance of well-respected *bhikkhu*s and *bhikkhunī*s in India. She noted,

> MBSI has already contributed a lot in education, in Buddha *sāsana*, charity, and also supporting the *bhikkhunī saṅgha*. With this opening of the International Bhikkhunī Training Center, with the cooperation between MBSI and UTBSI, we hope that we will all come together to contribute in our capacity to make this place become an international training center where all the *bhikkhunī*s and *samaneri*s can come to the land of the Buddha. We can stay here for one, two, or three months together to practice meditation, learn Pali, study Vinaya, and all. The place is very convenient and near all the Buddhist temples and not far from the main temple. We are so lucky to be in such a beautiful and very inspiring place. . . . We would like to express our gratitude to MBSI and we hope that together we can help develop our *bhikkhunī saṅgha*.[76]

More talks followed and the inauguration concluded with a ceremonial ribbon cutting and *saṅgha* members tossing celebratory marigold and jasmine flowers into the air. Attendees proceeded through the training center to the back garden for photos and conversation (see figure 3.4).

Figure 3.4. Participants at the Inauguration of the Bhikkhunī Training Center. Photo by Darcie Price-Wallace

Over the following days, members of UTBSI convened for ongoing training in the *Bhikkhunī Pātimokkha* (vows of individual liberation), written and oral examinations on these vows, *samaneri* re-ordination, the *upasampadā* (ordination) rehearsal, and then the two days of the higher ordination ceremony was held at the Wat Lao Buddhagaya International Temple. All members of the *sangha* who gave the *bhikkhunī* vows were from the Theravāda tradition.[77] These events concluded with two final days of seminars and workshops on the topic of "Staying on the Noble Path, the Opportunity of Going Forth." These workshops emphasized the necessity of gradual training, importance of staying with a teacher after ordination, relinquishing of assets and any property or money, achieving a harmonious *sangha*, importance of a teacher and discipleship, distribution of duties and responsibilities, community living and abiding by the Vinaya rules, importance of having competent *bhikkhu*s or *bhikkhunī*s for ordination, procedures for re-ordination into the Theravāda tradition, and living and abiding by the *Pātimokkha*. The week of events concluded with consideration of the way forward for the *bhikkhunī sangha* and with blessings for the successful 2022 ordination, indicative of the solidarity among all those present and how their solidarity serves their vision for the growing *bhikkhunī sangha*.

Co-seeing on pilgrimage underscores how religious traditions make the invisible into something visible.[78] Becoming a *bhikkhunī* remains an invisible possibility for many women, but it is continually made real through *bhikkhunī*s who co-see the fantastic and the mundane. As pilgrims, they experience the mundane, the gender asymmetries that they transform while sharing the Buddhist goal, alongside the fantastic, seeing the true nature of reality where the Buddha purely perceived peace and attained awakening. UTBSI and its pilgrims co-see the fantastic and mundane and in turn become exemplars for transforming the *bhikkhunī* path. They hold a vision for an enduring future filled with *bhikkhunī*s.

Conclusion: You Are Welcome Here, This Is Where You Belong

According to the *Mahāparinibbāna Sutta*, the Buddha stated he would not pass away until he established the fourfold *sangha* as "wise, well-trained, and self-confident."[79] These organizations uphold the Buddha's teachings through their co-seeing and co-facilitating of wise, well-trained, and self-confident *bhikkhunīs*. UTBSI and MBSI's solidarity is a testament to their generous envisioning of the longevity of the Buddha's dispensation. They co-see the fantastic within the teachings alongside the mundane gendered realities for Buddhist women; they make *bhikkhunīs* visible through their solidarity at a pilgrimage site.

Bhikkhunī Viditadhammā told me that "performing ordination at a pilgrimage site is very inspired because there is a connection with a strong lineage traced back to the Buddha and this is very sacred."[80] *Bhikkhunī* ordinations in pilgrimage sites facilitate "seeing-with, a double or binocular vision in which the pilgrim sees the site in two ways at once: the ordinary perception seen with the physical eye and the extraordinary vision seen in the mind's eye."[81] Co-seeing enables the succession of these ordination rituals as women see (and experience) the challenges of being "seen" as legitimate monastics in their respective communities where they face mundane gender asymmetries. The opening of the training center aims to mitigate discrepancies in training available to *bhikkhunīs* compared with their *bhikkhu* counterparts. They have an extraordinary vision for women practitioners enacted through *bhikkhunī* ordination. Their co-seeing on pilgrimage facilitates the fantastic as *bhikkhunīs* aspire for the extraordinary pure perception of the Buddha. As they shave their heads, wear robes, practice vows, and receive their ordination rites, they become visible exemplars for other Buddhist women.

The notion that "you are welcome here, this is where you belong" has textual precedent in the *Therīgāthā*, a collection of 522 verses compiled into seventy-three poems. This compilation of verses focuses exclusively on women's religious experiences.[82] Scholars of this body of literature from the Pali Canon suggest that these poems developed between the sixth and third centuries BCE,[83] and tradition holds that they were transcribed in the first century CE.[84] These verses call to mind the relationship between UTBSI and MBSI, and the solidarity that the fourfold *saṅgha* ideally symbolizes. This idea of welcoming and belonging in the *saṅgha* is present in Bhikkhunī Sundari's verses:

Sundari speaking to her preceptor
That eye that sees the invisible

I have cleansed through training,
I know my previous lives, honored one,
I know where I have lived before.

By relying on you, beautiful *therī*,
you who are an ornament to the sangha.
I know the three things that most don't know,
what the Buddha taught is done.[85]

Give me permission, honored one, to go to Savatthi,
I will roar like a lion in the presence of the Buddha

. . .

[and after she has approached the Buddha] *Sundari to the Buddha*
Sundari is your disciple, Great Hero,
she left Benares and came to where you are,
and now she bows to your feet.

You are the Buddha, you are my teacher,
Brahman, I am your daughter,
your own child, born from your mouth,
all that needs to be done has been done,
I am free from all that defiles from within.

Spoken by the Buddha to Sundari
Fortunate lady, *you are welcome here,*
this is where you belong,[86]
the same as those who have tamed themselves,
whose passion is gone, who are set free,
who have done what needs to be done
and are free from all that defiles from within,
Who all come and bow to the feet of the teacher.[87]

Sundari receives an invitation directly from the Buddha, who says to her, "you are welcome here, this is where you belong." Prior to this, Sundari cultivates her relationship with the *therī*, the senior *bhikkhunī*, who conferred her ordination. Sundari, the one who has tamed her mind, bows at the feet of the Buddha. These verses are Sundari's reflection on being welcome and belonging to the *saṅgha*. Contemporary *bhikkhunī*s can have a similar experience through multidirectional supports and a genealogy of ordinations and supporters that precede them.

Members of UTBSI also shared their own experiences of being welcome, belonging, and extending this type of solidarity in multidirectional ways. Bhikkhunī Viditadhammā reflects upon the collaborative effort and ongoing relationships necessary for Buddhist women's solidarity and strength. She states, "We are very united and cooperative. From the beginning, when I first established my nunnery here [in Vietnam] . . . [w]e invited Venerable Dhammananda and her *bhikkhunīs* from Songdhammakalyani Monastery [in Thailand] to come and help us establish the *sīmā*."[88] The senior *bhikkhunīs* in UTBSI have had an integral role in ordinations in their respective countries ranging from Vietnam, Malaysia, and Sri Lanka. They intentionally build solidarity. When she described the 2019 ordination, she said, "We all came to India to be together to cooperate with the support of the *bhikkhu saṅgha*. We organized international *bhikkhunī* ordination. So, unity and solidarity is our strength. We can break separate sticks, but we cannot break a bundle of sticks. So, sticking together, solidarity, being united is our strength of the *saṅgha*."[89]

Her words describe deep, generous connections that these *bhikkhunīs* foster. These connections are their strength and solidarity. They sustain this strength in their collaborative, transnational relationships forged in pilgrimage sites as they become ordained and ordain new *bhikkhunīs* in turn. They create and sustain possibilities for future *bhikkhunīs* through their co-seeing and solidarity. They extend the Buddha's words to Sundari into the present: "you are welcome here, this is where you belong."

Notes

1 Raymond Lam, "A New Era for the Women's Order: UTBSI's First International Bhikkhunī Ordination in Bodh Gaya," *Buddhist Door Global*, December 18, 2022, https://teahouse.buddhistdoor.net/a-new-era-for-the-womens-order-utbsis-first -international-bhikkhunī-ordination-in-bodh-gaya/.

2 This case study draws from in-person interviews and participant observation in Bodhgaya in November 2022 and digital ethnography conducted between November 2022 and September 2023.

3　Catherine Bell, "The Ritual Body and The Dynamics of Ritual Power," *Journal of Ritual Studies* 4, no. 2 (1990): 299–313, 308.

4　Karma Lekshe Tsomo, "Field Notes: Sakyadhita Pilgrimage in Asia—On the Trail of the Buddhist Women's Network," *Nova Religio: The Journal of Alternative and Emergent Religions* 10, no. 3 (2006): 102–16, 104. Bhikkhunī Kusuma, *The Dasil Nun: A Study of Women's Buddhist Religious Movement in Sri Lanka with an Outline of Its Historical Antecedents* (Sri Lanka: Buddhist Cultural Center, 2010), 68. Nirmala S. Salgado, *Buddhist Nuns and Gendered Practice: In Search of the Female Renunciant* (Oxford: Oxford University Press, 2013), 150–51. Susanne Mrozik, "Sri Lankan Buddhist Nuns: Complicating the Debate over Ordination," *Journal of Feminist Studies in Religion* 36, no. 1 (2020): 33–49.

5　Amy Allen, "Rethinking Power," *Hypatia* 13, no. 1 (Winter 1998): 21–40, 34–35.

6　*Therighata: Poems of the First Buddhist Women*, translated by Charles Hallisey (Cambridge: Murty Classical Library of India, Harvard University Press, 2015), 161–73.

7　Catherine Hartmann, "How to See the Invisible: Attention, Landscape, and Transformation of Vision in Tibetan Pilgrimage Guides," *History of Religions* 62, no. 4 (May 2023): 313–39.

8　Mrozik, "Sri Lankan Buddhist Nuns," 35–36.

9　Mrozik, "Sri Lankan Buddhist Nuns," 36–37, 48–49.

10　Mrozik, "Sri Lankan Buddhist Nuns," 36.

11　Tessa J. Bartholomeusz, *Women under the Bō Tree: Buddhist Nuns in Sri Lanka* (Boston: Cambridge University Press, 1994), 45–47.

12　Bartholomeusz, *Women under the Bō Tree*, 67.

13　Karma Lekshe Tsomo, ed., *Sakyadhītā: Daughters of the Buddha* (Ithaca, NY: Snow Lion, 1988).

14　Interview VPST, November 3–4, 2022.

15　Interview VPST, November 3–4, 2022.

16　Susanne Mrozik, "'We Love Our Nuns': Affective Dimensions of the Sri Lanka *Bhikkhunī* Revival," *Journal of Buddhist Ethics* 21 (2014): 57–95.

17　Mrozik, "'We Love Our Nuns,'" 87.

18　Tathāloka Therī, "Bodhgaya International Theravada Bhikkhunī Ordination January 2019," *Buddhist Door Global*, March 8, 2019, https://teahouse.buddhistdoor .net/bodhgaya-international-theravada-bhikkhunī-ordination-january-2019/ .

19　Tathāloka Therī, "Bodhgaya International Theravada Bhikkhunī Ordination January 2019."

20 Mission statement on UTBSI's Facebook, https://www.facebook.com/UTBSI (accessed July 22, 2023) and https://utbsi.org/ (accessed July 22, 2023).

21 Hartmann, "How to See the Invisible," 316–17.

22 Marlai Ouch, "Buddhist Women Completing the Fourfold Assembly of the Buddha: Cultivate Resilience and Seek Awakening for Themselves and Others," in *The Proceedings of 'Living in a Precarious World: Impermanence, Resilience, and Awakening' at the 18th Sakyadhita Conference*, June 23–27, 2023 (Korea: Sakyadhita International Organization of Buddhist Women, 2023), 119–22.

23 David Geary and Kiran Shinde, "Buddhist Pilgrimage and the Ritual Ecology of Sacred Sites in the Indo-Gangetic Region," *Religions* 12, no. 285 (May 2021): 1–21.

24 Geary and Shinde, "Buddhist Pilgrimage," 17.

25 David Geary, *The Rebirth of Bodh Gaya: Buddhism and the Making of World Heritage Site* (Seattle: University of Washington, 2017), 8.

26 Tathāloka Therī, "Bodhgaya International Theravada Bhikkhunī Ordination."

27 John Strong, "The Beginnings of Buddhist Pilgrimage: The Four Famous Sites in India," in *Searching for the Dharma, Finding Salvation—Buddhist Pilgrimage in Time and Space*, ed. Christoph Cueppers and Max Deeg (Lumbini: Lumbini International Research Institute, 2014), 49–63, 50–51.

28 Strong, "The Beginnings of Buddhist Pilgrimage," 51.

29 Strong, "The Beginnings of Buddhist Pilgrimage," 54–55.

30 Strong, "The Beginnings of Buddhist Pilgrimage," 54–55.

31 Interview KLT, July 11, 2023.

32 Interview KLT, July 11, 2023.

33 Strong, "The Beginnings of Buddhist Pilgrimage," 61.

34 Interview KLT, July 11, 2023.

35 Interview BVM, June 5, 2023.

36 Interview BVM, June 5, 2023.

37 Interview KLT, July 11, 2023.

38 Karma Lekshe Tsomo, "Sakyadhita Pilgrimage in Asia," *Nova Religio: The Journal of Alternative and Emergent Religions* 10, no. 3 (February 2006): 102–16.

39 Interview MO, September 8, 2023.

40 Ouch, "Buddhist Women Completing the Fourfold Assembly of the Buddha," 119–22.

41 Interview MO, September 8, 2023.

42 Ouch, "Buddhist Women Completing the Fourfold Assembly of the Buddha," 122.

43 Interview MO, November 7, 2022, and June 7, 2023.

44 Interview MO, September 8, 2023.

45 Victor Turner, "The Center Out There: Pilgrim's Goal," *History of Religions* 12, no. 3 (February 1973): 191–230, 197, 221–22.

46 Taiwanese-American Fo Guang Shan Community gave first *bhikkhunī* ordinations in 1988 in California. Tathālokā Therī's talk, Webinar: "The Significance and Challenges of the *Bhikkhunī Saṅgha*: Past, Present, and Future," September 20, 2021, https://www.youtube.com/watch?v=isOfVcWPTn0, 44.57–1.00.01 (September 12, 2023).

47 Tathaloka Theri, "Bodhgaya International Theravada Bhikkhunī Ordination."

48 The Budh-Gaya Temple Case. H. Dharmapala versus Jaipal Gir and others. Prosecution under sections 295, 296, 297, 143, and 506 of the Indian Penal Code (Calcutta: W. Newman and Company, 1895). Alan Trevithick, "British Archeologists, Hindu Abbots, and Burmese Buddhists: The Mahabodhi Temple at Bodh Gaya, 1811–1877," *Modern Asian Studies* 33, no. 3 (1999): 635–56.

49 Bartholomeusz, *Women under the Bō Tree*, 44–45.

50 Bartholomeusz, *Women under the Bō Tree*, 67, 71, 82–83. Salgado, *Buddhist Nuns and Gendered Practice*, 162–13. Alan Sponberg, "Attitudes toward Women and the Feminine in Early Buddhism," in *Buddhism, Sexuality, and Gender*, ed. José Ignacio Cabezon (Albany: State University of New York Press, 1992), 3–36.

51 Bartholomeusz, *Women under the Bō Tree*, 67.

52 Salgado, *Buddhist Nuns and Gendered Practice*, 162–65. MBSI was also involved in ordinations of European and American women in the early twentieth century. See Tathālokā Therī, "The Significance and Challenges of the *Bhikkhunī Saṅgha*: Past, Present, and Future," September 20, 2021, https://www.youtube.com/watch?v=isOfVcWPTn0, 44.57–1.00.01.

53 Bhikkhunī Kusuma, "How I Became a Bhikkhunī," *Sakyadhita Newsletter* 16, no. 2 (Summer 2008): 16–18.

54 Tyler Leher, "Global Networks, Local Aspirations: Gender, Lineage and Localization in Sri Lanka's Bhikkhunī Ordination Dispute." Masters of Arts Thesis, Boulder: University of Colorado, 2016, 62.

55 Leher, "Global Networks, Local Aspirations," 65–67.

56 Interview VPST, November 3–4, 2022.

57 Yuchen Li, "Ordination, Legitimacy, and Sisterhood: The International Full Ordination Ceremony in Bodhgaya," *Innovative Buddhist Women: Swimming*

against the Stream, ed. Karma Lekshe Tsomo (Richmond, Surrey: Curzon, 2000), 168–98, 172, 188.

58 Li, "Ordination, Legitimacy, and Sisterhood," 173.

59 Li, "Ordination, Legitimacy, and Sisterhood," 172–73.

60 Li, "Ordination, Legitimacy, and Sisterhood," 172.

61 Li, "Ordination, Legitimacy, and Sisterhood," 172.

62 Mrozik, "Sri Lankan Buddhist Nuns," 36.

63 Holly Hillgardner, "Comparative Theologies of Pilgrimage: Faith with Legs," *A Companion to Comparative Theology* (Brill, 2022), 300.

64 Hillgardner, "Comparative Theologies of Pilgrimage," 300.

65 Mrozik, "Sri Lankan Buddhist Nuns," 36.

66 Mrozik, "Sri Lankan Buddhist Nuns," 34–36. Tyler Leher, "Mobilizing Gendered Piety in Sri Lanka's Contemporary Bhikkunī Ordination Dispute." *Buddhist Studies Review* 36, no. 1 (2019): 101–2.

67 Bhikkhunī Viditadhammā, Webinar: "The Significance and Challenges of the *Bhikkhunī Saṅgha*: Past, Present, and Future," September 20, 2021, 2.28.20.

68 Tathāloka Therī, "Bodhgaya International Theravada Bhikkhunī Ordination."

69 Bhikkhu Bodhi, 2019, "A Buddhist Perspective on Women's Liberation," Buddhist Global Relief (July 10, 2019), https://buddhistglobalrelief.me/2019/07/10/a -buddhist-perspective-on-womens-liberation/.

70 Tathāloka Therī, "Bodhgaya International Theravada Bhikkhunī Ordination."

71 Interview VPST, November 3–4, 2022.

72 Bhikkhunī Viditadhammā, Webinar: "The Significance and Challenges of the *Bhikkhunī Saṅgha*: Past, Present, and Future," September 20, 2021, 20.00–21.44.

73 Rosemary Kellison, "Solidarity and Feminist Religious Ethics," chapter 1 of this volume.

74 "Theravāda Bhikkhunī Sangha: Past, Present, and Future: In Commemoration of 25 Years of Revival of Bhikkhunī Order in Modern Era (1996–2021)," November 17–19, 2021. https://www.youtube.com/watch?v=isOfVcWPTn0.

75 "Theravāda Bhikkhunī Sangha: Past, Present, and Future," 36.00–39.00.

76 Fieldnotes, November 8, 2022.

77 *International Theravāda Bhikkhunī and Sāmaṇerī Ordination Program, Bodhgaya, India.* November 6–14, 2022, Organized by Mahabodhi Society of India and United Theravāda Bhikkhunī Sangha International.

78 Hartmann, "How to See the Invisible," 337.

79 Bhikkhu Anālayo, "The Four Assemblies and Theravāda Buddhism." *Insight Journal* (2015). (September 29, 2023).

80 Interview BVM, June 5, 2023.

81 Hartmann, "How to See the Invisible," 337.

82 Kathyrn R. Blackstone, *Women in the Footsteps of the Buddha: Struggle for Liberation in the Therīgāthā* (New York: Routledge, 1998), 1.

83 Hallisey trans., *Therighata: Poems of the First Buddhist Women*, 161–73, xxxiii. Blackstone, *Women in the Footsteps of the Buddha*, 2–3.

84 Blackstone, *Women in the Footsteps of the Buddha*, 2.

85 *Tevijjā*—the three things that most don't know. These include the ability to know one's past lives, where and why other beings are reborn, and one's own moral corruptions. To know these things that most do not know signifies that one is awakened and will not be reborn (Hallisey, 279).

86 Emphasis added.

87 *Therighata: Poems of the First Buddhist Women*, translated by Hallisey, 169–73.

88 The *sīmā* refers to the boundary in which the monastic *saṅgha* performs specific formal acts such as ordination (*upasampadā*). See *Sīmā* and *Upasaṃpadā*, *The Princeton Dictionary of Buddhism*, ed. Robert E. Buswell Jr. and Donald S. Lopez Jr. (Princeton: Princeton University Press, 2014), 824, 941.

89 Bhikkhunī Viditadhammā, "The Significance and Challenges of the *Bhikkhunī Saṅgha*: Past, Present, and Future," September 20, 2021, 2.26.44–2.30.03.

References

Allen, Amy. "Rethinking Power." *Hypatia*, 13, no. 1 (Winter 1998): 21–40.

Anālayo, Bhikkhu. "The Four Assemblies and Theravāda Buddhism." *Insight Journal*, 2015. https://www.buddhistinquiry.org/article/the-four-assemblies-and-theravada-buddhism/.

Bartholomeusz, Tessa. *Women under the Bō Tree: Buddhist Nuns in Sri Lanka.* Cambridge: Cambridge University Press, 1994.

Bell, Catherine. "The Ritual Body and the Dynamics of Ritual Power." *Journal of Ritual Studies* 4, no. 2 (1990): 299–313.

Blackstone, Kathyrn R. *Women in the Footsteps of the Buddha: Struggle for Liberation in the Therīgāthā.* New York: Routledge, 1998.

The Budh-Gaya Temple Case. H. Dharmapala versus Jaipal Gir and others. Calcutta: W. Newman and Company, 1895.

Geary, David. *The Rebirth of Bodh Gaya: Buddhism and the Making of World Heritage Site.* Seattle: University of Washington, 2017.

Geary, David, and Kiran Shinde. "Buddhist Pilgrimage and the Ritual Ecology of Sacred Sites in the Indo-Gangetic Region," *Religions* 12, no. 285 (May 2021): 1–21, http://doi.org/10.3390/rel12060385.

Hallisey, Charles. Translator. *Therighata: Poems of the First Buddhist Women.* Cambridge, MA: Murty Classical Library of India, Harvard University Press, 2015.

Hartmann, Catherine. "How to See the Invisible: Attention, Landscape, and Transformation of Vision in Tibetan Pilgrimage Guides." *History of Religions* 62, no. 4 (May 2023): 313–39, https://doi.org/10.1086/724562.

Hillgardner, Holly. "Comparative Theologies of Pilgrimage: Faith with Legs." In *A Companion to Comparative Theology*, pp. 294–311. Brill, 2022. https://doi.org/10.1163/9789004388390_017.

International Theravāda Bhikkhunī and Sāmaṇerī Ordination Program, Bodhgaya, India. November 6–14, 2022, Organized by Mahabodhi Society of India and United Theravāda Bhikkhunī Sangha International.

Kellison, Rosemary. "Solidarity and Feminist Religious Ethics." In *Solidarity and Power: Feminist Approaches to Religious Ethics*, edited by Rosemary Kellison and Shannon Dunn. Lanham, MD: Rowman & Littlefield, 2025.

Kusuma, Bhikkhunī. *The Dasil Nun: A Study of Women's Buddhist Religious Movement in Sri Lanka with an Outline of Its Historical Antecedents.* Sri Lanka: Buddhist Cultural Center, 2010.

———. "How I Became a Bhikkhunī," *Sakyadhita Newsletter* 16, no. 2 (Summer 2008): 16–18.

Lam, Raymond. "A New Era for the Women's Order: UTBSI's First International Bhikkhunī Ordination in Bodh Gaya," *Buddhist Door Global*, December 18, 2022, https://teahouse.buddhistdoor.net/a-new-era-for-the-womens-order-utbsis-first-international-bhikkhunī-ordination-in-bodh-gaya/.

Leher, Tyler. "Global Networks, Local Aspirations: Gender, Lineage and Localization in Sri Lanka's Bhikkhunī Ordination Dispute." Masters of Arts Thesis, Boulder: University of Colorado, 2016.

———. "Mobilizing Gendered Piety in Sri Lanka's Contemporary Bhikkhunī Ordination Dispute." *Buddhist Studies Review* 36, no. 1 (2019): 99–121.

Li, Yuchen. "Ordination, Legitimacy, and Sisterhood: The International Full Ordination Ceremony in Bodhgaya." In *Innovative Buddhist Women: Swimming against the Stream*, edited by Karma Lekshe Tsomo, pp. 168–198. Richmond, Surrey: Curzon, 2000.

Mrozik, Susanne. "Sri Lankan Buddhist Nuns: Complicating the Debate over Ordination." *Journal of Feminist Studies in Religion* 36, no. 1 (2020): 33–49.

———. "'We Love Our Nuns': Affective Dimensions of the Sri Lanka *Bhikkhunī* Revival." *Journal of Buddhist Ethics*, 21 (2014): 57–95.

Ouch, Marlai. "Buddhist Women Completing the Fourfold Assembly of the Buddha: Cultivate Resilience and Seek Awakening for Themselves and Others." In *The Program Book and Proceedings of 'Living in a Precarious World: Impermanence, Resilience, and Awakening' at the 18th Sakyadhita Conference*, June 23–27, 2023, pp. 119–22. Korea: Sakyadhita International Organization of Buddhist Women, 2023.

The Princeton Dictionary of Buddhism, edited by Robert E. Buswell Jr. and Donald S. Lopez Jr. Princeton, NJ: Princeton University Press, 2014.

Salgado, Nirmala. *Buddhist Nuns and Gendered Practice: In Search of the Female Renunciant*. Oxford: Oxford University Press, 2013.

Sponberg, Alan. "Attitudes toward Women and the Feminine in Early Buddhism." In *Buddhism, Sexuality, and Gender*, edited by José Ignacio Cabezon, pp. 3–36. Albany: State University of New York Press, 1992.

Strong, John. "The Beginnings of Buddhist Pilgrimage: The Four Famous Sites in India." In *Searching for the Dharma, Finding Salvation–Buddhist Pilgrimage in Time and Space*, edited by Christoph Cueppers and Max Deeg, pp. 49–63. Lumbini: Lumbini International Research Institute, 2014.

Tathāloka Therī. "Bodhgaya International Theravada Bhikkhunī Ordination January 2019." *Buddhist Door Global*, March 8, 2019, https://teahouse.buddhistdoor.net/bodhgaya-international-theravada-bhikkhunī-ordination-january-2019/.

Trevithick, Alan. "British Archeologists, Hindu Abbots, and Burmese Buddhists: The Mahabodhi Temple at Bodh Gaya, 1811–1877." *Modern Asian Studies* 33, no. 3 (1999): 635–56.

Tsomo, Karma Lekshe. "Field Notes: Sakyadhita Pilgrimage in Asia–On the Trail of the Buddhist Women's Network." *Nova Religio: The Journal of Alternative and Emergent Religions* 10, no. 3 (2006): 102–16, 104.

———, ed. *Sakyadhītā: Daughters of the Buddha*. Ithaca, NY: Snow Lion, 1988.

Turner, Victor. "The Center Out There: Pilgrim's Goal." *History of Religions* 12, no. 3 (February 1973): 191–230.

4

Audre Lorde as Buddhist Ethicist

Toward a Practice of Tenderness, Accountability, and Solidarity

Rima Vesely-Flad

In this chapter, I uplift the voice of Audre Lorde as a feminist and Black freedom movement activist who developed psychological and emotional capacities for engaging nuanced dynamics in grassroots political communities. In so doing, I name Lorde as a cutting-edge voice who illuminates Buddhist doctrines and practices that buttress and sustain the difficult work of dismantling systems of oppression while cultivating respectful, enduring solidarity and community. I do not suggest that Audre Lorde self-identified as Buddhist, even as she was a prominent voice within the second-generation feminist movement.[1] To be sure, she was very clear about the identities she claimed: she self-identified as a warrior, a "Black lesbian feminist socialist mother of two."[2] She wrote of a deep spirituality connected to Dahomey and Yoruba deities in her book of poems, *The Black Unicorn*,[3] and quoted the *I Ching* in her essay "Eye to Eye: Black Women, Hatred, and Anger." She meditated while undergoing cancer treatment in Switzerland and occasionally referenced astrology.

Although she did not self-identify as Buddhist, I locate Lorde within emerging Buddhist ethics in the US context to argue that throughout her essays and interviews, Lorde illuminates core Buddhist teachings that, if practiced, help to cultivate personal and collective capacity to turn toward difficulty, embrace accountability, and genuinely practice solidarity within intersectional feminist and Black freedom movements. Furthermore, I argue that cultivating inner capacities moves feminist, anti-racist rhetoric past intellectual engagement into the difficult realm of skillfully engaging difficult emotions such as fear and anger. In this way, I identify Audre Lorde as a pivotal voice who expands Buddhist hermeneutics as well as activist practices in the distinctive context of the United States. Indeed, reading Buddhist doctrine through the lens of Audre Lorde illuminates the relevance of Buddhism in provocative ways. Finally, I posit that Lorde was deeply effective in challenging racism within the women's movement, and sexism and homophobia within the Black freedom movement, *precisely because* she turned toward suffering, impermanence, and compassion with perspectives and practices that are consistent with Buddhist teachings.[4] Audre Lorde may not have identified as a Buddhist practitioner, but, I argue, she clarifies for her intellectual descendants the power of Buddhist doctrines and practices for personal and collective liberation. In so doing, Lorde teaches us how to foster accountability, solidarity, and community within grassroots activist communities.

The Black Feminist Ethics of Audre Lorde

Before the term "intersectionality" was coined by Kimberlé Crenshaw in 1989, Audre Lorde parsed its definition. In 1980, she wrote:

> As a Black lesbian feminist comfortable with the many different ingredients of my identity, and a woman committed to racial and sexual freedom from oppression, I find I am constantly being encouraged to pluck out some one aspect of myself and present this as the meaningful whole, eclipsing or denying the other parts of self.[5]

Lorde went on to state that eclipsing and denying a part of herself resulted in inner destruction and fragmentation. To resist such inner annihilation required explicit and overt integration: bringing together the parts of herself that facilitated being "whole." Lorde wrote of this inner work as cultivating "energies." Furthermore, she routinely referred to the importance of integrated inner coherence as a service to others and, perhaps most importantly, as foundational for the larger struggle for justice.

She insisted on weaving together every aspect of her identity to achieve the fullest expression of her energy. In insisting on asserting all aspects of her identity, Lorde indicted members of the feminist and Black freedom movements who privileged gender over race. In her 1979 essay "The Master's Tools Will Never Dismantle the Master's House," Lorde wrote:

> If white American feminist theory need not deal with the differences between us, and the resulting difference in our oppressions, then how do you deal with the fact that the women who clean your houses and tend your children while you attend conferences on feminist theory are, for the most part, poor women and women of Color? What is the theory behind racist feminism?[6]

Lorde was unswerving in her commitment to challenging white women on their assumed privilege; similarly, she rejected the patriarchy, sexism, and homophobia endemic to the Black freedom struggle. In that vein, she mirrored sister Black feminists who similarly indicted the white feminist movement for its unacknowledged racism and lifted up an intersectional approach to dismantling oppression.

Lorde's challenge to white feminists is echoed in the writings of contemporary Black feminists. In 1973, a statement publicized by a group of Black women who identified themselves as the Combahee River Collective articulated a broad vision for Black feminism. In addition to identifying intersectionality as the pivotal point from which they articulated their analyses, the Combahee River Collective contested physical and sexual oppression by men, white and Black. They stated that the primary place from which one must act is from one's own identity.

> Above all else, our politics initially sprang from the shared belief that Black women are inherently valuable, that our liberation is a necessity not as an adjunct to somebody else's way because of our need as human persons for autonomy. . . . We realize that the only people who care enough about us to work consistently for our liberation are us. Our politics evolve from a healthy love for ourselves, our sisters and our community which allows us to continue our struggle and work.[7]

As did leading thinkers in the Black Power movement, the Combahee River Collective named psychological oppression as a central force against which to struggle. Their identification of "identity politics" springs from the fact that the very identities of Black women demarcate them as targets of marginalization and abuse. The writers stated:

> The psychological toll of being a Black woman and the difficulties this presents in reaching political consciousness and doing political work can never be underestimated. There is a very low value placed upon Black women's psyches in this society, which is both racist and sexist. As an early group member once said, "We are all damaged people merely by virtue of being Black women." We are dispossessed psychologically and on every other level, and yet we feel the necessity to struggle to change the condition of all Black women.[8]

Audre Lorde and the Combahee River Collective, alongside other Black feminists such as June Jordan, Angela Davis, and Sonia Sanchez, required accountability from white feminists. Rosemary Kellison notes in chapter 1 of this volume that "One of the most important tasks in building feminist solidarity, then, was for white feminists to address their own racism and for Black feminists to demand this accountability from them."[9]

Kellison points out—relying on analyses by women of color—that identity and solidarity are not intrinsically opposed. Lorde's writings buttress this claim by iterating that differences among women must be honored, and that honoring these differences requires cultivating emotional capacity to engage in the hard work of self-scrutiny and holding one another accountable.

But how do members of different groups who are struggling for similar goals internalize such priorities when dominant cultures—including the dominant cultures within political movements—disregard their voices? In other words, how can Black women honor their own voices and insist upon intersectionality within the feminist and Black freedom movements? Lorde and other Black feminists asserted a response to this question. Lorde in particular, in various essays and interviews, made clear: each member of the group should do the requisite internal work to acknowledge how dominant narratives of oppression are internalized, within themselves, whether they are members of the dominant culture or members of oppressed groups.

In turning toward their own self-expressions, Black feminists confronted the dominant cultures of the feminist and Black freedom movement and stated directly: white women and Black men should uplift the intersectional perspectives of Black feminists and be accountable for the harms they have enacted against Black women. Lorde further asserted that white feminists and Black men, steeped in the racism, sexism, and misogyny of the dominant culture, should reorient themselves and repair historical and prevailing harm. It was impossible, Lorde said, to establish sisterhood between Black and white women without genuine connection.[10] Furthermore, false sisterhood can be a source of suffering.[11] This is important to acknowledge because "society collectively erases the memory of suffering."[12]

And, the capacity to repair harm requires engaging in difficult internal reflection. In insisting on interiority, I argue, Audre Lorde illuminates early Buddhist doctrines and practices that foster the capacity to cultivate the requisite psychological "muscles" to engage in demanding accountability, being held accountable, engaging in solidarity, and cultivating community. The core Buddhist doctrines that I argue Lorde illuminates are the doctrines of suffering, impermanence, and compassion. It is important to locate the doctrines and practices as originating in the Buddhist tradition, to not perpetuate the erasure of a 2,600-year-old religious tradition that is often reduced to "mindfulness" without requisite respect for the Asian and Asian American Buddhist scholars and leaders whose emotional and practical labor has facilitated access to Buddhist texts and commentaries in contemporary Western societies.

The three aforementioned aspects of Lorde's writing that illuminate liberatory teachings in Buddhism also serve the purpose of cultivating accountability, solidarity, and community. In short, Lorde: (1) parsed the reality of suffering and in so doing, illuminates the Four Noble Truths; (2) embraced the doctrine of impermanence, including the fact of death; and (3) uplifted practices of compassion by employing maternal language that evokes the image of the Great Mother in Mahayana and Vajrayana Buddhism. In pointing to these three aspects of Lorde's writing, I argue that Lorde provided spiritual, theoretical, *and* practical blueprints in which feminist and Black freedom activists who are devoted to working in solidarity with other oppressed groups can cultivate the capacities for self-reflection, emotional transparency, and being accountable to one another.

Audre Lorde on the Nature of Pain and Suffering

Audre Lorde communicated extensive wisdom on the nature of pain and suffering. In a 1976 interview with Nina Winter, Lorde reflected:

> Pain is important: how we evade it, how we succumb to it, how we deal with it, how we transcend it. I always thought that I had a very low threshold for physical pain, that I could not take it and that was that. I did not know how to stand still gracefully when I got beaten, which was every day. I passed out in dentists' offices. And there was always the secret fear of it. Recently, I had a physical experience that was ghastly and terrible—and wonderful, because it taught me about pain.
>
> Not too long ago I unlocked the old window of my very old Victorian house on Staten Island. Somehow the chain broke and the window fell down immediately and caught my hand. There was no way to pull it out and everyone was gone for the weekend. I broke the window and called for help, and it was seven minutes before someone came. I have the scars to remind me. It was crucial, that seven minutes. In it I lived the whole history of pain from start to finish. The genesis of pain, where you put it, how you channel it and how you end it. The choice was immediate: to die, or to bear the pain. And what does bearing mean? It means changing, or going through. It is not death. It is an experience encapsulated. It could stop. It could be ended. By chewing off my arm, for example. But this was not possible for me. So the pain is transformed. The intensity changes. It has to stop or it has to change. This was a physical knowledge that I had not had before, that pain has a mutability. This is very, very important, and that is just as true about emotional pain: it will change or stop. And the worst thing that can happen is death, but that is a whole different thing to involve yourself in. I felt at that point that there was nothing I could not do, nothing that I could not deal with, because pain will always either change or stop. Always. I have tested this since then, and it is always clear and workable.
>
> . . . The confidence that it will change is what makes *bearing* possible. So pain is fluid. It is only when you conceive of it as something static that it is unbearable.[13]

The Buddhist scholar Peter Harvey attested that attaining perspective on the nature of suffering is the mark of an enlightened being. Harvey expounds that a spiritually ennobled person in the Buddhist tradition is a person who exhibits deep insight into the nature of reality, including the nature of suffering. In elaborating the Buddhist doctrine of suffering in his contemporary analysis of the Four Noble Truths, Harvey explains "The Four True Realities for the Spiritually Ennobled."[14] These "Realities for the Noble Ones" are, briefly:

1. *Dukkha*, "the painful," encompassing the various forms of "pain," gross or subtle, physical or mental, to which all human beings are subjected;
2. The origination of *dukkha*, which is craving;
3. The cessation of *dukkha* from the end of its cause, which is considered enlightenment or *nibbana*;
4. The Noble Eightfold Path, which delineates how to eliminate *dukkha*. The eight factors are broadly identified with wisdom, concentration, and ethics.[15]

Harvey elaborated on the doctrine of suffering by pointing out the nuances of suffering articulated in the sermons of Siddhartha Gotama, who was known as the "Buddha" (Enlightened One). As stated, the origin of suffering is craving (*tanha*), which is translated as "thirst." The first sermon given by the Buddha after his enlightenment demarcates three different kinds of craving: (1) desire for sensual pleasures, (2) drive for ego-driven identity, and (3) hunger for an unpleasant sensation or situation to change.[16]

In her essays, journal entries, and interviews, Lorde illuminated an inner capacity to turn toward these different dimensions of suffering and to know them intimately. As stated in the interview with Nina Winter, Lorde emphasized that pain is bearable, but one cannot avoid it; rather, one must "bear" or move through it. Such an approach to pain is not only physical; it is simultaneously psychological. It requires an inner capacity to stay with pain rather than attempt to evade it. Such capacity to stay with pain simultaneously requires self-reflection. Lorde wrote evocatively on the importance of self-scrutiny in her essay "Poetry Is Not a Luxury." She stated:

> The quality of light by which we scrutinize our lives has direct bearing upon the product which we live, and upon the changes we hope to bring about

through those lives. It is within this light that we form those ideas by which we pursue our magic and make it realized.[17]

Lorde associated self-scrutiny with flourishing. She used the language of "learning to bear the intimacy of scrutiny."[18] Furthermore, turning toward one's inner landscape and knowing it intimately expands an inner power and self-assurance. Women learn to transcend fear as they turn toward their own thoughts and feelings and embrace them. Silence imposed from above—racist, patriarchal, homophobic narratives—no longer threaten or assert control. Lorde employed the language of "power" as an internal force that propels Black women to "bear" suffering, and in so doing, to gain control over their lives. Bearing suffering does not relegate women to the position of a doormat; on the contrary, it requires strength that extends to every other aspect of daily life, including relationships. When women develop the capacity to bear suffering, such interior strength results in dismantling internalized narratives of the dominant culture as well as embracing new ways of being. In bearing suffering, the grip of fear lessens, and indeed, falls away. Lorde pointed to the fact that self-scrutiny and cultivating fearlessness were practices that shift psychological and relational patterns. In this way, I identify themes aligned with the Buddhist doctrine of the cessation of suffering and its requisite practices: the Third and Fourth Noble Truths.

Indeed, a contemporary application of wisdom, ethics, and concentration, as expounded in the Noble Eightfold Path, can be seen in Lorde's essay "Poetry Is Not a Luxury" and other writings. Lorde repeatedly redefines power as that which can be accessed by fearless confrontation with the intimidating messages and authority figures that have garnered strength by violent means. In confronting the internalized voices that women have been taught to fear, women evolve their capacity to define power on their own terms, distinct from the white, Western, patriarchal definitions of power. The patriarchal model uplifts ideas, thinking, and rationality. It privileges analysis and external structures. Lorde contested this definition of power by uplifting the importance of honoring feeling, *including the experience of suffering.* Power, for Lorde, does not revolve around intellectual presumptions, but rather, is found in creative, emotional intuitions and expressions that privilege one's interior life. In her focus on inner excavation, Lorde wrote that each person contains an inner "reserve" from which expression and power are held and can emerge. This inner spaciousness, for Lorde, is dark, ancient, and deep, far beyond Western intellectualism and judgment. This inner reserve privileges feelings, from which arise power, awareness, and stamina.[19]

Lorde, then, connected creativity and power with the examined life, with self-scrutiny and the willfulness to know one's interior being and to practice wisdom, concentration, and ethics. In her emphasis on inner excavation, she was clear that nothing is to be avoided, including painful experiences. Every aspect of life is instructive.

It was her advocacy for turning toward suffering, rather than evading or repressing it, that facilitated her capacity to be in relationships with other women, including women who have (consciously or unconsciously) committed harm. For Lorde, the commitment to addressing harm is a practice. Indeed, her emphasis on honoring suffering—on turning toward feelings, regardless of how excruciating or vile they might seem—facilitated her capacity to acknowledge harm without shutting down. For Lorde, the embrace (rather than rejection) of difficult emotions evolves a powerful capacity for fearlessness and growth. To align oneself with and to act from these feelings requires training and the capacity for meaningful self-expression.[20]

Giving oneself permission to *feel*, for Lorde, is liberation. And, as also seen in early Buddhist suttas,[21] she advocated training oneself to honor one's own emotions. Such training involves staying with one's feelings and allowing them to be articulated in language, rather than repressing them out of fear. Pain, Lorde mused, surfaces in dreams. Dreams, she believed, point the way to freedom. The recognition of the fact of suffering is the foundation for liberation. This is articulated as well in the Four Noble Truths. Therefore, honoring one's feelings, including painful ones, ultimately fosters the experience of liberation, for women, for queer persons, for Black people who have been oppressed by white, patriarchal social systems.

In numerous essays in *Sister Outsider*, Lorde uplifted the importance of cultivating the capacity to see clearly without rejection. Differences between women are to be named and embraced; indeed, in this way, Lorde was consistent in her orientation toward fearlessness. She refused to gloss over social meanings that have oppressed women based on their race, class, and sexuality. She similarly held herself accountable for ways in which she participated in oppression. She wrote in her essay "The Uses of Anger":

> Anger is loaded with information and energy. . . . The woman of Color who is not Black and who charges me with rendering her invisible by assuming that her struggles with racism are identical with my own has something to tell me that I had better learn from, lest we both waste ourselves fighting the truths between us. If I participate, knowingly or otherwise, in my sister's oppression and she calls me on it, to answer her anger with my own only blankets the substance of our exchange with reaction. It wastes energy. And yes, it is very difficult to stand still and to listen to another woman's voice delineate an agony I do not share, or one to which I myself have contributed.[22]

In this acknowledgment, Lorde conveyed how she practiced accountability, solidarity, and community. In her quest to acknowledge and name the complexity of what was taking place in her inner and outer worlds—including suffering that she may have herself provoked—from a place of inner mindfulness, Lorde illuminated how the recognition of the different dimensions of suffering espoused in the Buddhist tradition serves ethical practices of accountability and solidarity. These practices are rooted in deep inner clarity and the capacity to turn toward that which is unpleasant, even unbearable, and serve as a witness to the suffering that is unfolding. She simultaneously took responsibility for the harm that she herself caused.

Lorde's capacity to acknowledge, witness, and bear suffering, in turn, fostered her deep clarity about the evolution that must take place in the feminist and Black freedom movements for all experiences of oppression and all expressions of difference to be recognized and regarded.

> As women, we must root out internalized patterns of oppression within ourselves if we are to move beyond the most superficial aspects of social change. . . . Change means growth, and growth can be painful. But we sharpen self-definition by exposing the self in work and struggle together with those whom we define as different from ourselves, although sharing the same goals.[23]

Liberation, then, rests on awareness and *practice* of what is required for growth. It involves rooting out internalized oppression as well as recognizing how oppressed persons have been divided against each other and taught to fear the expressions of anger that may arise from confrontation and being held accountable for harm. Most importantly, liberation involves pain. Diving into pain—rather than avoiding it—cultivates fearlessness. This fearlessness can be practiced and consequently, cultivated, if pain can be acknowledged as useful.

Turning toward pain, then, is inseparable from gaining strength, and ultimately, interior and political freedom.

Lorde named growth that comes from confronting pain as a survival skill particularly honed by Black people. She wrote "One of the most basic Black survival skills is the ability to change, to metabolize experience, good or ill, into something that is useful, lasting, effective."[24] As Lorde focused on the specific oppressions encountered by Black people, she particularly honed in on internalized oppression. In her essay "Learning from the Sixties," she expanded the idea that it is not too narrow to focus only on political and social freedom:

> If our history has taught us anything, it is that action for change directed only against the external conditions of our oppressions is not enough. In order to be whole, we must recognize the despair oppression plants within each of us—that thin, persistent voice that says our efforts are useless, it will never change, so why bother, accept it. And we must fight that inserted piece of self-destruction that lives and flourishes like a poison inside of us, unexamined until it makes us turn upon ourselves in each other. But we can put our finger down upon that loathing buried deep within each one of us and see who it encourages us to despise, and we can lessen its potency by the knowledge of our real connectedness, arcing across our differences.[25]

The self-scrutiny that Lorde pointed to again and again rests upon training oneself to see clearly the origins of one's anger. Allowing oneself to *feel*, rather than repress; allowing oneself to *acknowledge*, rather than deny, evolves one's power and takes back the weapons from enemies' hands, especially the weapon of fear. If women are fearless, they can resist the messages and conditions of the dominant culture. "To search for power within myself means I must be willing to move through being afraid to whatever lies beyond. If I look at my most vulnerable places and acknowledge the pain I have felt, I can remove the source of that pain from my enemies' arsenals,"[26] Lorde wrote.

In short, Lorde was saying: we must turn toward our pain. All beings experience pain as endemic to life; pain is inevitable. But there is a distinction between pain and suffering. Pain is an experience often beyond one's control. Pain can be used for growth. But suffering is different from pain; it is useless." Lorde reflected:

> There is a distinction I am beginning to make in my living between *pain* and *suffering*. Pain is an event, an experience that must be recognized, named, and then used in some way in order for the experience to change, to be transformed into something else, strength or knowledge or action.
>
> Suffering, on the other hand, is the nightmare reliving of unscrutinized and unmetabolized pain. When I live through pain without recognizing it, self-consciously, I rob myself of the power than can come from *using* that pain, the power to fuel some movement beyond it. I condemn myself to reliving that pain over and over and over whenever something close triggers it. And that is suffering, a seemingly inescapable cycle.
>
> And true, experiencing old pain sometimes feels like hurling myself full force against a concrete wall. But I remind myself that I HAVE LIVED THROUGH IT ALL ALREADY, AND SURVIVED.[27]

For Lorde, awareness of survival, of allowing one's feelings to be known and refusing to suffer unnecessary psychological terror, results in ultimately embodying the capacity to honor differences between women. Lorde's ability to acknowledge her own suffering without judgment facilitated her capacity to honor the differences within and between women without fear. She wrote, poignantly, that women have been taught to dismiss differences, and yet, to do so is to evade lived experiences, identities, and social dynamics. Such avoidance breeds anger rather than ease and freedom.[28] Rather than deny that differences exist, Lorde stated illuminating them fuels creativity, insight, and power.[29]

In turning toward difference, pain, and anger—in short, aversion—Lorde illuminates the necessary practices for cultivating the capacity to hold feminist and Black freedom activists accountable while still committing to solidarity and collective liberation.

Audre Lorde on the Nature of Impermanence

Audre Lorde's preoccupation with pain and with developing her capacity for interior growth was inextricable from her confrontation with death. In her reflections on the nature of constant change, and the fact of suffering embedded in shifting phenomena, she illuminated the Buddhist doctrine of impermanence. Articulated in early Buddhist *suttas* on the nature of suffering, this doctrine states that all conditioned phenomena—including the human person—are subject to change.[30] All physical and mental properties constantly shift. The Buddha taught that the fact of inevitable change is, by its very nature, painful. Lorde experienced the fact of inevitable, painful change intimately. She acknowledged conditions that trigger pain, and that ruminating and seeking to avoid pain result in yet another level of suffering. Thus, denial of impermanence makes pain worse; grasping toward impermanent phenomena leads to further suffering.

Lorde's cancer diagnosis at age forty-four thrust the fact of impermanence and the reality of death suddenly and inescapably into her life. She stated in her introduction to *The Cancer Journals*, which chronicles her experiences of being diagnosed with breast cancer and undergoing a mastectomy in 1979, "I am a post-mastectomy woman who believes our feelings need voice in order to be recognized, respected, and of use."[31]

The terror Lorde experienced at the prospect of mortality led her to write evocatively of impermanence. Writing was a practice of self-soothing. It was also a way to be useful to women of color throughout the world who were similarly struggling with impending death, due to illness or mass violence. "I am learning to live beyond fear by living through it," Lorde wrote in *The Cancer Journals*, eighteen months after her mastectomy, "and in the process learning to turn fury at my own limitations into some more creative energy."[32] She further reflected:

> As women, we were raised to fear. If I cannot banish fear completely, I can learn to count with it less. For then fear becomes not a tyrant against which I waste my energy fighting, but a companion, not particularly desirable, yet one whose knowledge can be useful.[33]

For Lorde, the fear brought on by the ultimate fact of impermanence—death—was a state of mind to be known, embraced, and learned from. She wrote: "If I can look directly at my life and my death without flinching, I know there is nothing they can ever do to me again."[34]

When she was again diagnosed with cancer at age fifty—this time, cancer of the liver—the prospect of impending death opened up a wellspring of insights even as it provoked tremendous anxiety. But rather than resist death or repress debilitating feelings of terror, she sought to turn toward the reality of her diagnosis and to work with it skillfully. She embraced natural therapies, meditation, and a healthy diet. On November 19, 1979, she wrote: "There must be some way to integrate death into living neither ignoring it or giving into it."[35]

Acceptance of impermanence and its ultimate marker, death, became a daily work, a constant practice of attuning to her body and making wise choices: of what to eat, how to spend time, and how to learn from the reality of constant change. She acknowledged that resistance to death would only lead to more suffering. She wrote: "I must let this pain flow through me and pass on. If I resist or try to stop it, it will detonate inside me, shatter me, splatter my pieces against every wall and person I touch."[36]

Rather than undergo surgery for liver cancer, Lorde sought alternative treatments. Her journal entries from this time, published in *A Burst of Light*, relate the rising and falling thoughts of a mind grappling with the fact of pain and death. "As a living creature I am part of two kinds of forces—growth and decay, sprouting and withering, living and dying, and at any given moment of our lives, each one of us is actively located somewhere along a continuum between these two forces."[37]

As with her breast cancer diagnosis, Lorde turned toward the implications of her liver cancer: her fear, the fact of death, and the conviction that all of her pain and terror could be used for service and growth. On November 12, 1986, she wrote: "There is a terrible clarity that comes from living with cancer that can be empowering if we do not turn aside from it."[38] That clarity, for Lorde, was the awareness that life consisted of constant change, and that her precious life was most fully lived when she cared for her psyche and her body, surrounded herself with a community of loving women, and continued to write her personal truths. For Lorde, these truths were clearly interconnected: "Battling racism and battling heterosexism and battling apartheid share the same urgency inside me as battling cancer."[39]

The disproportionate violence and tragedy landing on Black women's backs ignited a sense of constant warfare. This was no less true with cancer. In the epilogue to *A Burst of Light*, Lorde wrote: "Overextending myself is not stretching myself. I had to accept how difficult it is to monitor the difference. Necessary for me as cutting down on sugar. Crucial. Physically. Psychically. Caring for myself is not self-indulgence, it is self-preservation, and that is an act of political warfare."[40] And, similarly to her work in the feminist movement—in which she elevated issues of racism, classism, and ageism alongside sexism—she treated cancer as something that had to be confronted. The presence of cancer required acknowledgment, even when she desperately feared the outcome. She mused:

> How do I hold faith with sun in a sunless place? It is so hard not to counter this despair with a refusal to see. But I have to stay open and filtering no matter what's coming at me, because that arms me in a particular Black woman's way. When I'm open, I'm also less despairing. The more clearly I see what I'm up against, the more able I am to fight this process going on in my body that they're calling liver cancer. And I am determined to fight it even when I am not sure of the terms of the battle nor the face of victory. I just know I must not surrender my body to others unless I completely understand and agree with what they think should be done to it. I've got to look at all of my options carefully, even the ones I find distasteful. I know I can broaden the definition of winning to the point where I can't lose.[41]

She approached her cancer in a familiar way: to turn toward the possibilities of inner and outer change, which, she acknowledged, are "not easy nor quick."[42] In this way, she embraced the fact of impermanence, and the suffering that it sometimes evoked. Lorde wrote in August 1987: "One of the hardest things to accept is learning to live within uncertainty and neither deny it nor hide behind it. Most of all, to listen to the messages of uncertainty without allowing them to immobilize me, nor keep me from the certainties of those truths in which I believe.[43]

She acknowledged that she did not control many of the levers of her life. Nonetheless, she still possessed power: to choose how to meet the fact of pain, of death. She could not control the reality of cancer, but she could determine how to turn toward it and not succumb to her fear.

At times, this took the form of joy. After leaving a Swiss alternative treatment center in January 1986, she traveled to the West Indies. She wrote: "This is the year I spent spring beachcombing in St. Croix . . . a loving context in which I fit and thrive."[44] She moved to St. Croix in late 1986, where she wrote about the lack of certainty in daily life amidst the commitment to living as fully as possible. She reflected: "I work, I love, I rest, I see and learn. And I report. These are my givens. Not sureties, but a firm belief that whether or not living them with joy prolongs my life, it certainly enables me to pursue the objectives of that life with a deeper and more effective clarity."[45]

The fact of impermanence and its final iteration, death, led Lorde to reflect on the reality of change.

Her capacity to hold complexity arose from her practice of self-scrutiny and resulted in an articulation of myriad forms of power. In November 1986, Lorde wrote: "Living a self-conscious life, vulnerability as armor."[46] She reflected on her approach to vulnerability in a 1989 interview with Laureen Greene: "We are always in training for the next step. Death is another step. Now that I have faced my mortality without embracing it, there is nothing anyone can do to me again."[47]

Lorde went on to reflect: "Living fully—how long is not the point."[48]

The commitment to living fully in the face of impermanence and death, the commitment to inner stamina while working for social change, and the embrace of community while honoring differences fostered a fearless way of being, regardless of context. And, crucially, Lorde's capacity for fearlessness was inseparable from her practice of self-compassion. In her commitment to exhibiting tenderness for herself and others, Lorde further pointed to Buddhist ethics of compassion.

Audre Lorde on the Nature of Compassion

Lorde's commitment to honoring differences among women arose from a tender relationship she fostered with her own complex identity. She was not afraid to insist that all parts of herself—Black, lesbian, poet, warrior, mother—be named and uplifted in social settings. Her refusal to leave different aspects of her identity in the background resulted from her wholesome desire to connect to her own voice and to connect to other women, especially Black women. She named the destructiveness of internalizing racist hatred, which ruptures connectedness to oneself and other Black women. Lorde's essay "Eye to Eye: Black Women Hatred, and Anger" provides a heart-wrenching acknowledgment of how hatred directed toward Black children is internalized and consequently manifests as anger and disconnection between Black women. She recognized how the nuances of anger between Black women must be named and confronted. Anger serves to connect when there is an ever-present threat. Yet it disconnects people who are attempting to bond on a deeper level; thus it can be ultimately debilitating when directed toward sister Black women. Lorde longed for intimacy and solidarity among Black women. She was not just oriented toward confronting oppressors. On a deeper dimension, sought to exhibit tenderness toward one another. She acknowledged that such a depth of relationality requires deep compassion.

In recognizing the difficulties of connecting to Black women, Lorde determined a way forward. She advocated "mothering ourselves." It is in this language that Lorde illuminated the Buddhist orientation toward cultivating and offering compassion.

Early Buddhism uplifts the *Brahmaviharas*: teachings and practices that include *metta* (translated as loving-kindness); *karuna* (compassion); *mudita* (empathetic joy); and *uppekha* (equanimity). Known as the "Four Immeasurables," the *Brahmaviharas* are identified as the "Four Faces of Love" of the Hindu god Brahma.

Additionally, the *Metta Sutta* states:
Even as a mother protects with her life
Her only child,

> So with a boundless heart
> Should one cherish all beings.[49]

In the Mahayana tradition, "the second turning of the wheel" that took place after the emergence of early Buddhism, different aspects of the Buddhist tradition were elaborated and depicted. The Mahayana Buddhist tradition emphasizes emptiness as well as skillful means, and the introduction of the Bodhisattva, an enlightened being who eschews *nirvana* to help suffering beings. The Bodhisattva is often depicted as a feminine image.

Alongside the Bodhisattva, the Mahayana tradition contains numerous descriptions and depictions of Tara, the female Buddha. Tara is compassionate, as well as sometimes wrathful and protective. Similarly, Vajrayana *dakinis*—wrathful, fierce, compassionate manifestations of energy—are depicted as simultaneously tender and indicting.

Alongside wrathful energies, the Mahayana and Vajrayana Buddhist traditions convey many maternal images, among them the Great Mother, *Prajnaparamita*.[50] *Prajnaparamita* is considered transcendental knowledge, an expression of that feminine principle called "mother." Lorde's writing evokes the image of *Prajnaparamita,* who is described as sometimes "depicted in human form, yet emphasizing vast and limitless qualities. . . . These forms are peaceful or wrathful and sometimes naked in order to highlight the qualities of uncloaked reality."[51]

The Vajrayana Buddhist tradition is replete with references to the Great Mother. Buddhist scholar Judith Simmer-Brown writes: "In Vajrayana the Mother is said to be powerful because of her unique abilities to express the vast, awesome, limitless (and genderless) nature of emptiness."[52] The writings of Tsongkhapa, a fourteenth-century Tibetan Buddhist scholar, contain a practice known as "Recognizing All Beings as Our Mothers," which fosters cultivating relative *bodhicitta*—heart energy—"at first through the ground of affection, recognition of the kindness of mother beings, and the sincere wish to repay them, which leads to love."[53]

For Lorde, who embraced mothering her two children, internalizing her own capacity to mother herself led to generative self-love that organically extended out toward Black women, even when she felt wounded by them. Indeed, for many of the women who encountered her within the second-wave feminist movement, Audre Lorde embodied mother energy. Lorde herself stated that she related to other women "in one of two ways, either as lover or as mother."[54] As Lorde took on a maternal role with women in her community, she also turned toward the difficult relationship she had with her biological mother, whom she experienced as distant, controlling, and abusive. Lorde's practice of nurturing herself and her female comrades was in essence a practice of healing the sense of alienation and disconnection she felt with her biological mother. For Lorde, the starting point for healing was mothering herself with a depth of tenderness that had eluded her in childhood.

Lorde's practice of self-mothering fundamentally rested upon embrace of all psychological states and feelings, regardless of how painful or messy they appeared to be. She uplifted self-scrutiny, allowing that which is painful and chaotic to be intimately known. In "Eye to Eye," she wrote:

> We will begin to see each other as we dare to begin to see ourselves; we will begin to see ourselves as we begin to see each other, without aggrandizement or dismissal or recriminations, but with patience and understanding for when we do not quite make it, and recognition and appreciation for when we do. Mothering ourselves means learning to love what we have given birth to by giving definition to, learning how to be both kind and demanding in the teeth of failure as well as in the face of success, and not misnaming either.

She went on to state:

> Mothering. Claiming some power over who we choose to be, and knowing that such power is relative within the realities of our lives. Yet knowing that only through the use of that power can we effectively change those realities. Mothering means the laying to rest of what is weak, timid, and damaged— without despisal—the protection and support of what is useful for survival and change, and our joint explorations of the difference.[55]

Mothering, for Audre Lorde, requires self-love and kindness toward sister Black women; it requires learning new ways of being, internalizing new narratives, and consistently practicing ancestral care and gentleness. Women wish for themselves the protection they offer young, vulnerable beings; they learn to turn compassion inward, and in so doing, expand compassion toward those whom they have been taught to despise. In her insistence on cultivating a practice of deep self-nurturing, Lorde helped all women—and particularly Black women—to see the possibility of deep self-intimacy and self-compassion as a way forward. Indeed, in Lorde's eyes, the practice of clearly seeing and turning toward one's own suffering can only be effective if women give themselves the tenderness and affection that they often desperately want from their mothers.

Lorde uplifts multiple quotations from different religious traditions in "Eye to Eye." At the time of writing, she had immersed herself in West African female imagery. Yet her reliance on the *I Ching* throughout "Eye to Eye" suggests that she also oriented herself toward Eastern spiritual writings. Womanist scholar Pamela Ayo Yetunde reflects:

> As I read and re-read [Lorde's] works with a Buddha eye this time, and for the first time encountered some of her unpublished works on spirituality, I understood more clearly and felt more strongly the emanation of the healing vibrations of Lorde's embedded nondualistic *I Ching* spirituality that led her to being the grandmother of intersectionality before Kimberlé Crenshaw coined the word in 1989. Lorde's *I Ching* is infused in her writings on justice, healing activism, romance, politics, parenting, psychology, poetry, and prose. Her ability to see the healing potential in various contexts and shape shift to meet the opportunity is the bodhisattva ideal manifested.[56]

For Yetunde, Lorde is a deeply maternal figure indebted to the wisdom teachings of the *I Ching* who conveys a self-compassion that extends to an expansive nurturing of all beings, with particular attunement to those who have internalized racism. Lorde's capacity to turn toward herself and state "When I can recognize my own worth, I can recognize yours" is, for Yetunde and other Black Buddhist practitioners, nothing short of the Bodhisattva vow: to offer boundless compassion for all beings. In other words, in this recognition of her own worth, Lorde extends compassion outward toward other Black women, as well as white women who seek to create solidarity within movement spaces.

Lorde makes clear that cultivating maternal compassion for herself facilitated inner spaciousness. The difficulties of navigating the world as a Black woman who suffered specific harms, who underwent two cancer diagnoses and sought numerous avenues for treatment, opened into an experience of emptiness and fearlessness. Internalized oppression met compassion and tenderness. In Lorde's practice of self-mothering, turning toward internalized hatred and anger made room for new narratives.

Thus the practice into which Lorde invited Black women is a practice of turning toward suffering and impermanence, deconstructing oppressive, internalized messages, and uplifting a self-compassion that radiates outward. She illuminated the Buddhist emphasis on wisdom and skillful means.[57] In so doing, she asked: How can Black women turn toward internalized self-hatred and fully know it? How can Black women turn toward self-hatred and investigate the anger they express toward those persons in closest proximity to them? How can Black women cultivate compassion and wisdom?

Lorde was focused on Black women's well-being, but she was also speaking to participants of the feminist and Black freedom movements. She challenged those who espouse freedom to move beyond intellect to embrace emotional complexity and healing. Can those who are committed to human freedom create spaciousness for new narratives and offer themselves compassion, Great Mothering? Can they internalize new narratives, emptiness beyond pretense? Can they offer compassion and support to one another? In short, can they cultivate the capacity to offer and accept accountability, work toward genuine solidarity, and manifest community?

Conclusion

In her essays and interviews, Audre Lorde illuminated insights and practices of several Buddhist doctrines. She demonstrated how these teachings facilitated her capacity to engage deeply in the second-generation feminist and Black freedom movements. In so doing, she held fellow activists accountable for their myopia, including racism and sexism, as her fellow activists insisted that solidarity was possible. For Lorde, liberation was internal and simultaneously political. It cannot *only* be political—focused on changing external conditions—nor can it be solely oriented toward interior life and shifting one's conditioning. Liberation involves changing conditions and conditioning at the same time.

In this way, Lorde's emphasis on cultivating awareness and self-compassion as foundational to political accountability and solidarity points to how Buddhist ethics can broaden feminist religious ethics. And, Lorde's writing also challenges Buddhist ethics' sometimes narrow framework of emphasizing liberation as experienced through the practice of the Noble Eightfold Path and the Bodhisattva vows. Liberation is personal and political; in Lorde's worldview, these interlocking facets of liberation are inseparable.

In sum, Lorde's writings on suffering, impermanence, and compassion uplift the interior work required for engaging in political movements; such an emphasis on interior reflection and practices fosters a new way of being that necessarily dismantles patriarchal, racist systems. "The Master's Tools Will Never Dismantle the Master's House," Lorde asserted. Indeed, for Audre Lorde, it is the dark, feminine mother warrior who uplifts feelings alongside rational thinking and who will lead a new political order.

At the same time, the capacity to privilege feeling requires sustained, consistent practices that I have argued are aligned with Buddhist doctrines and rituals. Indeed, the Buddhist doctrines illuminated by Lorde are:

- The Four Noble Truths: There is physical and psychological pain in life. Skillful means to work with pain requires turning toward it and knowing it fully. In so doing, one gives oneself permission to feel—rather than repress—one's pain.
- The distinction between pain and suffering: In language that is highly congruent with the Buddhist teaching of the "Two Arrows," Lorde observed that when a person feels the first arrow of affliction, it is a result of being injured. But individuals inflict the second arrow upon themselves when they ruminate and obsess.
- The Doctrine of Impermanence: Constant change is a fact of life. Material phenomena, feelings, and states of mind arise and fall away. The ultimate state of passing away is death. Human beings can cultivate the capacity to turn toward impermanence and death fearlessly, and thereby cultivate fearlessness in all aspects of life.

- Skillful Means: The fearlessness that arises with turning toward pain, suffering, impermanence, and death fosters a capacity to acknowledge harm and to hold those who commit harm accountable for their attitudes and actions.
- The Bodhisattva and Great Mother Archetypes: To meet pain and suffering, it is necessary to cultivate tenderness toward oneself that will naturally extend toward other people. Such compassion allows Black women to nurture themselves with a deep maternal energy that further allows Black women to cultivate solidarity with one another.

Lorde emphasized the importance of claiming inner wholeness in the quest for political liberation for all peoples. In this way, she did not privilege one aspect of her identity, but rather, integrated her gender, racial, sexual, and class identity into the second-generation feminist movement as well as the Black freedom struggle.

Even as she turned toward her own suffering, Lorde insisted that liberation is not solely individualistic. Liberation is communal and political. Yet to orient toward one another, activists must start with themselves. For power to be fully expressed, it must evolve from deep nurturing of one's inner life force. Embodying power requires deep listening and sharing of feelings.[58] And, for communal liberation to be authentic, indeed, truly rooted in solidarity, it requires cultivating the capacity to be held accountable for any harm that is committed, even unintentionally. Movement spaces must honor differences among people and acknowledge when members of the collective fall short. And honoring differences cannot solely be outward-facing work. Cultivating the interior capacity to honor differences and work through difficult dynamics—to be accountable and to be in solidarity—is rooted in the practice of turning toward one's own suffering, embracing the fact of impermanence and death, and consistently offering compassion to oneself and other beings.

As movement activists do the hard interior work of shifting oppressive narratives, nurturing themselves and each other, and confronting the status quo, an anti-racist, feminist political context will necessarily emerge. This liberatory context will contain the capacity to honor complexity: not just differing races, cultures, classes, genders, and sexualities, but also religious and ethical traditions, economic frameworks, and communal practices. Finally, this new way of being will insist upon honoring differences for the sake of individual and collective thriving and will resist extractive, exploitative relationships as the norm. For, as Lorde asserts, "The Master's Tools Will Never Dismantle the Master's House."

Notes

1 The second-generation feminist movement, which spanned the 1960s to the 1980s, focused on lesbian sexuality, challenges to traditional family structures, anti-racism, class dynamics, reproductive rights, international solidarity, and violence against women.

2 Audre Lorde, "Age, Race, Class, and Sex: Women Redefining Difference," *Sister Outsider* (New York: Crossing Press, 1984), 114.

3 Alexis de Veaux, *Warrior Poet: A Biography of Audre Lorde* (New York: W.W. Norton, 2004), 151.

4 Early Buddhism refers to the period of the institutionalization of Buddhism, beginning in the third century BCE during the Buddha's life and subsequently with the establishment of councils, philosophical schools, and the writing of the monastic discipline known as the *Vinaya* and the *suttas* (recitations of the Buddha's teachings). In referencing doctrines on suffering and impermanence, I rely upon early Buddhist *suttas*. In referencing images and practices of compassion later in this chapter, I rely primarily (but not exclusively) upon subsequent forms and images of Buddhism in Mahayana and Vajrayana lineages. See Peter Harvey, *An Introduction to Buddhism: Teachings, History, and Practices,* 2nd ed. (Cambridge, MA: Cambridge University Press, 2013), 88–113.

5 Lorde, "Age, Race, Class, and Sex," *Sister Outsider*, 120–21.

6 Lorde, "The Master's Tools Will Never Dismantle the Master's House," *Sister Outsider*, 112.

7 Combahee River Collective Statement. https://americanstudies.yale.edu/sites/default/files/files/Keyword%20Coalition_Readings.pdf. Accessed January 5, 2021.

8 Ibid.

9   Rosemary Kellison, "Solidarity and Feminist Religious Ethics," in *Solidarity and Power: Feminist Approaches to Religious Ethics,* eds. Rosemary Kellison and Shannon Dunn (Greenbelt, MD: Bloomsbury Academic, 2025), 6.

10 Aurora Celestin, "Buddha, Baldwin, and Lorde on How to Reduce Suffering," Unpublished Paper, September 14, 2023.

11 Ibid.

12 Ibid., 7.

13 Audre Lorde, "Audre Lorde," in *Conversations with Audre Lorde*, ed. Joan Wylie-Hall (Jackson: University Press of Mississippi, 2004), 16. Initially published in a volume of collected interviews by Nina Winter. See *Interview with the Muse: Remarkable Women Speak on Creativity and Power* (Berkeley, CA: Moon Books, 1978 [1976]).

14 Peter Harvey, "*Dukkha*, Non-Self, and the Teaching on the Four Noble Truths," in *A Companion to Buddhist Philosophy*, ed. Steven M. Emmanuel (New York: Wiley, 2013), 29.

15 Harvey, "Introduction," 74–75.

16 Ibid., 63.

17 Lorde, "Poetry Is Not a Luxury," *Sister Outsider*, 36.

18 Ibid.

19 Ibid., 36–37.

20 Ibid., 37.

21 See, as one example, the *Satipatthana Sutta.* https://accesstoinsight.org/lib/authors/nyanasatta/wheel019.html. Accessed August 13, 2024.

22 Lorde, "The Uses of Anger," *Sister Outsider*, 128.

23 Lorde, "Age, Race, Class, and Sex," *Sister Outsider*, 122–23.

24 Lorde, "Learning from the 60s," *Sister Outsider*, 135.

25 Ibid., 142.

26 Lorde, "Eye to Eye: Black Women, Hatred, and Anger," *Sister Outsider*, 146.

27 Ibid., 171–72.

28 Lorde, "Master's Tools," *Sister Outsider*, 112.

29 Lorde, "Uses of Anger," *Sister Outsider*, 131.

30 Harvey, *Introduction*, 55–57.

31 Audre Lorde, *The Cancer Journals* (New York: Penguin Books, 1980), 1.

32 Ibid., 8.

33 Ibid.

34 Ibid., 4.

35 Ibid., 5.

36 Ibid., 4.

37 Audre Lorde, *A Burst of Light* (Ithaca, NY: Firebrand Books, 1988), 79.

38 Ibid., 120.

39 Ibid., 116.

40 Ibid., 131.

41 Ibid., 60–61.

42 Ibid., 121.

43 Ibid., 132.

44 Ibid., 96.

45 Ibid., 134.

46 Ibid., 125.

47 Lorde, *Conversations*, 183.

48 Lorde, *A Burst of Light*, 126.

49 Metta Sutta, https://www.learnreligions.com/the-metta-sutta-450129.

50 *Prajnaparamita* is both feminine and also transcends gender.

51 Judith Simmer-Brown, *Dakini's Warm Breath: The Feminine Principle in Tibetan Buddhism* (Boulder, CO: Shambhala Press, 2002), 110.

52 Ibid., 115.

53 Jae Carey, "Recognizing All Beings as Our Mothers: Reflections on Mother-Practice Journeys and Bodhicitta," unpublished paper, June 2023, personal collection housing the material.

54 De Veaux, *Warrior Poet*, 241.

55 Lorde, "Eye to Eye," *Sister Outsider*, 173–74.

56 Pamela Ayo Yetunde, "Audre Lorde: Uncovering a Bodhisattva," in "Awakening Through Audre Lorde," *Lion's Roar*, May 15, 2022. https://www.lionsroar.com/awakening-through-audre-lorde/. Accessed August 13, 2024.

57 Simmer-Brown, *Dakini's Warm Breath*, 115.

58 Lorde, *Sister Outsider*, 58, 111.

References

Carey, Jae. "Recognizing All Beings as Our Mothers: Reflections on Mother-Practice Journeys and Bodhicitta." Unpublished Paper, June 2023, personal collection housing the material.

Celestin, Aurora. "Buddha, Baldwin, and Lorde on How to Reduce Suffering." Unpublished Paper, September 2023, personal collection housing the material.

Combahee River Collective. "Combahee River Collective Statement." 1977. https://americanstudies.yale.edu/sites/default/files/files/Keyword%20Coalition_Readings.pdf. Accessed January 5, 2021.

De Veaux, Alexis. *Warrior Poet: A Biography of Audre Lorde.* New York: W.W. Norton, 2004.

Harvey, Peter. "*Dukkha*, Non-Self, and the Teaching on the Four Noble Truths." In *A Companion to Buddhist Philosophy*, edited by Steven M. Emmanuel. New York: Wiley, 2013.

———. *An Introduction to Buddhism: Teachings, History, and Practices*, 2nd ed. Cambridge: Cambridge University Press, 2013.

Lorde, Audre. *A Burst of Light.* Ithaca, NY: Firebrand Books, 1988.

———. *The Cancer Journals.* New York: Penguin Books, 1980.

———. *Sister Outsider.* New York: Crossing Press, 1984.

Satipatthana Sutta. https://accesstoinsight.org/lib/authors/nyanasatta/wheel019.html. Accessed August 13, 2024.

Simmer-Brown, Judith. *Dakini's Warm Breath: The Feminine Principle in Tibetan Buddhism.* Boulder, CO: Shambhala Press, 2002.

Wylie Hall, Joan, ed. *Conversations with Audre Lorde.* Jackson: University Press of Mississippi, 2004.

Yetunde, Pamela Ayo. "Audre Lorde: Uncovering a Bodhisattva." In "Awakening through Audre Lorde," *Lion's Roar*, May 15, 2022. https://www.lionsroar.com/awakening-through-audre-lorde/. Accessed August 13, 2024.

5

Abolition Womanism

A Theological Account of Black Mothers' Unlawful Salvation

Nikia Smith Robert

A critical task for this chapter is to introduce Abolition Womanism, a novel construct situated at the intersections of religion, abolition, and Black womanhood. Abolition Womanism begins with the lived experiences of poor Black mothers who are criminalized for merely trying to survive and extends to the myriad ways Black women are blamed, condemned, and punished by systems of domination. Abolition Womanism aims to abolish death-dealing conditions by imagining emancipatory alternatives to repair harms, restore relationships, and rebuild more just and equitable systems. The teleological goal of Abolition Womanism is to co-create a world in which Black women can thrive beyond interlocking systems of oppression, including poverty, punishment, policing, and prisons.

Abolition Womanism is a comprehensive critical study that consists of theological, moral, legal, and political interventions related to Black women's experiences with survival in carceral contexts, domestically and globally. For the limited scope of this chapter, however, I focus on an aspect of a theological account that aims to justify Black mothers' lawbreaking in the United States. Here within, I argue that poor Black mothers who violate just, unjust, and unequally applied laws to survive and secure a quality of life for themselves and their families against unjust social conditions should not be punished when their lawbreaking is contextualized by three main criteria: (1) they are historically disadvantaged, (2) they have limited options to preserve themselves and family, and (3) they must secure life-generating resources out of necessity.

I draw from Delores Williams's exposition of the story of Hagar in connection to Black women who struggle to make an unlawful way out of no way by acting as self-legislator. I contend that Black women's grit to exercise moral agency and practical wisdom that transgresses dominant bounds is unequivocally consonant with Jesus, a first-century abolitionist. I also explore traditions of lawbreaking including the civil disobedience of Socrates and Martin Luther King. Moreover, I engage a comparative approach between Thomas Aquinas's natural law theory and Islamic law to present religious justifications for lawbreaking out of necessity.

This research contributes to the study of religion by advancing the first sustained theological and ethical conversation in womanist theory to center Black mothers' experience with carceral conditions. Importantly, Abolition Womanism is a theoretical *and* practical intervention to an urgent twenty-first-century moral crisis: the criminalization of impoverished Black motherhood. I aim to push womanist discourse beyond the ivory towers of academic study and into the streets that Black women walk struggling to find their next meal, pay rent, and feed their family when they do not have, what my mother would say, "a pot to piss in or a window to throw it out." This paradigmatic shift in religious studies and womanist theory is necessary to connect critical analysis to radical action and abolition to actualize more just and equitable systems. Importantly, Abolition Womanism is not essentialist. An argument justifying lawbreaking out of necessity can apply to other vulnerable groups. However, I focus on the lived experiences of Black mothers based on my personal story as a point of departure, but also because of a belief affirmed by the Combahee Collective that other groups are not free until Black women are free.

Law and Morality

A typology of law is important to establish how I am thinking about lawbreaking in the context of Black mothers' survival. I define a just law as universal and necessary to protect the common good (i.e., life and safety) and with regard for the human dignity and rights of all. For example, the imperative *do not steal* is a just law because if everyone stole then no one's property would be safe. However, even with universality binding, there are extreme cases that may call for an exception. For example, a hungry person may be morally permitted to steal food for self-preservation or to avoid death. Thomas Aquinas makes a similar claim in his natural law theory. Aquinas, in accordance with the Ten Commandments, believed that stealing is a sin. However, food belongs to the common good and no one should have excess while others are hungry. Thus, to avoid starvation one can take food that is not their own and not count it as theft. In the case of this exception, obeying a just law is not the right thing to do. In fact, disobeying the law may at times be morally permissible. Ergo, legality is not necessarily justice or the right thing to do.

Conversely, unjust laws are not universally recognized. There are many examples of unjust laws in the US legal system. Segregation laws in the Jim Crow South were unjust because they legislated the separation of whites and Blacks in schools, public education, marriages, churches, and other aspects of public life. These laws were unjust because they disregarded the humanity of marginalized groups and constructed them as inferior based on race and other social markers to deny civil and human rights. Martin Luther King, quoting Augustine and Aquinas, argued that an unjust law is no law at all and used this philosophy as a rationale to support civil disobedience. King believed segregation laws were unjust because they distorted the soul and damaged the personality.

Unequally applied laws are statutes that benefit some groups and disadvantage others, usually based on proximity to power and privilege. For example, the Stand Your Ground Law was unequally applied in the cases of George Zimmerman, who killed Trayvon Martin, and Marissa Alexander, who brandished her weapon against an abuser but killed no one. Both parties were tried in the State of Florida, the City of Sanford, by the same prosecutor, around the same time, and invoked the Stand Your Ground law as a defense, but the outcomes were drastically different. Zimmerman, a white-presenting Peruvian man and son of a judge, was acquitted. However, Alexander, a Black single mother, was initially sentenced to twenty years in prison. The variables of race and gender set these outcomes apart and demonstrate the unequal application of law.

The line between legality and morality is thin. Legal positivists have long argued for the rule of law that is exempt from the arbitrariness of morality. H. L. A. Hart, a proponent of legal positivism, supported the separation of "law as it is" and "law as it ought to be" (morality). Hart believed that the confusion of law and morality caused problems that could lead to anarchy. Hart's point is insufficient when considering power differentials between dominant society and marginalized groups. For example, acting autonomously, especially against unjust systems, is not to be confused with anarchy unless anarchy itself is something other than chaos such as radicalized resistance and revolution. Rather, tyranny is when people's noncompliance is driven by power because their positionality renders them above the law. These distinctions are important.

Early philosophical discourses have long revealed tensions between law and morality. Thomas Hobbes held that the law is a command that requires obedience and keeps us from returning to a state of nature or the human condition of barbarism and the code of kill or be killed. However, Hobbes also saw criminal law as amenable to self-preservation. He argued, "When a man is destitute of food, or other things necessary for his life, and cannot preserve himself any other way, but by some fact against the law, as in a great famine he takes food by force . . . which he cannot obtain from money nor charity . . . he is totally excused." Though Hobbes's philosophy of law requires obedience to keep the peace and civility, he understood when survival is at stake, individuals will do anything to avoid death even if it means breaking the law to take food when famished. Thus, Hobbes ultimately conflates law with moral reasoning.

Socrates also blurs law and morality and practices an earlier version of civil disobedience. On the one hand, Socrates believed in disobeying unjust laws to teach the youth and protect his freedom of speech. On the other hand, however, Socrates obeys unjust laws by not accepting his friend's offer to escape Athens to avoid death by a cup of poison hemlock. Socrates presents a moral dilemma within the gray area of whether to comply or not comply with Athenian law. Socrates's disobedience is an early precursor to civil disobedience.

In a *Letter from a Birmingham Jail*, King invokes Aquinas and Socrates in making a moral argument to defy the laws of segregation with civil disobedience. King responds to the question, "How can you advocate breaking some laws and obeying others?" On the one hand, he urged people to obey the Supreme

Court's 1954 decision outlawing segregation in public schools. On the other hand, King supported breaking (unjust) laws. Resolving this tension, King ascertained that there are two kinds of laws: just and unjust. King advocated for obeying just laws as a moral and legal responsibility, but he argued that one also has a moral responsibility to disobey unjust laws. Moreover, King exposed the double standards in society. Civil disobedience was deemed anarchist and insurrectionist, a claim Hart admonished against. However, dictators were ostensibly above the law. King reminds his readers that, "everything Hitler did in Germany was 'legal' and everything the Hungarian freedom fighters did in Hungary was 'illegal.' It was 'illegal' to aid and comfort a Jew in Hitler's Germany." These double standards in the legal system still exist today.

King continues in his letter, "even so, I am sure that had I lived in Germany at the time, I would have aided and comforted my Jewish brothers. If today, I lived in a Communist country where certain principles dear to the Christian faith are suppressed, I would openly advocate disobeying that country's antireligious laws." In the same tradition, it is quite possible that King would also support the justification of Black mothers' lawbreaking to survive and secure quality of life for themselves and their families against unjust social conditions. King concludes, "sometimes a law is just on its face and unjust in its application." In other words, everything that is legal is not always moral. Sometimes breaking the law is the right thing to do.

To be clear, I am not suggesting that Black mothers' lawbreaking is an act of civil disobedience. However, the reference to King provides support for the conflation between law and morality in maters of justice and human dignity for Black people. Hence, it is my stance that Black mothers are morally justified to break just, unjust, and unequally applied laws when motivated by preservation, need, and overcoming interlocking systems of oppression. In the negotiation of law and morality in the context of Black mothers' survival, it is important to reappraise Black mothers' moral decision-making as a source of moral worth, because when we allow the criminal system to enforce law and dictate the worth of Black women, we prioritize punishment over their accountability and care. Abolition Womanism shifts from individual blame to systems critique and identifies restorative ways to reappraise Black mothers' survival strategies while dismantling the systems that make survival nearly impossible in the first place.

A Gentrified El Barrio

I grew up against the backdrop of an unjust war on drugs, the crack epidemic, the criminalization of poverty and welfare, a burgeoning prison industrial complex, and the false convictions of five innocent boys dubbed the "Central Park Five."[1] I lived in Spanish Harlem. El Barrio was a mosaic of cultural fusions. Within a few short city blocks, I passed a church, a mosque, a Jehovah's Witness Kingdom Hall, and a private garden holding the Lucumí or Santeria ritual. At school, I was taught the revolutionary spirit of Black radical politics and the resistance of the Young Lords. Across from my buildings stood the first statue in the country honoring the Harlem Renaissance maestro Duke Ellington, and on the adjacent street loomed a green street sign named after the mambo musical genius Tito Puente. I heard Frankie Beverly and Maze play "Before I Let Go" from nearby apartments and cookouts and Joe Arroyo's song "Rebellion" belt out from bodegas and hair salons. I lined the streets during Harlem Week to see La Roc Bey's African troop dance to the djimbe drums and during Old Timers Day I watched Latino men play the congas while women shuffled their feet and hips with partners to Bachata, Salsa, and Meringue. I smelled the aromas of southern cuisine and *pollo con arrroz y habichuelas o gandules* while friends played basketball or stick ball and spades or dominoes. The East side of Harlem was fraught with abject poverty, but it was rich in communal ethos bringing together Puerto Rican (and Nuyorican), Mexican (and Chicano), Dominican, Black, African diasporic, immigrant, and undocumented neighbors—all vulnerable people who pooled resources together to survive and secure a higher quality of life.

However, processes of gentrification and eminent domain diminished the colorful vibrancy of our community. Racial capitalism threatened our collective ethic of solidarity with the counter values of individualism and corporate greed that displaced residents and replaced them with higher-income earners who could afford premium market-rate rents and mortgages. This intentional plan resulted in shifts in the neighborhood's demographics to enhance infrastructure and resources that benefited privileged incoming residents. I saw this unfold where I lived, as my mother and neighbors who occupied their apartments since the building's opening now struggled to remain and afford skyrocketing rent because they were no longer protected by rent stabilization.

Schomburg Plaza was a Mitchell-Lama residential complex named after the Afro Puerto Rican activist, Arturo Schomburg. The development complex consisted of three buildings including two identically brown thirty-five-storied octagonal towers overlooking a lap of luxury across 5th Avenue, the northern corner of Central Park, city-skyline, and a distant silhouette of New Jersey across the Hudson River. The West side of Central Park across the way was long considered prime real estate, but renters in affordable East Harlem benefited from the same views and accessible transportation. It was not long before profit-mongering businesses and powerful Realtors colluded with the market to outprice Harlem residents with privatization.

The Mitchell-Lama Housing Program, funded by New York state, offered a twenty-year tax subsidy to keep housing affordable.[2] However, many landlords prepaid or refinanced the mortgage, forfeited their return on investment, and removed their developments from the Mitchell-Lama program. Rentals built prior to 1974 were protected by rent stabilization, which meant the rent was set by the New York City Rent Guidelines Board. Rentals built post-1974 were not federally subsidized, which meant the rent was determined by the landlord. Consequently, tenants lost benefits such as the Housing Choice Voucher Program under Section 8 of the 1937 Housing Act. This meant that my mother would make too much to qualify for Section 8 vouchers, but not enough to afford market-rate rents. Contradistinctively, developers represented by nearby Columbia University, Mount Sinai Hospital, and New York University could afford to buy in the neighborhood and had no legal or economic interest in challenging gentrification because these corporate businesses benefited from the erasure of original residents and monetized their displacement. A once-forgotten El Barrio was now desired by the top bidders. Gentrification became colonization in new casings, and only a grim reality with faded memories of a once culturally vibrant and colorful community remained in the shadows.

This context highlights the systemic structures, such as gentrification, that make it hard for impoverished people to subsist. Racial capitalism is predicated on extraction, exploitation, and erasure that endangers poor Black mothers. As a last resort to overcome these death-dealing conditions, indigent Black mothers sometimes view breaking the law as more life-saving than following it in an unjust system that is stacked up against their survival.

First Criterion: Criminalizing Poor Black Motherhood

The first criterion to justify lawbreaking is to prove that Black mothers are uniquely burdened by historical and contemporary oppressions. In a recent study about Black motherhood by The Current Project, more than five hundred Black mothers of school-aged children were surveyed (N=504).[3] Most (60 percent) mothers' ages ranged from thirty to forty-four-years-old. They rented an apartment (67 percent) in urban areas (45 percent) and had at least one child. Sixty-nine percent of the mothers believed the country was going in the wrong direction to support their survival and quality of life. Fifty-five percent of the mothers described the job state as poor and believed local elected officials were not doing enough to respond to the issues that are important to Black single mothers. Sixty-six percent of the mothers barely had enough at the end of the month to cover basic expenses. In fact, in the last twelve months they indicated having difficulty finding enough food (51 percent) and healthy food (57 percent), paying weekly or monthly bills (81 percent), dealing with inflation and the rising cost of living (91 percent), accessing healthcare services (62 percent), and securing reliable transportation (53 percent). In the past year, 54 percent received or waited to receive cash assistance, food stamps, housing assistance, or childcare assistance. Importantly, these survival struggles and limited options deplete the quality of life. According to the study, conducted by a single Black mother, Alisha Gordon, impoverished conditions of Black mothers and the struggle to provide for their families cause insufficient sleep (66 percent) and an imbalance between work and family life (65 percent).

Gordon describes this economic state of in-betweenness using the term she coined, "Middlers." The Middler demographic is a group of mothers who often earn too much to qualify for government or public assistance but not enough to comfortably make ends meet. Middlers made up 77 percent of Black mothers surveyed in this study. Twenty-five percent of the mothers surveyed earned between $30,000 and $50,000. The Middler segment is important because it aptly describes a core group of Black mothers who are largely overlooked. As a result, Middler mothers consequently go without the help they need to survive.

My mother was a Middler mom. I watched my mother use a typewriter to fraudulently create W-2s that understated her income just to remain in our two-bedroom apartment and to avoid an astronomical rent increase. When rent was due and she could not afford to pay her bills, I saw my mother take manufactured paystubs to the daycare center to mitigate income-based tuition and cover my backup childcare. When that did not work, she forged doctors' notes to get paid time off work when there was a school holiday or an early dismissal. Still, empire is relentless. Eventually, my mother could no longer carry the burdens it took to try to beat the system. When she finally reported her full income, her rent skyrocketed by 300 percent because of the discontinuance of the Mitchell-Lama program and landlords charging market-rate rent. Sadly, while her cost of living increased, her quality of life, emotional state, and mental well-being sharply declined—perhaps even resulting in her premature death at the young age of sixty years old.

Indigent Black mothers who single-handedly provide for their families struggle to keep their homes and to survive against interlocking systems of oppression. Mothers, like my own, rightfully resist the coerced choice between two lesser evils and instead exercise practical wisdom to make a way out of no way, which sometimes means bending the rules and breaking laws to overcome limited options. In this sense, survival can lead directly to prison.

In a discussion about women offenders and economic barriers that impede survival, Barbara Bloom and Stephanie Covington observe that "Many women on the social and economic margins of society struggle to survive outside of legitimate enterprises, which brings them into contact with the criminal justice system."[4] Similarly, Angela Y. Davis argues that Black women become "perfect candidates for prison" due to a scarcity of "surviving social services" such as employment, economic resources, and education. Davis asserts, "huge numbers of people lose jobs and prospects for future jobs. Because the economic base of these communities is destroyed, education and other surviving social services are profoundly affected. This process turns the men, women, and children who live in these damaged communities into perfect candidates for prison."[5] At the 2016 Criminal Justice System Convening conference, US Attorney General

Loretta Lynch remarked, "Put simply, we know that when we incarcerate a woman we often are truly incarcerating a family, in terms of the far reaching effect on her children, her community, and her entire family network."[6]

This criminal system is an extension of slavery that treated Black bodies as chattel. In *Women, Race, and Class*, Angela Davis makes the point that Black mothers were also not viewed by their humanity but by their ability to reproduce. She states that the "ideological exaltation of motherhood—as popular as it was during the nineteenth century—did not extend to slaves. In fact, in the eyes of the slaveholders, slave women were not mothers at all; they were simply instruments guaranteeing the growth of the slave labor force. They were 'breeders'—animals, whose monetary value could be precisely calculated in terms of their ability to multiply their numbers."[7] When the European slave trade was abolished and the colonizers could no longer traffic human cargo, the colonies were forced to find new ways to sustain their profits from slave labor. The white slave owners turned to Black women's reproduction and ability to breed babies who would grow to work the fields for the exploitation of their labor and preservation of the slaveocracy. Thus, Black women were chattel and Black mothers were chattel and breeders to proliferate the slave labor force at the expense of their humanity. This historical context shows the unique burden of Black mothers who have always been disadvantaged by unjust systems.

It is critically important to reappraise dominant societal perceptions and judgments of deviance so that Black mothers are no longer punished for trying to overcome the unique burdens of historical disenfranchisement while still trying to care for their families and communities. When Black mothers act as self-legislators to save themselves and their families from death-dealing conditions, their extralegal survival strategies are not vice but virtue, and not deviant but divine. Society would easily condemn my mother's survival strategies as bad or criminal. However, her children viewed her wherewithal to make a way out of no way as a source of salvation. It saved our lives when she made the proverbial "dollar out of fifteen cents" and something out of nothing. She ensured we had food on the table, clothes on our backs, and a roof over our heads—her practical wisdom saved our lives. The unlawful survival strategies of poor Black mothers reveal more about a nefarious carceral system than they say about the moral integrity of Black women trying to make a way out of no way.

Second Criterion: Preservation

Punishing poor Black mothers for trying to persevere against hegemonic systems that impede survival is a social problem and a theological issue. I argue that preservation is connected to perception. This is to say, the social construction of Black mothers as deviant has repercussions for determining who is considered worthy or unworthy to save their lives for survival. More particularly, harmful Christian teachings of sin and sacrifice coalesce with practices of respectability to punish individuals who society perceives as inherently bad and unworthy of moral concern for transgressing acceptable standards and breaking the law to subsist. It is therefore necessary to take a closer look at doctrinal understandings of sin and atonement theology that have precluded preservation for Black women.

During the rise of the Roman empire in the fourth century CE, Saint Augustine (Aurelius Augustinus), an African Bishop of the early church, first conceptualized the theological category of original sin.[8] Responding to the Pelagian controversy of whether humanity is born perfect or as inherent sinners, Augustine believed that sin is inescapable and inherited. During the scholastic period, Saint Anselm of Canterbury interpreted original and personal sin to defend the purity of Christ. For Anselm, like Augustine, sin is corruption and separates fallen humanity from divine purity that only divine grace can repair and restore. During the Reformation period, John Calvin, a trained lawyer, applied a juridical lens to interpretations of sin to describe the distance between humanity and God. According to Calvin, God justly punishes human actions in the manner of judging a heinous crime to dispense divine wrath and condemnation. His contemporary, Martin Luther, held a view of sin that justified the death penalty to protect the safety of the common good.

Anselm's sacrificial atonement theology operationalized punishment within a feudal cosmology of salvation where lower serfs are sacrificed to restore the honor of an offended Lord. The hierarchy between serfs and lords created a social caste system. Marxist theory critiques a similar caste system in society that mirrors Anselm's soteriology. For Marx, the lower-class proletariats are exploited for the benefit of a higher-class bourgeoisie. Analogously, in *The New Jim Crow*, legal scholar Michelle Alexander argues there is a permanent underclass of poor Blacks who are disproportionately punished and sentenced more egregiously than whites in the US criminal system. Anselm's caste system is parabolic to today's underclass. Hence, there is a continuity among religious interpretations of sin and sacrifice in relationship to punishment that undergirds punishment, policing, and prisons in the US legal and criminal systems.

The formation of systems of punishment is an important additive because corporal punishment and later the penitentiary served as social and spiritual responses to individuals who needed to atone or make amends for their wrongdoing as an earthly indication of the divine wrath to come. Certainly, the birth of prisons is a theological project designed to punish people who sin against society. Solitary confinement was designed for malefactors to reflect on their sins and give penitence. Hence, the term "penitentiary." Isolating malefactors to reflect on wrongdoings was considered more humane than corporal punishment. The Quakers, a Pennsylvania-based pacifist religious group, were early abolitionists (of slavery) who joined in their support for solitary confinement at the Walnut Street Jail. Capital punishment was also deemed less harsh than hanging wrongdoers from the scaffold. In this regard, prisons began as not just a reform, but as religiously inspired reform. Protestant prison reformers conceived of new carceral technologies. From its architecture and design to the crucifixion and priest walking a malefactor to the gas chamber, the prison is a wholly religious edifice.

Womanist theologian Delores Williams criticizes both the doctrine of sin and atonement theory. She contends, "the theology in mainline Protestant churches (including African American ones) teaches believers that sinful humankind has been redeemed because Jesus died on the cross in the place of humans, thereby taking human sin upon himself."[9] In comparison to Black women, Williams looks at substitutionary atonement as when "Jesus represents the ultimate surrogate figure; he stands in the place of someone else: sinful humankind."[10] Williams argues that Jesus as surrogate reinforces Black women's exploitation and cannot have salvific power. Williams concludes that "redemption of humans can have nothing to do with any kind of surrogate or substitute role Jesus was reputed to have played in a bloody act that supposedly gained victory over sin and/or evil."[11] According to Williams, God did not want Jesus to die, and neither does God will for Black women to die in the role of surrogate.

Williams explores the motif of coerced and voluntary surrogacy in the biblical story of Hagar, the Egyptian slave of Abraham and Sarah. Williams argues that Hagar is prototypical of Black women's unique struggles with survival and quality of life. Black women, like Hagar, are often forced to take care of children that are not their own. In the Antebellum South, Black women performed coerced surrogacy as mammies and wet nurses. In the post-Antebellum period, Black women performed voluntary surrogacy as domestics. Hagar's surrogacy parallels Black women's unique suffering. Black women find themselves, like Hagar, in the wilderness facing death-dealing situations.

During Hagar's wilderness experience running away from the sexual violence and oppression of Abraham and Sarah, she encountered the Angel of God and received the resources she needed for her and her baby to survive. God saves Hagar but does not liberate her. Ultimately, God demands that Hagar return to her abuser and go back to the house of Abraham and Sarah. Williams concludes from the story of Hagar that survival is sometimes salvation but not always liberation. More specifically, God is not always a liberator. Williams problematizes atonement theory and the glorification of violent and vicarious requirements of death that are detrimental to Black women's survival and quality of life. She refutes the salvific value of the cross and any notion that suffering is redemptive. Williams therefore jettisons atonement theory altogether. Rather, she proposes a ministerial vision that focuses on the healings, miracles, and relationships Jesus demonstrates during his life and ministry instead of death and crucifixion.

Williams shows an alternative to punitive soteriology by pointing to restorative ways of viewing Black women's salvation as self-legislators when God is not a liberator. Williams redirects attention to the life-generating aspects of Jesus's ministry. A focus on Jesus's life is a focus on his ministerial purpose, which included clothing the naked, healing the afflicted, giving food to the hungry, providing drink to the thirsty, and setting the captives free. Jesus's life and ministry entailed revolutionary work to overturn the Roman empire and reorder society, using what Nietzsche called a *transvaluation of values*, or where the last becomes first, and victory is snatched from defeat. In this regard, Jesus was a first-century abolitionist.

In addition to the teachings of sin and atonement theories, the practice of respectability politics contributes to punitive responses that threaten poor single Black mothers' preservation. Religious historian Evelyn Higginbotham coined the term "politics of respectability" in her 1993 landmark text, *Righteous Discontent: The Women's Movement in the Black Baptist Church, 1880–1920*. At its best, respectability politics is contingent upon performance and aesthetics rooted in protest that is oriented toward a *telos* of justice. At its worst, respectability politics engenders conservative elements that hinge upon assimilationist ideals of white middle-class values. Subsequently, a dialectical relationship arises. Generally understood, respectability is either protest or proper behavior. A closer and more nuanced reading, however, renders a fuller account that is closest to Higginbotham's original intentions whereby respectability is *both* protest *and* conformity to proper behavior, which work together to inform Black women's fight for equality.

At the 1992 Republican Convention in Houston, George H. W. Bush gave a harsh and condemnatory message attacking homosexuality, feminism, abortion, and welfare. That same year, Bush addressed the Annual Convention of the National Religious Broadcasters stating, "the family is under siege."[12] He admonished that "Each one of us, parents, preachers, politicians, and teachers, must do our part to defend it."[13] Bush vowed to pass laws that fought back for the family; these became antecedents for later policies, such as welfare reform and the Christian Coalition's ten-point plan or the "Contract with American Families."[14] In 1995, Bill Clinton outlined a fourteen-point "American Family Values Agenda" that punished teenage pregnancy. Clinton's plan, like the Republicans', reflected that the standard for the nuclear family has theological connections to piety and punishment. These bipartisan policies served to define the American standard for the nuclear family and criminalized impoverished Black motherhood.

The perception of Black mothers as property and unworthy is reflected in public policies that are influenced by theological values and punitive outcomes. The 1996 Personal Responsibility and Work Opportunity Reconciliation Act transferred power to states to oversee welfare programs. As a result, welfare essentially criminalized poor single mothers and assigned them blame for emasculating men, isolating fathers, destroying the family, and morally corroding society. Black mothers were pathologized as inherently bad by the quasi-research of the Moynihan Report, and political leaders like Ronald Reagan made Black mothers synonymous with negative stereotypes, such as the Welfare Queen. Negative social constructions of Black motherhood resulted in burdensome policies that blamed single motherhood for the decline of family values, allocated punishment that criminalized poverty, and perpetuated the surrogate roles of Black mothers mandated to return to work to care for other people's children but leave their own at home just to qualify for government benefits.[15]

A closer look at welfare reform legislation reveals a hegemonic social imagination that is fascinated with notions of respectability and that blames single Black motherhood for the moral failings of society. According to the government findings in Title I of the Block Grants for Temporary Assistance for Needy Families, "Marriage is the foundation of a successful society."[16] However, the consequences of raising children in single-parent households contribute to dismal outcomes such as "Children of teenage single parents have lower cognitive scores, lower educational aspirations, and a greater likelihood of becoming teenage parents themselves."[17] Also, "Children of single-parent homes are 3 times more likely to fail and repeat a year in grade school than are children from intact 2-parent families."[18] Additionally, "Children from single-parent homes are almost 4 times more likely to be expelled or suspended from school."[19] Moreover, "Neighborhoods with larger percentages of youth aged 12 through 20 and areas with higher percentages of single-parent households have higher rates of violent crime."[20] Furthermore, "of those youth held for criminal offenses within the State juvenile justice system, only 29.8 percent lived primarily in a home with both parents. In contrast to these incarcerated youth, 73.9 percent of the 62,800,000 children in the Nation's resident population were living with both parents."[21] At the heart of welfare reform and its punishment of single Black motherhood is the politics of respectability that maintains white dominant norms as a standard of the American nuclear family.

The interplay of theology (i.e., sin and atonement theology) and public policy instantiates the role of punishment to allocate burdens that construct Black mothers as deviant, disrespectable, and not deserving of preservation. However, Black mothers who break the law to survive are not inherently bad or sinful and should not be punished for harm caused by their survival strategies. Rather, Abolition Womanism seeks to reappraise Black mothers from deviant to divine and to shift responses to harm from sin and punishment to accountability and restoration.

Third Criterion: Necessity

Black women are paid significantly less than Black men and white men. According to the Institute for Women's Policy Research, Black women earn 66.5 cents for every dollar earned by white men.[22] Single mothers in the United States have the highest poverty rates in comparison to those in all industrialized countries.[23] However, as the poorest of the poor, "eight out of ten (80.6 percent) Black mothers are breadwinners, who are either the sole earner or earn at least 40 percent of household income."[24] As the primary income earners, poor Black mothers still face significant economic hardships that make it nearly impossible to survive. Hence, Black mothers' struggles are not individualistic but communal. This is to say, when Black mothers are the primary caregivers and cannot make ends meet, their families also suffer and an entire ecosystem is decimated. This data shows the economic hardship for poor Black mothers who sometimes resort to underground economies and lawbreaking to meet their basic needs.

Thus, this third criterion relies on a comparative approach between Christianity and Islam to demonstrate varied religious responses to lawbreaking in the context of necessity. In the *Summa Theologiae*, Thomas

Aquinas advances a natural law theory that Christianizes Aristotelian ethics and appeals to practical reason using theologically infused virtues. Particularly germane is Aquinas's primary precept "good is to be done and pursued, and evil is to be avoided" (ST I-II, Q. 94, Art. 2). From the primary precept of self-preservation, other moral principles are derived, such as the right to food and adequate shelter. According to Aquinas, if someone is hungry and steals food to eat, they are not breaking the law but are instead morally justified to preserve their life. Aquinas makes the rationale that the right to food is a common good and there is a moral duty to give from overabundance.

Aquinas states, "In cases of need all things are common property, so that there would seem to be no sin in taking another's property, for need has made it common" (ST II-II, Q. 66, Art. 5). In this regard, all things belong to God and while it is permissible for humans to acquire property, they must not do so in abundance and in a way that is not common possession for others who are in need. Seen this way, a rich person does not act unlawfully if he precludes others from taking possession of something that was common, but he does act wrongfully if he indiscriminately prevents others from its use. Similarly, when the poor steal from those with abundance, it may look like theft from the outside, but they are not breaking the law because they have the right to self-preservation and food. In the end, when one person takes from the abundance of another person to alleviate a need, it is not stealing because distribution of God's property in accordance with God's will and purposes cannot qualify as theft.

Islamic law goes a bit further than individual cases and includes a systems critique to suggest that one's lawbreaking also signifies a social failure. I refer to Islamic law to show there are religious sources beyond Christianity that also support lawbreaking out of necessity and to overcome oppressive systems. Islamic law's higher objectives, known as the *Maqasid Al-Shari'a*, consist of five justifiable exceptions to break the law out of necessity. These objectives are: (1) to protect the soul (life), (2) to protect religion, (3) to protect offspring, (4) to protect property, and (5) to protect dignity. While the universal law holds that one should not steal, these five exceptions are possible to justify theft. The *Maqasid Al-Shari'a* states that each person has a right to do whatever is necessary to protect their life. Additionally, the overall objective is to preserve the good of society and the well-being of its citizenry. Thus, when someone steals food because they are hungry or their children are hungry, the person avoids punishment because their thievery reveals more about the community's failure to meet individuals' needs. Likewise, if a Muslim drinks wine or eats pork, though forbidden in normal circumstances, they are exempt from punishment due to necessity and the right to protect their life. Hence, natural law theory and the five objectives of Islamic Law provide religious support for breaking the law out of necessity and for the purpose of self-preservation that is relevant for a justification of Black mothers who contravene the law to survive.

Thus, a Black mother who steals food to eat is justified because "necessity knows no law." This Latin dictum points to a paradox. Political scientist Deborah Stone references this idiom when describing a policy paradox, or how social pressures lead to contradictions between law and morality when confronted with urgent survival needs. In *Policy Paradox*, Stone argues that there are rules in place for the good of society, but these rules are not always good for individuals to follow. Stone explains, "Slave narratives, Holocaust memoirs, and intimate stories of people in dire poverty all reveal this phenomenon: when survival is at stake, people will violate laws and their own deeply held moral principles." Stone continues, "Some of the greatest conundrums in moral philosophy stem from this question: is it ethical to lie, cheat, steal, betray a friend, or kill to ensure one's own survival?" "Necessity knows no law" implies that at some animal instinctive level, "humans know that survival is the necessity that invalidates all rules."[25] This axiom that justifies noncompliance is also, as argued, profoundly theological.

Additional examples of lawbreaking on religious terms can include civil disobedience when appealing to God's law as above human law and conscientious objection as a religious exemption to following the law. However, there is also a danger when religion is combined with hegemonic power to break the law. This is the caveat for all lawbreaking. When motivated by power, unilateralism, and authoritarianism, the act of survival to overcome oppression (first criterion) to save one's life (second criterion) out of necessity (third criterion) does not risk anarchy but tyranny. This is instantiated by white men proving to be above the law as Black women are thrown underneath the prison. For example, the forty-fifth President of the United States of America is a convicted felon but used his power to appoint Supreme Court justices who effectively legislated immunity to exempt him from federal charges as he ran for and won a second term as president. Meanwhile, Black women are punished for far less, including Vera Liddell for stealing chicken and sentenced to nine years in prison,[26] and Kelly Williams-Bolar for sending her child to a better school district and sentenced more harshly than Rebecca Loughlin and Felicity Huffman, who were convicted of admissions fraud,[27] and the Black woman braiding hair in the kitchen for supplemental income while receiving government help. No one should be punished, and Black women should not be punished, for trying to persevere against the death-dealing conditions of a double system of justice and a society that constructs them as inherently bad for wanting to survive and secure quality of life.

Abolition Womanism

Abolition is an answer. I define abolition as the process of repairing harms, restoring relationships, and rebuilding more just and equitable systems. Abolition Womanism returns to the lessons of Hagar to explore the human agency and salvific worth of Black motherhood. Hagar, the biblical African maidservant, teaches that wilderness experiences are sometimes caused by social *and* faith systems that would rather Black mothers merely survive death to return and oppressive conditions to care and nurture others than live whole and free for them and their families to thrive. An Abolition Womanist theological reading of the story of Hagar validates Black mothers as an embodiment of the divine and an orchestrator of unlawful salvation when making a way out of no way. Black mothers are theologically justified to act as their own liberators when survival is not promised, and freedom is not given.

An unlawful salvation is to do whatever is necessary, even it if means contravening laws, to save and liberate oneself out of a dire need for preservation against evil and oppressive systems. An Abolition Womanist theological approach validates human agency to transcend oppressive conditions and regressive systems designed to demonize and destroy Black motherhood over and against their God-given autonomy and practical wisdom to care for and protect themselves, their families, and their communities against all odds with an urgency that sometimes intervenes before answered prayers and societal support is rendered.

Importantly, Abolition Womanism justifies Black mothers who break the law to survive and points to the following three theological alternatives to harmful church teachings: (1) break the relationship between sin and punishment, (2) validate Black mothers' agentic survival practices as a source of unlawful salvation pointing to their participation in the divine, and (3) dismantle systems of domination that punish Black mothers for making an unlawful way out of no way and rebuilding something better. First, breaking the relationship between sin and punishment requires identifying alternative responses that are oriented toward restoration and healing harms. In indigenous traditions, healing circles are used to mediate injury between those who cause harm and individuals who experience harm. The US criminal system has adapted models of restorative justice as alternatives to punishment, as well as some schools to assist with conflict resolution. Restorative justice disrupts power dynamics between the victim and abuser. It gives equal voice to all parties and opens portals for mutual understanding. Restorative justice is not foolproof, but even in extreme cases of rape and murder, some families and victims feel a modicum of justice for going through the process.

Restorative justice is an alternative to draconian punishment that has theological resonance. In *The Little Book of Restorative Justice*, Howard Zehr explains that in addition to indigenous traditions, early Mennonite communities in the 1970s developed restorative practices. Zehr states, "Seeking to apply their faith as well as their peace perspective to the harsh world of criminal justice, Mennonites and other practitioners (in Ontario, Canada, and later in Indiana, U.S.A.) experimented with victim-offender encounters that led to programs in these communities and later became models for programs throughout the world."[28] As earlier mentioned, prisons are built on penitence and theological doctrine. However, their antidote is restorative justice as an application of liberative religious principles. The religion of white supremacy and carcerality harms and binds, but the religion of abolition heals and sets free.

Restoration played a vital role in the life and ministry of Jesus. Through his healing, miracles, and communal relationships, Jesus taught and practiced making people whole. In the synoptic gospels, Jesus saw a penitent thief on the cross and restored him to the *imago dei*. The Roman Empire had discarded this man and left him to die a criminal's death, but Jesus looked at the penitent thief and offered paradise, or salvation. Additionally, Jesus restored life in the dead and performed miracles to restore individuals from their affliction. Jesus is recorded as saying that one's faith has made them whole. The reimagining of using religion to heal harms without punishment is to see religion through the lens of abolition. In this sense, atonement is not a fixation on myopic interpretations of sacrifice and vicarious suffering, but an emphasis on making one whole as Jesus demonstrated in his life and ministry.

To disentangle sin and punishment is to move away from individual blame to communal responses and structural accountability. Poor Black mothers who break the law to survive are not bad people. Rather, indigent Black mothers navigate a nefarious system that uses dominant values to determine who is deserving of moral concern and help. Zehr states, "In short, the legal or criminal justice system centers around offenders and deserts—making sure offenders get what they deserve. Restorative justice is more focused on needs: those of victims, of communities, of offenders."[29] This distinction between desert and need is important. A hegemonic social imagination constructs narratives of deviance and perpetuates disparaging stereotypes to target Black mothers as undeserving. This is evident by the discussion on welfare reform and how Black mothers are pathologized as bad, stereotyped as Welfare Queens, and blamed for the moral failings of the family and society, which has resulted in burdensome policies and allocation of punishment that effectively criminalize impoverished Black motherhood.

Restorative justice asks different questions than apparatuses of punishment. Carceral systems ask, "How can we blame Black women for their own misfortune?" or "How can we use punishment as a deterrence and to create a permanent underclass?" and "How can we construct Black mothers as sinful, disrespectable, and undeserving to disqualify them from human dignity and communal flourishing?" In contrast, Abolition Womanism asks, "What do Black mothers *need* to be whole?" "How do we validate Black mothers' human agency and divine worth as instructive for healing harms and pointing toward abolitionist futures?" and "How do we overcome systems of domination so that the most vulnerable can survive and flourish in community?" Hence, making the shift from desert to need moves away from individual blame to a social critique that requires a response not of punishment but rather of restoration and transformation to repair harms, restore relationships, and rebuild more just and equitable systems for Black mothers and their families to live whole in communities of care.

In addition to restorative justice to address harms at the individual level, transformative justice is needed to interrogate the larger structures that make survival nearly impossible and create the conditions that lead Black mothers to break the law to meet their basic needs in the first place. I define abolition using the alliteration of three Rs: to repair harms, restore relationships, and rebuild more just and equitable systems for communal thriving. This definition harnesses reparative, restorative, and transformative justice. Ruth Gilmore reminds us that abolition is not just a negative project of tearing down but also a positive project of building up. Additionally, abolition does not only describe the problem; neither is abolition an answer. Rather, abolition is a process that invites us to think about overhauling oppressive systems with alternative solutions that only our collective imagination can conjure and summon this world anew.

Second, instead of interpreting original sin to construct Black bodies as inherently bad and guilty *a priori*, Abolition Womanism begins with seeing Black women as not only restored but as a reflection of the divine and a source of unlawful salvation. On March 13, 2020, in Louisville, Kentucky, seven police officers used a no-knock warrant to forcibly enter a home and fatally shoot a twenty-six-year-old Black woman, Breonna Taylor, who was previously asleep with her partner.[30] During the same year, in October 2020, Black Lives Matter Los Angeles created the campaign, "Black Women Are Divine" to recognize Breonna Taylor's angelversary, the date her life was stolen by the police, and to celebrate the divinity of Black women killed by state violence. According to the Black Lives Matter website, "police and white supremacy stole Breonna's life and justified themselves in doing so because this world tries to make Black women into mules—*tried to make Breonna into a mule*—mules like the ones Zora

Neale Hurston writes about. We are reminded by Alice Walker, though, that 'a woman . . . unless she submits . . . is not a mule . . . although she may suffer.'" The assertion of Black women's divinity is an acknowledgment of suffering, but not the glorification of it as interpreted by most Western Christian atonement theories. Rather, the Black women's divinity is a reclamation of their human dignity and the determination to live and thrive beyond suffering.

The divination of Black womanhood is a foreign concept in dominant Western Christianity, perhaps because of its fixation on sin and punishment that has sanctioned slavery, built prisons, and exculpated white privilege. Contradistinctively, in other traditions such as Eastern orthodoxy and African spirituality, the reclamation of humanity's divine qualities is centrally accepted. *Deification* is a concept central to Eastern Orthodoxy's theology that emphasizes the divine restorative qualities of human nature to the *imago dei*. This concept provides a model of redemption that Eastern church fathers understood as restoring the divinity within human activity. Irenaeus's argument of recapitulation emphasized the restoration of humanity to the image of God. Origen of Alexandria (c. 186–255), likely the most influential of all Greek theologians, argued for the process of deification where "Christians can be transformed into the likeness of Christ. Human nature can now be divinized because God, in Jesus, came into human nature."[31] Athanasius (c. 296–373), a Bishop of Alexandria in Egypt and chief architect of the Nicene faith, stated, "The Incarnation is the key to the restoration of the human race to the divine life."[32] *Deification* is central to Eastern Orthodoxy's theology, and it emphasizes the divine restorative qualities of human nature.

Divinization is not exclusive to Christianity. In some practices of African diasporic traditions—Brazilian Candomblé, Cuban Lucumí (or Santeria), Haitian Voodoo, and Nigerian Yoruba—experience of divination is a ritual reserved for women, who are considered more susceptible to divine manifestations as mediums and portals to communicate to their communities. Namely, Mãe Stella, a prominent Candomblé priestess, states that "women make better leaders in Candomblé because of their natural 'mothering' qualities, as well as their ability to be responsive to the demands of the *orixá*. The skills required to manage and sustain the *terreiro*'s intricate dynamics of interpersonal relations, hierarchy, and spiritual powers are perhaps cultivated more consistently and effectively among female leaders."[33] According to Stella's experience with the Candomblé spiritual tradition, women are viewed as more receptive to spiritual manifestations and divination than their male counterparts. This makes women, particularly mother figures, communicate with their village and conduct business on behalf of divine directives they encounter firsthand. In this sense, women are indispensable to village life and the preservation of communities. They are the carriers of not just progeny, but their people's stories, customs, and traditions. Women are conduits of the divine and caretakers of their village. This reverence for women leaders in Candomblé is very different from the demonization of womanhood by doctrines of sin in Christianity. Despite Augustine's roots in the continent, his conception of original sin counters African religions' emphasis on the divine qualities of humanity and the belief that women are among the closest to the divine. It makes sense that Christianity's alignment with empire would maintain a dissonance with religions that predate colonialism and imperialism.

This leads to the third point. Abolition Womanism calls for the dismantling of systems of domination that punish Black mothers for trying to survive and secure a higher quality of life for themselves and their families. The gentrification of Harlem and the displacement of poor and Middler mothers are perpetuated by racial capitalism, neoliberalism, and greed. Abolition is a negative project to destroy oppressive structures, but it is also a positive project to rebuild something better in its place. Thus, a conversation about dismantling the carceral state must follow a discussion about creating alternatives. Instead of capitalistic motivations that make gentrification possible, an alternative approach is to build mutual aid societies focused on solidarity. According to Dean Spade, mutual aid moves toward the goals of building "a society organized by collective self-determination where there is a wide range of options beyond 'sink or swim.'"[34] Black mothers have always participated in mutual aid—from borrowing sugar to bartering services, to leading the church fish-fry for the building fund. However, Black mothers have not been awarded for this communal ethic because capitalism recognizes the values of individualism and greed. Contradistinctively, Black mothers are punished for pooling their resources because this practice counters self-responsibility.

Abolition is not only a negative project but a positive one that calls us to do more than tear down but to build a better world. This practice is one of reimagining, which is social but also religiously apocalyptic and futuristic inviting us to look beyond to create a better world we can behold here and now (i.e., "I saw a new heaven and a new earth . . . "). Abolition Womanism should prompt inquiry signifying a dissatisfaction with current conditions of carcerality with the hope for abolitionist futures. What would a society look like where Black women can do more than survive but thrive beyond poverty, punishment, policing, and prisons? What would our communities look like if they were driven not by capitalism but by mutual aid? What would churches look like that no longer taught atonement theologies and doctrines of sin used to condemn, judge, and blame Black mothers for trying to make a way out of no way? What would a legal system look like that did not rely on punishment but instead used restorative practices that held people accountable to heal harms? What if there were no police? What if Black women were socially constructed as worthy and deserving of flourishing, freedom, and fullness of life?

Conclusion

I began this chapter with my experiences of growing up with a single poor Black mother in Harlem New York who sometimes contravened rules and laws to survive against the backdrop of capitalism, carceral, and cruelty. This context provided an occasion to further explore the criminalization of Black mothers' survival using a theological and abolitionist lens. Punishment is a religious concept with connections to sin, atonement, and respectability, and it is used to support harmful teachings and practices that harm Black mothers who transgress "acceptable" norms. Punishment also functions to perpetuate unjust social systems through regressive laws, policies, and regulations that proliferate policing, prisons, and perceptions of Black mothers as deviant and undeserving. Thus, punishment is a theological issue and a social problem used to respond to harm by blaming Black mothers for their misfortune without structural critique of the root causes that led to their survival strategies in the first place.

Abolition Womanism is a counter theology that is interreligious, intersectional, and interconnected. The three problems that Abolition Womanism addresses are how Black women are punished because they are historically and contemporarily disadvantaged by unique burdens, denied preservation based on perceptions of deviance that are reinforced by theological interpretations and public policies, and unable to access the resources they need to survive. In contradistinction, Abolition Womanism as a theological construction responds with a threefold prescription that aims to dismantle punitive systems of domination, disentangle religious interpretations of sin or wrongdoing from punishment, and validate Black mothers' agentic survival practices as a source of unlawful salvation. Abolition Womanism solicits solidarity in a faith-based movement to ensure that Black mothers can survive and thrive as self-legislators, liberated, and as an embodiment of the divine.

Notes

1 In 1989, Kevin Richardson, Yusef Salaam, Corey Wise, Raymond Santana, and Atron McCray, five Black teenage boys ages fourteen to sixteen, were arrested, interrogated, forced to give false statements, indicted, wrongfully convicted, and sentenced to seven to thirteen years in prison for raping a twenty-eight-year-old white female jogger, Trisha Meilli, in Central Park, New York. Donald Trump spent $85,000 on full-page advertisements calling for the reinstatement of the death penalty in four New York newspaper outlets (*New York Times, The Daily News, New York Post,* and *New York Newsday*). The advertisements were all titled, "Bring Back the Death Penalty. Bring Back Our Police!" In 2001, more than twenty years later, Matteo Reyes was imprisoned with Corey Wise. As a result of Reyes's moral consciousness, he confessed to raping Meilli. Reyes served no additional time due to the statute of limitations. However, the five Black boys, dubbed the "Central Park Five," moved to vacate the charges and sued the city for its wrongdoings. Upon winning a $41 million settlement, the Central Park Five now embrace the moniker, the "Exonerated Five." Kevin Richardson lived next door to me, Korey Wise and Steven Lopez lived in the same residential building, and Antron and Raymond lived nearby.

2 According to New York State Homes and Community Renewal, "The Mitchell-Lama Program provides housing across New York State that is affordable to the middle class. It was created by the Limited Profit Housing Act in 1955, which was championed by Manhattan State Senator MacNeil Mitchell and former Brooklyn

Assemblyman Alfred Lama. New York State Homes and Community Renewal plays an oversight role for existing Mitchell-Lama developments (privately owned and managed), and works with owners as they near the end of their 20-year affordability requirements to provide low-cost financing tools that help maintain the developments while also extending their affordability." "Mitchell-Lama Program," Homes and Community Renewal, accessed February 25, 2024, https://hcr.ny.gov/mitchell-lama-program.

3 "Data Research/TCP," The Current Project, accessed February 25, 2024, https://www.thecurrentproject.org/dataresearch.

4 Barbara Bloom and Stephanie Covington, "Addressing the Mental Health Needs of Women Offenders," in *Women's Mental Health Issues Across the Criminal Justice System*, ed. R. Gido and L. Dalley (Columbus, OH: Prentice Hall, 2008), 160–76.

5 Angela Y. Davis, *Are Prisons Obsolete?* (New York: Seven Stories Press, 2003), 16.

6 "Attorney General Loretta E. Lynch Delivers Remarks at the White House Women and the Criminal Justice System Convening," March 30, 2016, https://www.justice.gov/opa/speech/attorney-general-loretta-e-lynch-delivers-remarks-white-house-women-and-criminal-justice. Accessed August 15, 2024.

7 Angela Yvonne Davis, *Women, Race & Class* (New York: Vintage Books, 1983), 10.

8 Matthew Fox, *Original Blessing: A Primer in Creation Spirituality: Presented in Four Paths, Twenty-Six Themes, and Two Questions* (New York: Jeremy P. Tarcher/Putnam, 2000).

9 Delores S. Williams, *Sisters in the Wilderness: The Challenge of Womanist God-Talk*, Nachdr. (Maryknoll, NY: Orbis Books, 1993), 161–62.

10 Ibid., 162.

11 Ibid., 165.

12 "Public Papers of the Presidents of the United States: George H. W. Bush (1992, Book I)—Remarks at the Annual Convention of the National Religious Broadcasters," accessed May 8, 2024, https://www.govinfo.gov/content/pkg/PPP-1992-book1/html/PPP-1992-book1-doc-pg151.htm.

13 Ibid.

14 Alison Mitchell, "On Issue of Family Values, Clinton Unveils an Agenda of His Own," *New York Times*, July 29, 1995, sec. U.S., https://www.nytimes.com/1995/07/29/us/on-issue-of-family-values-clinton-unveils-an-agenda-of-his-own.html (Accessed May 7, 2024).

15 In *Disruptive Christian Ethics*, Traci West traces the biblical antecedents of welfare reform when looking at the role of Mary in the Magnificat. Also, in

Unfinished Business, Womanist theologian Keri Day explores interpretations of the Protestant Work Ethic in connection to the Prosperity Gospel to blame Black mothers for their calamity because of the belief that God punishes the poor and idle but rewards those who work and have abundance. These theological rationales figure into welfare policies that justify blaming and punishing poor Black mothers for their misfortune rather than critique the systems that make survival nearly impossible.

16 U.S. Congress, House, *Personal Responsibility and Work Opportunity Reconciliation Act of 1996*, August 22, 1996, https://www.congress.gov/bill/104th-congress/house-bill/3734/text. Accessed August 15, 2024.

17 Ibid.

18 Ibid.

19 Ibid.

20 Ibid.

21 Ibid.

22 "Black Women's Equal Pay Day: How Segregation in the U.S. Labor Market Affects Black Women's Earnings Now and (Potentially) in the Future," Institute for Women's Policy Research, August 22, 2019, https://iwpr.org/Black-womens-equal-pay-2019-one-pager/.

23 Timothy Casey and Laurie Maldonado, *Worst Off—Single-Parent Families in the United States: A Cross-National Comparison of Single-Parenthood in the U.S. and Sixteen Other High-Income Countries*, 2012, https://doi.org/10.13140/RG.2.1.3863.6885. Accessed August 15, 2024.

24 "The Status of Black Women in the United States," Women in the States, June 8, 2017, https://statusofwomendata.org/report/status-Black-women-united-states/. Accessed August 15, 2024.

25 Deborah Stone, *Policy Paradox: The Art of Political Decision Making*, 3rd ed. (New York: W.W. Norton, 2012), 152.

26 Alexandra E. Petri, "Woman Sentenced to Nine Years for Stealing $1.5 Million in Chicken Wings," *New York Times*, August 15, 2024, sec. U.S. https://www.nytimes.com/2024/08/14/us/chicago-school-chicken-wings-theft.html. Accessed August 15, 2024.

27 Kelley Williams-Bolar, "Kelley Williams-Bolar: I Am a 'Criminal' Because I Wanted a Good Education for My Girls," *The Skanner News*, August 20, 2012, https://www.theskanner.com/opinion/commentary/15478-kelley-williamsbolar-i-am-a-criminal-because-i-wanted-a-good-education-for-my-daughters-2012-08-20. Accessed August 15, 2024.

28 Howard Zehr, *The Little Book of Restorative Justice*, revised and updated (Intercourse, PA: Good Books, 2014), 13.

29 Ibid., 18.

30 Richard A. Oppel Jr., Derrick Bryson Taylor, and Nicholas Bogel-Burroughs, "What to Know about Breonna Taylor's Death," *New York Times*, December 13, 2023, sec. U.S., https://www.nytimes.com/article/breonna-taylor-police.html. Accessed June 6, 2024.

31 Stephen Finlan, *Problems with Atonement: The Origins of, and Controversy about, the Atonement Doctrine* (Collegeville, MN: Liturgical Press, 2005), 67–68.

32 Ibid., 68.

33 Rachel Elizabeth Harding, "É a Senzala: Slavery, Women, and Embodied Knowledge in Afro-Brazilian Candomblé," in *Women and Religion in the African Diaspora: Knowledge, Power, and Performance* (Baltimore: Johns Hopkins University Press, 2006), 12.

34 Dean Spade, *Mutual Aid: Building Solidarity during This Crisis (and the Next)* (London: Verso, 2020), 36.

References

Bloom, Barbara, and Covington, Stephanie. "Addressing the Mental Health Needs of Women Offenders," in *Women's Mental Health Issues Across the Criminal Justice System*, ed. R. Gido and L. Dalley. Columbus, OH: Prentice Hall, 2008.

The Current Project. "National Data Survey of Black Single Mothers." 2023. Accessed February 25, 2024. https://www.thecurrentproject.org/dataresearch.

Davis, Angela Y. *Are Prisons Obsolete?* New York: Seven Stories Press, 2003.

———. *Women, Race and Class*. New York: Vintage Books, 1983.

Finlan, Stephen. *Problems with Atonement: The Origins of, and Controversy about, the Atonement Doctrine*. Collegeville, MN: Liturgical Press, 2005.

Fox, Matthew. *Original Blessing: A Primer in Creation Spirituality: Presented in Four Paths, Twenty-Six Themes, and Two Questions*. New York: Jeremy P. Tarcher: Putnam, 2000.

Harding, Rachel Elizabeth. "É a Senzala: Slavery, Women, and Embodied Knowledge in Afro-Brazilian Candomblé," in *Women and Religion in the African Diaspora: Knowledge, Power, and Performance*, ed. R. Marie Griffith and Barbara Dianne Savage. Baltimore: Johns Hopkins University Press, 2006.

Homes and Community Renewal. "Mitchell-Lama Program." Accessed February 25, 2024. https://hcr.ny.gov/mitchell-lama-program.

Mitchell, Alison. "On Issue of Family Values, Clinton Unveils an Agenda of His Own." *New York Times*, July 29, 1995, sec. U.S. Accessed August 15, 2024. https://www.nytimes.com/1995/07/29/us/on-issue-of-family-values-clinton-unveils-an-agenda-of-his-own.html.

Oppel, Richard A., Derrick Bryson Taylor, and Nicholas Bogel-Burroughs. "What to Know about Breonna Taylor's Death." *New York Times*, December 13, 2023, sec. U.S. Accessed August 15, 2024. https://www.nytimes.com/article/breonna-taylor-police.html.

Petri, Alexandra E. "Woman Sentenced to Nine Years for Stealing $1.5 Million in Chicken Wings." *New York Times*, August 15, 2024, sec. U.S. https://www.nytimes.com/2024/08/14/us/chicago-school-chicken-wings-theft.html.

"Public Papers of the Presidents of the United States: George H. W. Bush (1992, Book I)—Remarks at the Annual Convention of the National Religious Broadcasters." Accessed May 8, 2024. https://www.govinfo.gov/content/pkg/PPP-1992-book1/html/PPP-1992-book1-doc-pg151.htm.

Spade, Dean. *Mutual Aid: Building Solidarity during This Crisis (and the Next)*. London: Verso, 2020.

Stone, Deborah. *Policy Paradox: The Art of Political Decision Making*. 3rd ed. New York: W.W. Norton, 2012.

U.S. Congress. House. *Personal Responsibility and Work Opportunity Reconciliation Act of 1996*. 104th Congress. August 22, 1996. Accessed August 15, 2024. https://www.congress.gov/bill/104th-congress/house-bill/3734/text.

West, Traci C. *Disruptive Christian Ethics: When Racism and Women's Lives Matter*. Louisville, KY: Westminster John Knox Press, 2006.

Williams, Delores S. *Sisters in the Wilderness: The Challenge of Womanist God-Talk*. Nachdr. Maryknoll, NY: Orbis Books, 1993.

Williams-Bolar, Kelley. "Kelley Williams-Bolar: I Am a 'Criminal' Because I Wanted a Good Education for My Girls." *The Skanner News*, August 20, 2012. Accessed September 14, 2020. https://www.theskanner.com/opinion/commentary/15478-kelley-williamsbolar-i-am-a-criminal-because-i-wanted-a-good-education-for-my-daughters-2012-08-20.

Women in the States. "The Status of Black Women in the United States," June 8, 2017. Accessed August 15, 2024. https://statusofwomendata.org/report/status-black-women-united-states/.

Zehr, Howard. *The Little Book of Restorative Justice*. Revised and Updated. Intercourse, PA: Good Books, 2014.

Section 3

Organizing, Activism, and Protest as Solidarity

6

Against Alienation

Anger and Solidarity in Protest and Social Movements

Candace Jordan

In September 2022, twenty-two-year-old Kurdish-Iranian Mahsa Amini died three days after her arrest by the morality police in Tehran. She was detained for improperly covering her hair with her hijab. Eyewitnesses reported that Amini appeared to have been beaten while being taken into custody.[1] Amini's killing outraged Iranians and sparked nationwide and worldwide protests. Following Amini's death, feminist protesters in Iran shouted "Jin, Jiyan, Azadî," or "Woman, Life, Freedom," protesting not only Amini's death but also what scholar Haidar Khezri calls the Islamic Republic of Iran's gender apartheid.[2] Scholar of civil rights, women's issues, and political developments in the Gulf Rafiah Al Talei explains the protests this way,

> As the protests intensified, videos of women cutting their hair and burning their hijabs spread, acts which served as both an expression of anger directed towards the morality policy responsible for Mahsa Amini's death, and a rejection of the policy of compulsory hijab more generally. However, the acts of hijab burning, and hair cutting did not merely launch a rebellion against government-imposed dress codes, but also came to symbolize broader demands for fundamental political and economic reforms.[3]

Social movements are a useful site for studying emotions. Anger is pervasive in movements aimed at resisting systemic injustice and inspiring reform. In recent years, scores of people have organized in response to systemic injustice. The Movement for Black Lives has protested the murder of Black people by the police. Social media hashtags such as #BlackLivesMatter and

#AbolishThePolice amplify the value of Black life at a time when Black people are more than three times as likely as white people to be killed during a police encounter.[4] While seemingly hostile displays of anger may seem to threaten potential solidary bonds (among protesters, their targets, bystanders, and even among protesters themselves), expressing anger in protest can actually foster solidarity by undermining various forms of alienation experienced by marginalized persons.

Anger and Solidarity Contested

In feminist philosophical and moral psychological literature, much has been written about the moral status of anger and other so-called hostile or negative emotions. As these accounts see it, negative emotions such as anger have an important role to play in responding to gender oppression. Arguments in defense of anger in the feminist literature posit that anger is a basic way to protest injustice and that it can help motivate social change. Feminist poet and scholar Audre Lorde writes, "Every woman has a well-stocked arsenal of anger potentially useful against those oppressions, personal and institutional, which brought that anger into being. Focused with precision it can become a powerful source of energy serving progress and change."[5] Writing within the tradition of feminist theorists who have argued for the value of anger in response to oppression, Myisha Cherry gives an extended account of Lordean rage, named for Lorde's influential essay "The Uses of Anger." Focusing on anger in the context of racial injustice, Cherry argues that Lordean rage works toward moral and social progress that would be hard to generate without it. She writes, "Anger makes us attentive to wrongdoing and motivates us to pursue justice."[6]

Many are critical of this line of thought. One common criticism of anger is that it alienates potential allies in the pursuit of just social change. In *Anger and Forgiveness* (2016), Martha Nussbaum argues that anger should be avoided as a response to political injustice because, in favoring personal vengeance, it undermines the pursuit of just outcomes.[7] Those derisive of anger stage their condemnation of it in the form of pleas to forgo violence and work toward social harmony. Sharing Nussbaum's concerns, Glen Pettigrove recommends the virtue of meekness in place of anger, while Nussbaum recommends civic love, as practiced by exemplars like Martin Luther King Jr. and Gandhi.[8]

To be sure, even for some committed to an account of anger where the desire for payback is partly constitutive of anger, there are reasons yet in favor of anger—that it articulates self-respect and that when anger rightly decries injustice it expresses something true.[9] These benefits, however, are outweighed by reasons against anger, such as political inefficacy, perpetuating cycles of payback, and making oneself more miserable. In line with scholars in feminist philosophical and moral psychological literature, I explore the value of anger for forging solidary bonds among marginalized persons.

Evaluations of anger ought not to lose sight of the large range of goals that protesters have, not all of which are material advantages for a group or its members. Leaders and organizers intentionally use emotional displays to coordinate action, attract participants, retain members, and persuade or implicate those who may be ignorant of or hostile to their central aims. Further, I argue for the value of expressions of anger as capable of generating and sustaining solidarity among marginalized persons. Solidary bonds, forged and sustained in part through rituals of anger in organizing and protest can enable previously frustrated activities, such as assembly, social participation, and authentic emotional expression. Expressions of anger in protest and organizing can draw persons together, healing through anger the very alienation caused by deriding anger in the first place. Anger can also claim, and sometimes receive, the recognition of bystanders.

In this chapter, I sketch three types of alienation that solidary bonds, forged in part through angry protest, stand to pierce. These are alienation from oneself, alienation that forestalls connection among people who share social identities in common, and alienation of an individual or group from the mainstream. Then, I explore how stigmatizing expressive practices can give rise to alienation. Finally, I explore the range of techniques deployed in rituals of anger, focusing especially on the confrontational activism of the AIDS Coalition to Unleash Power (ACT UP). I do so with an eye to how these practices contravene the varieties of alienation sketched.

Three Varieties of Alienation

Alienation from Oneself

Feminist philosopher Alison Jaggar, in her 1989 "Love and Knowledge: Emotion in Feminist Epistemology," argues that emotions are shaped in part by certain social conventions and rules.[10] In learning the language of emotion, Jaggar argues, we absorb the standards and values of our society, and those standards are "built into the foundation of our emotional constitution."[11] Jaggar and others argue, and I agree, that a society's predominant values often serve the interests of dominant groups. It is not hard to identify or imagine how emotions that go against the dominant emotions in various contexts can serve to isolate persons or mark them out as other. And this othering is not just the result of feeling emotions that are out of step with one's social milieu. Alienation can result from identifying differently from a dominant social group. The difference, coupled with lack of acceptance and compounded by isolation, can fuel alienation from oneself.

Consider a queer person living in a social milieu where gender is conceived of as strictly binary and language of and acceptance for gender fluidity is not prevalent. Their physical isolation from other queer persons can contribute to not understanding parts of their identity that are out of step with their social milieu. Such an experience of difference without a community of others to help make sense of an identity that is often stigmatized or downgraded can be isolating. This isolation can make it difficult for such a person, who may feel compelled to hide their identity out of concern for safety or in pursuit of social belonging, to come to know important parts of their identity. Such a person may have difficulty expressing or even understanding parts of their identity that are out of step with the community around them. Stigmatizing treatment communicated in various subtle and overt ways can weaken people's sense of self, causing them to internalize stigmatizing messages surrounding them. I count this internalization as one sort of alienation, especially given stigma's capacity to obscure persons from themselves. Internalizing negative messages about one's identity—messages that communicate that one does not count in the same way as others—can precipitate feelings of shame and humiliation.

The alienated person, more than just being physically isolated, may also lack a community of similar others to help interpret experiences relevant to their identity. Not being in a community with similarly identified others contributes to a person's lack of fully inhabiting what might be otherwise important features of one's identity.

My account of alienation can include being isolated or physically separated from others, but importantly it is not defined primarily by one's physical proximity to like others.[12] Rather, I mean alienation to describe a state in which one has only opaque access to oneself, including a lack of self-understanding, and self-judgment or self-hatred of those non-normative feelings and characteristics that are out of step with dominant society. Jaggar approximates the psychic dimension of alienation I have in mind, arguing that it can arise from a person expressing emotions that are out of sync with the larger society from which they are isolated (where the alienating mechanism is the friction created by experiencing unconventional emotion in isolation). She writes, "When unconventional emotional responses are experienced by isolated individuals, those concerned may be confused, unable to name their experience; they may even doubt their own sanity."[13]

Alienation from Similar Others

The alienated person, more than just being physically isolated, may lack a community of similar others to help interpret experiences relevant to their identity. Not being in a community with similarly identified others contributes to a person's lack of fully inhabiting what might be otherwise important features of one's identity.

Consider for example the #MeToo movement, founded by activist Tarana Burke, which draws attention to the sexual abuse and thwarted attempts for redress that have isolated women and girls from each other. The movement draws attention in part to this second kind of alienation: alienation among similar others. #MeToo highlights how women are kept from coalescing due to being coerced into silence, having their testimonies derided, or wanting to avoid further stigma. Women who have spoken out about assault in high-profile cases were often disparaged (many times by other women) for lying, embellishing, or even inviting advances. Kate Manne describes this feature of misogyny's logic as "himpathy," where sympathy is extended to male perpetrators and withheld from testifying women.[14]

Jaggar, and later Miranda Fricker in her work on hermeneutical injustice, describe the injustice that occurs when one is unable to understand or articulate a harmful experience due to a structural identity prejudice that excludes groups from participating in knowledge practices.[15] Alienation from similarly identified others might look like women not coalescing around each other to yield a better understanding of their experiences of sexual assault. It was precisely this alienation from other women that the women's movement of the 1960s and 1970s strove to overcome.

Consider two final examples of alienation from like others. Audre Lorde writes in "Eye to Eye: Black Women, Hatred, and Anger" about her broken relationship with Black women, resulting in part from her internalized hatred of herself qua Black woman. She queries,

> Other Black women are not the root cause nor the source of that pool of anger. . . . Then why does that anger unleash itself most tellingly against another Black woman at the least excuse? Why do I judge her in a more critical light than any other, becoming enraged when she does not measure up?[16]

Lorde suggestively hints at the cause of her deep well of anger toward other Black women. Lorde identifies the source of her internalized hatred as "that societal deathwish directed against us from the moment we were born Black and female in America."[17] The hatred and contempt Lorde felt as early as childhood, "from the time [she] could see," permeated news media, film, religious iconography, and everyday encounters with racist white people.[18] Though Black women aren't the source of her anger, Black women especially draw Lorde's ire. Her hostility toward Black women, purportedly through no fault of their own, constitutes an inability to connect charitably with other Black women. The societal hatred of Black women educates Lorde on how she regards herself and other Black women as contemptible. Of that internalized hatred, she writes, "Echoes of it return as cruelty and anger in our dealings with each other."[19] Lorde's anger toward and contempt for Black women illustrates marginalized people's vulnerability to being recruited into maintaining and perpetuating their own oppression.

Similarly, María Lugones's *Pilgrimages/Peregrinajes: Theorizing Coalition against Multiple Oppressions* describes her inability to love her mother and her inability to recognize herself similarly to how I have typified alienation from self and related others. This inability to love was born of the ways she was educated to instrumentalize and ignore working-class women of color. Lugones writes, "I was disturbed by my not wanting to be what [my mother] was. I had a sense of not being quite integrated, my self was missing because I could not identify with her, I could not see myself in her, I could not welcome her 'world.' I saw myself as separate from her, a different sort of being, not quite of the same species."[20] Even as she identifies as a woman of color reared by a working-class woman of color, Lugones has adopted the mode of perception pervading her cultural milieu, which is to instrumentalize and ignore these women. Lugones is hesitant to associate herself with her mother, because she does not want to risk being seen (and seeing herself) as like her mother.

Alienation from a Larger Community

Alienation of marginalized persons from their larger community will consist in the paucity of counter-publics that counter dominant modes of being and feeling. It might look like queer persons alienated from their larger heterosexual social milieu, a person of color alienated from a dominant white supremacist society, or women living in patriarchal and misogynist communities. This type of alienation can consist in the lack of recognition of a person or group by a larger community of others, especially given the practices that inhibit the emergence of alienated individuals in larger social milieus. More than theorizing their alienation from their beloveds, Lugones's and Lorde's treatises speak to the reduplication of these interpersonal alienations between and among social groups.[21]

Stigmatizing Expressive Practices as a Technique of Alienation

Stigmatizing expressions communicated in various subtle and overt ways can weaken people's sense of self, causing them to internalize the messages surrounding them. I count this internalization as one sort of alienation, especially given stigma's capacity to obscure marginalized persons from themselves. Gay men, for example, have long suffered being pejoratively deemed effeminate, weak, or perverse. Internalizing such characteristics can precipitate feelings of shame and humiliation. Myriad other examples abound. In a patriarchal American context, women are often deemed hysterical, irrational, and overly emotional. These stigmatizing scripts can make it harder for women to interpret their own experiences apart from the stigmas directed toward them. In other words, stigmatizing scripts can inhibit marginalized persons from understanding their own experiences and from joining together with others to identify cultural and structural factors contributing to their suffering. This social stigma can also lead to discrimination in other domains, such as healthcare, housing, or employment. These mechanisms can make stigmatized, discriminated against, and marginalized persons vulnerable to individual and collective harm, such as discriminatory legislation, hate crimes targeted at individuals or groups, or even atrocities such as genocide.

A person's grasp of their own identity, where identity is, as Charles Taylor writes, "a person's understanding of who they are, of their fundamental defining characteristics as a human being," is importantly tied to the ways that they are recognized or misrecognized by others.[22] Taylor's account of the distortion caused by nonrecognition and misrecognition is especially insightful for describing the damage caused to individuals and groups of people, what I call alienation. He writes,

> A person or group of people can suffer real damage, real distortion, if the people or society around them mirror back to them a confining or demeaning or contemptible picture of themselves. Nonrecognition or misrecognition can inflict harm, can be a form of oppression, imprisoning someone in a false, distorted, and reduced mode of being.[23]

One way that society mirrors back contemptible and confining pictures of persons or groups is through stigmatizing expressions. Supreme Court Justice Brett Kavanaugh's September 2019 confirmation hearing was interrupted when his former classmate Dr. Christine Blasey Ford accused him of sexual assault while they were in high school in 1982. While Dr. Ford's account was in part interpreted by Republican politicians as a political ploy by Democrats to derail Kavanaugh's confirmation, Dr. Ford's testimony was met with suspicion, and she was demeaned qua woman upon seeking redress. When Dr. Ford's allegation was made public, South Carolina Senator Lindsey Graham said that he would "listen to the lady, but we're going to bring this to a close."[24] Senator Orrin Hatch described Dr. Ford as "mixed up" regarding how she remembered the details of her assault.[25] At a 2018 rally in Southaven, Mississippi, President Donald Trump imitated Dr. Ford during her testimony, mocking her for not remembering answers to questions such as how she arrived at the party where Brett Kavanaugh allegedly sexually assaulted her. Trump acted out a series of questions put to Ford and her congressional testimony. He mocked, to laughter and applause from the crowd,

> "I had one beer." Right? "I had one beer." How did you get home? "I don't remember." How'd you get there? "I don't remember." Where is the place? "I don't remember." How many years ago was it? "I don't know. I don't know. I don't know. I don't know." What neighborhood was it in? "I don't know." Where's the house? "I don't know." Upstairs, downstairs, where was it? "I don't know. But I had one beer. That's the only thing I remember."[26]

Notice here that there is more at issue than credibility.[27] Withholding granting women credibility in their testimonies to sexual assault is generated in part due to the stigmatizing practices that shape how they, and thus their testimonies, are viewed. Subtle expressive practices impact how women (and their capacity to testify to their experiences) are regarded. Rather than calling Dr. Ford by her honorific, Senator Graham calls her dismissively "the lady." Senator Hatch's claim that Ford is "mixed up" reinforces the stereotype that women are illogical and confused. Trump reinforces this stereotype when he mocks Dr. Ford, suggesting in his dismissive tone that she is flighty and unserious.

What the backlash against Dr. Ford belies is how her demeanor during the Senate Judiciary Committee hearing expressly did *not* challenge common tropes of how "good women" behave. *Time* magazine notes that during Dr. Ford's testimony, she remained "unflaggingly gracious, soft-spoken and deferential."[28] Dr. Ford never interrupted a Senator, and she never refused to answer a question.[29] At one point, Dr. Ford described herself as "used to being collegial."[30] By contrast, Kavanaugh wept openly, repeatedly interrupted his questioners, and became angry throughout his testimony. Although Dr. Ford did not present herself in ways stereotypic of women (such as angry or hysterical) that are often stigmatized, she was nevertheless derided by being mocked as unserious in ways stereotypic of women. By contrast, Kavanaugh deployed a range of emotions that would have likely harmed Dr. Ford's public perception but instead seemed to enhance his credibility.[31]

Many stereotypes that plague women generally were leveraged against Ford. Her stigmatization was accomplished through sexist rhetoric, mocking tones, dismissive gestures, and derisive laughter. Ford and countless other female victims of sexual assault, qua woman, suffer negative stereotypes (e.g., that women are prone to hysteria, misinterpret male attention, invite male advances, or do not clearly communicate consent). These stereotypes diminish self-understanding, discourage communicating experiences with other women potentially suffering similar abuse, and dissuade women from seeking public redress. Stigmatizing practices like these (i.e., the behaviors that result from negative stereotyping) can yield the varieties of alienation previously described. Maligning women or queer persons, for example, can make them less able to understand and name their experiences. Pervasive misrecognition damages the ability to accurately interpret one's experiences. These practices can alienate persons by lowering self-esteem, weakening self-confidence, and undermining self-respect.

Further, stigmatizing expressive practices can isolate individuals from those who suffer similar stigmas. In lowering one's self-esteem and self-respect, stigmatizing practices can even conscript victims to participate in disciplining other members of their social group. Examples of this technique of alienation from self and its potential to fracture social bonds with like others include internalized racism, internalized homophobia, and misogyny.[32] Similarly to Lugones, Audre Lorde writes about how she was educated to hate Black women. She writes,

> When I started to write about the intensity of the angers between Black women, I found I had only begun to touch one tip of a three-pronged iceberg, the deepest understructure of which was Hatred, that societal death

wish directed against us from the moment we were born Black and female in America. From that moment on we have been steeped in hatred—for our color, for our sex, for our effrontery in daring to presume we had any right to live.[33]

Not only do stigmatizing expressions demean and downgrade the marginalized individual, but these practices can also recruit victims into following suit, thus foreclosing opportunities to coalesce around shared oppression.

Finally, stigmatizing expressions also yield alienation of individuals and groups from a larger community of others. Such practices can block important contributions from these persons and groups. As a result, these persons are limited in their capacity to contribute to the social and epistemic landscape in similar ways as those who do not suffer harmful stigmas. The confining or demeaning images of marginalized persons and groups can crowd out the availability of counter-narratives. Totalizing narratives can become entrenched, and failure to respect people's privileged access to themselves can cause folks to miss out on knowledge about marginalized persons and groups. Further, dominant publics can be stunted in their ability (and motivation) to recognize their own complicity in enacting and perpetuating these totalizing scripts via stigmatizing practices.[34]

Anger and Solidarity in Protest and Social Movements

Fortunately, the variety of disciplinary mechanisms that yield alienation is not total. Just as stigmatizing techniques can structure relationships of grievous injustice, Black folk, women, and lesbian feminist scholars, writers, and activists have demonstrated that affect can be leveraged toward just social change. Focusing on ACT UP's confrontational AIDS activism, this section analyzes the techniques deployed by protest movements, to produce, emit, and amplify those feelings, ideas, values, and practices that can contravene alienation. These techniques include the deployment of facial expressions, bodies oriented toward each other, synchronized movement and singing, and chants. It also includes material ephemera, like leaflets, fact sheets, t-shirts, stickers, buttons, posters, banners, and quilts brought together in protest movements. I explore how leaders and organizers enact rituals of anger that motivate solidarity and heal alienation.

ACT UP, a direct-action AIDS movement, deployed confrontational activism in the fight for recognition and improving the care of persons living with HIV/AIDS. Deborah Gould, in her masterful tome *Moving Politics* (2009), argues that ACT UP's emergence was facilitated by the shifting emotional habitus in lesbian and gay communities with the arrival of the Supreme Court's *Bowers v. Hardwick* decision in 1986.[35] Up to then, grief was the central emotion animating AIDS activism. Later, ACT UP would deploy anger in its confrontational political strategy, complementing ritual expressions of mourning with anger.

Consider the candlelight vigils and commemorative AIDS quilts that lesbian and gay persons used to grieve and remember those who died from AIDS-related complications. In a 1987 viewing of the quilt, which included 1,920 panels listing names memorializing the dead, names were read aloud continuously for more than three hours.[36] ACT UP sought to complement grieving the dead with confrontational activism. AIDS activists assembled in Washington, D.C., in October 1988 where the Names Project quilt was displayed on the National Mall. To draw the attention of the FDA, ACT UP leaders distributed leaflets at the quilt that read on one side, "SHOW YOUR ANGER TO THE PEOPLE WHO HELPED MAKE THE QUILT POSSIBLE: OUR GOVERNMENT."[37] Gould argues that through this act of confrontational activism, the AIDS quilt moved from being seen as a memorial to a record of murder.[38]

Here is a prescient example of the power of material ephemera to transform the emotion of grief through the ritual production of anger.[39] The emotional work of direct activism here complemented mourning rituals with anger to help facilitate the assignment of blame for government negligence that contributed to the AIDS-related deaths of those memorialized. I extend Gould's analysis by arguing that through speeches, demonstrations, and synchronized locomotion and singing, AIDS activists were able to puncture the alienation of the individual from themselves (through uncovering suppressed anger), from similarly identified others (as a group denied their rightful anger), and from wider society.

Techniques deployed include a shared focus of attention, bodies oriented toward each other, and synchronized movement and singing. Movements experiment with emotion through rhetoric, images (including posters, banners, and insignias), and bodily displays in both strategic and spontaneous ways. I argue that expressions of anger (manifest in protests, leafleting, banners, posters, meetings, visualizations, and healing circles) can function to produce and amplify the sentiments and values appropriate to more liberatory ways of being. These rituals can even incite attempts to figure out what one is feeling at all. Organized to imagine and bring about more just worlds, social movements can counter dominant habits of feeling and emoting, normalize and authorize anger, practice nonhierarchical leadership formations, and induce experiencing and being changed by new feelings. These practices can offer participants practice defying authority and produce the pleasures of activism and solidary bonds.

The women's movement of the 1960s and 1970s also harnessed anger in yet another unique way. Women's anger expressed and discovered during grassroots consciousness-raising groups was essential in bringing to social consciousness women's political, social, sexual, and economic subordination. Expressing anger was essential to forging solidarity among women, not just educating the larger publics about the subordinate treatment of women. As Naomi Scheman has argued, it was through consciousness-raising and the hard work of feminist activists in the women's movement that women learned to express their anger, to understand themselves, and to interpret their experiences through those expressions of anger. The women's movement provided opportunities and encouragement for women to share their experiences, naming themselves and their experiences as "angry," and thus they began "to see things differently, as it were through the anger."[40] Countless feminist philosophers aptly identify the epistemic lacunae wrought by various forms of domination. Jaggar articulates especially powerfully that resisters continue to confront totalizing scripts defining the appropriate bounds of self-expression. She writes, "the hegemony that our society exercises over people's emotional constitution is not total."[41] Nurses Bonnie Moore Randolph and Clydene Ross-Valliere wrote of their experiences in consciousness-raising groups: "To feel the support, acceptance, and permission of other women is a powerful tool for growth"; further, "and for many, a first-time experience of the celebration and joy in being a woman."[42]

Here is yet another example of women confronting totalizing scripts that define the appropriate bounds of self-expression.

Continuous with the insights of consciousness-raising groups and countless other forms of grassroots organizing, feminist philosophical literature illuminates the information that hostile emotions carry. Marilyn Frye writes, "in each of our lives, others' concepts of us are revealed by the limits of the intelligibility of our anger. Anger can be an instrument of cartography."[43] Given that women's anger receives uptake as anger in limited circumstances, Frye argues that anger reveals the sorts of relations possible in the "world of male-supremacy."[44] In addition to anger's epistemic value in providing unique insight into sexist and racist oppression, anger is epistemically valuable in that it reveals that marginalized people, especially women and people of color, are less successful in their anger-receiving uptake as anger; further, their anger is less often seen as justified.[45]

Numerous practices have facilitated the crucial process of overcoming alienation from self and others. We saw in the case study of the AIDS memorial quilt and complementary leaflet that the emotional segue of grief into anger was an important way to attend to governmental negligence. Consider one final example of the value of rituals of anger outside the context of protest movements. In a study of women incarcerated for infanticide, social psychologists Verta Taylor and Lisa Leitz show that writing to pen pals helped the women locate untreated postpartum depression as an impetus for their actions. Letter writing, the authors write, "allowed women to minimize their shame and emotional distress and to shift blame for their actions to the medical and legal systems, enabling them to remake their identities as mothers."[46] Letter writing provided another emotional segue (from shame to anger about unsupported illness) that allowed writers to begin to pierce the alienation from their identities as mothers. Further, it allowed them to circulate (among each other and their pen pals) a counter-narrative that authorized an alternative vision of motherhood (taking as valid that "woman" and "mother" can include women suffering from severe postpartum depression). Christina Sharpe's *In the Wake* articulates this identity-making task, albeit in a different context. She queries, "What does it mean to be a 'former mother' when one has never been able to lay claim to how mother means in the world?"[47] The generation of certain feelings and the suppression of others is a critical effect of the ritual practices I have here discussed. The ability to express anger is critical to leading full emotional lives.[48]

Foregrounding anger can enable previously frustrated activities, such as assembly, social participation, and authentic emotional expression. It can draw members together with similar others, and, it can claim, and sometimes receive, the recognition of bystanders. As illustrated by Lugones's and Lorde's overcoming internalized hatred, anger can establish solidarity within a group whose members are victims of a particular injustice. Further, it can reinforce within-group unity.[49] Rituals of anger can clarify for individuals the social and structural oppression that underly experiences of interpersonal harm. Remember how this functioned in the transformation of the mourning ritual (grieving individual AIDS-related deaths) into expressions of anger at government negligence for producing and exacerbating the structural injustice that precipitated those deaths.

Anger and other protest emotions surely yield instrumental goods. Anger can recruit bystanders and complicit bystanders in their liberatory projects. Rather than necessarily foreclosing valuable political friendships, anger among a group can invite non-group members to act on a group's behalf from a place of recognition of the group's entitlement to social participation and deference to the way angry groups push back against their thwarted abilities to speak and be heard. And yet, affective pleasures are irreducible to the instrumental upshots of emotions in activism. Protest movements deploy rich and diverse ways of emoting: from facial expressions to the material objects brought together in memorials.[50] While an angry chant might orient participant and bystander anger toward rightful targets, chants might also fulfill a felt need to express anger or be in sync (vocally, bodily, and emotionally) with comrades. Refusing to evaluate anger solely based on its productivity allows us not to lose the sensuous experience of feelings, its power to facilitate solidary bonds among persons, and its ability to puncture alienation.

Conclusion

That anger is often described as deleterious in the political sphere yet still finds meaningful expression in egalitarian social justice movements makes it worthy of continued attention. Confrontational AIDS activism, grassroots organizing by women, and numerous other protest strategies are grounded in the demand for recognition, a yearning for solidarity, and a refusal of techniques of alienation. Expression of anger and other affects produced, sometimes for their own sake, the sensual and pleasurable experience of protest. A diverse group of poets, scholars, feminists, and LGBTQ folks constituted various counter-publics that deployed affects of all sorts, including anger, pride, and mourning, to chart a fundamental transformation between the intimate and the political. These counter-publics were fueled in part by archival silences, vicious disciplinary practices, lazy epistemic practices, and the institutions that constrained the radical ideas and authentic self-presentation of marginalized persons. These mechanisms profoundly distorted the ability of the lived realities of women, LGBTQ persons, and Black people to surface. Feminists and writers including Marilyn Frye, María Lugones, and Audre Lorde, along with numerous protest organizers and leaders, literally stage multimodal interventions that disrupt the effacing techniques that facilitate their alienation—from themselves, similarly identified others, and from larger publics.

Notes

1 Ardeshir Tayebi, "Iranian Medical Official Says Amini's Death Caused by Head Injury, Rejects Official Version," September 20, 2022. https://www.rferl.org/a/iran-amini-death-head-injury-doctor/32042587.html (Accessed June 5, 2023).

2 Haidar Khezri, "Unrest across Iran Continues under State's Extreme Gender Apartheid." The Conversation, September 27, 2022. https://theconversation.com/unrest-across-iran-continues-under-states-extreme-gender-apartheid-183766 (Accessed June 5, 2023).

3 Rafiah Al Talei, "Hijab in Iran: From Religious to Political Symbol," Carnegie Endowment for International Peace, October 13, 2022, https://carnegieendowment.org/sada/88152 (Accessed June 5, 2023).

4 Gabriel L. Schwartz, and Jaquelyn L. Jahn, "Mapping Fatal Police Violence across U.S. Metropolitan Areas: Overall Rates and Racial/Ethnic Inequities, 2013–2017," *PLoS ONE*, 15, no. 6 (June 24, 2020): e0229686, https://doi.org/10.1371/journal.pone.0229686 (Accessed January 5, 2023).

5 Audre Lorde, "The Uses of Anger," *Women's Studies Quarterly*, 25, no. 1/2 (1997): 278–85, 280.

6 Myisha Cherry, *The Case for Rage: Why Anger Is Essential to Anti-Racist Struggle* (Oxford: Oxford University Press, 2021), 31.

7 Martha Nussbaum, *Anger and Forgiveness: Resentment, Generosity, Justice* (New York: Oxford University Press, 2016), see especially chapter 7. Philosophers are divided about whether a retributive component is a constitutive feature of anger. Those who argue that anger fundamentally involves a retributive element (a wish that the perceived offender suffers somehow), which they find normatively bad, include contemporary philosophers such as Martha Nussbaum, Owen Flanagan, and Glen Pettigrove as well as ancients such as Seneca. See Nussbaum, *Anger and Forgivenes*; Owen Flanagan, *The Geography of Morals* (New York: Oxford University Press, 2016); Glen Pettigrove, "Meekness and 'Moral' Anger," *Ethics* 122, no. 2 (2012): 341–70; Lucius Annaeus Seneca, trans. Robert A. Kaster and Martha C. Nussbaum, *Anger, Mercy, Revenge* (Chicago: University of Chicago Press, 2010). Others, such as Myisha Cherry, argue that a desire for revenge is not essential to anger. See Cherry, *The Case for Rage*. Further still, some find that anger has a retributive element that is not disqualifying, but rather can be appropriate. See Macalester Bell, "Anger, Virtue, and Oppression," in *Feminist Ethics and Social and Political Philosophy: Theorizing the Non-Ideal*, ed. Lisa Tessman (New York: Springer, 2009). While I do not in this chapter take a stand on whether anger fundamentally includes a retributive component, I am in favor of an account of anger that can, but need not, include a desire for retribution. Such desires that anger can include, for example, are recognition or authentic self-expression.

8 Pettigrove, "Meekness and 'Moral' Anger," 341–70.

9 Nussbaum, *Anger and Forgiveness*, 211.

10 Alison M. Jaggar, "Love and Knowledge: Emotion in Feminist Epistemology," *Inquiry* 32, no. 2 (1989): 151–76, 165.

11 Ibid., 165.

12 I do not want to diminish more extreme examples of alienation from self, occurring under regimes of extreme oppression or near total domination.

13 Jaggar, "Love and Knowledge: Emotion in Feminist Epistemology," 166.

14 See Kate Manne, *Down Girl: The Logic of Misogyny* (2018), esp. chapter 6.

15 See Miranda Fricker (2007), especially chapter 7. Where I use the language of alienation from self, Fricker uses the language of preventing the construction of selfhood.

16 Audrey Lorde, "Eye to Eye," in *Sister Outsider: Essays and Speeches* (Trumansburg, NY: Crossing Press, 1984), 145.

17 Ibid., 146.

18 Ibid., 147.

19 Ibid., 146.

20 María Lugones, *Pilgrimages/Peregrinajes: Theorizing Coalition against Multiple Oppressions* (Oxford: Rowman & Littlefield, 2003), 82.

21 See Marilyn Frye's *The Politics of Reality: Essays in Feminist Theory* (1983) and María Lugones' *Pilgrimages/Peregrinajes* (2003) on the constrained emergence of counter-publics yielded from white/Anglo society's "arrogant perception."

22 Charles Taylor, "The Politics of Recognition," in *Multiculturalism*, ed. Charles Taylor (Princeton, NJ: Princeton University Press, 1994), 25.

23 Ibid., 25.

24 Ryan Bort, "Sen. Lindsey Graham Is Melting Down in Real Time over the Kavanaugh Hearings," *Rolling Stone*, September 27, 2018, https://www.rollingstone.com/politics/politics-news/lindsey-graham-christine-blasey-ford-730157/ (Accessed November 30, 2022).

25 Ibid.

26 Allie Malloy, Kate Sullivan, and Jeff Zeleny, "Trump Mocks Christine Blasey Ford's Testimony, Tells People to 'Think of Your Son,'" CNN, October 3, 2018, https://www.cnn.com/2018/10/02/politics/trump-mocks-christine-blasey-ford-kavanaugh-supreme-court/index.html (Accessed November 30, 2022).

27 For more on the epistemic injustice of credibility distortions, see Miranda Fricker's *Epistemic Injustice* (2007); José Medina's "*The Epistemology of Resistance*" (2013).

28 Haley Sweetland Edwards, "Why Americans Are Still Grappling with Christine Blasey Ford's Legacy," *Time*, December 11, 2018, https://time.com/5476021/christine-blasey-ford-legacy/. Though initially Dr. Ford was commended as a compelling, upon Kavanagh's eventual confirmation, Donald Trump would later mock Dr. Ford for her inability to remember specific details of the alleged assault. (Accessed November 30, 2022).

29 Ibid.

30 David Crary, "Kavanaugh-Ford Hearing: A Dramatic Lesson on Gender Roles," *Associated Press*, September 28, 2018, https://apnews.com/article/c3bd7b16ffdd4320a781d2edd5f52dea (Accessed November 30, 2022).

31 See Kate Manne, *Down Girl: The Logic of Misogyny* (2018), esp. chapter 6, for a discussion of "himpathy," where sympathy is extended to male perpetrators and withheld from testifying women.

32 For more on internalized hatred vis-à-vis race, see Audre Lorde's "Eye to Eye: Black Women, Hatred, and Anger" (1983). For more on internalized homophobia, see Eve Sedgwick's *Epistemology of the Closet* (Berkeley: University of California Press, 1990). See also Maria Lugones on "arrogant perception" in *Pilgrimages/Peregrines*.

33 Lorde, "Eye to Eye," 146.

34 Consider Assistant Secretary of Labor Daniel Patrick Moynihan's controversial "Moynihan Report," which discussed racial inequality primarily in terms of family structure. For example, the report condemned so-called unwed single mothers without recognizing how Black women often innovated in their parenting to secure the support and wisdom of intergenerational networks of mothers, grandmothers, aunts, and sisters.

35 Deborah Gould, *Moving Politics: Emotion and ACT UP's Fight against AIDS* (Chicago: University of Chicago Press, 2009), 121. The August 1982 arrest of Michael Hardwick led him to challenge in court Georgia's anti-sodomy statute. The Supreme Court upheld the Georgia statute, confirming that the state of Georgia did not need to offer any compelling reason for the statute apart from the moral sense that sodomy is wrong. See Lisa M. Keen, "High Court Upholds Sodomy Law," *Washington Blade*, July 4, 1986, p. 6.

36 Anne-Christine d'Adesky and Phil Zwickler, "The Names Project: The Quilt That Woke Up America; 1,920 Panels Memorialize PWAs," *New York Native*, October 26, 1987, p. 6.

37 ACT UP/NY, "Show Your Anger to the People Who Helped Make the Quilt Possible: Our Government," leaflet, October 1988. Leaflet accessed in Deborah Gould's personal archive.

38 Gould, *Moving Politics*, 226.

39 Social scientists Lively and Heise discuss emotional segues, such as the important transformation of shame or fear into anger. See K. J. Lively and D. R. Heise, "Sociological Realms of Emotional Experience," *American Journal of Sociology* 109 (2004): 1109–36.

40 Naomi Scheman, "Anger and the Politics of Naming," in *Women and Language in Literature and Society*, ed. N. Furman, R. Borker, and S. McConnell (New York: Praeger, 1980), 22.

41 Jaggar, "Love and Knowledge," 166.

42 Bonnie Moore Randolph and Clydene Ross-Valliere, "Consciousness Raising Groups," *American Journal of Nursing* 79, no. 5 (1979): 922–24.

43 Frye, *The Politics of Reality*, 93–94.

44 Ibid., 90. Frye writes that for women to presuppose their own respectability and claims upon respect through their anger is "at best potentially problematic and at worst incomprehensible in the world of male-supremacy where women are Women and men are Men. A man's concept of Woman and of Man, and his understanding of what sorts of relations and connections are possible between beings of these sorts, to a great extent determine the range of his capacity to comprehend these claims, and hence of his capacity to give uptake to women's anger" (p. 90). Further, she credits women reformers of the nineteenth century with extending the range of tolerance of women's anger.

45 Mariana Alessandri powerfully finds that a racist society that "strains to associate dark skin with wisdom also has a hard time pairing a dark mood like "anger" with "healthy" or "justified." Mariana Alessandri, *Night Vision: Seeing Ourselves through Dark Moods* (Princeton, NJ: Princeton University Press, 2023), 17. For more on how Black women's anger in particular is derided, see Brittney Cooper, *Eloquent Rage: A Black Feminist Discovers Her Superpower* (New York: St. Martin's Press, 2018).

46 V. Taylor and L. Leitz, "From Infanticide to Activism," in *Social Movements and the Transformation of American Health Care*, ed. J. C. Banaszak Holl, S. R. Levitsky, and M. N. Zald (New York: Oxford University Press, 2010).

47 Christina Sharpe, *In the Wake: On Blackness and Being* (Durham, NC: Duke University Press, 2016), 77.

48 Such an account finds support from theorizing about affective injustice, defined as the foreclosure of one's basic human entitlement to lead full emotional lives and exercise one's capacity to respond to the world aptly. For more on affective injustice, see Amia Srinivasan's "The Aptness of Anger," *Journal of Political Philosophy* 26, no. 2 (2018): 123–44.

49 Social scientific studies (in addition to the feminist philosophical literature, affective theoretical literature, ritual studies literature, and social movement literature) bear out the ability of successful ritual performance and the good moods they produce to boost feelings of group efficacy and motivate political action. For more, see H. J. Smith and T. Kessler, "Group-Based Emotions and

Intergroup Behavior," in *The Social Life of Emotions*, ed. L. Z. Tiedens and C. W. Leach (New York: Cambridge University Press, 2004).

50 See José Esteban Muñoz, "Feeling Brown, Feeling Down: Latina Affect, the Performativity of Race, and the Depressive Position," *Signs* 31, no. 3 (2006): 675–88. Muñoz describes how groups are in opposition to the dominant class not simply through the fact of identity but rather in the way they perform affect. This ethnic difference and resistance, articulated through feeling and affect, stands in opposition to the "national affect" of a hegemonic class.

References

Alessandri, Mariana. *Night Vision: Seeing Ourselves through Dark Moods*. Princeton, NJ: Princeton University Press, 2023.

Al Talei, Rafiah. "Hijab in Iran: From Religious to Political Symbol." *Carnegie Endowment for International Peace*, October 13, 2022, https://carnegieendowment .org/posts/2022/10/hijab-in-iran-from-religious-to-political-symbol?lang=en.

Bell, Macalester. "Anger, Virtue, and Oppression." In *Feminist Ethics and Social and Political Philosophy: Theorizing the Non-Ideal*, edited by Lisa Tessman. New York: Springer, 2009.

Bort, Ryan. "Sen. Lindsey Graham Is Melting Down in Real Time over the Kavanaugh Hearings." *Rolling Stone*, September 27, 2018, https://www.rollingstone .com/politics/politics-news/lindsey-graham-christine-blasey-ford-730157.

Cherry, Myisha. *The Case for Rage: Why Anger Is Essential to Anti-Racist Struggle*. Oxford: Oxford University Press, 2021.

Cooper, Brittney. *Eloquent Rage: A Black Feminist Discovers Her Superpower*. New York: St. Martin's Press, 2018.

Crary, David. "Kavanaugh-Ford Hearing: A Dramatic Lesson on Gender Roles." *Associated Press*, September 28, 2018, https://apnews.com/article/c3bd7b16ffd d4320a781d2edd5f52dea.

d'Adesky, Anne-Christine, and Phil Zwickler. "The Names Project: The Quilt That Woke Up America; 1,920 Panels Memorialize PWAs." *New York Native*, October 26, 1987.

Edwards, Haley Sweetland. "Why Americans Are Still Grappling with Christine Blasey Ford's Legacy." *Time*, December 11, 2018, https://time.com/5476021/ christine-blasey-ford-legacy/.

Flanagan, Owen. *The Geography of Morals: Varieties of Moral Possibility*. New York: Oxford University Press, 2016.

Fricker, Miranda. *Epistemic Injustice: Power and the Ethics of Knowing*. New York: Oxford University Press, 2007.

Frye, Marilyn. *The Politics of Reality, Essays in Feminist Theory*. Berkeley, CA: Crossing Press, 1983.

Gould, Deborah. *Moving Politics: Emotion and ACT UP's Fight against AIDS*. Chicago: University of Chicago Press, 2009.

Jaggar, Alison M. "Love and Knowledge: Emotion in Feminist Epistemology." *Inquiry* 32, vol. 2 (1989): 151–76.

Khezri, Haidar. "Unrest across Iran Continues under State's Extreme Gender Apartheid." *The Conversation*, September 27, 2022, https://theconversation.com/ unrest-across-iran-continues-under-states-extreme-gender-apartheid-183766.

Lively, K. J., and Heise, D. R. "Sociological Realms of Emotional Experience." *American Journal of Sociology*, 109 (2004): 1109–36.

Lorde, Audre. "Eye to Eye." In *Sister Outsider: Essays and Speeches*. Trumansburg, NY: Crossing Press, 1984.

———. "The Uses of Anger: Women Responding to Racism." *Women's Studies Quarterly* 25, no. 1/2 (Spring/Summer 1997): 278–85.

Lugones, María. *Pilgrimages/Peregrinajes: Theorizing Coalition against Multiple Oppressions*. Oxford, UK: Rowman & Littlefield, 2003.

Malloy, Allie, Kate Sullivan, and Jeff Zeleny. "Trump Mocks Christine Blasey Ford's Testimony, Tells People to 'Think of Your Son.'" *CNN*, October 3, 2018, https://www.cnn.com/2018/10/02/politics/trump-mocks-christine-blasey-ford -kavanaugh-supreme-court/index.html.

Manne, Kate. *Down Girl: The Logic of Misogyny*. New York: Oxford University Press, 2018.

Medina, José. *The Epistemology of Resistance: Gender and Racial Oppression, Epistemic Injustice, and Resistant Imaginations*. New York: Oxford University Press, 2013.

Muñoz, José Esteban. "Feeling Brown, Feeling Down: Latina Affect, the Performativity of Race, and the Depressive Position." *Signs* 31, no. 3 (2006): 675–88.

Nussbaum, Martha. *Anger and Forgiveness: Resentment, Generosity, and Justice*. New York: Oxford University Press, 2016.

Pettigrove, Glen. "Meekness and 'Moral' Anger." *Ethics*, 122, no. 2 (2012): 341–70.

Randolph, Bonnie Moore, and Clydene Ross-Valliere. "Consciousness Raising Groups." *American Journal of Nursing* 79, no. 5 (1979): 922–24.

Scheman, Naomi. "Anger and the Politics of Naming." In *Women and Language in Literature and Society*, edited by N. Furman, R. Borker, and S. McConnell-Ginet. New York: Praeger, 1980.

Schwartz, Gabriel L., and Jaquelyn L. Jahn. "Mapping Fatal Police Violence across U.S. Metropolitan Areas: Overall Rates and Racial/Ethnic Inequities, 2013–2017." PLoS ONE 15(6): e0229686, June 24, 2020, https://doi.org/10.1371/journal.pone.0229686.

Sedgwick, Eve. *Epistemology of the Closet*. Berkeley: University of California Press, 1990.

Seneca, Lucius Anneaus. *Anger, Mercy, Revenge*. Translated by Robert A. Kaster and Martha C. Nussbaum. Chicago: University of Chicago Press, 2010.

Sharpe, Christina. *In the Wake: On Blackness and Being*. Durham, NC: Duke University Press, 2016.

Smith, H. J., and T. Kessler. "Group-Based Emotions and Intergroup Behavior." In *The Social Life of Emotions*, edited by L. Z. Tiedens and C. W. Leach. New York: Cambridge University Press, 2004.

Srinivasan, Amia. "The Aptness of Anger." *Journal of Political Philosophy* 26, no. 2 (2018): 123–44.

Tayebi, Ardeshir. "Iranian Medical Official Says Amini's Death Caused by Head Injury, Rejects Official Version." *Radio Free Europe*, September 20, 2022, https://www.rferl.org/a/iran-amini-death-head-injury-doctor/32042587.html.

Taylor, Charles. "The Politics of Recognition." In *Multiculturalism*, edited by Charles Taylor. Princeton, NJ: Princeton University Press, 1994.

Taylor, V., and L. Leitz. "From Infanticide to Activism." In *Social Movements and the Transformation of American Health Care*, edited by J. C. Banaszak-Holl, S. R. Levitsky, and M. N. Zald. New York: Oxford University Press, 2010.

7

Ritual, Protest, and the Relational Ethics of Solidarity

Molly Farneth

A few months before I finished writing this chapter, I got a call from an organizer with Jews for Racial and Economic Justice (JFREJ). JFREJ is a New York City–based nonprofit that organizes on the Jewish left to combat economic inequality and racial violence. JFREJ was preparing for its big annual awards ceremony and fundraiser, and the organizer was calling to find out if I would attend the event or contribute to the organization. As these calls usually go, the organizer said many compelling things about the mission of the group, the urgency of the issues, and the promise of the grassroots organizing that JFREJ was involved in at the time. In the course of this call, he said one phrase that was particularly striking to me: "our fights for bodily autonomy are all interconnected."

Now, at first, this might sound like typical political language—from the martial metaphor ("the fight"; see also: the struggle, the war, the battle) to the reframing of particular issues as part of, and inseparable from, a larger political vision. Nevertheless, what I was struck by in this phrase, and what remains compelling about it to me, was how it held together the individual and the collective, autonomy and interconnection. The phrase got me thinking, for that reason, about how JFREJ embodies this "holding together" in its political organizing work.

This was the summer of 2023. The US Supreme Court decision in *Dobbs v. Jackson Women's Health*, which had overturned *Roe v. Wade*, was only a year old. In that context, the JFREJ organizer's reference to "bodily autonomy" as among the values that the organization tries to uphold in and through its solidarity work felt particularly resonant. The pro-choice movement has often used that phrase to characterize what was at stake in the long-standing efforts to overturn *Roe* and revoke the Constitutional right to abortion. "Bodily autonomy," and the closely related phrase "women's right to choose," cast people's decisions about whether or not to carry a pregnancy to term as a matter of individuals' sovereignty over their own bodies. Such language is often associated with liberal politics that imagine the sovereign individual as the locus of rights and political decision-making. By noting that people's "fights for bodily autonomy" are intertwined with one another, however, JFREJ appears to accept the idea that *one* aim of politics is to secure such rights, while also resisting the idea that politics are therefore exhausted by this individual rights-based framework. The phrase turns from the rights of sovereign individuals to the solidarity of relational subjects.

JFREJ is itself committed to a pluralist Judaism that encompasses multiple racial, ethnic, and national identities. Its membership is diverse, along multiple dimensions of identity. Moreover, JFREJ rarely works on a political issue or campaign in isolation from other organizations. Instead, its organizing model is one of relationship-building and coalitional politics. Organizing across religious, racial, and class differences, JFREJ commits to learning from the perspectives and experiences of diverse neighbors and allies and to being accountable to them. With its partners, JFREJ aims to build solidarity and generate effective, democratic, political power.

Notably, JFREJ is also one of a handful of organizations on the contemporary Jewish left that has made ritual and liturgy central to its political organizing.[1] One of the three pillars of JFREJ's strategy is this:

> We create the world as it should be. JFREJ will continue to grow the New York Jewish Left by creating a welcoming, vibrant home for our city's multiracial, multiethnic, intergenerational, progressive Jewish community. We invest in education, artmaking, ritual, and joyful celebrations that bring us into new ways of relating to one another through Jewish culture with all our diasporic languages, traditions, and texts.[2]

JFREJ is committed, in other words, to ritual and other forms of cultural expression as part of a project of progressive Jewish world-making, prefiguring the forms of Jewish and communal life that the organization and its members seek in their politics.

Rituals feature not only in the organization's celebrations but also in its protests and direct action. When the holiday of Sukkot fell in the middle of a housing justice campaign, for example, JFREJ erected a public sukkah—the temporary dwelling where Jews eat and commune throughout the week-long holiday—and they made the sukkah a place for organizing around and affirming a commitment to fair housing policies. In another protest, when a Grand Jury decided *not* to indict the New York City police officer who had killed Eric Garner, an unarmed Black man in Staten Island, members of JFREJ gathered in the street to recite the Mourner's Kaddish, the prayer that observant Jews recite at the death of close kin.[3] In these and other cases, JFREJ and its members have emphasized the public enactment of Jewish ritual as a *political* act—and, more specifically, as an act of *solidarity*.

This isn't a chapter about JFREJ, not really, but I take their organizing and their political vision as a starting point for thinking about rituals and their relationship to solidarity. What do rituals like those that JFREJ enacts in its protests and political campaigns have to do with the idea that "our fights for bodily autonomy are all interconnected"? How might rituals actually help to create the relationships and solidarity groups that realize that interconnectedness? As I will argue, the promise of such ritual or liturgical activism lies in rituals' ability to embody a relational ethic that is central to creating and sustaining solidarity.[4] What I'll call *rituals of solidarity* can create these solidary relationships in the context of political protests and social movements while also exemplifying the more just and democratic world that protesters imagine and seek.

Rituals as Performative and Prefigurative

Rituals are complex series of acts that usually include a combination of speech or other vocalizations, postures, gestures, and bodily movements. These series of verbal and gestural acts are routinized or scripted. Their order is set; to perform the ritual is to follow the routine. For this reason, a ritual can be enacted over and over again in more or less the same way.

Understood in this way, rituals are a type of social practice, among the shared activities of a group. Members of the group care about them, and they care about getting them right—that is, about following the routine or script in the right way. This is not least because rituals encode, express, and enact some of the most significant norms of the group, including norms concerning such things as gender roles and power relations. People also care about their rituals, and about getting them right, because rituals are part of how such groups sustain their collective norms over time.

Two features of rituals are worth drawing out here: their performativity and their prefigurative capability. When rituals not only symbolize the norms of a group, but actually bring about a change in the social world, we can call them *performatives*. In one common use of that term, something performative is insincere, a kind of virtue signaling. That's not at all what I mean here. Rather, I'm drawing on the philosopher of language J. L. Austin's conception of performatives as utterances that *do* something in and through the act of speaking.[5] In and through a speech act of this kind, a person can be named, an invitation can be issued, a couple can be wed, a promise can be made. For example, if I say to you, "I promise to show up for the protest tomorrow," I am not naming or describing a promise that I have made. By saying the words, I'm making the promise. And, in making the promise, I am issuing new obligations and entitlements that did not exist beforehand. I create an obligation (mine) to show up for the protest and an entitlement (yours) to expect me to be there.

Rituals, whether or not they involve speech, can function similarly to these sorts of speech acts, bringing about changes in the social world. Among the most important changes that rituals can bring about are alterations in the roles, statuses, and corresponding obligations and entitlements of the people participating in them. This is most obvious in the case of rites of passage, in which a person who participates in the ritual goes from having one role or status at the beginning of the ritual to having a different role or status at the end of the ritual. In the case of a coming-of-age ritual, for example, it is in and through a person's participation in the ritual that they move from the status of a child to that of an adult, gaining the obligations and entitlements that characterize adulthood in their particular community. In the case of an initiation ceremony, to take another example, it is in and through participation in the ceremony that a person goes from being an outsider to the group to being a member of it, with all of the obligations and entitlements, the rights and responsibilities, that come with membership. The initiate might gain power that they did not have before; they might be expected to act in ways that they were not before. Notice that these shifts in a person's role, status, obligations, and entitlements aren't merely symbolic; they're *real* effects. They change the relationships and the distribution of power and other goods among the members of a group. Notice, too, that it is not only the central participant in the rite of passage who has new obligations and entitlements—*others* are now expected to see them as having a new status and treat them accordingly, which is to say that these others now have new obligations and entitlements with respect to the person who underwent the rite of passage. In and through the ritual, the structure of their relationship has changed.

Although rites of passage may be the most straightforward examples of rituals' performative structure, other kinds of rituals can work this way, too. When a person participates in a mourning ritual, for instance, they express and enact their grief at the death of a person who matters to them. One of the many things that a mourning ritual does is communicate the mourner's grief, by making it visible to others. People who witness the ritual, then, are entitled—and perhaps even obligated—to treat that person as a mourner. The mourner's social status shifts, and other people in the community are, in the ordinary course of things, expected to treat them differently at least for a time. What, exactly, this treatment entails depends on the community in question.

Often, as rituals function performatively, they do so in ways that change the roles, statuses, and corresponding obligations and entitlements of the people who participate in the ritual, while also reinforcing the norms of a broader society. The heir to the British throne undergoes a coronation ceremony and thereby becomes the king. His status certainly changes. He gains power and authority that he did not have before. But his own status change doesn't change the power of the monarchy. If anything, the rules and norms of the social and political institutions are reinforced through the performance of the coronation ceremony that invokes them. This is often how rituals work—changing individual statuses and obligations while strengthening or solidifying the norms of the group.

But that's not always the case. Sometimes, rituals can function performatively in ways that are also *prefigurative*. In such cases, rituals and their participants enact roles, statuses, and relationships that are *not* yet in effect more broadly. The term "prefigurative" comes from political analysis, as a way of describing the political tactics of (typically) left protests and social movements that seek to embody in their own ranks the sorts of communities that they are working to achieve at a societal level.[6] So, for instance, when the feminist consciousness-raising groups of the 1970s eschewed hierarchical leadership and decision-making, even as they turned toward political action, they sought to embody and enact in their own relationships and practices the egalitarian communities that they sought through political means as well. This was a kind of prefigurative politics. Or when the Occupy Movement used the "human microphone" to amplify the voice of speakers to an assembled crowd, they sought to embody the kind of inclusive and participatory ethos in their communicative practice that they sought in economic relations. This, too, was a prefigurative politics.

Rituals can also be prefigurative, as when they enact, say, beloved community, or when they affirm a set of relations that *don't* actually obtain in society or, really, outside of the context of the ritual community. As I noted earlier, JFREJ lists ritual-making as one of its strategies for "creating the world as it should be."[7] The idea is that rituals, along with art and other cultural forms, can embody, even temporarily, the world as it *should* be in the midst of the world as it is. A sukkah, that temporary dwelling-place, that is open to all comers—Jews of multiple races, genders, sexualities, nationalities, and class positions gathering along with their diverse neighbors to share a meal—enacts in ritual form a joyful, pluralist, and radically hospitable political community. In this way, rituals can generate and sustain countercultural norms, enacting them and reinforcing them in the confines of a group that hopes or believes that they might one day take root in society.[8]

These two features of rituals—their performativity and their prefigurative capability—are related in ways that help us to understand what rituals and liturgies are doing in the context of protest and social-movement building. If rituals can prefigure relationships and practices that are not yet widely held, and if they can actually bring about changes in the social world, then we ought not to think of them as simply expressing a political vision that will ultimately be achieved through other (more explicitly political) means. Rather, we ought to recognize rituals as among the ways people can bring about changes in the norms, relationships, and practices that characterize a group, including whatever aspirational norms, relationships, and practices characterize *solidary* groups.

Rituals and Political Solidarity

It's a commonplace idea in the study of religion that rituals foster solidarity. This idea has its roots in the work of Émile Durkheim. According to Durkheim, religions are significant sources of social cohesion, even in modern societies otherwise characterized by individualism. Rituals, in particular, are powerful engines of social cohesion because of the way they subordinate individuals' concerns and judgments to those of the group. Through their ritual actions and experiences, otherwise disparate individuals become bound to one another. "By shouting the same cry," Durkheim writes, "pronouncing the same words, making the same gesture to the same object, [individuals] become and feel as one."[9] When people enact a ritual together, Durkheim argues, they are joined in a collective experience around shared symbols and objects. This experience, as Durkheim puts it, "sets the collectivity in motion."[10] Notice the double meaning of this phrase. Durkheim alludes to the coordinated physical movement that often characterizes rituals: when people perform rituals, they move their bodies in sync. They are a collectivity, in motion together. At the same time, however, he points to the group-forming work performed by rituals; when people perform rituals together, they become a group. They are a collectivity *on account of their collective action*, the group's very existence set in motion by ritual. Through shared movement, rituals create the group and sustain it over time.

Many of those who follow this Durkheimian tradition think about rituals in terms of symbols and symbolic action to consider how and why it is that rituals are effective in creating solidarity. Shared symbols can powerfully consolidate and communicate social or political ideas or ideals. Symbolic actions give rise, then, to collective effervescence—the intense feeling of unity that can be experienced by the people who participate in a ritual together. David Kertzer has developed these Durkheimian ideas about ritual and solidarity in relation to protest and social movements, writing that "if they are to be successful, social movements must create their own *esprit de corps*. . . . People must have a feeling of belonging together and participating in a common effort if their commitment to the movement is to be strong."[11] Like Durkheim, Kertzer argues that rituals can foster this feeling of unity or belonging. "Ritual," Kertzer continues, "by inducing people to take public action that identifies them with a political group, serves to build and reinforce the attachment the person has to the group."[12]

This way of thinking about ritual and solidarity tends to emphasize the feeling or experience of unity. But this feeling of unity is only one part of what constitutes solidarity in political life.[13] Political solidarity also involves commitments and the obligations that follow from those commitments. Sally Scholz's influential account of solidarity is helpful here. Scholz defines solidarity in terms of a form of unity that mediates between the individual and the community and entails positive moral obligations. While Scholz's emphasis on unity and individual-community mediation echoes Durkheim's, her inclusion of *obligation* takes us in a different direction. People who are in relationships of solidarity have obligations to one another and to the group of which they are a part.

Political solidarity, in particular, is a form of unity that is based on the shared commitments of members of the solidary group—shared commitments to alleviate or rectify a situation of oppression or injustice. Political solidarity, according to Scholz, is inherently justice-seeking. It involves commitments to a just cause and to other people who have also committed to that cause. These commitments establish the nature of solidarity's positive moral obligations. As Scholz writes, "a commitment to a cause establishes voluntary relations and obligations to that cause. The commitment is a sort of agreement to act in such a way that the pursuit of the cause or goal informs one's actions. But the commitment also informs other relations."[14] The commitment creates a kind of voluntary association, a group of people who have made the same commitment, and it creates ancillary obligations to other members of the group—new social relationships characterized by these positive moral obligations.

Scholz's emphasis on the role of shared commitment and obligation in political solidarity reveals something significant about the structure of the relationships that characterize this political formation. Conceived in this way, solidarity is not only about the feeling or experience of unity or belonging. Solidarity also involves commitments, and those commitments generate obligations: obligations to act in ways that support the goal to which one has committed oneself, and obligations to stand alongside others who have committed themselves to that goal. Relatedly, then, solidarity involves entitlements: entitlements to expect others who have committed themselves to the goal and to the solidary group to act similarly, and to hold them responsible for their actions to that end.[15] In solidarity, these commitments, obligations, and entitlements are often directed toward or focused on what people are doing with their bodies—commitments, for instance, to *stand* alongside others, both literally and figuratively, often putting one's body on the line with, or in the place of, another who is vulnerable.

The commitment to action makes solidarity quite different from, say, empathy or compassion, which involves feelings or affective experiences (feeling with or for another), but which does not necessarily involve making commitments or generating obligations to act with or for another. When I say that I am in solidarity with you, I am not saying, "I feel your pain." I'm saying, "I will stand alongside you." In turn, when I say that "I will stand alongside you," I am committing to actually doing so—to showing up, to standing or marching beside you, to joining my voice with yours. By making this commitment, I am also entitling you to believe that I will do what I have said I'll do and to hold me accountable if I do not.

Now, it is fairly straightforward to make commitments to others with whom we are already in some direct contact or relationship. We sign a contract with a business partner or an employer, thereby making a commitment that spells out what each of us is obligated to do and entitled to expect from the other. Or we make a promise to a friend, committing to do something in the future and creating various obligations and entitlements between us, relative to that commitment. But one of the challenges of political solidarity is its scale. Political solidarity typically involves commitments, obligations, and entitlements to people with whom one is *not* already or often in close contact. It extends one's responsibility and accountability to others—sometimes others who are quite differently situated from oneself in social and political space— with whom one may or may not interact directly. If solidarity is not only about *feeling* bound together but actually creating and sustaining the obligations and entitlements that go with a certain kind of relationship and status, well, that is a difficult thing to do *en masse*.

Rituals can help. Rituals can express and enact these sorts of obligations and entitlements—can actually create them—on a group level in a way that is not possible with the formation of direct interpersonal relationships. A group of people who do not know one another personally can nevertheless, through rituals, signal their shared commitments and take on the obligations that go with them. This makes rituals well-suited to the enactment of a kind of civic friendship, in which it is precisely *not* the affective experience of love that characterizes the relationship but its structure of mutual recognition that makes it worth calling friendship. That is the peace that rituals can bring about. They can set the collectivity—a collectivity with shared commitments, and obligations to one another relative to those commitments—in motion. And, in doing so, they can bring about relationships of solidarity. They can signal commitment (identification with a cause and with the group centered around that cause) and they can also enact that commitment, leaving people with new obligations and entitlements toward one another.

To put the point in the language of rituals' performative structure, when rituals bring about a change in the social world, sometimes that change is the creation of *solidarity*. Rituals can do this in a way that is not unlike what I have described in talking about the act of promising or the coming-of-age ceremony: they shift people's normative statuses and issue obligations and entitlements that reshape people's relationships with one another. These rituals express one person or group's commitment to stand with or in the place of another, in the face of threat or harm. In addition to expressing this commitment, they enact, and bring about, obligations to act in the service of that commitment and to be held accountable if one does not.

Enacting Our Interdependence

Rituals and solidarity, both, mediate between the individual and the collective. They put people into relationships, aligning individuals' actions—postures, gestures, movements, speech—with collective norms. Rituals *of* solidarity, then, are those rituals that make this connection explicit by expressing a commitment to stand alongside one another for the sake of a shared cause. Such rituals *express* this commitment, but we ought not to think of them solely as expressive or communicative. They also *enact* this commitment—bring it into being—by issuing new obligations and entitlements that change the relationships among the members of the solidary group. Their new obligations and entitlements are the normative stuff that binds the solidary group together: obligations to show up for one another and entitlements to expect one another to do so. By virtue of having enacted the ritual, people come to have new relationships to one another—relationships of accountability.

Rituals of solidarity, therefore, are among the practices in which political actors relate to and act alongside others. In and through such rituals, they enact their co-authorship of, and mutual responsibility for, the world they seek to build. In doing so, rituals of solidarity perform and prefigure a set of *relational* norms that emphasize interdependence and mutuality.

These relational norms, fundamental to feminist ethics, capture the notion that human beings are relational subjects rather than isolated individuals. They recognize that human beings are shaped by, engaged in, and defined in terms of a web of relationships with others, that people are subjects always and only in relation to other subjects. This feature of human beings—our profound relationality rather than our radical independence—is an ethical matter. We are responsible to and for one another. As relational subjects, we are also accountable subjects.[16] Our commitments, claims, and actions are ours, certainly, in the sense that we are typically responsible for them, but this responsibility makes sense only in relationship to others—those who are in a position to hold us accountable, that is, our fellows.

When the Supreme Court released its decision in *Dobbs v. Jackson Women's Health*, overturning *Roe v. Wade* and abandoning the idea of a federal right to abortion, I anticipated a wave of protest. I expected that, like some other recent protest movements, the reproductive justice movement would engage in rituals and other symbolic actions to express protesters' ethical and political commitments and to forge solidarity among them. But the protests of the *Dobbs* decision were neither as widespread and sustained as I had imagined they would be nor was ritual a significant feature of them. Was this an example of the exhaustion of mass protest after the anti-racism protests of 2020 changed so little? Or could it be explained by reproductive justice organizers' emphasis on local actions to protect and preserve individuals' access to abortion and other reproductive health services on the ground? I suspected that each of those factors was at play. But there was something else happening, too, since even those mass protests that did take place largely lacked the ritualized actions or the widely shared symbols that have characterized other recent social movements in the United States and abortion-rights protests in other countries.

Protests of US immigration policies, for instance, have often been ritualized. Some examples include the annual protest at the US-Mexico border fence known as the Posada sin Fronteras, which draws on the Posadas (the reenactment during Advent of Mary and Joseph's search for hospitality in Bethlehem) to draw attention to the lack of hospitality and failures of neighbor-love at the border, as well as the many border Eucharists, which perform the communion at and across the US-Mexico border, that take place each year. Progressive Jewish organizations have enacted the Tisha B'Av liturgy at US Immigration and Customs Enforcement (ICE) offices and related sites to mark and mourn the death of immigrant children in ICE custody. Meanwhile, protests against anti-Black racism and police violence have often drawn on Black homegoing traditions and the history of political funerals to integrate memorial practices and rituals of mourning into political actions.

By contrast, why has the reproductive justice movement in the United States shied away from rituals? I have two hypotheses about why this might be. The first is that there is widespread skepticism in the movement about institutional religion and its associated practices, given the history of Roman Catholic and conservative evangelical opposition to abortion, contraception, and other reproductive health services. For that reason, the fight for reproductive rights and reproductive justice has been more likely to take institutional religion as its target (as in protests at Roman Catholic churches and religiously affiliated pro-life organizational headquarters) than as a source of inspiration for any organizing or mobilizing tactics. Because of the association of rituals with organized religion and, in the United States, with conservative Christianity in particular, protesters may be likely to view religion with skepticism if not outright hostility.

A second possible reason—and more to the point here—may be that the movement, particularly in its liberal strands, is often framed around the demand for "bodily autonomy" and individual choice. As I suggested at the outset, these phrases can be associated with liberal politics that emphasizes the sovereign individual as the locus of rights and political decision-making. (Contrast this with the framing of, for instance, immigration protests, which are more likely to invoke relational norms—interdependence, interconnectedness, mutuality, responsibility for one another—than individualist ones.) If that's right, if one of the dominant normative frameworks for the reproductive justice movement is individual rather than collective, it should come as no surprise that the movement would eschew rituals, which, as we have seen, align the individual with *collective* norms.

But if we return to the idea that "our fights for bodily autonomy are all interconnected," and if we see this not simply as a political slogan but as an articulation of a relational norm that informs both the ends and means of solidarity, then we might see ritual as a fruitful site for this mediation of the individual and the collective. This is the insight of groups like JFREJ, who view ritual as an embodiment of that relational norm and integral, therefore, to a politics of solidarity.

This is the insight, too, of a group that periodically gathers for a modified Shacharit service on Shabbat mornings outside of the offices of a health center and abortion provider in northern Virginia. The Shacharit is the first and the longest of the daily prayer services in Judaism. The service is typically communal, performed with and alongside others, and it is liturgical or scripted. Participants recite blessings and prayers together, in a set and prescribed order, sitting, standing, and bowing at the appointed times. The Shacharit service includes several of the central prayers of Judaism.

Beginning in the summer of 2023, members of five local synagogues, in partnership with the National Council of Jewish Women, began to gather outside of Falls Church Healthcare Center on Saturday mornings to join together in songs and prayers drawn from this service. Participants congregate and stand side-by-side along the front of the health center, facing outward toward those who might arrive to protest abortion as well as those who might approach to enter the clinic. Many of the participants hold signs that name abortion access as a Jewish issue as well as a matter of religious freedom. Meanwhile, they sing *niggunim*, traditional wordless melodies, and recite the Shacharit blessings and prayers. Their gathering has a ritual structure. It is not spontaneous but scripted, and the words spoken and acts undertaken are not individual but communal. In fact, one of the prayers of the Shacharit service, the *Shema*, begins: "Hear, O Israel!" With these words, participants in the prayer service hail, or call upon, themselves *as* a collective entity, not as a collection of isolated individuals.

This creation and affirmation of community is significant. Participants stand together at the clinic, joining their bodies and their voices in the postures and words of the liturgical script. And, in so doing, they also frame their protest in terms of collective norms rooted in Jewish ritual and tradition. They commit *as* Jews to a shared cause—abortion access—and they embody that commitment by showing up, speaking and standing in unison, and positioning their bodies and their prayers to receive and safeguard those entering the clinic. After one Shabbat morning service at the center, the health center's director of operations noted that "usually on Saturday morning, we see a lot of people who are using their prayer as a form of control, as a form of hatred. Today, we were able to see something very different. We were able to see a *kehilat ahava, kehilat chesed*, a compassionate community, who is very supportive of autonomy, of reproductive freedom."[17] His characterization of the gathering echoes what I said earlier about rituals of solidarity—that they enact and embody a set of relational norms that emphasize interdependence and mutuality. In part because of its ritual structure, the Shabbat morning service at the abortion clinic enacts and embodies the commitment to do the thing that the participants have already begun to do by showing up: to stand with and alongside others.

I don't know what the outcome of these gatherings will be. As they hold space for people to commit to a shared cause and shared relational norms, they may generate new relationships and coalitions in the struggle for reproductive justice. Or they may give way to other forms of activism and politics. In the meantime, I believe, we can think of them as rituals of solidarity, drawing on shared norms and collective action to forge new ways of being with and for one another.

Acknowledgments

Many thanks to Fannie Bialek, Rosemary Kellison, and Shannon Dunn for helpful feedback on a draft of this chapter.

Notes

1   Jewish Voice for Peace and IfNotNow, for instance, have enacted Jewish rituals and liturgies in their organizing for solidarity with Palestine; see Atalia Omer's *Days of Awe: Reimagining Jewishness in Solidarity with Palestinians* (Chicago: University of Chicago Press, 2019), 133ff. Omer also briefly discusses this in her chapter in this volume. I've also written elsewhere about the use of the Tisha B'Av liturgy in protests organized against US Immigration and Customs Enforcement in 2019 by a coalition of progressive Jewish organizations; see "For These Progressive Jews, Prayer Is Part of the Protest," *ARC Magazine*, September 10, 2019, https://arcmag.org/for-these-progressive-jews-prayer-is-part-of-the -protest/ (Accessed December 9, 2024).

2   JFREJ Member Handbook 2022–2023, https://jfrej-web-assets.nyc3 .digitaloceanspaces.com/2022/JFREJ-Member-Handbook_Oct2022.pdf.

3   I discuss this protest throughout *The Politics of Ritual* (Princeton, NJ: Princeton University Press, 2023).

4   I draw the phrase "liturgical activism" from C. Melissa Snarr's work on the living wage movement. She highlights the role of religious rituals and liturgies in creating collective identity among activists, lowering the perceived barriers to political participation for those familiar with the rituals, and negotiating the

boundaries of what is considered to be sacred and profane. See Snarr, *All You That Labor: Religion and Ethics in the Living Wage Movement* (New York: New York University Press, 2011), 122–39. A similar idea is captured by Rev. Bill Wylie Kellerman's "liturgical direct action." Kellerman, *Seasons of Faith and Conscience: Explorations in Liturgical Direct Action* (Eugene, OR: Wipf & Stock, 1991).

5 J. L. Austin, *How to Do Things with Words* (Cambridge: Harvard University Press, 1975). I discuss this conception of performatives at length in *The Politics of Ritual*, esp. 91–103.

6 To my knowledge, the term "prefigurative politics" was coined by the sociologist Wini Breines in her analysis of the New Left; see *The Great Refusal: Community and Organization in the New Left, 1962–1968* (New York: Praeger, 1982).

7 JFREJ Member Handbook.

8 Francesca Polletta, *Inventing the Ties That Bind: Imagined Relationships in Moral and Political Life* (Chicago: University of Chicago Press, 2020), 163.

9 Émile Durkheim, *The Elementary Forms of Religious Life*, trans. Carol Cosman, ed. Mark Cladis (Oxford: Oxford University Press, 2001), 175.

10 Durkheim, *Elementary Forms of Religious Life*, 258.

11 David Kertzer, *Ritual, Politics, and Power* (New Haven, CT: Yale University Press, 1988), 73.

12 Ibid.

13 Leah Hunt-Hendrix's dissertation on the ethics of solidarity provides a detailed account of three major strands of nineteenth- and twentieth-century thinking about the concept, and it includes a lengthy discussion of Durkheim. See *The Ethics of Solidarity: Republican, Marxist, and Anarchist Interpretations* (PhD dissertation, Princeton University, 2014).

14 Sally J. Scholz, *Political Solidarity* (University Park, PA: Penn State Press, 2008), 73. Scholz distinguishes among three types of solidarity: social solidarity, political solidarity, and civic solidarity. She identifies Durkheim and those in the sociological and anthropological tradition that follows from him with the first, which is a kind of social cohesion based on shared identity. I have some quibbles with Scholz's characterization of Durkheim, for whom I think shared identity is less crucial for the formation of solidarity than a shared conception of the sacred. For this reason, I believe that his conception of solidarity is more akin to what Scholz calls political solidarity, which involves shared commitment to a cause, than Scholz herself suggests. Nevertheless, because Scholz explicitly thematizes commitment and obligation (much more than

feeling, which is so central to Durkheim), I follow her account of political solidarity here.

15 The content and limits of these obligations are worked out in social practice, which is to say that they can always be a matter of deliberation, debate, and contestation. No one person's claim about what solidarity requires has prima facie authority over the others, except as that's negotiated and recognized by others in the course of things.

16 Ann Russo considers what such responsibility-holding looks like when it is embedded in relationships (including relationships of solidarity) rather than applied or enacted as in a juridical framework. The accountability involved in relationships of solidarity isn't typically the institutional accountability of courts and law, but the mutual and relational accountability of communities. See Russo, *Feminist Accountability: Disrupting Violence and Transforming Power* (New York: New York University Press, 2019).

17 Temple Micah, "Shabbat Morning Gathering," https://www.templemicah.org/events/abortion-clinic-shabbat-morning-4/ (Accessed April 5, 2024).

References

Austin, J. L. *How to Do Things with Words.* Cambridge: Harvard University Press, 1975.

Breines, Wini. *The Great Refusal: Community and Organization in the New Left, 1962–1968.* New York: Praeger, 1982.

Durkheim, Émile. *The Elementary Forms of Religious Life.* Translated by Carol Cosman. Edited by Mark Cladis. Oxford: Oxford University Press, 2001.

Farneth, Molly. "For These Progressive Jews, Prayer Is Part of the Protest." *ARC Magazine,* September 10, 2019, https://arcmag.org/for-these-progressive-jews-prayer-is-part-of-the-protest/ (Accessed December 9, 2024).

———. *The Politics of Ritual.* Princeton, NJ: Princeton University Press, 2023.

Hunt-Hendrix, Leah. *The Ethics of Solidarity: Republican, Marxist, and Anarchist Interpretations.* PhD dissertation, Princeton University, 2014

JFREJ Member Handbook 2022–2023, https://jfrej-web-assets.nyc3.digitaloceanspaces.com/2022/JFREJ-Member-Handbook_Oct2022.pdf.

Kellerman, Bill Wylie. *Seasons of Faith and Conscience: Explorations in Liturgical Direct Action.* Eugene, OR: Wipf & Stock, 1991.

Kertzer, David. *Ritual, Politics, and Power*. New Haven, CT: Yale University Press, 1988.

Omer, Atalia. *Days of Awe: Reimagining Jewishness in Solidarity with Palestinians*. Chicago: University of Chicago Press, 2019.

Polletta, Francesca. *Inventing the Ties That Bind: Imagined Relationships in Moral and Political Life*. Chicago: University of Chicago Press, 2020.

Russo, Ann. *Feminist Accountability: Disrupting Violence and Transforming Power*. New York: New York University Press, 2019.

Scholz, Sally J. *Political Solidarity*. University Park: Penn State Press, 2008.

Snarr, Melissa C. *All You That Labor: Religion and Ethics in the Living Wage Movement*. New York: New York University Press, 2011.

8

Defending Secularism through Islam

American Muslims' Opposition to the *Dobbs* Decision

Maria Tedesco

In the aftermath of the US Supreme Court decision overturning *Roe v. Wade*, political cartoons depicting Supreme Court justices and politicians in beards and turbans popped up on social media. Tweets mentioned the Christian Taliban and American shari'a. "Y'all Qaeda" jokes floated around the internet. The "Talibanization" of America was referenced.[1] The *Atlanta Journal-Constitution* published a cartoon depicting two women in black burqas with a speech bubble above them reading: "Pray for Texas women."[2] An *Arizona Republic* opinion column titled "Texas goes Taliban on abortion rights. Is Arizona next?" made the case that the new Texas law—which bans abortions as early as six weeks into a pregnancy—"seems to have less to do with the U.S. constitution than with shari'a law."[3]

Muslim experts and activists around the country reacted by pointing out that these comparisons are not only inaccurate but also further perpetuate Islamophobia. Moreover, they claimed that this comparison minimizes the role of Christianity and US systems that led to severely restrictive abortion bans in Texas, Alabama, and Mississippi and to the overturning of *Roe*.[4] Such commentaries reveal indeed a fundamental misunderstanding of the nature and functioning of Islamic law, of Islamic regulations concerning abortion, and of the stance that the majority of American Muslims take on reproductive justice.

In a *Religious Landscape Study* conducted in 2007 and 2014 by the Pew Research Center, 59 percent of American Muslims declared that abortion should be legal in all/most cases, 37 percent declared that abortion should be illegal in all/most cases, and 9 percent declared that they did not know.[5] Along the same line, a study conducted in 2022 by the Institute for Social Policy and Understanding shows that 56 percent of American Muslims think that abortion should be legal in all or most cases and 42 percent think that abortion should be illegal in all or most cases. Of this 42 percent, 26 percent think abortion should be illegal in most cases, and only 16 percent think that abortion should be illegal in all cases.[6] These trends are reflected in the open letters and public statements issued in 2022 by several American Muslim organizations condemning the *Dobbs* decision as an infringement of constitutionally granted freedoms of religion and conscience.

In this chapter, I analyze in depth the statements issued by HEART Women and Girls, KARAMAH: Muslim Women Lawyers for Human Rights,[7] AMBA Legal (American Muslim Bar Association), Muslims for Progressive Values (MPV), Women's Islamic Initiative in Spirituality and Equality (WISE Women), and Queer Crescent.[8] I also discuss Muslim participation in interfaith initiatives in support of reproductive justice, such as the Religious Coalition for Reproductive Choice, and Amici Curiae. Employing this analysis and on six interviews conducted with members of some of the above-mentioned organizations, I show how in the process of defending abortion rights and promoting reproductive justice, American Muslims develop Islamic arguments in favor of secularism and religious pluralism and build interfaith and interracial coalitions with non-Muslim actors.[9] Moreover, I argue that the formation of these networks of solidarity hinges upon three aspects of the worldview of the organizations under study: their intuitive inclination toward feminism and secularism; their methodological approach to Qur'anic interpretation, derived in part from the history of intellectual exchanges between Jewish, Christian, and Muslim feminist theologians in the United States; and their understanding of their own communities as the coming together of multiple perspectives and experiences. All these elements combined enable these Muslim activists to strike a balance between identity and coalition, and sameness and difference, while pursuing political alliances with non-Muslims.

Arguing for Reproductive Rights from Inside and Outside Islam

From the documents and the interviews, four main sets of arguments emerge in favor of reproductive justice: traditional Islamic jurisprudence's stance on abortion, divinely granted bodily autonomy, protection of secularism, and care for the oppressed. While the discussion regarding the legality and morality of abortion in Islamic law is obviously carried out exclusively from an Islamic perspective, in the articulation of the other three sets of arguments, activists incorporate into Islamic modes of thinking values and principles expressed in the American Constitution and Declaration of Independence, as well as frameworks and ideas borrowed from non-Muslim thinkers and social movements. I maintain that it is precisely this ability to argue simultaneously from inside and outside of Islam that allows these activists to build interfaith and intersectional alliances in which "differences are celebrated and not erased because people reach the same conclusions starting from different departure points."[10]

I now turn to an overview of the arguments that American Muslims use in opposition to the *Dobbs* decision. In traditional Islamic jurisprudence, there is no notion that life begins at conception, and there are no references to fetal rights.[11] The Qur'anic verses describing fetal development are the following: "He makes you in the wombs of your mothers in stages, one after another, in three veils of darkness" (Qur'an 39:6) and "[We] then formed the drop into a clot and formed the clot into a lump and formed the lump into bones and clothed the bones in flesh; and then brought him into being as another creature. Blessed be Allah, the Best of Creators!" (Qur'an 23:14). The Hadith that complements these verses is: "(As regards to your creation), every one of you is collected in the womb of his mother for the first 40 days, and then he becomes a clot for another 40 days, and then a piece of flesh for another 40 days. Then Allah sends an angel to breathe the soul into his body" (narrated by Abdullah, recorded in *Sahih Bukhari*, vol. 4, book 55, no. 549).

Taken together, these verses and Hadith have been interpreted to indicate that a fetus becomes a human being at the time of ensoulment. A pre-ensouled fetus has traditionally been considered a biological entity, not a legal-moral one, and abortion has traditionally been deemed legal without restrictions before ensoulment. There is, however, a divergence of opinions among legal scholars with regard to when a fertilized egg reaches ensoulment. A majority of scholars calculate ensoulment at 120 days based on the Hadith quoted earlier. More stringent interpreters rely on another tradition that states that after the first forty days, an angel endows the fetus with hearing, sight, skin, flesh, and bones. Finally, a minority opinion forbids abortion altogether based on the notion that the fetus is potentially human from the moment of conception.[12]

The statements made by the organizations listed above add to the reasoning of classical jurisprudence and several other arguments derived from the Islamic tradition. For example, they highlight that Islam has a positive view of human sexuality and perceives sex as aimed at fostering emotional intimacy, not exclusively procreation.[13] They emphasize that the Qur'anic condemnation of the killing of children (cf. Qur'an 6:137, 17:31, and 60:10) refers to infanticide, not abortion.[14] They use the Surah Maryam, in which God talks about the hardship of the Virgin Mary when she gave birth to Jesus, and the verse "We instructed the human being to honor his parents. His mother bore him with hardship, gave birth to him in hardship" (Qur'an 46:15) to point out that women's pain must be taken into consideration first and foremost when discussing abortion, and the final decision about bringing a child into this world must be theirs.[15] The statements also discuss the practice, common in traditional Muslim societies, of accepting the testimony of a midwife for settling inheritance disputes. Fetuses were not automatically considered as humans and therefore eligible to inherit, so midwives had to testify whether the fetus had taken a breath upon birth and therefore was a human entitled to inheritance or if they were stillborn and therefore not eligible for inheritance.[16] Finally, to reaffirm that Islamic traditions did not traditionally consider the fetus a legal person, they quote a Hadith in which two women fought and one of them, along with her unborn child, died. The Prophet ordered her killer to pay *diya* (blood money for a legal person) for the victim's death and a *ghurra* (calculated usually as a tenth of the *diya*) for the miscarried fetus.[17]

Activists define bodily autonomy as "the right of a person to govern what happens to their body, without external influence, pressure, or coercion."[18]

They recognize that bodily autonomy is not a term used in the Qur'an,[19] but they claim that the concept is inherently Islamic and reflected in divinely granted freedom of religion.[20] They emphasize the need to use a contemporary vocabulary to articulate Islamic concepts in a way that allows Muslims to reach a wider audience and participate in conversations with non-Muslim actors and organizations.[21]

Bodily autonomy is founded on the religious freedom enshrined in the Qur'anic verse, "Let there be no compulsion in religion" (Qur'an 2:256), and is encouraged through the Islamic principle of *ijtihad*, which calls on individuals to practice independent reasoning. These principles endow all individuals with the right to be free from coercion of any kind, but especially from religious coercion. Such freedom affords all Muslims the right to make their own choices. Independent reasoning is the cornerstone of human freedom, which can only be practiced if one is free from coercion and can exercise their free will. Likewise, coercing an individual and limiting their free will to maintain bodily dignity through legislation of any kind, religious or secular, violates an individual's right to *ijtihad*.[22] Moreover, the verse "No soul shall be compelled beyond capacity, neither the mother made to suffer for the child or the father for his offspring" (Qur'an 2:233) is a reminder that God wishes only ease for the believers, and that ease is nowhere to be found without bodily autonomy and reproductive freedom.[23]

Bodily autonomy is also founded on *karamah* (dignity), *khilafah* (individual moral agency before God), *hurma* (sacred boundaries of each body), and *ridha* (choice and consent). In Islam, the human body is considered a divine miracle. God commands the individual to maintain dignity over their body, by caring for it as they see fit. As "vicegerents" (*khalifah*) of God on Earth, humans are responsible for recognizing injustice and taking care of each other and themselves. When applying this principle to the work of advancing reproductive justice, believers must address the systemic injustice facing our society and work toward equity. Here activists quote scholar Sa'diyya Shaikh's argument that for Muslim women in particular to fulfill their role as *khalifahs* on this earth, they must "realize their full potentials for intellectual, economic, and social agency."[24] Giving Muslim people with wombs access to reproductive rights can help them embody their roles as *khalifas*, allowing them to make empowered and informed decisions, and reach their full potential, whether as parents or not.[25]

The notion of *hurma* or sacred inviolability is inspired by scholar Ingrid Mattson's Hurma Project, an organization that fights against sexual assault, abuse, and gender-based violence as "grave violations of the sacred inviolability of a person."[26] Everyone is a sacred being and if harm comes to them, it is a grave injustice. If their bodies are violated, it is incumbent upon the Muslim community to challenge those who bring about such harm and center the healing of the individual that was violated. To argue for the importance of *ridha* or consent, activists recall that when the Prophet married Saffiyah, she declined to engage with him in sexual intimacy on their wedding night. The Prophet responded with respect toward this decision. Following the prophetic example, Muslims must uphold individual agency and practice consent.[27]

Finally, activists emphasize the notion of *rahma*, or compassion. They point out that Muslims invoke Allah by using the Names *ar-Rahman, ar-Rahim,* the most merciful, the compassionate, and claim that it is not a coincidence that the word *rahma* and the Arabic word for womb—*rahm*—have the same root.[28] They emphasize that this sacred part of the body should be honored and that all matters of the womb should be met with compassion. Further, they adopt the framework of "responding with *rahma*" elaborated by the Hurma Project to respond to individual disclosure of experiences of sexual violence to instruct community members on how to react to stories of abortion.[29] In this framework, RAHMA stands for Respond by listening; Affirm and believe; Honor cultural and religious context; Maintain privacy; and Assist with providing resources.[30]

The defense of secularism is at the core of another set of arguments put forward by the organizations under study. Their view of secularism points not to a system where religion is discredited and put under the control of the state, but to a system where expression of religious beliefs is tolerated, even encouraged, and protected against encroachment from state authorities. One interviewee, for example, declared: "America is losing one of the things that made it great, that is, the practice of highly valuing religion and at the same time keeping it out of politics."[31] In support of secular law, organizers argue that by disregarding the diversity of religious viewpoints on when life begins, the abortion ban denies the values of religious pluralism and religious freedom, which are enshrined in the US Constitution, particularly through the Establishment Clause ("Congress shall make no law respecting an establishment of religion"). Moreover, by elevating a particular religious viewpoint and restricting the ability of women to act according to their own faith, the *Dobbs* decision threatens the freedom of all religious communities. The abortion ban is thus contrary to the founding principles of the United States and inconsistent with America's pluralistic society, which is averse to legislating morality.[32]

A defense of secular law—the argument goes—is also in keeping with Islamic traditions of governance. In the premodern period, the pluralism of shari'a law gave a Muslim individual discretion to choose, in consultation with religious scholars and spiritual guides, which legal opinion to follow from a variety of different equally valid opinions. No state or executive authority could dictate the opinion that a Muslim woman must follow. Premodern Muslim governments did not have the authority to declare a particular legal opinion correct over all the others, and even less to enforce it over the entire population. When they did force a rule on the people, it had to be justified as serving the common good (*maslaha 'amma*). This is also what protected non-Muslims living in safety under Muslim rule: they could follow their own religious laws as long as such laws did not conflict with the general good.[33]

Documents and interviewees show that people in marginalized communities are disproportionally harmed by the abortion ban and emphasize that serving and supporting the vulnerable and the disenfranchised is a central tenet of Islam. For example, one of the statements issued by the organizations under study claims: "We as Muslims and moral agents of God, must act to defend and uplift the rights of those among us who are most oppressed. We are entrusted by our Creator with doing so with our hands, our tongues, and our hearts, following the example of our Prophet (peace be upon him) and our ancestors."[34] Thus, Muslims have a moral obligation to protect, succor, uplift, and advocate on behalf of those who are poor and low-income and those who have historically been disenfranchised and discriminated against, including people of color, people with disabilities, immigrants, and LGBTQ+ individuals. This charge includes ensuring that individuals from these communities have the same access to healthcare and the same freedom to make decisions concerning their reproductive health, including the right to abortion—something that the ban puts into jeopardy.[35]

All the organizations in this study embrace the broader framework of reproductive justice inspired by professor and women's rights activist Loretta Ross as a tool that allows them to care for the oppressed.[36] SisterSong, founded by Ross, defines Reproductive Justice as "the human right to maintain personal bodily autonomy, have children, not have children, and parent the children we have in safe and sustainable communities.[37] HEART expands on that by stating: "We believe this [using the reproductive justice framework] includes examining the multiple intersections that individuals cross every day that can have a profound impact on one's sexual health: such as access to culturally and linguistically appropriate healthcare, a living wage job, quality education, freedom from discrimination, violence, and other systems of oppression, and communities that support healing, empowerment, and self-determination."[38]

In a document titled *The Islamic Principle of Rahma: A Call for Reproductive Justice*, authored by AMBA and HEART and signed by a coalition of Muslim and non-Muslim organizations, activists make references to the Birth Justice Framework developed by the Southern Birth Justice Network, an organization that strives to make midwife and doula care accessible to all birthing people, especially people of color and LGBTQ+ communities. The framework "includes the right to choose whether or not to carry a pregnancy, to choose when, where, how, and with whom to birth, including access to traditional and indigenous healers, such as midwives and other birth workers, and the right to breastfeeding support. The complete range of pregnancy, labor, and birth options should be available to everyone as an integral part of reproductive justice. These are our rights as mothers and parents."[39] AMBA and HEART also support the call from the Black Midwives Alliance to remove state restrictions on midwifery care so midwives can support birthing people in safely giving birth outside of hospital settings without civil or criminal penalties. Pregnant people, they claim, must be afforded the ability to experience safe births that are respectful of their decisional autonomy and in ways that meet their needs. This entails providing opportunities for diverse sources of healthcare including funding midwives and doulas through legislation.[40] Some of the interviewees linked this support for the re-introduction of midwifery as a form of culturally sensitive healthcare to a desire to "decolonize" healthcare within Muslim communities,[41] as midwifery was widely practiced in Muslim countries before colonialism and then severely curtailed by the latter in favor of Western, allopathic medicine.[42]

In terms of action, the organizations under study have embarked on a series of educational, social, and legal initiatives to protect and strengthen reproductive rights in the United States. Educational initiatives aim at instructing the Muslim community and decolonizing Islamic thought and reproductive justice. They include activities such as distributing pamphlets and short articles, hosting panels and discussions, developing workshops, and seeking the support of imams in these educational efforts. Social initiatives include sharing abortion access stories to spread awareness, integrating sexual and reproductive healthcare into zakat-eligible funds, creating and distributing care packages to those who have experienced reproductive and sexual health struggles, and responding with RAHMA to disclosures of abortion, pregnancy loss, and reproductive/sexual health struggles.

Finally, the legal initiatives focus on supporting legislation for abortion access. These include inviting Muslims to use toolkits to ask their representatives to pass the EACH Act,[43] the WHPA Act,[44] and the Black Maternal Health Momnibus Act.[45] Further, Muslims for Progressive Values together with Amici Curiae, an interfaith coalition of religious leaders who acknowledge the diversity of views regarding when life begins and affirm abortion rights in the United States, filed an amicus brief in the 2017 case *Whole Woman's Health v. Hellerstedt*. In the brief, the authors objected to the Texas law that provided that, to protect the "sanctity of life," after the termination or loss of *any* pregnancy, the embryonic fetal tissue must be treated like human remains; that is, it must be buried or cremated. The brief affirmed women's right to decide, in accordance with their beliefs, how to dispose of fetal tissue following the loss or termination of pregnancy.[46] In 2022 numerous other Muslim associations, including KARAMAH, HEART, and AMBA Legal, joined Amici Curiae in filing an amicus brief for *Dobbs v. Jackson*. The authors of the brief, once again, reaffirmed women's right to terminate a pregnancy in the light of the freedom of conscience and equal protections under the laws enshrined in the American Constitution.[47]

Feminism, Secularism, and the Construction of Solidarity

Contrary to a broad literature that questions the compatibility of Islam with feminism and secularism on the grounds that they represent for Muslims "difficult double commitments," the activists of the organizations under study assume rather than argue for such compatibility.[48] Their advocacy for both feminism and secularism seems to stem organically out of their faith. For example, in reference to feminism, one interviewee recalled that her journey as a Muslim feminist began when a friend, to whom she had confided her desire to find ways to help women in Muslim communities, suggested that she read the writings of the Suffragettes. She had some reservations at first because in her community feminism was perceived as something Western and alien, but she went ahead and studied those writings anyway. Upon reading, she was thrilled to have found "such a clear articulation of women's rights that was coming from a faith perspective" and told herself: "Yes, I am a Muslim suffragette!"[49] This story indicates how the feminism the activist encountered immediately made sense to her because it was religiously informed (inspired by Christianity) and provided a model for a parallel endeavor in Islam.

This openness toward "foreign" concepts allows these activists to move beyond what American scholar Gisela Webb calls a "siege mentality." Webb points out that such a mentality is one of the unfortunate consequences of misrepresentations of Muslims in the West and that it contributes, in turn, to an "occidentalist" view that perpetuates "othering" constructs focused on Western immorality, greed, and brute force. The dichotomous categorization of "Islam versus the West" results in monolithic constructions that efface the complex nature of realities and multiple ethical discourses prevalent in both Muslim and Western societies.[50] The advocates I worked with represent instead an "interpretative community" that rejects such a dichotomous outlook and builds meaning in conversation with a variety of religious and secular constituencies.[51] This in turn allows them to build coalitions with non-Muslim groups while expanding their ethical repertoire and at the same time holding tight to their Islamic worldviews.

The creation of alliances, exchanges, and mutually enriching interactions among Muslim and non-Muslim women was spearheaded by the emerging field of Islamic feminist theology in the United States, within which, I claim, the work of the organizations under study should be positioned. All the interviewees emphasized that their worldviews and moral stances are derived first and foremost from the Qur'an, but they also mentioned, as a source of inspiration for their activism, the work of Muslim feminist scholars such as Fatima Mernissi,[52] Aziza al-Hibri,[53] Zahra Ayubi,[54] Riffat Hassan, and Sa'diyya Shaikh.[55] This field of Islamic feminist theology, concerned primarily with reinterpreting Islamic traditions from feminist perspectives, is in part the product of a fruitful dialogue among Jewish, Christian, Muslim, and secular scholars. For example, Sa'diyya Shaikh, whose academic work informs the activism of HEART, uses the concept of "multiple critique" introduced by feminist scholar miriam cooke, which entails a multi-headed approach based on a simultaneous critique of the many communities and discourses in which Muslims find themselves positioned.[56] Further, in reconstructing her own genealogy, Shaikh recalls the impact imprinted on her thinking by Denise Ackermann, a leading Anglican feminist theologian, and by her participation, under Ackermann's mentorship, in the Circle of Concerned African Women Theologians, a continental interfaith group founded by Ghanaian theologian Mercy Amba Oduyoye. These two intellectual experiences provided Shaikh with tools for the critical analysis of gender power relations.[57] Azizah al-Hibri, the founder of KARAMAH, references African American Christian feminist theology by adopting the term "womanism" to describe her re-reading of the Qur'an.[58] Like Jewish and Christian feminist theologians, the theologians who inspire the organizations under study use the concept of "herstory" (the recovery of important female figures, their activism, and their literary production) to rediscover the role of women in religious traditions.[59] They also embrace a "hermeneutics of suspicion"—a phrase coined by Catholic feminist theologian Elisabeth Schüssler Fiorenza—and call for the reinterpretation of the Qur'an in the light of the experience of Muslim women and queer Muslims. In doing so, they criticize the treatment of cisgender, heterosexual men's experience as normative.[60]

One of the most striking aspects of the influence of Islamic feminist theology on the organizations under study is the fact that the latter treat women's experiences as epistemology. This methodological stance, when applied to the issue of reproductive justice, hinges in particular on Saʿdiyya Shaikh's notion of "*tafsīr* of praxis" and on Zahra Ayubi's and Ingrid Mattson's questioning of male-dominated *fiqh* as the sole source of reasoning regarding medical ethics in Islam. Shaikh, in examining the ethical and exegetical dilemmas of South African Muslim women confronted with spousal abuse, contends that the experiences of the women, and their subsequent grappling with Qur'anic verses such as 4:34 ("Those [women] whose *nushūz* [disagreement between husband and wife] you fear, admonish them, and abandon them in bed, and strike them") constitute a form of *tafsīr* that is separate from the textual and patriarchal approaches of men in the Muslim communities these women are part of.[61] Drawing on feminist theory on experience and female subjectivity, she claims that Muslim feminist exegetes of the Qur'an can utilize this practical approach to challenge patriarchal interpretations. Zahra Ayubi[62] and Ingrid Mattson[63] instead argue for the incorporation into *fiqh* of other considerations such as spiritual matters and the circumstances of the life of a woman to decide about medical procedures, including abortion. The driving framework of discourse, their argument goes, should not be exclusively juridical, but also ethical and philosophical. The incorporation of women's experiences and concerns into medical ethics would counterbalance the narrowly theoretical and male-biased attitude of the jurists.

This approach is reflected in HEART's digital handout on what to do when seeking an abortion and in the interviewees' claim that the "decision of getting an abortion is between a woman and God."[64] HEART invites women to ask themselves the following questions when trying to decide to terminate: What medical information do you need? What are your religious and spiritual values? What is the geography and sociopolitical context you live in? Do you have access to the necessary insurance or funds needed for abortion? Who are the people you can trust? How will the decision impact your personal mental, spiritual, and physical health?[65] This series of questions demonstrates a more nuanced and gender-sensitive way of dealing with abortion that moves beyond the dichotomous *haram-halal* style of thinking and the prefabricated responses regurgitated by the jurists. Along these lines, one interviewee claimed: "We should not conflate the legality and morality of abortion. Abortion should be legal in the United States so that women can have the freedom to decide about the morality of terminating a pregnancy in consultation with their legal and spiritual advisors and based on their life circumstances and their legal stance."[66] Like the digital handout, this quote indicates that, although *fiqh* remains a starting point for reflections on ethical behavior, activists do not consider *fiqh* regulations as the only element to be taken into account when deciding about abortion.

For the advocates in these organizations, making religiously informed ethical decisions regarding medical procedures presupposes a secular law. All the interviewees claimed that they see no tensions between Qur'anic values and the values enshrined in the American Constitution and Declaration of Independence and that they perceive secularism as fundamentally compatible with Islamic teachings because the Qur'an gives people the freedom to believe or not to believe. One interviewee stated: "Of course, we see the abortion ban as an infringement of religious freedom. We all know that this country was founded by people who were escaping religious persecution and who established secularism to protect freedom or religion from the encroachment of the state. The plurality and multivocality of shari'a law also entail that no legal opinion can prevail over another and obviously this means we need a secular law."[67] In a TED Talk titled "Islam: As American as Apple Pie," Ani Zonneveld, the founder of Muslims for Progressive Values, stresses that the establishment of justice—mentioned fifty-two times in the Qur'an—and the pursuit of happiness are what makes Islam "American."[68] Along the same lines, one interviewee claimed:

These issues [related to reproductive rights] are relevant to us because we are Americans. We are an American organization that happens to be Muslim. This means that our relationship to this country is defined by our citizenship, not by our religion. So, it is really important for us as Muslims living in America to understand the common denominator: there is justice, there is the pursuit of happiness, the pursuit of lineage, and the pursuit of property rights. There are principles of the Declaration of Independence and are also the *maqaṣid al-shari'ā* (objectives of the *shari'ā*).[69] Within this framework, we believe that depriving women of their bodily autonomy is against American and Islamic values because it means depriving them of their happiness.[70]

The ease and instinctiveness with which these activists can translate Islamic concepts into American values, and vice versa, is one more element that contributes to their ability to build intersectional and interfaith coalitions while achieving a balance between identity and solidarity.

Finally, some attention needs to be paid to how the organizations under study conceptualize their own identity. The emphasis they place on *ijtihad* (independent reasoning), *khilafa* (individual moral agency before God), the impossibility of reaching a definitive interpretation of the law, and the interconnectedness of ethical stances and subjective experiences all point to the multivocality of Islam as a central tenet in their worldview. This way of embodying Islam as a dynamic interpretation rather than static dogma, coupled with an awareness of power dynamics and relations of privilege and oppression within Muslim communities (see their discussion on the care for the oppressed), indicates an understanding of Muslim identity as intersectional, varied, and in motion. This, I claim, is the third element that facilitates these Muslim activists' participation in interfaith and interracial alliances. The work of Anna Carastathis on identity categories in potential coalitions represents a useful tool to grasp the political implications of the organizations' understanding of their Muslim identity.[71] Drawing from the thought of Kimberlé Williams Crenshaw[72] and embracing an intersectional critique of identity, Carastathis claims that "identity remains a useful basis for political organizing as long as identity categories are conceptualized as coalitions"— that is, as an amalgam of positionalities that come together not through similarity and seclusion, but through difference and confrontation.[73] Viewing identities as plural enables envisioning "movements premised on finding the interconnections of struggles by forming relationships of accountability and compassion across lines of difference and dominance internal as well as external to group identities."[74] Recognizing groups as internally heterogeneous does not mean that members of a social group have nothing in common with one another, or that their experiences are entirely unique. Rather, it means to focus simultaneously on intragroup and intergroup differences and to avoid the pitfall of thinking about groups in essentialist terms.[75] One of the interviewees clearly expressed the relevance of coalition-building and of acknowledging multiplicity within groups. She stated: "There is not one Islam in Islam. We all come from a variety of perspectives and cultural backgrounds. We realize that it is the same for other religions as well, and they understand this about us. So, collaborating with different religious communities has actually been pretty easy because the purpose is to maintain this diversity and to make sure that each member of all of our communities can act upon it."[76] Thus, the recognition of differences *within* communities is pivotal in the creation of forms of solidarity that embrace differences *across* communities.

Conclusion

In this chapter I have shown how American Muslim organizations that opposed the *Dobbs* decision have developed arguments in favor of reproductive justice that combine Islamic legal and moral stances with non-Islamic approaches to sexual ethics and reproductive health. Moreover, I have claimed that they were able to build networks of solidarity with non-Muslims thanks to three interlocking systems of thought: their incorporation of the teachings of Muslim feminist theologians into their religious interpretations and sociopolitical activism, their endorsement of feminism and secularism, and their understanding of their own communities as coalitions of multiple voices.

The discourses and the educational, social, and legal initiatives of the organizations under study represent the turning into practice of the normative claims Muslim feminist scholars have been making over the past decades. The two most striking features of this intellectual legacy are the centering of women's experiences in the interpretation of the Qur'an and the application of *fiqh*, and the construction of meaning in dialogue with non-Muslim feminist thinkers and women's movements (see, for example, the adoption of the reproductive justice framework developed by Loretta Ross and the support for the Southern Birth Justice Network's initiatives). This methodological approach, coupled with the activists' endorsement of secularism and foundational American values, allows them to argue in favor of reproductive rights simultaneously from inside and outside of Islam and to develop a repertoire of ethical stances that, while rooted in Islam, can transcend Islam. Moreover, following Anna Carastathis, I claim that the organizations under study conceptualize Muslim identity "coalitionally," that is, as marked by internal differences and dissonances as well as by internal and external relations of power. This awareness of, and appreciation for, heterogeneousness shields them from the dangers of political alliances premised on homogeneous or essential identities, against which intersectionality as a political project warns us.

Such narratives and initiatives, while still on the fringes of the national political discourse, have the potential to produce expressions of social responsibility, a commitment to secularism and pluralism, as well as political alliances that surpass race, gender, class, and religion. A secular state, founded on the necessity of negotiating differences, is a central tenet of this political project, and a prerequisite for Muslims to practice Islam properly, that is, according to the dictates of their conscience and without state imposition. Moreover, precisely because of the recognition of both religious diversity and diversity within religions, this approach can fortify ethical thinking. The care for the oppressed envisioned by the organizers fosters a feeling of connection with the Other that recognizes alterity. In this sense, it is a seed that carries the possibility of moving towards political coalitions where a sense of "otherness" is celebrated and not erased and where the religious self is built relationally, in solidarity with the religious Other.

Notes

1 Sarah Mushtaq, "Enough with the Islamophobic Takes on Abortion." *Tvo Today*, July 6, 2022, https://www.tvo.org/article/enough-with-the-islamophobic-takes-on -abortion.

2 Mike Luckvovic (@mluckovicajc), "Pray for Texas Women," X, September 1, 2021, https://twitter.com/mluckovichajc/status/1433169465806622720.

3 EJ Montini, "Texas Goes Taliban on Abortion Rights. Is Arizona Next?" *Az Central*, September 1, 2021, https://www.azcentral.com/story/opinion/op

-ed/ej-montini/2021/09/01/texas-abortion-law-supreme-court-arizona-next
/5683457001/.

4 Alejandra Molina, "Comparing Texas' Abortion Ban to Islamic is Inaccurate, Perpetuates Islamophobia, Experts Say," *Religion News Service*, September 3, 2021, https://religionnews.com/2021/09/03/texas-abortion-ban-comparisons-to -islamic-law-are-innacurate-and-perpetuate-islamophobia-experts-say/.

5 "Religious Landscape Study: Views about Abortion," Pew Research Center, https://www.pewresearch.org/religion/religious-landscape-study/views-about -abortion#views-about-abortion (accessed March 21, 2024).

6 "The Majority of American Muslims Believe Abortion Should Be Legal in All or Most Cases," American Muslim Poll, https://www.ispu.org/2022-abortion-data/ (accessed March 21, 2024).

7 KARAMAH (dignity) is a reference to the Qur'anic verse: "We have given dignity (*karamah*) to the Children of Adam" (Q. 17:70), https://karamah.org/about/ #mission-vision (accessed August 13, 2024).

8 All the organizations under study promote women's rights and LGBTQI+ rights, including sexual and reproductive rights, from a Muslim perspective. Except for KARAMAH, which was founded by Muslim feminist theologian Azizah al-Hibri, all the organizations were founded and are run by human rights activists and lawyers. KARAMAH, HEART, and Muslims for Progressive Values, have nevertheless advisory boards comprised of academics. They all endorse very progressive Muslim values, and some of their positions, particularly those of Queer Crescent, are not mainstream among American Muslims. Taken together, however, these organizations represent a growing movement within the American Muslim community, and many of their initiatives to enhance women's rights, for example, through cooperating with religious leaders and through using the vernacular of Islam, have been successful both in the United States and in Muslim countries. Finally, while interfaith dialogue is not the primary focus of any of these organizations, they all cooperate with non-Muslim actors on a variety of issues and on an ad-hoc basis. WISE Women and Muslims for Progressive Values, in particular, have a long history of interfaith community engagement.

9 None of the interviewees were scholars; three were lawyers and three were human rights activists; two were born in Muslim countries and emigrated to the United States in their youth; four were second-generation Muslim immigrants born in the United States; five identified as women and one identified as a man.

10   Interview no. 3, November 3, 2023.

11   Leila Hessini, "Abortion and Islam: Policies and Practices in the Middle East and North Africa," *Reproductive Health Matters* 15, no. 29 (2007): 75–84; Sachedina Abdulaziz, *Islamic Biomedical Ethics: Principles and Applications* (Oxford: Oxford University Press, 2009).

12   Hessini, "Abortion"; Abdulaziz, *Islamic Biomedical Ethics.*

13   The following verse is used to support that claim: "And among His Signs is this that He created for you mates from among your-selves that you might find tranquility with them, and He has put love and mercy between your (hearts); verily in that are Signs for those who reflect" (Qur'an 30:21, quoted in Religious Coalition for Reproductive Choice, "Islam and Reproductive Choice"; HEART, "*Roe v Wade* Statement").

14   For example, Q. 17:31 says: "Kill not your children for fear of want: We shall provide sustenance for them as well as for you: verily the killing of them is a great sin."

15   "Islam and Reproductive Choice," Religious Coalition for Reproductive Choice, https://rcrc.org/muslim/ (accessed March 21, 2024); "MPV's Stance on Reproductive Justice," Muslims for Progressive Values, https://www.mpvusa.org/reproductive-justice (accessed March 21, 2024).

16   Religious Coalition for Reproductive Choice, "Islam"; Muslims for Progressive Values, "MPV's Stance."

17   Religious Coalition for Reproductive Choice, "Islam"; Muslims for Progressive Values, "MPV's Stance."

18   Muslims for Progressive Values, "MPV's Stance."

19   Interview no. 2, November 1, 2023; interview no. 3; interview no. 5, November 9, 2023.

20   "*Roe v. Wade* Statement," HEART, https://hearttogrow.org/roe-v-wade-statement/ (accessed March 21, 2024); "Reproductive Justice Fund," HEART, https://hearttogrow.org/learn-more-about-hearts-rj-fund/; Muslims for Progressive Values, "MPV's Stance" (accessed March 21, 2024).

21   The same logic is applied to the vocabulary used around issues concerning LGBTQI+ rights in Islam. Interview no. 2, November 1, 2023; interview no. 3, November 3, 2023; interview no. 5, November 7, 2023.

22   Muslims for Progressive Values, "MPV's Stance."

23   "MPV's statement on *Dobbs vs Jackson*," Muslims for Progressive Values, https://www.mpvusa.org/reproductive-justice (accessed March 21, 2024).

24   Muslims for Progressive Values, "MPV's Stance."

25 Muslims for Progressive Values, "MPV's Stance."

26 "About Us," Hurma Project, https://hurmaproject.com/about-us/ (accessed March 21, 2024).

27 Interview no. 4, November 6, 2023; HEART, "Reproductive Justice Fund."

28 Interview no. 3, HEART, "Reproductive Justice Fund."

29 "Responding with RAHMA: Removing Roadblocks for Muslim Survivors of Sexual Violence," Hurma Project, https://hurmaproject.com/wp-content/uploads/2021/03/Responding-with-RAHMA-Removing-Roadblocks.pdf (accessed March 21, 2024).

30 HEART, "Reproductive Justice Fund"; "The Islamic Principle of *Rahma*: A Call for Reproductive Justice," AMBA Legal, https://www.ambalegal.org/ambainthenews/the-islamic-principle-of-rahma-a-call-for-reproductive-justice (accessed March 21, 2024).

31 Interview no. 6, January 12, 2024.

32 Abed Awad, "Alabama's Abortion Law Is Not 'Christian Sharia', Professor Says. Shari'a Isn't as Inflexible as Draconian," *NJ.com True Jersey*, May 23, 2019; https://www.nj.com/opinion/2019/05/alabamas-abortion-law-is-not-christian-sharia-professor-says-sharia-isnt-as-inflexible-as-draconian.html; Molina, "Comparing Texas' Abortion Law"; https://religionnews.com/2021/09/03/texas-abortion-ban-comparisons-to-islamic-law-are-innacurate-and-perpetuate-islamophobia-experts-say/ (accessed August 13, 2024); Muslimgirl, "Why Muslims Must Oppose the Abortion Ban," https://muslimgirl.com/why-muslims-must-oppose-the-abortion-ban/ (accessed March 21, 2024); "Amicus Brief for Whole Woman's Health vs Hellerstedt," Amici Curiae, https://www.supremecourt.gov/DocketPDF/18/18-1323/124071/20191202140741883_2019-12-2%2018-1460%20WWH%20amici%20Final.pdf (accessed March 21, 2024); "Amicus Brief for *Dobbs vs Jackson*," Amici Curiae, https://www.supremecourt.gov/DocketPDF/19/19-1392/192909/20210920125441954_191392%20Thomas%20E%20Dobbs%20v%20Jackson%20Womens%20Health%20Brief%20of%20Amici%20in%20Support.pdf (accessed March 21, 2024); interview no. 1, October 31, 2023; interview no. 2.

33 Awad, "Alabama Abortion Law"; Muslimgirl, "Why Muslims Must Oppose"; interviews no. 1 and 2.

34 HEART, "*Roe v. Wade*."

35 AMBA Legal, "The Islamic Principle."

36 Interviews no. 1, 3, and 6.

37	Loretta Ross, "Conceptualizing Reproductive Justice Theory: A Manifesto for Activism," in *Radical Reproductive Justice: Foundations, Theory, Practice, Critique*, ed. Loretta Ross, Lynn Roberts, Erika Derkas, Whitney Peoples, and Pamela Bridgewater (New York: Feminist Press at City University of New York, 2017), 170–232; Sistersong, "Reproductive Justice," https://www.sistersong.net/reproductive-justice (accessed March 21, 2024).

38	HEART, "Reproductive Justice Fund."

39	AMBA Legal, "The Islamic Principle."

40	"Campaigns," Black Midwives Alliance, https://blackmidwivesalliance.org/campaigns (accessed March 21, 2024).

41	Interviews no. 1 and 3.

42	See for example, Leila Ahmed, *Women and Gender in Islam* (New Haven, CT: Yale University Press, 1992); Zahra Ayubi, "Authority and Epistemology in Islamic Medical Ethics of Women's Reproductive Health," *Journal of Religious Ethics* 49, no. 2 (2021): 245–69.

43	Introduced in January 2023 in the US House of Representatives, the Equal Access to Abortion Coverage in Health Insurance (EACH) Act, aims at removing bans on abortion coverage for Federal Health Programs.

44	Introduced in June 2023 in the US House of Representatives, the Women's Health Protection Act (WHPA) aims at reestablishing a nationwide right to abortion after *Roe.*

45	Reintroduced in May 2023 in the US House of Representatives, the Black Maternal Health Momnibus Act addresses the crisis of the high maternal mortality rate in the United States through investments that comprehensively address every driver of maternal mortality, morbidity, and disparity in the United States.

46	Amici Curiae, "Amicus Brief for *Whole Woman's Health vs Hellerstedt*," https://www.supremecourt.gov/DocketPDF/18/18-1323/124071/20191202140741883_2019-12-2%20181460%20WWH%20amici%20Final.pdf (accessed March 21, 2024).

47	Amici Curiae, "Amicus Brief for *Dobbs vs Jackson*," https://www.supremecourt.gov/DocketPDF/19/19-1392/192909/20210920125441954_19-1392%20Thomas%20E%20Dobbs%20v%20Jackson%20Womens%20Health%20Brief%20of%20Amici%20in%20Support.._.pdf (accessed March 21, 2024).

48 Saʿdiyya Shaikh, "Transforming Feminisms: Islam, Women, and Gender Justice," in *Progressive Muslims: On Justice, Gender, and Pluralism*, ed. Omid Safi (Oxford: Oneworld, 2003), 146–62.

49 Interview no. 6.

50 Gisela Webb, "Teaching Islam as a World Religion to Undergraduates: Challenges and Opportunities in the Age of Globalization and Multiculturalism," *Religion and Education* 25 (1998): 1–2.

51 Julianne Hammer, "Activism as Embodied Tafsīr: Negotiating Women's Authority, Leadership, and Space in North America," in *Women, Leadership, and Mosques: Changes in Contemporary Islamic Authority*, ed. Masooda Bano and Hilary E. Kalmbach (Leiden: Brill, 2011), 457–80.

52 Interview no. 2.

53 Interview no. 1.

54 Interview no. 3.

55 Interviews no. 4 and 5.

56 Shaikh, "Transforming Feminisms."

57 Shaikh, "Transforming Feminisms."

58 Aysha Hidaytullah, "Muslim Feminist Theology in the United States," in *Muslima Theology: The Voices of Muslim Women Theologians*, ed. Ednan Aslan, Marcia Hermansen, and Elif Medeni (Frankfurt: Peter Lang Edition, 2013), 81–99.

59 Azizah al-Hibri, "A Study of Islamic Herstory: Or How Did We Ever Get into This Mess?" *Women's Studies International Forum* 5, no. 1 (1982): 212–15; AMBA Legal, "The Islamic Principle."

60 Marcia Hermansen, "Introduction: The New Voices of Muslim Women Theologians," in *Muslima Theology: The Voices of Muslim Women Theologians*, ed. Ednan Aslan, Marcia Hermansen, and Elif Medeni (Frankfurt: Peter Lang Edition, 2013), 11–34; al-Hibri, "A Study of Islamic Herstory"; Hidaytullah, "Muslim Feminist Theology."

61 Saʿdiyya Shaikh, "A *Tafsīr* of Praxis: Gender, Marital Violence, and Resistance in a South African Muslim Community," in *Violence against Women in Contemporary World Religions: Roots and Cures*, ed. Daniel C. Maguire and Saʿdiyya Shaikh (Cleveland, OH: Pilgrim Press, 2007), 66–89.

62 Ayubi, "Authority and Epistemology."

63 Ingrid Mattson, "Gender and Sexuality in Islamic Bioethics," in *Islamic Bioethics: Current Issues and Challenges*, ed. Alireza Bagheri and Khalid Alali, vol. 2, 57–84 (Hackensack, NJ: World Scientific, 2018).

64　Interviews no. 3 and 4.

65　HEART, "Abortion: Terminating a Pregnancy," https://hearttogrow.org/wp -content/uploads/2021/12/Abortion-Resources.pdf (accessed March 21, 2024).

66　Interview no. 1.

67　Interview no. 1.

68　Ani Zonneveld, "Islam, as American as Apple Pie," filmed May 4, 2016, at TEDxOccidentalCollege, Los Angeles, CA, video 15:24, https://www.youtube .com/@TEDx/search?query=islam%2C%20as%20american%20as%20apple %20pie (accessed August 13, 2024).

69　The notion of *maqasid* was first clearly articulated by al-Ghazali (d. 1111), who argued that *maslaha* (common good) was God's general purpose in revealing the divine law, and that its specific aim was preservation of five essentials of human well-being: religion, life, intellect, lineage, and property.

70　Interview no. 2.

71　Anna Carastathis, "Identity Categories as Potential Coalitions," *Signs: Journal of Women in Culture and Society* 38, no. 4 (2013): 941–65.

72　Kimberlé Williams Crenshaw, "Mapping the Margins: Intersectionality, Identity, Politics, and Violence against Women of Color," *Stanford Law Review* 43, no. 6 (1991): 1241–99.

73　Carastathis, "Identity Categories," 941.

74　Carastathis, "Identity Categories," 942.

75　Carastathis, "Identity Categories," 945.

76　Interview no. 4.

References

Abdulaziz, Sachedina. *Islamic Biomedical Ethics: Principles and Applications.* Oxford: Oxford University Press, 2009.

Ahmed, Leila. *Women and Gender in Islam.* New Haven, CT: Yale University Press, 1992.

Al-Hibri, Azizah. "A Study of Islamic Herstory: Or How Did We Ever Get into This Mess?" *Women's Studies International Forum* 5, no. 1 (1982): 212–15.

AMBA Legal. "The Islamic Principle of *Rahma*: A Call for Reproductive Justice." Accessed March 21, 2024. https://www.ambalegal.org/ambainthenews/the-islamic -principle-of-rahma-a-call-for-reproductive-justice.

American Muslim Poll. "The Majority of American Muslims Believe Abortion Should Be Legal in All or Most Cases." Accessed March 21, 2024. https://www.ispu.org/2022-abortion-data/.

Amici Curiae. "Amicus Brief for *Dobbs vs Jackson.*" Accessed March 21, 2024. https://www.supremecourt.gov/DocketPDF/19/19-1392/192909/20210920125441954_19-1392%20Thomas%20E%20Dobbs%20v%20Jackson%20Womens%20Health%20Brief%20of%20Amici%20in%20Support.._.pdf.

———. "Amicus Brief for *Whole Woman's Health vs Hellerstedt.*" Accessed March 21, 2024. https://www.supremecourt.gov/DocketPDF/18/18-1323/124071/20191202140741883_2019-12-2%2018-1460%20WWH%20amici%20Final.pdf.

Ayubi, Zahra. "Muslim Biomedical Ethics and Neonatal Care: Theory, Praxis, and Authority." In *Religion and Ethics in the Neonatal Intensive Care Unit*, edited by Ronald M. Green and George A. Little, 94–109. Oxford: Oxford University Press, 2019.

———. "Authority and Epistemology in Islamic Medical Ethics of Women's Reproductive Health." *Journal of Religious Ethics* 49, no. 2 (2021): 245–69.

Awad, Abed. "Alabama's Abortion Law Is Not 'Christian Sharia', Professor Says. Shari'a Isn't as Inflexible as Draconian." *NJ.com True Jersey*, May 23, 2019. Accessed August 13, 2024. https://www.nj.com/opinion/2019/05/alabamas-abortion-law-is-not-christian-sharia-professor-says-sharia-isnt-as-inflexible-as-draconian.html.

Carastathis, Anna. "Identity Categories as Potential Coalitions." *Signs: Journal of Women in Culture and Society* 38, no. 4 (2013): 941–65.

Crenshaw, Kimberlé Williams. "Mapping the Margins: Intersectionality, Identity, Politics, and Violence against Women of Color." *Stanford Law Review* 43, no. 6 (1991): 1241–99.

Hammer, Julianne. "Activism as Embodied Tafsīr: Negotiating Women's Authority, Leadership, and Space in North America." In *Women, Leadership, and Mosques: Changes in Contemporary Islamic Authority*, edited by Masooda Bano and Hilary E. Kalmbach, 457–80. Leiden: Brill, 2011.

HEART. "Abortion: Terminating a Pregnancy." Accessed March 21, 2024. https://hearttogrow.org/wp-content/uploads/2021/12/Abortion-Resources.pdf.

———. "Reproductive Justice Fund." Accessed March 21, 2024. https://hearttogrow.org/learn-more-about-hearts-rj-fund/.

———. "*Roe v. Wade* Statement." Accessed March 21, 2024. https://hearttogrow.org/roe-v-wade-statement/.

Hermansen, Marcia. "Introduction: The New Voices of Muslim Women Theologians." In *Muslima Theology: The Voices of Muslim Women Theologians*, edited by Ednan

Aslan, Marcia Hermansen, and Elif Medeni, 11–34. Frankfurt: Peter Lang Edition, 2013.

Hessini, Leila. "Abortion and Islam: Policies and Practices in the Middle East and North Africa." *Reproductive Health Matters* 15, no. 29 (2007): 75–84.

Hidaytullah, Aysha. "Muslim Feminist Theology in the United States." In *Muslima Theology: The Voices of Muslim Women Theologians*, edited by Ednan Aslan, Marcia Hermansen, and Elif Medeni, 81–99. Frankfurt: Peter Lang Edition, 2013.

Hurma Project. "Responding with RAHMA: Removing Roadblocks for Muslim Survivors of Sexual Violence." Accessed March 21, 2024. https://hurmaproject .com/wp-content/uploads/2021/03/Responding-with-RAHMA-Removing -Roadblocks.pdf.

Luckvovic, Mike (@mluckovicajc). "Pray for Texas Women," X, September 1, 2021. Accessed August 13, 2024. https://twitter.com/mluckovichajc/status /14331694658066222720.

Mattson, Ingrid. "Gender and Sexuality in Islamic Bioethics." In *Islamic Bioethics: Current Issues and Challenges*, edited by Alireza Bagheri and Khalid Alali, vol. 2, 57–84. Hackensack, NJ: World Scientific, 2018.

Molina, Alejandra. "Comparing Texas' Abortion Ban to Islamic is Inaccurate, Perpetuates Islamophobia, Experts Say." *Religion News Service*, September 3, 2021. Accessed August 13, 2024. https://religionnews.com/2021/09/03/texas-abortion -ban-comparisons-to-islamic-law-are-innacurate-and-perpetuate-islamophobia -experts-say/.

———. "On Abortion, Muslim Americans Say Islamic History Is on the Side of Mercy." *Washington Post*, June 24, 2022. Accessed August 13, 2024. https://www .washingtonpost.com/religion/2022/06/24/abortion-muslim-americans-say -islamic-history-is-side-mercy/.

Montini, EJ. "Texas Goes Taliban on Abortion Rights. Is Arizona Next?" *Az Central*, September 1, 2021. Accessed August 13, 2024. https://www.azcentral.com/story/ opinion/op-ed/ej-montini/2021/09/01/texas-abortion-law-supreme-court-arizona -next/5683457001/.

Mushtaq, Sarah. "Enough with the Islamophobic Takes on Abortion." *Tvo Today*, July 6, 2022. Accessed August 13, 2024. https://www.tvo.org/article/enough-with-the -islamophobic-takes-on-abortion.

Muslimgirl. "Why Muslims Must Oppose the Abortion Ban." Accessed March 21, 2024. https://muslimgirl.com/why-muslims-must-oppose-the-abortion-ban/.

———. "Why We Need to Stop Trying to Overturn *Roe v Wade*." Accessed March 21, 2024. https://muslimgirl.com/why-we-need-to-stop-overruling-roe-v-wade/.

Muslims for Progressive Values. "MPV's Stance on Reproductive Justice." Accessed March 21, 2024. https://www.mpvusa.org/reproductive-justice.

———. "MPV's Statement on *Dobbs vs Jackson*." Accessed March 21, 2024. https://www.mpvusa.org/reproductive-justice.

Pew Research Center. "Religious Landscape Study: Views about Abortion." Accessed March 21, 2024. https://www.pewresearch.org/religion/religious-landscape-study/views-about-abortion#views-about-abortion.

Religious Coalition for Reproductive Choice. "Islam and Reproductive Choice." Accessed March 21, 2024. https://rcrc.org/muslim/.

Ross, Loretta. "Conceptualizing Reproductive Justice Theory: A Manifesto for Activism." In *Radical Reproductive Justice: Foundations, Theory, Practice, Critique*, edited by Loretta Ross, Lynn Roberts, Erika Derkas, Whitney Peoples, and Pamela Bridgewater, 170–232. New York: The Feminist Press at City University of New York, 2017.

Shaikh, Sa'diyya. "Embracing the *Barzakh*: Knowledge, Being, and Ethics." *Journal for Islamic Studies* 39, no. 1 (2021): 28–48.

———. "Exegetical Violence: *Nushūz* in Quranic Gender Ideology." *Journal for Islamic Studies* 17, no. 1 (1997): 49–73.

———. "A *Tafsīr* of Praxis: Gender, Marital Violence, and Resistance in a South African Muslim Community." In *Violence against Women in Contemporary World Religions: Roots and Cures*, edited by Daniel C. Maguire and Sa'diyya Shaikh, 66–89. Cleveland: Pilgrim Press, 2007.

———. "Transforming Feminisms: Islam, Women, and Gender Justice." In *Progressive Muslims: On Justice, Gender, and Pluralism*, edited by Omid Safi, 147–62. Oxford: Oneworld, 2003.

Webb, Gisela. "Teaching Islam as a World Religion to Undergraduates: Challenges and Opportunities in the Age of Globalization and Multiculturalism," *Religion and Education*, 25 (1998): 1–2.

Zonneveld, Ani. "Islam, as American as Apple Pie," filmed May 4, 2016, at TEDxOccidentalCollege, Los Angeles, CA, video 15:24. Accessed August 13, 2024. https://www.youtube.com/@TEDx/search?query=islam%2C%20as%20american%20as%20apple%20pie.

9

Solidarity and Ethics of Care

Muslim Feminist Reflections on Sexual Violence and on Palestine

Juliane Hammer

What is solidarity in the face of genocide? As I write this question in February 2024, more than thirty thousand Palestinians have been killed by the Israeli army, with hundreds of thousands more displaced, starving, dying of thirst and lack of even basic medical care, exposed to the elements, and further bombings without shelter and aid. What can I do in this darkness? Do words even make sense? Do they mean anything, do anything? I channel my grief and rage into these pages, not to offer profound theoretical insights or sophisticated analysis but to bear witness and as a promise that I will not stop talking about Palestine. We are watching ethnic cleansing and genocide in real time and most of us are powerless to stop it. The magnitude of human suffering and loss, especially in Gaza, is hard to comprehend.

I come from a Palestine studies background, a field that I reluctantly shifted away from when I moved to the United States in 2002 as even then, American academia was quite hostile to an academic focus on Palestine and Palestinians. I lived in the West Bank for both my master's and PhD research projects in the 1990s and wrote my first book, *Palestinians Born in Exile*, about Palestinians as well. The connecting piece between Palestine studies and the study of US Muslim communities with a focus on gender and sexuality was an interest in US Muslim organizations that engaged in pro-Palestinian solidarity work: in the early 2000s, American Muslims for Jerusalem; since 2006, American Muslims for Palestine. My work in and about US Muslim communities has moved from exploring feminist Qur'anic exegesis and the debate about woman-led prayer to how Muslims organize efforts against gender-based violence (GBV) in their communities and families.

While my work is not theologically normative, I have been a feminist longer than I have been a Muslim. I also grew up in a socialist country (the German Democratic Republic) and have always had a particular attachment to the concept of solidarity. It felt self-evident to me that solidarity meant affirming everyone's right to fight for justice and to recognize that social justice struggles are interconnected, or in the words of Fannie Lou Hamer, "but the changes we have to have . . . are going to be for liberation of all people—because nobody's free until everybody's free."[1] Socialist internationalism was still a big deal when I was growing up and I have found it easy to connect my commitment to justice as active and activist to my understanding of the fight for justice in this world as an ethical imperative and impulse at the heart of (my) Islam. Activism as a critique of what is and as a struggle for something different is by its very nature normative, even if not framed as traditional theological normativity. Thus, I have been studying activism and movement-building toward world-changing for a very long time, and I have been an activist and then a scholar-activist for even longer. And that activism has always included Palestine and Palestinian liberation.

When I wrote an essay on intersectional solidarity and religion in 2020, which focused on the Muslim activist leaders in the 2017 Women's March and the specter of Palestine, I wanted to resist the idea that solidarity can be broken, can fail, or even have limits and thus be conditional. The volume the essay appeared in ended up being called *Religion and Broken Solidarities*, but I saw myself highlighting the centrality of the notion of solidarity for the Women's March by refusing to take its meaning for granted.[2] Instead of deciding whether the Women's March was an example of failed or unrealized solidarity, or alternatively celebrating it as the epitome of feminist and intersectional solidarity, I considered the history of the march as an opening toward further reflection on solidarity, movement and coalition building, and accountability. As I look around in 2024, especially in feminist circles and networks, I wonder whether it is in fact "solidarity except for Palestine" that we are seeing in sharp relief in this historical moment.

Since 2020, I have been working on a participatory research project with a US Muslim organization, HEART to Grow, which was founded in 2009 in Chicago by a group of Muslim women of color to address issues of sexual abuse in Muslim communities and to offer Islamically framed sex education to Muslims in the United States. HEART's commitment to justice as an Islamic ethical principle and core value encompasses feminism, intersectionality, anti-racism, and queer inclusivity as active solidarity with those most marginalized in ways that align with my own values. Working with HEART has been an inspiration and a continuing lesson in how to practice both solidarity and care.[3]

In the time since October 7, 2023, I have continued to research sexual violence and efforts against it in Muslim communities, while also bearing witness to the slaughter of Palestinians in Gaza, and raising awareness of both issues in my teaching, scholarship, and activism. The political climate in the United States and in my native Germany is oppressive toward those demanding a ceasefire and even more so toward those who insist on protesting more than seventy-five years of Israeli dispossession of Palestinians, denying them land, statehood, and recognition as human beings. Palestine solidarity work has always carried risks, and we are fighting for Palestinian lives and freedom under the constant threat of being accused of antisemitism, which has had practical consequences for many. In what follows, I connect my work on and against sexual violence in Muslim communities with Palestine solidarity work and point to several parallels and overlaps that strike me as important as we consider how to do the work of intersectional solidarity and movement building for the liberation of all of us.

Before I share my reflections on these parallels, I need to acknowledge and name the fact that in both arenas, anti-Muslim hostility and racism loom large. Working against GBV in Muslim communities puts activists and scholars in a double bind "between imperialism and gender injustice," as Rochelle Terman has put it. "In an age of Islamophobia, how does one engage in a feminist critique of women's status in Muslim contexts without providing ideological fuel for undesired political ambitions? When the United States invokes the oppression of Muslim women to justify war, how do we practice feminist solidarity without strengthening orientalism and imperialism?"[4] Similarly, advocating for Palestinian survival and liberation is often represented as synonymous with antisemitism rather than as a critique of Israeli policies, denying the possibility and indeed necessity of responsible and multiple critiques. It has turned out to be rather difficult, even in academic contexts, to convince people that gender-based injustices in Muslim contexts and anti-Muslim racism are not mutually exclusive. Why else do we have to name anti-Muslim hostility as so pervasive that it is always already in the room with us, as much as GBV is always present, with both survivors and perpetrators in our midst? In addition, anti-Palestinian and anti-Arab racism overlap with anti-Muslim hostility in both discourse and practice.

In what follows, I focus on three parallel challenges in work against sexual violence and Palestine solidarity work that are worth pondering together even if they are not the same: silence and silencing, the demand for perfect victims, and the focus on perpetrators of violence.

HEART to Grow and Ethics of Care

HEART is an acronym that stands for "health education, advocacy, research and training," and the work of the organization since its inception in 2009 has revolved around core values including compassion, justice, accountability, and gratitude, as well as humility and empathy. The organization works "to promote sexual health, uproot gendered violence, and advance reproductive justice by establishing choice and access for the most impacted Muslims."[5]

HEART offers workshops and training across the United States, including the training of young Muslim leaders in Muslim sexual health and sex education, in Muslim communities and on college campuses especially. The organization also offers direct support and services to Muslim survivors of sexual violence. In response to the 2022 US Supreme Court decision that overturned the 1973 *Roe v. Wade* ruling and thus limited abortion access in the United States by moving regulation of abortion from the federal to the state level, HEART expanded its efforts to include reproductive justice frameworks, awareness work, and financial support for Muslims seeking abortion access. HEART has participated in solidarity networks with other organizations, especially of women of color, such as SisterSong,[6] to further joint work on reproductive justice issues and GBV.

Late in October 2023, HEART announced the creation of the "INAYA Care Fund" ("Inaya" means care in Arabic) and posted the following description on its social media channels:

> As a team dedicated to care work, we heard your stories. We grieved with the families impacted by the siege on Gaza and the West Bank, and asked ourselves "how can we help?" Our answer: The INAYA Care Fund.
>
> The INAYA Care Fund is a grassroots fund for US-based Muslims in need of financial assistance as they navigate grief, organizing, and transitions. We aim to connect those seeking help with an ummah of accomplices motivated to show up with love. This fund will increase our communities' capacity to mourn and respond to violence by prioritizing our grief, care, and wellness. Individuals in our community are emotionally exhausted from the loss of loved ones, constant organizing, and impacts of retaliation. With your help, we can bridge the resource gap and ensure every call for help is met with action. Anyone can engage with this project: whether you're directly impacted or wanting to show solidarity, there is room in this movement for you![7]

It is this announcement that inspired the notion of "ethics of care" in the title of this chapter. The HEART advocates clearly see an organic link between work against GBV that centers on support and care for survivors of such violence and the ongoing trauma of genocide in Palestine for Palestinians around the globe. For me, HEART's work is a model of feminist and Muslim solidarity work, guided by an ethic of care and by their focus on those most affected by violence. Rather than putting HEART at the center of my research as a research subject, I am continuously learning from them as both activists and producers of knowledge who model world-changing and radical empathy and solidarity.

Silence and Silencing

From the outset, HEART has identified "silence" as a significant issue and as one of the reasons the founders of the organization came together. In the brief history of the organization's website, they write:

For years, they had heard Muslims covertly share their stories and struggles with sex, relationships, and all too often, sexual violence. They often spoke of not having access to culturally-sensitive information and resources, and many more expressed their fears and apprehension about seeking out existing resources and services because of the shame and stigma associated with discussing sex and sexual violence in their communities. Though very different with respect to race, socioeconomic status, geography, and day-to-day religious practice, these individuals shared something in common: many desired to have greater access to resources and language to think critically about their bodies, sexual violence, and faith and how it all intersects. Often, they navigated these life experiences alone, and in silence.

This silence is unjust and contributes to the gender inequities and violence in our communities. At the root of this silence is decades of systemic oppression: patriarchy, racism, white supremacy, classism, and Islamophobia, which has enabled gender inequities and gender-based violence to continue.[8]

In light of my earlier remarks on anti-Muslim hostility it is worth mentioning that sexual violence in Muslim communities is not "special" but is rather one part of a broad and all-pervasive set of systemic issues—so much of what I say here holds true for the rest of our society. Some of my insights are inspired by other scholars and advocates in the "Religion and Sexual Abuse Project" who work in and on other religious communities.[9]

The silence around sexual violence in and beyond Muslim communities is loud once a person becomes aware of its existence. Often, this silence is manufactured and enforced by expending significant effort, because once the silence is broken and sexual violence is acknowledged, individuals, communities, and institutions can no longer ignore its existence and need to respond. Our communities are split between those who have experienced or witnessed sexual violence and those who claim to have no knowledge of its existence, let alone its prevalence. Recognizing sexual violence might mean confronting perpetrators in our midst, affirming and supporting survivors, and considering the systemic nature of its causes.

HEART's approach to sexual violence is explicitly survivor-centered and includes both communal and societal awareness work and care efforts, always most concerned with those most marginalized, in Muslim communities and beyond. They have developed three interconnected frameworks that center around three Islamic ethical concepts: RAHMA (mercy), AMANAH (trust or faith), and ADALAH (justice). Each of these frameworks is aimed at a specific level of awareness and care work: Rahma on the individual level, Amanah on the community level, and Adalah on the institutional level. RAHMA stands for "Responding by listening, Affirm and believe, Honor cultural and religious contexts and values, Maintain privacy, Assist with providing resources." On the level of the individual, the ethic of care for survivors is clearly outlined. AMANAH stands for "Acquire knowledge; Mobilize community care funds and resources, Ally with trained professionals, Normalize seeking help, information and services, Address root causes, Handle reporting through trauma-informed processes. Amanah, too, is survivor-centered and trauma-informed and encourages communities to come together in support of survivors of sexual violence. On the institutional level, ADALAH calls institutions to "Allocate financial and human resources, Determine victim-centric restorative practices, Accommodate victim needs, Look beyond the perpetrator, Assess risk to community and create action plan, Honor transparency, confidentiality, and accountability." Taken together, these three frameworks are intended to break the pervasive silence around sexual violence in Muslim communities.

There is another way in which silence (and acts of silencing) appear in the work of HEART and others addressing sexual violence. The individual advocates and the organization both risk shaming and attacks on them coming from a spectrum of adversaries that include perpetrators and their allies, those in communities who are uncomfortable acknowledging sexual violence and would rather silence those who raise awareness of it than address the problem, and those who fear that making sexual violence in Muslim communities public will increase anti-Muslim hostility by confirming prevalent stereotypes about Muslim men as more violent than other men.

As the genocide of Palestinians in Gaza (and the West Bank) continues, there are many people (but not many governments and people in power) who are speaking out, protesting, educating, and resisting their silencing. At the same time, even a brief look at mainstream US media outlets makes it very clear that there is an active and pervasive silencing of Palestinians and their allies at work. That silence is demanded by the current US government which has put its weight and power in the service of the state of Israel.[10] Palestinian experiences, casualty counts, and Palestinian suffering and losses are either erased from media representations or diminished and belittled in favor of attention to the Israeli victims of the Hamas attacks on October 7, as well as the Israeli hostages and sometimes their families. This selective media coverage mirrors that in Israeli media, which, as Rebecca Stein has argued, has relied on a strategy of "unseeing Gaza" long before the events of October 2023.[11]

Social media outlets have engaged in extensive policing of pro-Palestinian content and even more broadly in "shadow banning" whereby the reach of certain posts is limited. Palestinian and pro-Palestinian content producers have reported that their reach of followers is dramatically diminished in numbers and that social media platforms also often delay posts, which in the active stages of genocide means that information reaches social media users too late to act, participate in events, or organize responses.

Those engaging in Palestine solidarity activism, on college and university campuses and elsewhere, as they educate, protest, support students, and mourn the rapidly growing number of Palestinians killed by Israel, find themselves navigating already treacherous campus climates, attempting to assess the risks in speaking out publicly. The possibility of being accused of antisemitism now always hangs over our heads, with little room for even discussing what antisemitism means. Any critique of Israel and of Zionism is routinely equated with antisemitism. Pro-Israel voices claim the right to free speech and academic freedom for themselves but successfully limit that same right when said speech is pro-Palestinian, anti-Zionist, and/or critical of Israel. It is with a distinct sense of irony that I write these words in an academic publication while fighting for my right to pro-Palestine speech on my own campus. Similarly, accusations of hate speech are leveled against some but not others. Even our affect is being policed, with those on the pro-Israeli side being able to voice their feelings of fear, anxiety, terror, and grief, while Palestinians and their allies are denied such feelings and with that often their very humanity.

As the slaughter goes on, the silence from the liberal US public, from media outlets and journalists, from academic professional organizations, from colleagues and (former) friends gets louder and louder. When colleagues from three academic organizations of ethicists, the Society for Christian Ethics, the Society for Jewish Ethics, and the Society for the Study of Muslim Ethics, met in Chicago in January 2024, I looked in vain for Palestine anywhere on their conference programs. Gaza was mentioned a few times in sessions I attended. Perhaps all the talk was in those sessions I did not attend, but I sincerely doubt it. If religious ethicists could not manage to be in conversation (I would have taken two-sided conversations over the silence), then how can we expect solidarity to flourish and work, and how can we expect our ethics to do work in the world? Is it a lack of care? Or is our/their ethic of care conditional?

Demanding Perfect Victims

As I ponder solidarity and the ethics of care, I am reminded of one of HEART's core principles: "people who are most impacted are the experts and at the center of our work."[12] The HEART advocates also speak of investing in communities of care. Perhaps because of the ways in which sexuality and religion are intertwined, scholars and advocates seem to consider sexual violence in religious communities as somehow special. Within a feminist framework of diagnosing the roots and causes of GBV, patriarchy as the culprit is central, and much of secular feminist theory has assumed religion (regardless of which one) to be essentially patriarchal, and thus always a roadblock to addressing GBV. Much of my work has tried to move from that assumption to an argument that "religion" can be a roadblock for sure, but it also can be and is a resource for some advocates, as is clear from my presentation of HEART's framework and advocacy efforts.

It is worth mentioning as well that I see a distinction between solidarity and care in that care can, but does not have to, produce a potentially hierarchical relationship between the carer and the person or community being cared for, as the carer has the power to decide who is deserving of their care. It may be that this problem is also related to the fact that care is more easily connected to an individual, where solidarity has an obvious communal dimension to it. Solidarity, in contrast to care, is not unconditional but embedded in a systemic critique of structural injustices.

Regardless of whether GBV, including sexual violence and abuse, takes place in religious contexts or communities, once the pervasive silence is broken, it is still hard to navigate the murky waters of whom to blame and how to both address violence already committed and prevent more of it from happening. I will say more about the focus on perpetrators of such violence later in this chapter but want to focus here on the demand for perfect victims. It serves our desire for a neat ethical picture, and so we tend to expect that victims of sexual violence are only victims: helpless, innocent, and undeserving of such violence. Relatedly, it is much easier to condemn sexual violence when the perpetrator is perfectly evil, rather than complicated.

In a recent conversation, Megan McCabe formulated explicitly what I had known implicitly from other work on sexual abuse in Catholic contexts: that in dealing with sexual abuse in Catholic communities, a tendency has been evident to focus on children as victims of such abuse even though such abuse has also been inflicted on adults. The reason, as she stated, is that children are most easily presented as perfectly innocent and thus as perfect victims, while adult survivors of sexual violence, within and beyond the Catholic Church, are more often not believed or interrogated as to their own partial culpability. We have all seen the vicious questioning of survivors who come forward and are interrogated as to their clothing, their sexual history, their behavior around the events, which spaces they moved in, and so on.[13] Even sexual violence prevention training, such as all first-year students at my institution have to pass, focuses on consent, but pays much attention to alcohol and drugs as risk factors and suggests safety planning measures that at least imply a victim's partial culpability if they do not follow such advice.

In a poignant footnote to her article on rape culture as a social sin on college campuses, McCabe addresses the issue of victimization and rejects a binary between that and the agency of survivors:

> By centering victimization, I do not intend to deny the agency, especially the moral agency, of those who have experienced victimization. Although it is outside the scope of this particular project to develop fully, I do not accept an opposition between "victimization" and "agency" that is so typically put forward, even by feminists. Such language, while attempting to recognize the agency of women, unwittingly re-inscribes victim-blaming discourses,

suggesting that those who are victimized are those who lack agency, or if they had proper agency they would not have suffered. Moreover, I would argue that naming the experience of sexual violence precisely as a form of victimization is, itself, an act of agency. Such language recognizes the violation of this form of experience. In it, a woman (or other victimized person) asserts, with agency, that such an act of violation is wrong and ought not be accepted.[14]

An additional dimension of the demand for perfect victims is Miranda Fricker's concept of "testimonial injustice," which she explains both in epistemological and judicial terms.[15] She contends that testimonial injustice occurs when a witness has, for reasons related to their identity and experiences, a credibility deficit, meaning that their testimony is not perceived as credible, and their knowledge of events and experiences is denied significance for addressing the injustice that occurred. I want to reiterate the quote from HEART's value statement that "people who are most impacted are the experts and at the center of our work." HEART does recognize survivors as those holding knowledge, which recognizes the agency that McCabe insists on as well.

Abolitionist organizing led by Black advocates and the political and intellectual framing of such efforts teach us that "there are no perfect victims," which is also the title of Part II of Mariame Kaba's 2021 book, *We Do This 'Til We Free Us.*[16] In her essay, "Black Women Punished for Self-Defense Must Be Freed from Their Cages," Kaba writes about the history of the US criminal injustice system recognizing Black women's rights to resist their oppression and violation. She argues, "While self-defense laws are interpreted generously when applied to white men who feel threatened by men of color, they are applied very narrowly to women and gender nonconforming people, and particularly women and gender nonconforming people of color trying to protect themselves in domestic violence and sexual assault cases."[17]

In the context of Palestine and Palestine solidarity work, the juxtaposition of perfect victimhood and any form of resistance appears configured even more starkly. On October 10, 2023, Noura Erakat published a short essay on *Jadaliyya*, titled, "The Violence of Demanding Perfect Victims." In it, she predicts the level of bloodshed and destruction later inflicted on Palestinians in Gaza, but also critically points out that Israel has inflicted seventy-five years of structural violence on Palestinians which "has condemned Palestinians to a slow death." She points to the catastrophic conditions in Gaza, from environmental degradation, poor water quality and Palestinian lack of control over water, electricity, and telecommunications, to direct military assaults, before the Hamas attack on October 7. Erakat argues that Palestinians have collectively been blamed for electing Hamas in 2006 and for any expressions of resistance to Israeli occupation from the Boycott, Divestment, and Sanctions (BDS) movement to the March of Return in 2018–2019, thereby "fixating on Palestinians as imperfect victims," which amounts to "absolution of, and complicity with, Israel's colonial domination." Later in the article, she writes: "The message to Palestinians is not that they must resist more peacefully but that they cannot resist Israeli occupation and aggression at all." The failure (or rather refusal) to recognize and consider the history of Palestinian dispossession and occupation, the seventy-five-year history of Israeli violence then is "tantamount to telling Palestinians that they must die quietly."[18] I am struck by the resurfacing of the notion of silence here.

There are also, as in sexual violence, distinctions between victims. I have caught myself emphasizing the number of Palestinian children and women who have been killed, with the expectation that the killing of children would elicit the shock and outrage necessary to jolt people into action, protest, something beyond erasure, refusal to see, silence. If to be perfect victims, Palestinians are not allowed to resist in any way, then children make for perfect victims and women are assumed to only partake in nonviolent forms of resistance. However, as we saw in Erakat's formulation, even nonviolent forms of resistance detract from Palestinians' potential to be credible victims.

In the Israeli government's "justification" for the assault on Gaza, the argument that everyone in Gaza either is part of Hamas, or supports Hamas, or is used as "a human shield" by Hamas, has been presented and repeated for months. This framing of Palestinians embraces racist and anti-Muslim tropes of Arab/Muslim men as terrorists, as inherently violent, and thus as undeserving of the status as victims. In an *Al Jazeera* article from January 2024, Yousef Al Helou, Meena Masood, and Leah de Haan argue that "Muslim men are not 'terrorists in the making,'" so the title of the piece. They, too, point to the emphasis on "the ever increasing number of dead Palestinian women and children," and concern about them even from some governments that are allied with Israel. They write:

> Through this refusal to explicitly count and grieve their deaths, Palestinian men are denied civilian status. Their humanity is erased and they are portrayed collectively as "dangerous brown men" and "potential terrorists." This, in turn, permits Israel's killing of Palestinian men. Their killing is permitted precisely because they are Palestinian men. Their gendered and racialised status, specifically their blanket designation as "Hamas terrorists," eclipses their civilian status, deeming them killable and un-grievable. Their killing is excused and justified within the context of "counterterrorism." . . .
>
> The blanket demonisation of men—underpinned by narratives about brown, especially Arab, men being inherently untrustworthy, dangerous and radical—is not new. These narratives, currently being used by Israel and its allies to excuse genocidal violence in Palestine, have consistently been used to justify the mass killing of brown men and boys over the years, including in the context of the so-called global "War on Terror" and the illegal invasions of Iraq and Afghanistan.[19]

Thus, there are at least two layers to the impossible demand for perfect victims: that they are innocent, free of blame, and nonresisting, and that children and women are in categories closer to the possibility of perfect victimhood, while Palestinian men cannot be accepted into such status. In writing about gendered anti-Muslim hostility, I have argued that the white (often women) savior complex that propelled the narrative of oppressed and silent Muslim women in need of liberation, including military invasion of their countries, no longer even works for all Muslim women. The Trump administration's so-called Muslim ban did not distinguish between men, women, and children. In the wake of the Orlando shooting in 2016, we saw the wife of the shooter investigated and indicted as an accessory. Muslim women activists, such as Linda Sarsour, have been denied their claim to being feminists; they are attacked for their social justice activism, and end up also falling outside of the group boundaries of Muslim women who can be saved.[20] We come full circle then with Noura Erakat's argument that no Palestinian can be recognized as a perfect victim, which in turn puts all Palestinians outside of the frame of care and solidarity, and to put it even more starkly, outside of their recognition as fully human.

It goes with the territory when discussing sexual violence that matters are complex and, as I said earlier, murky. I would be remiss if I did not acknowledge that sexual violence was committed on October 7 during the Hamas attack. We must be open to multiple critiques or risk being hypocritical in our care for and affirmation of survivors.[21] Simultaneously, but much more slowly, it has emerged that the Israeli army and prison system have committed sexual violence, since October 7, but also long before then. For example, in February 2024, the United Nations called for an investigation into allegations of violations of the rights of Palestinian women and girls.[22]

In an initiative that recognizes the need for multiple critiques, a group of US-based anti-Zionist Jewish feminists has formulated a letter to "to the Israeli and US governments and others weaponizing the issue of rape," that has garnered many signatures since it was first posted in mid-February 2024. The authors of the letter write on the website: "All too often in the fog of war, the brutality of sexual assault and rape is lost in the public eye, and bringing these abuses to light is something for which feminists have fought for decades. Complicating this issue, however, is the fact that accusations of sexual assault have also been wielded as a tool of war—and as an (often lethal) weapon of racism and colonialism."[23]

The insistence on perfect victims, in cases of sexual violence and in Palestine, is a tool to dismiss the demands of victims for recognition of the injustice they have suffered. It also precludes both solidarity and care for them.

Focus on Perpetrators

Academic work on sexual violence as well as public discourse on the issue have often focused on the perpetrators of such violence. That is especially true when the alleged perpetrator is a celebrity of some kind. In advocacy spaces, the reverse is sometimes the case: the focus is on supporting victims and survivors, with little space left to consider work with perpetrators or resources for such engagement. When the focus is on perpetrators in academic analysis, we can assume that the purpose is an analysis of structures and systems that produce individuals who commit sexual violence. The purpose of such analysis, I would hope, is not to excuse or explain away the abuse perpetrated. At times, the express purpose of academic and advocacy work on sexual violence is to hold perpetrators accountable and even to achieve justice for their victims. I am thinking here of restorative justice projects and approaches as represented in the work of Mariame Kaba and others.

In public discourse, even during the height of the second wave of the #MeToo movement,[24] we saw an inordinate amount of attention paid to perpetrators, in tandem with the demand for perfect victims as I described in the previous section. Such attention to perpetrators of sexual violence often revolves around exaggerated concern for the impact of false accusations, even though a tiny fraction of sexual assault and abuse allegations are actually false. And the potential impact on the personal life, as well as career of the perpetrators concerns people more than the impact of actual sexual violence on its victims. This phenomenon speaks volumes as to who matters and who is deserving of (our) care. More broadly though, a focus on the perpetrators of sexual violence in public discourse has tended to explain, and with that, excuse such violence.

The Israeli assault on Gaza after the October 7 attack has been justified, by the Israeli government and military, as well as by other states, including the United States and Germany, among others, using the violence inflicted upon Israeli citizens on October 7. The Israeli government has used the October 7 attacks as justification for the Israeli army's ongoing human rights abuses, and the Israeli army is carrying out its campaign of genocidal violence with complete impunity. Israel has refused to consider its actions as violations of international law. In January 2024, a case was brought to the International Court of Justice by South Africa, which accused Israel of committing genocide in Gaza. While the court found that Israel was not committing genocide, "the ICJ ordered Israel to refrain from any acts that could fall under the Genocide Convention and to ensure its troops commit no genocidal acts against Palestinians." In March 2024, South Africa "asked the International Court of Justice (ICJ) to order additional emergency measures against Israel over its war on Gaza, . . . In its application, South Africa warned that Palestinians in

Gaza were facing starvation and asked the court to order that all parties cease hostilities and release all hostages and detainees."[25]

Another strategy by Israel and its allies has been to deny the extent of violence inflicted on Gaza. An early example is the claim that the Israeli army did not bomb al-Ahli Arab Hospital on October 17, 2023. Rather, the casualties and damage to the hospital were allegedly caused by an explosion of ammunition belonging to Hamas. Since then, the Israeli army has bombed, invaded, put under siege, and at least partially destroyed most other hospitals in Gaza. The very significant international media attention and efforts of the Israeli government to prove that the October 17 bombing was not committed by the Israeli army can be contrasted with the multiple hospital bombings and destruction that have followed and been met with relative silence; this strategy thus enables minimization and denial of responsibility. Such denial of violence and responsibility for it is reminiscent of cases of sexual violence in which the perpetrator claims the consent of their victim. This replicates the power dynamic by which powerful men abuse less powerful others and are not held accountable.

While HEART does not specifically focus its efforts on perpetrators of sexual abuse in Muslim communities, they have acknowledged the particular dynamics of "power-based violence" as they intersect with the responsibility of Muslim organizations and communities to address such violence, especially when it involves religious and community leaders. In 2019, in response to an increase in discussion of sexual violence in the US Muslim public square, HEART issued a statement, discussing the definition of power-based violence and emphasizing the need for victim-centered approaches by institutions and organizations. The relevant portion for my discussion here reads:

> When such allegations involve leaders of institutions, many questions arise about institutional accountability and organizational responsibility towards those who have been harmed.
>
> To prevent future harm, institutions must respond in a timely, transparent, and victim-centered process. Unfortunately, organizational responses to a leaders' wrongdoings too often focus on protecting an institution's short-term reputation and can ultimately re-traumatize those who experienced harm. Incidents of power-based violence in our communities frequently result in uproar, misinformation, and rampant victim-blaming, but rarely

is there any substantive institutional change. This can mean people in an institution who allowed abuse to go on despite evidence of wrongdoing can be left free of any accountability, and it leaves communities vulnerable to future abuse. Until those in leadership positions commit to addressing this epidemic of abuse and exploitation of vulnerable community members head on, in partnership with trained experts, we will not be able to eradicate power-based violence.[26]

This level of community engagement is also addressed in the ADALAH framework I introduced earlier. The framework emphasizes accountability over punitive measures and embraces the idea of restorative and transformative justice as proposed and advocated for by abolitionist justice organizations and advocates.[27]

In Conclusion?

I have written three books since I moved to the United States. In my second and third books, instead of a conclusion chapter, I wrote what I saw as an opening for further reflection and an invitation for conversation. In this last section of my chapter, I want to circle back to the question of solidarity.

My involvement in the Religion and Sexual Abuse Project, including participation in the 2022 conference on Religion and Sexual Abuse, has allowed me to read, learn, and discuss my work on efforts against sexual violence in Muslim communities with colleagues in academia and with advocates. In those contexts, I have experienced amazing solidarity and mutual support as we all navigate in different ways the pressures to be silent, the weight of the problem, and in many cases the layers of trauma. Many colleagues in the project engage in survivor-centered research and writing, and many would be comfortable with the identifier "feminist" or the broader and less fraught notion of the struggle for gender justice that is at the heart of our work against GBV.

I have also been involved in Feminist Studies in Religion (FSR) since 2019, including for almost five years on the board of the FSR Co-Laboratory.[28] While Palestine advocacy (or any discussion of Palestine-Israel) was not at the center of my work with FSR, it also did not feel like a space where that topic could not be discussed at all. It has been hard and painful to see the complete silence of the organization on the events in Gaza since early October 2023. How am I to read that silence? It could reflect the idea that "it's complicated." Or, it could be fear of upsetting some of our colleagues and friends who are Jewish (which also uncritically makes the assumption that they are in support of Israel and/or Israel's indiscriminate killing of Palestinians). Or, it could be a refusal to make or see Palestine as a feminist issue. To be sure, there is the unacceptable conflation of Palestine-Israel with Judaism and Islam, forcing a framework of religious conflict rather than occupation, dispossession, and settler-colonialism. To me, Palestine is a feminist issue not only because of the ways it has affected Palestinian women but because I see any injustice as intersecting with my commitment to social justice regardless of who is committing the injustice.[29]

To be sure, other feminists have spoken out as heartening statements by several Women and Gender Studies Departments have shown. The National Women's Studies Association issued a strongly worded statement on October 13, 2023, which was endorsed and adopted by many Women's, Gender, and Sexuality Studies (WGST) departments and scholars.[30] That statement did not mince words and engaged in the kind of solidarity work that I am still hoping to see from so many more people and institutions. The statement calls for the US government to cease its support of Israeli apartheid:

> As feminists, we recognize that violence and war often inflict gendered and sexualized harms on women and queer, trans and non-binary people. We cannot look away while this violence destroys people's lives. The struggle for Palestinian liberation and for a just and lasting peace in the region is intertwined with the liberation and resistance movements led by other indigenous, colonized, and oppressed peoples everywhere. Today, we reaffirm our unwavering support for the Boycott, Divestment, and Sanctions (BDS) resolution, which NWSA passed in 2015. We pledge to continue to work as hard as we can to educate ourselves and our communities about the historic injustice, suffering, and resistance of Palestinians.

My own institution's WGST department also issued a statement but was forced to remove it from the official department website by the university administration.

Alongside solidarity with Palestinians and their allies, since October 2023 we have also witnessed a glaring lack of public interest and response, and certainly a realization that efforts to lobby the US government to change its policy of supporting Israel without any regard for Palestinian lives are severely limited. We see widespread erasure of Palestinians from institutional and public discourse as well as a dramatic increase in anti-Palestinian and anti-Arab racism, and by extension and intentional conflation, an increase in anti-Muslim hostility. As the violence continues unabated, I feel hopelessness, grief, and rage. I attend events, organize some, and support students on our campus. I feel anger at the way the university that employs me denies free speech to some of us but not others and cares more about its reputation and funding than about the most vulnerable in this current moment, Palestinians in Gaza.

I think a lot about an ethic of care that does not patronize or disempower, that does not talk over those most affected, but rather prioritizes acts of listening and supporting. There is, I think, much to learn from organizations like HEART in this endeavor. We need to reflect but also need to act. I continue to hold onto hope that solidarity in action will make a difference in the lives of those harmed by violence and apathy. Inshallah.

Notes

1 Fannie Lou Hamer, "Nobody's Free Until Everybody's Free," Speech Delivered at the Founding of the National Women's Political Caucus, Washington, DC, July 10, 1971, in *Speeches of Fannie Lou Hamer: To Tell It Like It Is*, ed. M. P. Brooks, D. W. M. P., Houck, and D. W. Houck (Jackson: University Press of Mississippi, 2010), 137.

2 Juliane Hammer, "The Women's March: A Reflection on Feminist Solidarity, Intersectional Critique, and Muslim Women's Activism," in *Religion and Broken Solidarities: Feminism, Race, and Transnationalism*, ed. A. Omer and J. Lupo (South Bend, IN: University of Notre Dame Press, 2022), 51–85.

3 This participatory project with HEART is partly funded through a sub-grant that I have been awarded from the Luce Foundation supported Religion and Sexual Abuse Project, https://www.religionandsexualabuseproject.org/. I have learned

so much already from other scholars involved in the RSA project, especially Ann Gleig and Amy Langenberg.

4 Rochelle Terman, "Islamophobia, Feminism, and the Politics of Critique," *Theory, Culture and Society* 33, no. 2 (2016): 78.

5 HEART, "Our Values," https://hearttogrow.org/mission/. Accessed March 14, 2024.

6 "SisterSong's mission is to strengthen and amplify the collective voices of indigenous women and women of color to achieve reproductive justice by eradicating reproductive oppression and securing human rights." https://www .sistersong.net/.

7 HEART, "The Inaya Care Fund," https://sites.google.com/heartwomenandgirls .org/inayacarefund/home/about-the-fund. Accessed March 14, 2024.

8 HEART, "Our History," https://hearttogrow.org/our-history/. Accessed March 14, 2024.

9 See Religion and Sexual Abuse Project, https://www.religionandsexualabusep roject.org/. Accessed December 18, 2024.

10 See for critical examples: Chris McGreal, "CNN Staff Say Network's Pro-Israel Slant Amounts to 'Journalistic Malpractice'," *The Guardian*, February 4, 2024, https://www.theguardian.com/media/2024/feb/04/cnn-staff-pro-israel-bias; Human Rights Watch, "Meta's Broken Promises: Systemic Censorship of Palestine Content on Instagram and Facebook," December 21, 2023, https://www.hrw .org/report/2023/12/21/metas-broken-promises/systemic-censorship-palestine -content-instagram-and-facebook; Rami G. Khoury, "Watching the Watchdogs: Fear in Newsrooms Silences Pro-Palestine Voices," *Al Jazeera*, November 1, 2023, https://www.aljazeera.com/opinions/2023/11/1/watching-the-watchdogs-fear-in -newsrooms-silences-pro-palestine-voices. Accessed March 14, 2024.

11 Rebecca. L. Stein, "How to Unsee Gaza: Israeli Media, State Violence, Palestinian Testimony," in *Gaza on Screen*, ed. Nadia Yaqub (Durham: Duke University Press, 2023), 172–86.

12 HEART, "Our Mission," https://hearttogrow.org/mission/. Accessed March 14, 2024.

13 See this factsheet from the Maryland Coalition against Sexual Assault for an explanation of what amounts to victim blaming: https://mcasa.org/assets/files/ Victim_Blaming_Fact_Sheet_2022.pdf. Accessed March 14, 2024.

14 Megan McCabe, "A Feminist Catholic Response to the Social Sin of Rape Culture," *Journal of Religious Ethics* 46 no. 4 (December 2018): 635–57, 638.

15 Miranda Fricker, *Epistemic Injustice: Power and the Ethics of Knowing* (Oxford: Oxford University Press, 2007).

16 Mariame Kaba, *We Do This 'Til We Free Us: Abolitionist Organizing and Transforming Justice* (Chicago: Haymarket Books, 2021), 29.

17 Kaba, *We Do This 'Til We Free Us*, 50–51.

18 Noura Erakat, "The Violence of Demanding Perfect Victims," *Jadaliyya*, October 10, 2023, https://www.jadaliyya.com/Details/45383. Accessed March 14, 2024.

19 Yousef Al Helou, Meena Masood, and Leah de Haan, "Palestinian Men Are Not 'Terrorists in the Making'" *Al Jazeera*, January 1, 2024, https://www.aljazeera.com/opinions/2024/1/1/palestinian-men-are-not-terrorists-in-the-making. Accessed March 14, 2024.

20 Juliane Hammer, "Muslim Women, Anti-Muslim Hostility, and the State in the Age of Terror," in *Muslims and Contemporary US Politics*, ed. Mohammad Khalil (Cambridge, MA: Harvard University Press, 2019), 104–26.

21 Questions have been raised as to the veracity of reports in October that there was widespread sexual assault committed by Hamas on October 7. See, Jeremy Scahill, Ryan Grim, Daniel Boguslaw, "The Story Behind the *New York Times* October 7 Exposé," *The Intercept*, February 28, 2024, https://theintercept.com/2024/02/28/new-york-times-anat-schwartz-october-7/. Accessed March 14, 2024.

22 UN News, "Rights Experts Call for Probe into Alleged Violations against Palestinian Women and Girls," February 19, 2024, https://news.un.org/en/story/2024/02/1146667.

23 https://stopmanipulatingsexualassault.org/#home. Accessed March 14, 2024.

24 Tarana Burke, a social activist and community organizer, began using the phrase "Me Too" in 2006, on the Myspace social network to promote "empowerment through empathy" among women of color who have been sexually abused. By the second wave I mean the awareness movement around the issue of sexual harassment and sexual abuse of women in the workplace that grew to prominence in 2017 in response to news reports of sexual abuse by American film producer Harvey Weinstein.

25 Al Jazeera, "South Africa Asks ICJ for More Measures against Israel over Gaza 'Famine,'" March 6, 2024, https://www.aljazeera.com/news/2024/3/6/south-africa-asks-icj-for-more-measures-against-israel-over-gaza-famine. Accessed March 14, 2024.

26 HEART, "Institutional Accountability and Victim-Centered Practices: Power-Based Violence," https://hearttogrow.org/institutional-accountability-being-victim-centered/. Accessed March 14, 2024.

27 See Kaba, *We Do This 'Til We Free Us.*

28 See Feminist Studies in Religion, https://www.fsrinc.org/. Accessed March 14, 2024.

29 I am inspired in this conviction by a talk Cornel West gave at UNC Chapel Hill on January 30, 2024.

30 National Women's Studies Association, "National Women's Studies Association releases statement about the violence in Gaza and Israel," https://wgss.umd.edu/news/nwsa-calls-ceasefire-and-negotiations-end-gaza-siege-and-israeli-apartheid. Accessed March 14, 2024.

References

Al Jazeera. "South Africa Asks ICJ for More Measures against Israel over Gaza 'Famine.'" March 6, 2024. https://www.aljazeera.com/news/2024/3/6/south-africa-asks-icj-for-more-measures-against-israel-over-gaza-famine.

Erakat, Noura. "The Violence of Demanding Perfect Victims." *Jadaliyya.* October 10, 2023. https://www.jadaliyya.com/Details/45383.

Fricker, Miranda. *Epistemic Injustice: Power and the Ethics of Knowing.* Oxford: Oxford University Press, 2007.

Hamer, Fannie Lou. "Nobody's Free Until Everybody's Free," Speech Delivered at the Founding of the National Women's Political Caucus, Washington, DC, July 10, 1971, in *Speeches of Fannie Lou Hamer: To Tell It Like It Is*, edited by M. P. Brooks, D. W. M. P., Houck, D. W. Houck. Jackson: University Press of Mississippi, 2010.

Hammer, Juliane. "Muslim Women, Anti-Muslim Hostility, and the State in the Age of Terror." In *Muslims and Contemporary US Politics*, edited by Mohammad Khalil, 104–26. Cambridge, MA: Harvard University Press, 2019.

———. "The Women's March: A Reflection on Feminist Solidarity, Intersectional Critique, and Muslim Women's Activism." In *Religion and Broken Solidarities: Feminism, Race, and Transnationalism*, edited by Atalia Omer and Joshua Lupo, 51–85. South Bend, IN: University of Notre Dame Press, 2022.

Helou, Yousef Al, Meena Masood, and Leah de Haan. "Palestinian Men Are Not 'Terrorists in the Making.'" *Al Jazeera.* January 1, 2024. https://www.aljazeera.com/opinions/2024/1/1/palestinian-men-are-not-terrorists-in-the-making.

Human Rights Watch. "Meta's Broken Promises: Systemic Censorship of Palestine Content on Instagram and Facebook." December 21, 2023. https://www.hrw.org/report/2023/12/21/metas-broken-promises/systemic-censorship-palestine-content-instagram-and-facebook.

Kaba, Mariame. *We Do This 'Til We Free Us: Abolitionist Organizing and Transforming Justice.* Chicago: Haymarket Books, 2021.

Khoury, Rami G. "Watching the Watchdogs: Fear in Newsrooms Silences Pro-Palestine Voices." *Al Jazeera.* November 1, 2023. https://www.aljazeera.com/opinions/2023/11/1/watching-the-watchdogs-fear-in-newsrooms-silences-pro-palestine-voices.

McCabe, Megan. "A Feminist Catholic Response to the Social Sin of Rape Culture." *Journal of Religious Ethics* 46, no. 4 (December 2018): 635–57.

McGreal, Chris. "CNN Staff Say Network's Pro-Israel Slant Amounts to 'Journalistic Malpractice.'" *The Guardian.* February 4, 2024. https://www.theguardian.com/media/2024/feb/04/cnn-staff-pro-israel-bias.

Scahill, Jeremy, Ryan Grim, and Daniel Boguslaw. "The Story Behind the *New York Times* October 7 Exposé." *The Intercept.* February 28, 2024. https://theintercept.com/2024/02/28/new-york-times-anat-schwartz-october-7/

Stein, Rebecca. L. "How to Unsee Gaza: Israeli Media, State Violence, Palestinian Testimony." In *Gaza on Screen*, edited by Nadia Yaqub, 172–86. Durham, NC: Duke University Press, 2023.

Terman, Rochelle. "Islamophobia, Feminism, and the Politics of Critique." *Theory, Culture and Society* 33, no. 2 (2016): 77–102.

UN News. "Rights Experts Call for Probe into Alleged Violations against Palestinian Women and Girls." February 19, 2024. https://news.un.org/en/story/2024/02/1146667.

Challenging Exclusionary Forms of Solidarity

10

From Bypass Roads' Feminism to Decolonial Judaism

A Feminist Reading of Jewish Religious Ethics and Solidarity

Atalia Omer

No "God Tricks"

"No, You Can't Be a Feminist and a Zionist," writes Mariam Barghouti in an opinion piece by that title.[1] A Palestinian American journalist and activist residing in the West Bank, Barghouti conveys the inconsistency between feminist ethics and militancy and oppression. Indeed, the title of her piece captures nationalism and, in this instance, Zionism as an obstacle to a "true" feminist intersectional analysis, solidarity, and emancipatory visions of liberation. The piece describes a female soldier's humiliating treatment of Palestinians at checkpoints, putting into sharp relief that feminist liberation which entails the oppression of an occupied and uprooted people is neither liberationist nor feminist. The situation is even more complicated because of the ideological blinder, a nationalist discourse of self-defense, and a militarist ethos that belonging to Zionism entails being embedded within a particular interpretation of Jewish history and destiny. The presumed solidarity of the female soldier at the checkpoint with all women (considering that her inclusion in the military may be interpreted as a feminist achievement) is obviously blocked by her Zionism and her commitment to "Jewish self-defense," which translates in practice to the right to occupy and displace another people. At the time of finalizing this contribution, the Nakba or the Palestinian catastrophe (a word referring to the mass depopulation of 1948 but also to ongoing realities of displacement and entrenched military occupation) escalated into a prolonged genocide against Gazans in the aftermath of the Hamas attack on southern Israeli communities on October 7, 2023.

The feminist normativity to resist oppression is obscured by the soldier's presumed Jewish normativity authorizing domination, even if the soldier's participation in the military itself conveys a departure from the patriarchal norms undergirding Jewish tradition. If intersectionality denotes a matrix linking various sites of oppression, "bypass roads" for Jews only in Palestine/Israel invisibilized and literally drive over such intersections, rendering feminist politics of solidarity across geopolitical terrains incoherent.[2] Bypass roads cut through the West Bank. They were constructed to facilitate an illusion of safety and to consolidate the de facto annexation of the illegal settlements in the territories Israel occupied in 1967 to "Israel proper," a reference to the territories acquired in 1948–1949. Bypass roads' feminism amplifies and normalizes Jewish supremacy, ethnocentric solidarity, and settler colonial and annexionist practices in Palestine. At the same time, anti-Zionist queer and feminist diasporic Jewish ethics combats supremacist Judaism with *Other*-centric rather than *ethnocentric* articulations of Jewishness. This chapter grapples with the tension between queer diasporic other-centric and intersectional Jewishness that rearticulates itself in solidarity with Palestinians and feminist, decolonial, and Mizrahi Israeli Jewish efforts to reconfigure the horizons of democratic politics and historical accountability.

This volume asks us to think of normativity in the study of religion and, specifically, religious ethics in ways that center feminist ethics and the insights propelling coalitional politics, oriented by demands to rectify conditions of injustice. This volume argues that scholars of religion should not shy away from normativity and, far from reinventing the wheel, feminist ethicists, religious feminists, and womanist thinkers already have demonstrated normativity and hermeneutical scholarly rigor (e.g., see Kellison in this volume). Religious ethics, therefore, ought to be feminist and thus unabashedly normative and situated (embodied) rather than assuming an Archimedean pretense or what Donna Haraway has called a "god trick."[3] The figure of the female soldier at the Israeli checkpoint in Palestine exposes why the absence of normativity or the scientific distance/gaze through the presumption of descriptive scholarship can become complicit in violence and oppression. Neither feminist ethics nor Jewish ethics, in this instance, can be articulated in abstraction from the on-the-ground dynamics of settler colonialism, apartheid, military occupation, and genocide or in abstraction from Palestinian grievances and demands. My case study of Palestine/Israel clarifies why this volume's effort to center feminist conceptions of solidarity in rearticulating the domains of the study of religion, in general, and religious ethics, in particular, as politically normative requires a situated, relational, dialectical, and sociological/ethnographic approach to intersectional knowledge production about religion.

Focusing on the concrete case of Jewish Palestinian solidarity and the co-resistance struggle against the Israeli regime of apartheid, settler colonialism, and Jewish Zionist supremacy, I show how unlearning Zionism as a form of exclusionary Jewish solidarity involves feminist, decolonial, and religious hermeneutics. Yet not all ingredients are always foregrounded. The role of religion and religious ethics is only clarified when the anatomy of secular Zionism is exposed for its political theology. In what follows, I examine two cases of American Jews and Israeli Jewish anti-occupation mobilization, which have entailed an interrogation and reconfiguration of the Jewish meanings of Israel through an ethical retrieval and rewriting of Jewish belonging and ethics. I show why the one instance of ethical reimagining is also centrally feminist and queer, whereas the other is pronouncedly not.[4] I argue that this discrepancy is an outcome of context and of the question of who the Jewish activists engage in building ethical and political belonging, even if both communities (in Israel and the United States) mobilize in response to how the occupation and a supremacist Jewish regime reflect on their identity as Jews.

Drawing on my extensive ethnographic research for my recent book *Days of Awe: Reimagining Jewishness in Solidarity with Palestinians*,[5] and my other scholarship on Jewish Israeli peace and justice praxes,[6] I structure this chapter around three questions asked by the ancient Rabbi Hillel, who was active during the period of the *Tanaaim*, or transmitters of the Oral Law, around the first century BCE and first century CE. The three questions, for Hillel, summed up what the Torah is about. They go as follows: If I am not for myself, who will be for me? If I am only for myself, who am I? And if not now, when? A feminist prism deepens the responses to Hillel's questions and subsequent accounts of political ethics. Given that the questions are interrelated, I am going to move from the ethical urgency of the moment to the reconfiguration of the question "Who am I" as an elastic, context-dependent, situated, and relational ethical process of becoming.

On their own, the questions convey a feminist potentiality because they capture relationality and solidarity as central dimensions for constituting the normative self and for building coalitions across identitarian grounds without an erasure of difference or the creation of bypass roads. It is, therefore, no wonder that Rabbi Hillel's three questions provide a general technology for community organizing. Indeed, Marshall Ganz, a veteran community organizer in the migrant farmworkers' movement and a Harvard professor at the Kennedy School of Government, centers the three questions in his public narrative methodology, which translates values into action through stories that explain the *why* of community organizing. Ganz's public narrative approach grounds itself in the story of the *self* (Hillel's first question) and how to connect the self (including what gives the self hope) to the stories of the broader community and how our stories become an *us* describing who we are—not in terms of phenotypes, but in terms of the values, challenges, and aspirations around specific issues we share as *us* (Hillel's second question). The stories of *self* and *us* finally connect to the story of *now*, always with urgency, that details the consequences of inaction as catastrophic (Hillel's third question). Through creating a sense of hope and urgency, the solidarity action of the *us* is galvanized to move power and transform social realities.[7]

My examination of Jewish anti-occupation activism in Palestine/Israel and the United States shows that asking Hillel's second question, "If I am only for myself, who am I?" rotates back to the first question, "If I am not for myself, who will be for me?" revealing a feminist insight where the "self" (who am I?) is only truly human if she is relationally accountable for another. When this insight is integrated into the social movement mobilization of young American Jews, it facilitates their questioning of the narrative into which their institutions and elders socialized them, namely, that to be Jewish in the aftermath of the Holocaust means to prioritize exclusionary forms of solidarity, to be *only* for oneself with a reified assumption of what this "self" means as embodied in Palestine/Israel. Critically, what the process of ethical outrage and the dissolution of cognitive dissonance regarding Israel and Zionism does for American Jews is to redirect their affective attachment and solidarity as they reimagine and re-script an alternative self (a response to the question who am I?). Their solidarity is redirecting from the Zionist teleological and homogenizing construction of the Jews as a "nation" associated intimately (regardless of where they are) with a State and its policies to Palestinians whose oppression they are complicit in and whose oppression connects to a broader global analysis of coloniality and a Jewish commitment to stand with the oppressed.

American Jewish solidarity with Palestinians is interconnected with broader anti-racist struggles and a Jewish self-understanding of being on the side of justice, not domination and whiteness or the curious civilizational construct "Judeo-Christian."[8] Next, I show that reorienting the locus of affective loyalties also entails constructing a new anti-Zionist Jewish *us* within the diasporic context. In distinction, anti-occupation Israeli Jews have differently situated selves that also require them to hermeneutically interrogate the sacred meanings of the Land of Israel outside a settler colonial and supremacist paradigm without erasing such significances and without erasing their actual bodies that inhabit the space and cannot exit from it as a matter of theoretical decree. Likewise, they need to decolonize Jewishness to reconfigure ethical frameworks of living together with Palestinians and redressing historical crimes. While American Jews can imagine the *us* in the form of a synagogue or a "faith community," working for justice everywhere and in solidarity with all those who are marginalized and oppressed, but with particular attention to those in whose oppression they are directly ethically implicated, Israeli Jews need to think politically along questions of democratic citizenship and political solidarity with Palestinians. I trace below why feminist prisms inform or interact (albeit differently) with both instances of relationally reimagining the *us*.

If Not Now, When?

Hillel's questions pertain directly in the contemporary moment to American Jews who have been socialized into a narrative that prescribes an exclusionary form of Jewish solidarity, which has been translated into a chauvinistic and reductive account of Jewishness, one that is only for itself as demonstrated by statements issued in the aftermath of the October 7 Hamas attack and the subsequent indiscriminate Israeli assault on Gaza. Such statements only affirmed and mourned Jewish life and became exclusively concerned with antisemitism (defined problematically as the same as offering criticism of a nation-state) on American campuses, abstracting the horrific Hamas assault from a deeper context of occupation, siege, and up-rootedness going back seventy-five years. It is no wonder then that one of the main organizations created by young Jews who felt betrayed by their elders in the face of obvious Israeli assaults on the dignity and life of Palestinians took one of Hillel's questions as its name. If Not Now (INN) captures the moral urgency these activists experienced in the face of periodic assaults on Gaza. INN was formed during the 2014 attack on the besieged Gaza Strip. The activists respond to Hillel's first question by underscoring Jewish diversity, plurality, and intimate historical familiarity with the experience of being oppressed. This plurality and history define their stories of self, which then leads them to conclude, in response to Hillel's second question, that oppressing others is inconsistent with Jewish liberation.[9] This also leads them to express grief and outrage aimed primarily at the Jewish community for its disregard for Palestinian lives and to challenge their elders and the institutions that produced them. They do so by confronting and shaming them with the inconsistency of their unconditional support of belligerent Israeli policies that contradict what they were taught about their Jewish values and dedication to justice and solidarity with the oppressed.

One of INN's first political actions during the Gaza massacre of 2014 was to recite publicly the Mourner's Kadish for those who were killed and to read all their names. The act of Jewish ritual mourning inclusive of Palestinians re-signifies and re-narrates conceptions of ethical solidarity.[10] Ganz's public narrative methodology explains why the emotion of ethical outrage, which entails a particular experience of values, propels people to act urgently: *if not now, when?* Ethical outrage, however, is not instinctive, but rather a product of long, multipronged processes of unlearning and politicization, which I trace in my book *Days of Awe*. This process results in rescripting what it means to be us or what are the values and histories that constitute the public Jewish narrative. The emotive experience of shame and ethical outrage is also a product of a feedback loop process with critical hermeneutical retrieval of alternative prophetic rather than chauvinistic accounts of Jewishness.[11]

American Jewish education romanticizes Jewish participation in solidarity work during the civil rights movement as proof of the Jewish ethical vocation as prophetic, standing, and marching with the oppressed. The image of the prophetic, however, does not compute with the images of routine human rights violations done in the name of all Jews in Palestine/Israel and presumably for the sake of Jewish safety/redemption. The dissonance between the two images of a Judaism of force and tanks, and a Judaism of prophetic ethics (of speaking truth to power) and creating a human chain to block the violent Jewish-Kahanist flag parade in occupied East Jerusalem on Jerusalem Day, has been accomplished through a variety of discursive mechanisms, such as orientalism, Islamophobia, and an ethnocentric reading of Jewish history that negates Jewish diasporic learnings and histories. Accordingly, for Jews to rearticulate their community as ethical and anti-racist, the activists recognize their need to decolonize and de-orientalize the scaffolding of modern Jewish history[12] and to trace the discursive and semiotic moves that assimilated Jews into a civilizational euro-centric discourse.[13] Unsurprisingly, James Baldwin's essay that rendered the whitening of Jews in America as a moral choice that (white) American Jews made is a frequent reference in the grassroots ethical rescripting critical Jews engage in.[14] To decolonize, as I elaborate here, for American Jews, means to disassimilate from whiteness, which also entails necessarily dezionizing Jewish public narratives.

Questioning exclusionary accounts of Jewish solidarity can be feminist, decolonial, or both, with an understanding that the decolonial move is not necessarily feminist. Zionism has relied on a biblical script, which the Jewish Israeli scholar Amnon Raz-Krakotzkin explains is a form of Euro-Christian colonization of the Jewish imagination wherein Jews read the Bible through Christian interpretations about the Jews, the Land, and the promise of return and the ingathering of the exiles. This biblical-centric interpretation also rendered the Jews of Europe as foreigners, illuminating the close links between Christian Zionism (presumed Philo-semitism) and antisemitism and its genocidal upshot. Raz-Krakotzkin's work retrieves the possibility of Jewish exilic life in historic Palestine by interrogating an alternative Jewish modernity that consolidated in the Palestinian Ottoman city of Safed in the sixteenth century.[15] This was a time of convergence of Eastern and Western Jewish communities upon the expulsion of the Jews from Portugal and Spain and their settling in Palestine and the broader region. It was also when Jewish mysticism and legal learning in Safed were standardized, printed, and circulated broadly. Raz-Krakotzkin juxtaposes Safed's midrashic or Mishnaic model of Jewishness incubated in Safed (one centering hermeneutical praxis) with the biblical or Mikraic model that centers a "literal reading" of the Torah, which underlie a Zionism cradled in Christian Europe (upon all of Europe's ills). For Raz-Krakotzkin, decolonizing Jewishness means dispelling the hold of the Christian Zionist imagination shaping Jewish meanings and political horizons. The Safed model has been eclipsed and downplayed within the Zionist ethos and later the nationalist Jewish Israeli discourse. For Raz-Krakotzkin, decolonizing Jewishness means retrieving an alternative Jewish modernity and an exilic reading of Jewish life in Zion, outside of a European settler colonial narrative, which has defined European Zionism since at least the Balfour Declaration of 1917, written by a British lord, embedded within a Christian Zionist restorationist imagination as well as the interest of an empire, who "gave" the land to the Jews.

Raz-Krakotzkin's decolonial move reclaims the three interrelated negations that define the Zionist monopoly over Jewish meaning, namely: the negation of exile/diaspora, which entails an internalized antisemitic discourse about the "sickly and passive" Jews roaming around, as if outside history; the negation of the East, including the many manifestations of flourishing Jewish life in Asia, Africa, and Arab and Islamic lands; and the negation of the indigenous Palestinians who lived in the Land to which Jews "returned" in a reenactment of a biblical script, which itself depends on a Christian biblical and prophetic imagination of a Jewish return. Raz-Krakotzkin's interrogation and retrieval of Jewish exilic life in the Land, through the model of Safed and its Mishnaic hermeneutical praxis, constitutes a nonfeminist decolonial move ethically accountable to the normative demands of Palestinians on Jewish accounts of the question "If I am only for myself, who am I?" Influenced deeply by

Walter Benjamin's reading of Paul Klee's painting *Angel of History*, blown backward by civilizational progress and facing piles of debris in its aftermath, Raz-Krakotzkin's retrieval of Safed resonates with a feminist epistemology from the margins. He seeks to articulate a decolonial approach and dialectic accountability to Arab Jews, Palestinians, and the colonization of the Jewish tradition—these are the debris. His hermeneutical move, however, is not feminist, per se, because the Mishnaic model of sixteenth-century Safed, which Raz-Krakotzkin retrieves, is hetero-patriarchal. The decolonial move, therefore, is not necessarily feminist, even if, in the case of Raz-Krakotzkin, it denotes dialectical Benjaminian attention to the (Jewish and Palestinian) debris left by the "progress" of political Zionism.[16]

Recognizing the piles of debris as sites of harm and violence is a normative position from where Raz-Krakotzkin's hermeneutical and historical work amounts to Jewish ethics, which is also concerned with rearticulating the question "Who are we?" This question is urgent in the Jewish Israeli context because Israeli Jews cannot stop being Jewish and Israeli by reclaiming the diaspora as most authentically Jewish and their true home.[17] They must ascertain from their situatedness (rather than through "god tricks") how to be Jewish in the land without being hegemonic and beholden to a settler colonial and Jewish Zionist supremacist logic. Supremacist logic constitutes a form of exclusionary solidarity; naming such chauvinism wrong is a normative claim. Likewise, exposing how chauvinistic articulations of Jewish identity eclipse other Jewish meanings, possibilities, and histories is a normative and hermeneutical counter-archival praxis. That such hermeneutics goes to the debris or the margins constitutes a feminist ethical move, even if the focus of such a move is not necessarily feminist and intersectional.

In distinction, the diasporic American Jewish anti-occupation and anti-Zionist movements are centrally embedded in queer and feminist positionalities. Their fundamental questions revolve relationally around the recognition of sinfulness vis-à-vis what is being done to the Palestinians in the name of all Jews. Unlike the Jewish Israeli task of scripting another way of being ethically Jewish in the land and through historical accountability to Palestinians, diaspora Jews' main impetus is to feel belonging (as Jews) within social justice and anti-racist circles. To do so, the activists I interviewed and accompanied needed to relinquish Zionism and whiteness. My ethnographic work with American Jewish activists reveals a gradual (but sometimes sudden) erosion of cognitive dissonance between presumptions around Jewish normativity and progressive values around feminism and gender and the support for the occupation of Palestinians.

Many activists I interviewed needed to unlearn the discursive violence underpinning their prior ethnoreligious centric solidarity with Israel (or "the Jews"). This amounted to a critique of Zionism's euro-centricity, internalized forms of Christian European antisemitism, assimilation into whiteness, the negation of the Jewish tradition itself through the ethos of the negation of exile and diaspora, the transvaluation of Jewish masculinity, and the creation of the "new Hebrew," muscled and suntanned. The activists I depict in my book have realized that the storyline concerning the Jewish redemption in Palestine in the aftermath of the Shoah, in fact, entailed the Nakba or Catastrophe for the Palestinians and their subsequent uprooting and exile. This historical injustice and the ongoing, entrenched dynamics and structures of the Israeli settler colonial, military occupation, and apartheid regime cannot be justified on human rights grounds, regardless of the aftermath of the Nazi genocide against the Jews and the legacies of antisemitism. One injustice cannot be redressed through another injustice, and no right, such as "the right to self-determination," can be understood abstractly and nonrelationally outside its very particular historical and political contexts. Jewish self-determination as a Jewish majority nation-state meant the Nakba because there were people in the land.

If I Am Only for Myself, Who Am I?

My book *Days of Awe* shows, through extensive ethnographic work, how the meaning of Jewish belonging and solidarity reconfigured from ethnocentric to *other*-centric, relational, intersectional, and accountable to how the oppression of Palestinians as well as their dislocation and uprooting is done and justified in the name of Jews. The activists reclaimed Jewish ethics by first declaring in outrage that occupation is not *their* Judaism and then by reimagining their Jewishness otherwise. My in-depth interviews with American Jews who shifted their affective loyalties from Israel (and Zionist ethnocentric conceptions of solidarity) to the Palestinian struggle reveal that one of the most predictable mechanisms for politicization on questions about the occupation of Palestinians and how it has been justified morally through a Jewish nationalist discourse is through sensitization into feminist and queer theories, identities, and praxes. Indeed, the Judaism reimagined from within the social movement is queer, multiracial, multigender, and feminist. It is a Judaism of solidarity with the oppressed and the marginalized, one seeking to disengage from the assimilation of Jews into whiteness and a civilizational discourse.

A case study that I feature in the book and that most explicitly captures the "product" of the relational and intersectional meaning-making process of responding to the question: "What is my Judaism?" is the case of Tzedek Chicago. Tzedek Chicago (founded in 2015) is a prefigurative Jewish community that, under the leadership of Rabbi Brant Rosen, deliberately rereads the tradition by innovating its liturgy through a relational engagement with Palestinians and other victims of injustice. Rosen and community members devised a set of values to define the community's Judaism as antimilitarist, spiritual, ethical, un-chosen, diasporic, multiracial, and postnationalist. Tzedek's diasporic Judaism centers and retrieves the Eastern European notion of *doikayt* or "hereness," signaling a commitment to stand and fight in solidarity with *all* of one's neighbors, not just Jewish ones, thereby rejecting Zionism and diasporic enclave practices. *Doikayt*, in this instance, was available as archival "debris" for contemporary reclaiming and reshaping as an ethical Jewish principle conducive to relinquishing nationalist, exclusionary, and territorial conceptions of solidarity.

Hence, Tzedek's diasporism inverses the Zionist negation of exile by underscoring Tzedek's at-homeness in Chicago. Since the publication of my book, Tzedek officially shifted its self-definition from non-Zionist to anti-Zionist. In 2022, the community affirmed anti-Zionism as a communal core value through a multipronged voting process. Before this final vote, the board facilitated various communal discernment channels. In the rationale for the decision, the leadership of Tzedek Chicago clarified its relational approach:

Zionism, the movement to establish a sovereign Jewish nation-state in historic Palestine, is dependent upon the maintenance of a demographic Jewish majority in the land. Since its establishment, Israel has sought to maintain this majority by systematically dispossessing Palestinians from their homes through a variety of means, including military expulsion, home demolition, land expropriation, and revocation of residency rights, among others. It is becoming increasingly difficult to deny the fundamental injustice at the core of Zionism.[18]

The drafters of the statement conclude by echoing Angela Davis who famously said, "In a racist society, it is not enough to be non-racist; we must be anti-racist."

In the same way, Tzedek Chicago now feels that "the neutral term [non-Zionist] fails to honor the central anti-racist premise of the movement [signaling the location of Tzedek within a broader contested social movement field]." The community concurrently affirms its commitment to diasporism: "At Tzedek Chicago, we seek to develop and celebrate a diasporic consciousness that joyfully views the entire world as our homeland." Further, the statement reads, "We also believe that Jewish diasporic consciousness has the real potential to help us reach a deeper solidarity with those who have been historically colonized and oppressed." Diasporism, therefore, is the antidote for Zionism and offers a resource for American Jews to disengage from their assimilation into whiteness. In another sermon for Rosh Hashanah 5777 (2016), Rosen defends the earlier choice of defining the community as "non-Zionist." He retrieves the Jewish tradition of how God exiled together with the Jews, which for him "represents the intrinsic beauty and genius of the Jewish conception of peoplehood: we used our own unique experience to make a spiritual statement about the human condition."[19] We may observe a shift to universalizing and metaphoricizing the Jewish experience and the basic terms of Zion and diaspora, a metaphoricization that is not inconsistent with the Christian supersessionist spiritualization of Zion and a modernist rendering of religion as a set of values.

Rosen continues his hermeneutical maneuvers: "Whether we are Jewish or not, we are all, in a sense, wanderers. One way or another, we all know the experience of being strangers in a strange land." This last point echoes feminist philosopher Judith Butler's account of dispersion and alterity as the foundations of Jewish ethics. Butler's account of Jewish ethics decenters Jewish subjectivity and, in the process, reclaims it anew as alterity rather than at-homeness. However, while retrieving this notion of being a stranger in a strange land, Rosen is also interested in telling the world how comfortable he is in the diaspora, which is *his* home. He feels at home in Chicago through a universalizing reversal of the Zionist ethos of the negation of diaspora. However, the dependency of his diasporism on the metaphoricization of Zion (and on the literalism of a conception of home in Chicago) renders him unconcerned with Zion as a place that also constitutes a site of multiple Jewish meanings and histories of dislocations (such as that of Arab Jews) as well as a home, the meaning of which ought to resignify. Rosen's anti-Zionist diasporism is unconcerned with Jewish Israeli margins (such as Mizrahi and Ethiopian) on their own terms, beyond the struggle of Palestinians. But his diasporism nevertheless emphasizes Jewish and non-Jewish epistemologies from the margins, which otherwise unsettle Ashkonormative conceptions of Jewishness, highlighting lived and embodied multiracial and multigendered Jewish positionalities.

Dialoguing with broader social movement actors and contentious debates, Tzedek's intervention, therefore, is relational and intersectional. Interrogating white supremacist and heteropatriarchal motifs within the Jewish community, Tzedek expands the boundaries of Jewish normativity while reinscribing a binary negation of a negation of exile (central to the Zionist ethos) that represents Tzedek's complicity with erasures, nevertheless: inversing the Zionist ethos of the negation of exile or diaspora flips the valued side of the binary without interrogating the binary itself. On one occasion, I was part of a conversation where community members discussed with sadness how the sacred language of Hebrew had become triggering to Palestinians. The discussion revolved around whether protest actions in Chicago involving prayers across community lines should eliminate Hebrew, considering many Palestinians and Arab Americans partake in the mobilization of such broad-based coalitions. However, a fundamental concept in peace research tells us that such an erasure (in this case, of Hebrew) replicates rather than transforms injustice. The transformative question for Jews is how to inhabit Hebrew justly.

Tzedek Chicago's negation of the euro-Zionist negation of exile reclaims exile as a site of historical meaning for Jews. However, it falls short of decolonizing the Jewish imagination in ways that would disrupt an internalized Christian supersessionist account of Zion, as Raz-Krakotzkin does. Retrieving exile, for Raz-Krakotzkin, as I noted, is not a reactionary escape route, but rather an unrealized source for imagining a binational alternative future in Palestine/Israel and a concurrently alternative, de-orientalized Jewish modernity. However, unlike Butler and the movement of American Jews that Rosen embodies and their sense of complicity and responsibility toward the Palestinian other, remaining in a theological/epistemological remembrance mode, as Raz-Krakotzkin does, risks glossing over historical accountability for redressing Palestinian moral and political claims as the point of departure of the restorative/reparative process in the present.

Focusing on Europe as ground zero of intellectual, theological, political, imperial, and genocidal culpability for both the repression of Safed *and* Palestinian displacement diminishes Jewish Israeli/Zionist agency, responsibility, and historical accountability. Ironically, it also reinstates the positionality of Jews (and the Jewish tradition) as victims, even while, regarding their structural situatedness in the racialized political geography of Palestine/Israel, they inhabit the location of perpetrators and beneficiaries of violence, including Mizrahi and Ethiopian marginalized communities. Therefore, while foregrounding binationalism as a decolonial ethics, Raz-Krakotzkin's conceptual moves are not reparative because they invest responsibility and locate agency in Christian European modernity. In distinction, Amos Goldberg and Bashir Bashir, in their book *The Holocaust and the Nakba*, understand binational decolonial ethics as also necessarily about interrogating *dialogically* what Jews did to others and what shape Jewish historical accountability should take.[20] The praxis of remembrance (as in Raz-Krakotzkin's deployment of a Benjaminian lens) also stops short of intersectionally interrogating, for example, the patriarchal normativity of the model of Safed. This similarly demobilizes its reparative traction as a sociological future-oriented dialectical force for decolonial rescripting from the ground up.[21]

In activist Jewish Israeli circles, the organization Zochrot (literally, "they remember" in the feminine conjugation) focuses on remembrance and accountability for the Nakba as an event in time, but also as an ongoing reality of displacement, erasure, and replacement of the indigenous people. Over the decades, Zochrot has deepened its sphere of activism from a focus on ethnic cleansing (teaching Israeli Jews about the erased and denied history of the Nakba) to an analysis of settler colonialism going back to the establishment of the still-operating Jewish National Fund tasked with the colonization of Palestine. The organization has also grappled with its own Ashkonormativity as well as Mizrahi critiques and narratives of dislocation that are interlaced with the Palestinian Nakba.[22] Over the decades of the "peace process" (which itself became a form of further entrenching the occupation and annexationist designs), the Israeli peace movement often bracketed the "domestic" social justice issue concerning marginalized communities who were the targets of orientalist and discriminatory attitudes by the Ashkenazi hegemony from the "conflict" with the Palestinians, which was posited as a "foreign policy" issue.[23]

Upon the growing realization that the "peace process" is neither of its two terms, international and Israeli human rights organizations finally joined Palestinians in naming the entire geography from the Jordan River to the Mediterranean Sea an "apartheid" Jewish supremacist regime. In this stretch of land, the logic of apartheid operates differently depending on whether we are discussing Palestinians within the territories of 1948 or "proper Israel," the territories of the West Bank occupied in 1967, occupied East Jerusalem where Palestinians have only residency cards, and the most massive open-air prison of Gaza, which turned, after October 7, 2023, into a killing field.[24] Naming the issue is critical because of the ethical implications it evokes if we can all agree that the privileging of one group over another because of their identity is wrong. Beyond the question of privilege, "Jewish" warrants are deployed to dominate, imprison, displace, annihilate, and deny the humanity of Palestinians.

The feminism of Zochrot functions as a clarifying lens, exposing the definitional realities of violence. The feminine conjugation of the organization's name denotes the possibility of an alternative memory to the "heroic" masculinity that populates the Zionist ethos of defense and conquest. Feminism and peace in the context of the Israeli peace movement, however, have been deeply implicated in Ashkonormativity and in the binarization of "domestic issues" and "foreign affairs"—a conceptual binarization enabled by the Green Line, a demarcation that refers to the temporary armistice line achieved in 1949, but whose erosion the many apartheid reports show clearly. The bifurcation of "domestic issues," often framed along the discourse of ethnic tensions or cleavages and the occupation of Palestinians in 1967, enraged Mizrahi populations (or those communities who trace their roots to Arab and Islamic countries and who were subjected to racist practices within the Israeli context). Many Mizrahim saw the "peace movement" as an Ashkenazi (or euro-Zionist) discourse that overlooked their own experiences of inter-generational injustice and marginalization within the racialized political geography of Palestine/Israel. Further, peace mobilization became a feminist issue dominated by Ashkenazi and often Anglo-Saxon women who engaged in various activities with Palestinian women, but without connecting the dots between the occupation of Palestinians and what came to be articulated as the "ongoing Nakba" and Mizrahi marginalization. Drawing on the extensive history of radical Mizrahi protest, including the legacy of the Israeli Black Panthers of the 1970s, Mizrahi feminists have been challenging the myopic function of the Green Line for decades.[25]

Further, while the stories of the dislocation of Arab Jews from inhabiting the MENA region as indigenous communities and their assimilation into a settler colonial Euro-Zionist discourse are intertwined with the Palestinian Nakba, Mizrahi communities within the racialized context of Israel became beneficiaries of and complicit with a supremacist Jewish Zionist regime. The travel, physically and metaphorically on bypass roads, embodies the logic of Jewish supremacy and the racialization process whereby Arab Jews needed to self-alienate from their Arabness to assimilate. Their socialization, like that of Ethiopian Israelis, entails underscoring their Jewishness over and against their Arabness[26] and, in effect, alienated them from their roots as indigenous to and interwoven within the region's pluralistic social fabrics, which predated the violent epistemic and identitarian sectarianism engineered by Western Christian colonial forces.[27] For years, the Green Line constituted not only a geopolitical but also a normative, boundary, helping Israeli Jews to render only what was happening on the other side of the line (in 1967 occupied territories) as wrong and corrupting, such as the messianic settlement or colonization project. The Green Line myopically concealed the Nakba and normalized "proper Israel" as "Jewish and democratic," an appearance and contradiction that became impossible to maintain. The margins of the mass mobilization against the "judicial coup" of 2023 capture this foundational contradiction in the slogan: "no democracy with occupation." This is where Zochrot's primary work in teaching the Nakba in Hebrew enters the field as a disruption of Israeli Zionist historiography about 1948.

In a 2023 interview, Rachel Beitarie, the CEO of Zochrot, explains that anti-occupation work and feminism are intertwined.[28] In conversation with Palestinian feminist mobilization, Zochrot understands Palestine as a feminist issue because any struggle that demands liberation from oppression, and the dismantling of supremacist structures, gender-based or ethnonational, constitutes a feminist struggle. Supremacist configurations of power, accordingly, are all interrelated forms of oppression. Beitarie reflects: "The belief that men are superior to women or that women should occupy only certain places that they ought not to transgress is just like the belief that Jews are superior to Palestinians and deserve more rights."[29] Echoing Barghouti, Beitarie identifies the glorification of militarism in Israeli society and the recruitment of women into this military as antithetical to feminism. Women's military accomplishments only make them complicit in the occupation and the oppression of Palestinians. The occupation, which depends on a Jewish supremacist ideology and regime, corrupts feminist possibilities and harms women, LGBTQIA+ people, and other marginalized communities. The increased ethnocentricity and supremacist policies indicative of the formation of an extremist government late in 2022 also came with explicit and intensifying homophobia and anti-women policies.

While Zochrot's feminism is foregrounded, the organization's main issue is dismantling the occupation and the apartheid regime. The normative urgency is located in working to dismantle the occupation. Feminist ethics and positionality are pivotal in unlearning Zionism and in dismantling Jewish Zionist supremacism by literally and figuratively deconstructing bypass roads that fragment communities, divide potential allies, and harm ethically and physically, depending on one's location along the matrix of domination.[30] Still, the question is whether imagining Jewish ethical life in the land also requires a positive Jewish normativity—one that, like Raz-Krakotzkin's decolonial move, understands itself as Jewish in Palestine meaningfully, outside the settler colonial and ethnocentric paradigm, but not through erasure. Unlike Tzedek Chicago, such normativity cannot simply rely on the "diasporic" ethics of solidarity with anti-racism and *doikayt* where Judaism can be retrieved as postnationalist, queer, and feminist as the binary antidote to ethnocentric Zionist conceptions of solidarity.

If I am only for myself, who am I? This question certainly animates the Jews in Tzedek Chicago, but it also finds an intricate manifestation in the much more complicated Jewish terrains of Palestine/Israel, where feminist Jewish solidarity with non-Jews has to be worked out through different mechanisms and frames that cannot quite easily conjure up a post-nationalist diasporic positionality. The Mizrahi Civic Collective, which consolidated during the early days of the Israeli Jewish uprising against the "judicial coup" that was orchestrated by the extremist annexionist and conservative coalition, formed late in 2022 as a result of multiple and frequent election cycles. Drawing on decades of critical Mizrahi scholarship and activism, the Mizrahi Collective rejected the myopic romanticism regarding the presumed "democracy" that the judicial reform would demolish by significantly diminishing the independence of the Supreme Court. The Supreme Court, which the protesters see themselves as defending, has sanctioned the occupation. The "old order" was not only "democratic only for Jews," but also extremely discriminatory toward nonnormative Jewish citizens. Hence, the Mizrahi Collective mobilized to offer both a rejection of the "judicial reform" and a return to the "good old" nondemocracy.

The vision document of the Mizrahi Collective explains as follows:

Today, we do not lament: "There goes democracy . . ." as many other Israelis are doing right now. The reason is that full democracy for Mizrahim, Palestinians, Ethiopians, and immigrants from the former Soviet Union was never really in place—so where could such "democracy" possibly go?! The current crisis presents an opportunity to envision a real democratic horizon—not one that longs for an imagined past but one that strives instead to transform the oppressive power structures at their core for the benefit of everyone who inhabits this land.[31]

The Mizrahi Collective proceeded to produce a series of position papers. Of particular relevance to the analysis here is their position paper on traditionalism or *masortiyut* as conservative or emancipatory.[32] The challenge is to disrupt and decolonize the modernist frame that posits Ashkenazi as "secular" and peace-loving, juxtaposed to the religious "peace spoilers," such as the settlers in the occupied territories of 1967. The position paper, written collectively by major critical Mizrahi thinkers, retells how the history of anti-hegemonic Mizrahi mobilization, in its various modalities since the 1950s, often drew on traditionalism.[33] However, over the decades appeals to Mizrahi traditionalism became coopted into Jewish supremacist, anti-women, and anti-LGBTQIA+ agenda.

Against this cooptation, the Mizrahi Collective seeks to reclaim *masortiyut* committed to dismantling the oppressive dynamics, relational patterns, and structures in Palestine/Israel. Accordingly, the position paper clarifies that secularist/modernist analytic frames attributing blame to religion as a peace spoiler and engine for supremacist politics conceal how "religion" authorized the state.

Raz-Krakotzkin observed the striking contradiction inherent in "secular" forms of political Zionism. It is summed up in this statement of his: "We don't believe in God, but God promised us the land."[34] Over the decades and partly due to the prolonged occupation, explicitly religious justifications, messianic visions, and sacred warrants have gained momentum.[35] Rejecting the instrumentalization of the Torah into a supremacist nationalist discourse and its domestication as "sweet" and "moderate," the Mizrahi Civic Collective underscores *masortityut* as a source of hope for shaping a democratic horizon, recognizing that this entails a particular feminist interpretation of *masortiyut* itself rather than its reified characterization. Specifically, dispelling the diffusion and mirroring of American neo-conservativism about anti-women and anti-LGBTQIA+ "family values" outlooks, a Mizrahi democratic approach unsettles a presumption that the struggle against patriarchy is to be waged by the "secular" state over and against "religion." Instead, the fight against patriarchy and gender-based violent structures is all-encompassing, and the rhetorical appeal to a "defense of traditional values" as a form of Jewish authenticity, which coopts Mizrahi *masortiyut* as a new buttressing of ethnocentric Jewish politics, contributes to reinforcing male Mizrahi hegemony and patriarchal interpretations of tradition along with the Jewish supremacist political regime upon its ethnocentric, racist, and messianic impulses (which I have already traced to Christian European genealogies, histories, and ideologies).

While inclusive of some female Mizrahi cultural producers, this coopted Mizrahi traditionalist approach, the authors of the Mizrahi Civic Collective's position paper write, blocks non-elitist feminist and queer Mizrahi voices that challenge heteropatriarchal normativity. Furthermore, the cooptation of Mizrahi *masortiyut* does not translate into any actual investment in social justice issues that have inflicted marginalized communities, such as public housing, education, and poverty. The latter connects complexly with the Palestinian experience because Mizrahim often were put in Palestinian homes or in their ruins, only to be displaced later from such locations due to gentrification processes. Unlike the Ashkenazi in the Kibbutzim and their land theft from Palestinians, the Mizrahi did not get "ownership" over the "nationalized" or "Judaized" land and property into which they were relocated; thereby, they found themselves with significantly less intergenerational wealth. Of course, if the Mizrahi struggles for equity, equality, and affirmative action do not also connect the dots to the dispossession of the Palestinians from their lands and property,[36] these struggles become, like women serving in the occupying military, a demand to have a larger portion in an oppressive unjust regime. Indeed, the position paper on *masortityut* rejects the deployment of tradition to sanction the settler colonial link between nationality and citizenship; rather, it aspires to dismantle this link as a scaffolding for a future of total civic equality between Palestinians and Jews in the land. This will not translate into an erasure of Jewishness since the synonymizing of citizenship and Jewish belonging will be disrupted as a decolonial act. As in Raz-Krakotzkin's retrieval of Mishnaic Judaism in Ottoman Palestine, the position paper draws on alternative Jewish archives of centuries of Jewish life in Palestine outside of a settler colonial and modernist/secularist European nationalist discourse where Jews were interwoven into the local Ottoman milieus, living with a sense of the sacredness of the place and yet in persistent exile, not seeking a Zionist reenactment of a biblical script.

The critical Mizrahi intervention seeks to build on the histories and memories of Jewish life in the region and to reclaim from the euro-centric Zionist colonial logic of fragmentation and division their sense of belonging to Arabic as evident in the (unsuccessful) Mizrahi litigation against the Jewish Nation-State Law (passed in 2018), which demoted the status of Arabic, along with declaring that Israel is the State of Jews and Jews only.[37] The drafters of the position paper highlight how Mizrahi erasure and Palestinian erasure are interconnected, despite the physical and metaphorical bypass roads; this recognition is at the foundation of rewriting and retrieving alternative Jewish history and ethics. Likewise, the critical delinking between citizenship and nationality will have implications for Jewish discourse around gender, conversion, and other critical issues, which are now beholden to a nationalist supremacist frame, even if those are analytically bracketed to discuss feminist practice and gendered dimensions of disputes over the sacred spaces in the Western Wall and the Haram al-Sharif/Temple Mount, for example.[38] This exposition of the position paper illuminates the impossibility of isolating feminist religious ethics from an interrogation of the occupation and apartheid regime within which such a discussion unfolds. It also shows why anti-occupation and anti-colonial feminist ethics are incomplete without a Jewish sociological, historical, and hermeneutical reclaiming of alternative archives as resources for reparative future horizons.

If I Am Not for Myself, Who Will Be for Me?

Often Hillel's questions are deployed to illuminate how the nature of one group's liberation is entangled with all other liberation struggles. Yet they still presume heteropatriarchal normativity. Recognizing that my oppression connects to your oppression does not mean I can recognize all facets of this interconnectedness. For example, I may recognize how Black Americans' struggle against police brutality connects to the Israeli occupation and policing of Palestinians or the wall on the Mexico-US border. But I may not recognize how both instances of oppression also convey capitalist greed and toxic masculinity in addition to racial profiling, xenophobia, and necropolitical control. In other words, a Palestinian man can identify with the image of George Floyd, but the resonance that the killing of Floyd evokes in him does not necessarily invite interrogation of hetero-patriarchal norms and feminist emancipatory scripts. Nevertheless, Hillel's three questions do capture a feminist insight concerning the importance of identity (knowing who you are) to solidarity work seeking to join a coalition of actors mobilized against systemic oppression and injustice. The act of knowing who one is furnishes one's particular accounts of not only their oppression but also of their conception of freedom. The question is not only about the structures that oppress me, how they constitute the matrix of domination inflicted on other people, and how this oppression is spun as normative and ethical and necessary. The question is also about how knowing who I am or reimagining it anew as pivotal to my ability to imagine the future outside the structures of oppression, radically and particularly.[39]

To interrogate the nationalistic and identitarian limits of bypass roads' feminist solidarity in Palestine/Israel and the underlying settler colonial dynamics, one needs to engage in what I called elsewhere the "hermeneutics of citizenship" or reinterpreting the meanings and thresholds of belonging to the nation.[40] For feminist ethics to be emancipatory in this context, it needs to be decolonial, not only through an abstract global analysis of coloniality/modernity[41] (coloniality/modernity is a term of art in decolonial scholarship, denoting the constitutive relation between the violence of Western Christian colonialism and the lofty values of liberal modernity[42]), but also specifically through decolonizing the Jewish imagination and the political discourse framing ethnocentric accounts of Jewish solidarity. Bargouti's insight with which I opened this chapter not only reveals an inconsistency between feminist normativity and the participation of Jewish women in the occupying force (oppressing men, women, and other genders alike), but it also conveys that this participation entails particular accounts of these women's Jewishness. Grappling with Bargouti's thesis means recognizing that controlling an entire population for another to feel safe is wrong. Not only that, the feeling of safety itself is fallacious and dependent upon walls, tanks, weapons, surveillance, bypass roads, and other technologies not of safety, but of violence and domination. What grounds do I have to make this claim? The very articulation of such a question intimates the privilege that one enjoys in Anglophone or

French seminar rooms. Suppose you are a Palestinian crossing a checkpoint and subjected to the arbitrariness of a regime of permits. In that case, you just know that someone's boot is constantly on your neck and that this is wrong and antithetical to your humanity. This should be the relational ethical starting point.

To render a situation where Palestinians are routinely surveilled, their movement is constrained, and their homes are demolished, among other atrocities, as oppressive and wrong is to be normative. For religion scholars like myself, this analysis requires interrogating the emergence and consolidation of teleological, belligerent, and exclusionary accounts of Jewish identity and solidarity and identifying sites of disruption where religion is imagined relationally and intersectionally rather than chauvinistically through the prism of defense, revenge, and domination, underwritten by messianic and apocalyptic motifs that trump "ordinary" morality (i.e., "don't steal," "don't kill"). Such interrogation of *If I am not for myself, who will be for me?* (the self) is the work of critique where feminist methodologies, such as intentionally centering epistemologies from the margins, illuminate counter-hegemonic public narratives of us (*if I am only for myself, who am I?*).

Critique, however, is not sufficient for imagining social and political horizons outside the conditions of one's oppression. This is where alternative, obscured, and negated archives, such as Black and Mizrahi Jewish geographies of Jewish life outside the euro-Zionist paradigm, or diasporic conceptions of Judaism are retrieved and become pivotal for reimagining Jewishness outside whiteness. In my analysis of the Mizrahi Civic Collective and Tzedek Chicago, albeit differently, I showed how eclipsed, marginalized, and denied historical and cultural memories can populate alternative ethical resources for Jewish rescripting of the story of us, to recall Ganz's methodology of public narrative. The search for such margins constitutes feminist and decolonial potentialities, though they are not always self-evident or consistent with one another. The religion scholar analyzing sociologically and ethnographically alternative Jewish ethics is not less rigorous for being attuned to the oppression experienced by Palestinians, namely, violence sanctioned by particular appeals to Jewish narratives and warrants. Likewise, feminist mobilization and ethics may inflict their omissions, as Barghouti succinctly states.

Religion and coopted forms of traditionalism through a nationalist discourse of authenticity, as implicated in political boundaries and ideologies, are central to why cross-cutting solidarity does not always materialize across national divides, regardless of the cross-cutting presence of heteropatriarchal normativity. At stake is the question of identity versus difference within coalitional spaces and contexts defined by discursive violence. The role of religion in constituting political belonging is also under scrutiny and subject to rescripting, which is why an analysis of feminist conceptions of solidarity can never be articulated in abstraction from political positionality. This entails interrogating the "we" or "us" as well as the political theology buttressing it. Likewise, even if feminism is, by definition, normative, injustice and oppression are not abstract targets of normative work for coalition-building. Indeed, a simplistic appeal to a coalitional sisterhood across Palestinian and Jewish Israeli thresholds of bypass roads and checkpoints is laughable and myopic of power relationships.

Feminist (and queer) solidarity in the Israeli context is myopic if it only focuses on "women's liberation," without also unlearning exclusionary and racialized Zionist accounts of Jewish solidarity. Indeed, bypass roads' feminism and queer discourse, undergirded by orientalist scaffolding (exemplified, for instance, in a branding campaign showing images of male-presenting Israeli soldiers kissing or holding hands, accompanied by a caption indicating that Israel is the only place in the region where such a thing can happen), has facilitated the violent dynamics of pinkwashing the occupation on the critical level of narratives. Queer Palestinian scholar Sa'ed Atshan, however, challenges what he calls the "purist positionality" of an "empire of critique," which mobilized against pinkwashing for diminishing queer Palestinian individual struggles and suffering by subordinating them to anti-colonial and anti-imperialist international solidarity discourse.[43] Feminist ethics and queer solidarity, therefore, constitute a critical anti-colonial and decolonial methodology without necessarily also specifically accounting for the lives of women and queer individuals within broader narratives of colonial violence. Zochrot's decolonial praxis of remembering denied and erased Palestinian narratives understands itself as feminist, but it similarly subsumes the story of Palestinian women to the broader narrative of the Palestinian Nakba and their experience of settler colonialism.

Zochrot's example of deploying a feminist prism to expose a denied "generic" rather than feminist Palestinian story and to decolonize Jewish Israeli self-understanding illuminates how and why political (national) urgency operates to de-individualize LGBTQIA+ communities and women. At the same time, I traced how the regime of bypass roads literally prevents the emergence of an intersectional imagination within and across ideational lines in Palestine/Israel. Far from an exceptional case,[44] the identitarian limits of Israeli bypass roads' feminism point not only to the presumed tensions between religious ethics and feminist ethics (as if womanist and feminist religious hermeneutics can be bracketed). It also points to how both are entangled within ideological and colonial discursivity. The case study I feature in this chapter reveals that feminist normativity cannot perform "god tricks" because it is always entangled within webs of particularities constituted by religio-cultural and historical meanings as well as political conceptions of belonging and nonbelonging.

This volume's efforts to bring religious ethics into conversation with feminist normativity and broad-based solidarity mobilizing against oppression and injustice shed light on how and why the convergence of feminist and religious ethics requires ethnographic and sociological methodologies. These methodologies must examine how people on the ground and in the margins disentangle exclusionary accounts of solidarity, whether feminist emancipatory visions propel this disentanglement, and where is it coopted into or complicit with structures of injustice, which are themselves beholden to exclusionary forms of solidarity. The case of unlearning Jewish nationalism or Zionism and reimagining Jewishness as anti-occupation, feminist, and anti-racist happens through cross-learning within social justice spaces. It is a fluid process, undetermined in advance, thereby defying reified accounts of normativity and solidarity. Anti-occupation and anti-racist Jewish ethics, in other words, happen on the ground, relationally and dialectically, thereby intimating feminist methodologies and potentialities.

This chapter showed why the crucial conversation between feminist ethics and religious ethics requires attention to and embeddedness in the actual dynamics on the ground of social movements and meaning-making grassroots activists. In the United States, the main emphasis is on disengaging from whiteness and ethnonationalist accounts of Jewishness to link into a global social justice movement and its "empire of critique." In contrast, in the Israeli context, the key focus is on decolonizing Jewishness to facilitate the imagination of nonhegemonic Jewish life in the land and to create a reparative and democratic political imagination together with Palestinians. The distinctions between the two Jewish contexts and their ethical mobilization complicate purist and abstract analyses of ethical mobilization against oppression, particularly where political ideologies are entangled in ethnoreligious narratives about the "we" (the "who are we" question). My findings show that decolonial Jewish ethics in Israeli circles is not necessarily feminist, even if it could be amenable to growing in this direction. At the same time, decolonial and feminist Jewish diasporic ethics is not necessarily fully accountable to Jewish hermeneutics or interpretative methodologies, relying instead on secular (or Christian modernist) accounts of universalism, religion, and humanism. Both cases show why explicating one's normative situatedness is critical for scholarship in religion and that naming oppression and the matrices of violence and their transformation call for feminist and decolonial methodologies.

Notes

1 Mariam Barghouti, "No, You Can't Be a Feminist and a Zionist," *The Forward*, November 27, 2017, https://forward.com/opinion/387675/no-you-cant-be-a -feminist-and-a-zionist/. Accessed August 10, 2024.

2 See, for example, Gil Hochberg, *Visual Occupations: Violence and Visibility in a Conflict Zone* (Durham, NC: Duke University Press, 2015).

3 Donna Haraway, "Situated Knowledges: The Science Question in Feminism and the Privilege of Partial Perspective," *Feminist Studies* 14, no. 3 (1988): 575–99.

4 Queer and feminist theories are interconnected and both disrupt binaries and essential accounts of sexuality and gender. American Jewish critics of Zionism and Israeli policies reach their critique by also undoing the toxic masculinity inherent in militarist accounts of Jewish redemption embodied in images of state violence. My findings also illuminate that many young people who politicize on issues related to Zionism undergo prior politicization on gender and sexuality.

5　Atalia Omer, *Days of Awe: Reimagining Jewishness in Solidarity with Palestinians* (Chicago: University of Chicago Press, 2019).

6　For example, Omer, *When Peace Is Not Enough: How the Israeli Peace Camp Thinks about Religion, Nationalism, and Justice* (Chicago: University of Chicago Press, 2013) and Omer, "Restorative Justice Pathways in Palestine/Israel: Undoing the Settler Colonial Captivity of Jewishness," *Shofar: An Interdisciplinary Journal of Jewish Studies* 41 no. 2 (2023): 154–85. *Project MUSE*, https://doi.org/10.1353/sho.2023.a911223.

7　Marshall Ganz, "Public Narrative, Collective Action, and Power," in *Accountability through Public Opinion: From Inertia to Public Action*, ed. Sina Odugbemi and Taeku Lee (Washington, DC: World Bank, 2011), 273–89.

8　See, for example, Shaul Magid, "The Judeo-Christian Tradition," in *Theologies of American*, ed. Winnifred Sullivan and Elizabeth Shakman Hurd (Bloomington: Indiana University Press, 2021), https://publish.iupress.indiana.edu/read/theologies-of-american-exceptionalism/section/0bebab72-c6b6-4839-a58a-4c86ea2fc977.

9　Omer, *Days of Awe*, 49.

10　Ibid., 51.

11　Ibid., 50.

12　Ibid., especially 211–43.

13　See Santiago Slabodsky, *Decolonial Judaism: Triumphal Failures of Barbaric Thinking* (New York: Palgrave Macmillan, 2014), and Houria Bouteldja, *Whites, Jews, and Us: Toward a Politics of Revolutionary Love* (South Pasadena, CA: Semiotext(e), 2017).

14　James Baldwin, "On Being White . . . And Other Lies," *Essence* (1984), https://www.cwsworkshop.org/pdfs/CARC/Family_Herstories/2_On_Being_White.PDF. Accessed on August 10, 2024. For his deployment in American Jewish rescripting of their public narrative, see Brant Rosen, "The Uprooted and Unwanted: A Sermon for Tzedek Chicago's first Yom Kippur Service," *Shalom Rav*, September 25, 2015, https://rabbibrant.com/2015/09/25/the-uprooted-and-unwanted-a-sermon-for-tzedek-chicagos-first-yom-kippur-service/. Accessed on August 10, 2024.

15　Amnon Raz-Krakotzkin, *Mishna Consciousness, Biblical Consciousness: Safed and Zionist Culture* (Jerusalem: Van Leer Institute Press/Hakibbutz Hameuchad Publishing House, 2022), in Hebrew.

16　See also Raz-Krakotzkin, "Secularism, the Christian Ambivalence toward the Jews, and the Notion of Exile," in *Secularism in Question: Jews and Judaism in*

Modern Times, ed. Ari Joskowicz and Ethan Katz (Philadelphia: University of Pennsylvania Press, 2015), 276–98.

17 See, for example, Judith Butler, *Parting Ways: Jewishness and the Critique of Zionism* (New York: Columbia University Press, 2012).

18 Tzedek Chicago, "Tzedek Chicago Adds Anti-Zionism to Our Core Values Statement," n.d., https://www.tzedekchicago.org/updates/tzedek-chicago-affirms -anti-zionism-as-a-core-value. Accessed on August 10, 2024.

19 Brant Rosen, "Celebrating a New Jewish Diasporism," *Shalom Rav*, n.d., https:// rabbibrant.com/2016/10/04/celebrating-a-new-jewish-diasporism-a-sermon-for -rosh-hashanah-5777/. Accessed August 10, 2024.

20 Bashir Bashir and Amos Goldberg, eds., *The Holocaust and the Nakba: A New Grammar of Trauma and History* (New York: Columbia University Press, 2018).

21 See also Atalia Omer, "What Is 'Jewish' about the Jewish Left in Palestine/Israel?" *Critical Research on Religion*, forthcoming, published in advanced here: https:// doi.org/10.1177/20503032241267233.

22 Ella Shohat, "Sephardim in Israel: Zionism from the Standpoint of Its Jewish Victims," *Social Text* 19/20 (1988): 1–35.

23 Atalia Omer, Diane L. Moore, and Hilary Rantisi, "Touring Absences, Erasures, and Futures in the Unholy Land: Religiously Literate Diasporic Reading of Palestine/Israel," *Palestine/Israel Review* (accepted for publication January 15, 2024). Available in advance here: https://doi.org/10.5325/pir.1.2.0003.

24 For example, B'tselem, "A Regime of Jewish Supremacy from the Jordan River to the Mediterranean Sea: This Is Apartheid," January 12 , 2021, https://www.btselem .org/publications/fulltext/202101_this_is_apartheid. Accessed August 10, 2024.

25 Smadar Lavie, "Where Is the Mizrahi-Palestinian Border Zone? Interrogating Feminist Transnationalism through Bounds of the Lived," *Social Semiotics* 21, no. 1 (2011): 67–83.

26 Yehouda Shenhav, *The Arab Jew: A Postcolonial Reading of Nationalism, Religion, and Ethnicity* (Stanford, CA: Stanford University Press, 2006).

27 See Ella Shohat, "On Orientalist Genealogies: The Split Arab/Jew Figure Revisited," in *The Arab and Jewish Questions: Geographies of Engagement in Palestine and Beyond*, ed. Bashir Bashir and Leila Farsakh (New York: Columbia University Press, 2020), 89–121.

28 Orna Raz, "Feminism of Care," *Politically Correct*, February 28, 2023, https:// politicallycorret.co.il/feminism-of-care/ (in Hebrew). Accessed on August 10, 2024.

29 Ibid., my translation.

30 The "matrix of domination" is an analytic conceptualization developed by Patricia Hill Collins in her *Black Feminist Thought: Knowledge, Consciousness, and the Politics of Empowerment* (New York: Routledge, 2008).

31 Mizrahi Civic Collective, "A Democratic Mizrahi Vision," https://mizrahinationlaw .com/a-democratic-mizrahi-vision/, n.d. Accessed August 10, 2024.

32 See also my analysis of the Mizrahi Civic Collective in Atalia Omer, "What Is 'Jewish' about the Jewish Left in Palestine/Israel?" *Critical Research on Religion* (2024) 12.2: 227–42.

33 Almog Behar, Avi-ram Tzoreff, Hila Dayan, and Moshe Behar, "Position Paper: Masortiyut as Conservative or Liberatory," *Mizrahi Civic Collective*, n.d., https:// mizrahinationlaw.com/ש-או-כשמרנות-מסורתיות.-בעניין-עמדה-נייר/ (in Hebrew). Accessed August 10, 2024.

34 See Youssef Hijazi, "I Feel Responsible for the Victims of Zionism: An Interview with Amnon Raz-Krakotzkin," Qantara, August 13, 2004, https://en.qantara.de/ content/interview-amnon-raz-krakotzkin-i-feel-responsible-for-the-victims-of -zionism. Accessed August 10, 2024.

35 For example, Nadim N. Rouhana and Nadera Shalhoub-Kevorkian, eds. *When Politics Are Sacralized: Comparative Perspectives on Religious Claims and Nationalism* (Cambridge: Cambridge University Press, 2021).

36 See, for example, Itamar Mann, "Disentangling Displacements: Historical Justice for Mizrahim and Palestinians in Israel," *Theoretical Inquiries in Law* 21, no. 2 (2020): 427–58.

37 Jen Marlowe, "Israel's Mizrahi Activists Are Fighting the Racist Nation-State Law," May 27, 2020, *The Nation*, https://www.thenation.com/article/world/israel -racism-mizrahis-palestinians/. Accessed August 10, 2024.

38 See Lihi Ben Shitrit, *Women and the Holy City: The Struggle over Jerusalem's Sacred Space* (Cambridge: Cambridge University Press, 2021). Ben Shitrit, however, demonstrates how and why gendered dynamics and feminist agendas of religious women's contestations and practices in the sacred site of the Haram al-Sharif/Dome of the Rock and the Western Wall intensify rather than diminish the ethnoreligious centric logic of Israeli nationalism.

39 See also Jakeet Singh, "Religious Agency and the Limits of Intersectionality," *Hypatia* 30, no. 4 (2015): 657–74.

40 Omer, "When Peace Is Not Enough," esp. 93–114.

41	See, for example, Maria Lugones, "Toward a Decolonial Feminism," *Hypatia* 25, no. 4 (2010): 742–59.

42	See Santiago Slabodsky, "Seeing the Old in the New: The Coloniality of the Liberal-Populist Marriage," in *Religion and Colonialism*, ed. Atalia Omer and Joshua Lupo (Notre Dame: University of Notre Dame Press, 2024) pp. 25–48.

43	Sa'ed Atshan, *Queer Palestine and the Empire of Critique* (Stanford, CA: Stanford University Press, 2020).

44	For examples of broken and ephemeral solidarities, see Atalia Omer and Joshua Lupo, eds., *Religion and Broken Solidarities: Feminism, Race, and Transnationalism* (Notre Dame: University of Notre Dame Press, 2022).

References

Atshan, Sa'ed. *Queer Palestine and the Empire of Critique* (Stanford, CA: Stanford University Press, 2020).

Baldwin, James. "On Being White . . . And Other Lies," *Essence* (1984), https://www.cwsworkshop.org/pdfs/CARC/Family_Herstories/2_On_Being_White.PDF.

Barghouti, Mariam. "No, You Can't Be a Feminist and a Zionist," *The Forward*, November 27, 2017, https://forward.com/opinion/387675/no-you-cant-be-a-feminist-and-a-zionist/. Accessed August 10, 2024.

Bashir, Bashir, and Amos Goldberg, eds. *The Holocaust and the Nakba: A New Grammar of Trauma and History* (New York: Columbia University Press, 2018).

Behar, Almog, Avi-ram Tzoreff, Hila Dayan, and Moshe Behar. "Position Paper: Masortiyut as Conservative or Liberatory," *Mizrahi Civic Collective*, n.d., https://mizrahinationlaw.com/ש-או-כשמרנות-מסורתיות.בעניין-עמדה-נייר/ (in Hebrew). Accessed August 10, 2024.

Ben Shitrit, Lihi. *Women and the Holy City: The Struggle over Jerusalem's Sacred Space* (Cambridge: Cambridge University Press, 2021).

Bouteldja, Houria. *Whites, Jews, and Us: Toward a Politics of Revolutionary Love* (South Pasadena, CA: Semiotext(e), 2017).

B'tselem. "A Regime of Jewish Supremacy from the Jordan River to the Mediterranean Sea: This Is Apartheid," January 12, 2021, https://www.btselem.org/publications/fulltext/202101_this_is_apartheid. Accessed August 10, 2024.

Butler, Judith. *Parting Ways: Jewishness and the Critique of Zionism* (New York: Columbia University Press, 2012).

Ganz, Marshall. "Public Narrative, Collective Action, and Power." In *Accountability through Public Opinion: From Inertia to Public Action*, edited by Sina Odugbemi and Taeku Lee, 273–89 (Washington, DC: World Bank, 2011).

Haraway, Donna. "Situated Knowledges: The Science Question in Feminism and the Privilege of Partial Perspective." *Feminist Studies* 14, no. 3 (1988): 575–99.

Hijazi, Youssef. "I Feel Responsible for the Victims of Zionism: An Interview with Amnon Raz-Krakotzkin." Qantara, August 13, 2004, https://en.qantara.de/content /interview-amnon-raz-krakotzkin-i-feel-responsible-for-the-victims-of-zionism. Accessed August 10, 2024.

Hill Collins, Patricia. *Black Feminist Thought: Knowledge, Consciousness, and the Politics of Empowerment* (New York: Routledge, 2008).

Hochberg, Gil. *Visual Occupations: Violence and Visibility in a Conflict Zone* (Durham, NC: Duke University Press, 2015).

Lavie, Smadar. "Where Is the Mizrahi-Palestinian Border Zone? Interrogating Feminist Transnationalism through Bounds of the Lived." *Social Semiotics* 21, no. 1 (2011): 6783.

Lugones, Maria. "Toward a Decolonial Feminism." *Hypatia* 25, no. 4 (2010): 742–59.

Magid, Shaul. "The Judeo-Christian Tradition." In *Theologies of American Exceptionalism*, edited by Winnifred Sullivan and Elizabeth Shakman Hurd (Bloomington: Indiana University Press, 2021), https://publish.iupress.indiana.edu/read/theologies-of -american-exceptionalism/section/0bebab72-c6b6-4839-a58a-4c86ea2fc977.

Mann, Itamar. "Disentangling Displacements: Historical Justice for Mizrahim and Palestinians in Israel." *Theoretical Inquiries in Law* 21, no. 2 (2020): 427–58.

Marlowe, Jen. "Israel's Mizrahi Activists Are Fighting the Racist Nation-State Law." May 27, 2020, *The Nation*, https://www.thenation.com/article/world/israel-racism -mizrahis-palestinians/. Accessed August 10, 2024.

Mizrahi Civic Collective. "A Democratic Mizrahi Vision." https://mizrahinationlaw .com/a-democratic-mizrahi-vision/, n.d. Accessed August 10, 2024.

Omer, Atalia. *Days of Awe: Reimagining Jewishness in Solidarity with Palestinians* (Chicago: University of Chicago Press, 2019).

———. "Restorative Justice Pathways in Palestine/Israel: Undoing the Settler Colonial Captivity of Jewishness." *Shofar: An Interdisciplinary Journal of Jewish Studies* 41 no. 2 (2023): 154–85. *Project MUSE*, https://doi.org/10.1353/sho.2023.a911223.

———. "What Is 'Jewish' about the Jewish Left in Palestine/Israel?"

———. *When Peace Is Not Enough: How the Israeli Peace Camp Thinks about Religion, Nationalism, and Justice* (Chicago: University of Chicago Press, 2013).

Omer, Atalia, Diane L. Moore, and Hilary Rantisi. "Touring Absences, Erasures, and Futures in the Unholy Land: Religiously Literate Diasporic Reading of Palestine/

Israel." *Palestine/Israel Review* (accepted for publication January 15, 2024). Available in advance here: https://doi.org/10.5325/pir.1.2.0003.

Omer, Atalia and Lupo, Joshua, eds. *Religion and Broken Solidarities: Feminism, Race, and Transnationalism.* Notre Dame: University of Notre Dame Press, 2022.

Pontifical Council for Justice and Peace. *Compendium of the Social Doctrine of the Church.* Washington, DC: U.S. Conference of Catholic Bishops, 2004.

Raz-Krakotzkin, Amnon. *Mishna Consciousness, Biblical Consciousness: Safed and Zionist Culture* (Jerusalem: Van Leer Institute Press/Hakibbutz Hameuchad Publishing House, 2022), in Hebrew.

———. "Secularism, the Christian Ambivalence toward the Jews, and the Notion of Exile." In *Secularism in Question: Jews and Judaism in Modern Times*, edited by Ari Joskowicz and Ethan Katz, 276–98 (Philadelphia: University of Pennsylvania Press, 2015).

Raz, Orna. "Feminism of Care." *Politically Correct*, February 28, 2023, https:// politicallycorret.co.il/feminism-of-care/ (in Hebrew). Accessed on August 10, 2024.

Rosen, Brant. "Celebrating a New Jewish Diasporism." *Shalom Rav*, n.d., https:// rabbibrant.com/2016/10/04/celebrating-a-new-jewish-diasporism-a-sermon-for -rosh-hashanah-5777/. Accessed August 10, 2024.

———. "The Uprooted and Unwanted: A Sermon for Tzedek Chicago's First Yom Kippur Service." *Shalom Rav*, September 25, 2015, https://rabbibrant.com/2015/09 /25/the-uprooted-and-unwanted-a-sermon-for-tzedek-chicagos-first-yom-kippur -service/.

Rouhana, Nadim N., and Nadera Shalhoub-Kevorkian, eds. *When Politics Are Sacralized: Comparative Perspectives on Religious Claims and Nationalism* (Cambridge: Cambridge University Press, 2021).

Shenhav, Yehouda. *The Arab Jew: A Postcolonial Reading of Nationalism, Religion, and Ethnicity* (Stanford, CA: Stanford University Press, 2006).

Shohat, Ella. "On Orientalist Genealogies: The Split Arab/Jew Figure Revisited." In *The Arab and Jewish Questions: Geographies of Engagement in Palestine and Beyond*, edited by Bashir Bashir and Leila Farsakh (New York: Columbia University Press, 2020), 89–121.

———. "Sephardim in Israel: Zionism from the Standpoint of Its Jewish Victims," *Social Text* 19/20 (1988): 1–35.

Singh, Jakeet. "Religious Agency and the Limits of Intersectionality." *Hypatia* 30, no. 4 (2015): 657–74.

Slabodsky, Santiago. *Decolonial Judaism: Triumphal Failures of Barbaric Thinking* (New York: Palgrave Macmillan, 2014).

———. "Seeing the Old in the New: The Coloniality of the Liberal-Populist Marriage." In *Religion and Colonialism*, edited by Atalia Omer and Joshua Lupo (Notre Dame: University of Notre Dame Press, 2024): 25–48.

Tunu, Wilhelmina Uhai. "*Caritas in Veritate* and Cultural Development," in *Modern Catholic Family Teaching: Commentaries and Interpretations,* ed. Jacob M. Kohlhaas and Mary M. Doyle Roche. Washington, DC: Georgetown University Press, 2024.

Tzedek Chicago. "Tzedek Chicago Adds Anti-Zionism to Our Core Values Statement." n.d., https://www.tzedekchicago.org/updates/tzedek-chicago-affirms-anti-zionism-as-a-core-value. Accessed on August 10, 2024.

11

Rethinking Solidarity in Families

Contributions from Catholic Ethics

Emma McDonald Kennedy

The Catholic tradition envisions the family as a fundamental unit of society concerned both for the welfare of its members and for the wider world. The emphasis on the family as inextricably connected to the common good in global solidarity provides a necessary and helpful challenge to the dominant cultural understanding of the insular, nuclear family. Yet the same documents that promote an outward-facing family betray an implicit reliance on the nuclear family that, I argue, does not take seriously the diversity of family configurations that enact the very solidarity they summon. Analyzing the theological paradigm adopted in Catholic teaching on the family, this chapter illustrates how heterosexual marriage and biological procreation are presumed ideals. Official Catholic teaching on marriage and the family adopts a particular natural law approach that asserts the existence of complementary male and female bodies "naturally" unified through sexual intercourse, which is in turn interpreted as reflecting divine ideals for human relationality.[1] Not only does this approach hinder the Church's teaching from recognizing developments in understandings of gender identity, intersex embodiment, and sexual orientation, but it also shapes the Church's negative reception of families that depart from this normative structure.

While papal documents flag evolving dynamics in marriage and family structure as threats to society, an intersectional methodology aligned with Gospel-grounded commitments to challenging unjust hierarchies in family structures demonstrates how the nuclear family ideal assumed in Church teaching has itself contributed to exclusion and marginalization. I find that an emphasis on the narrow nuclear ideal is an ineffective foundation for solidaristic family formation: not only does it encourage adherence to a family structure that has proved exclusionary historically, but it also limits focus to spousal and biological parent-child relationships with limited recognition of other family relationships. These limitations weaken the Church's petition to families to embody outward-facing solidarity, through both a failure to question the exclusivity and insularity common in a nuclear family model and a lack of recognition of the many families that show how different family configurations function well—and often better—as "schools of solidarity."[2] Families' creative responses to social exclusion and marginalization related to race, migration status, sexual orientation, infertility, and gender-based violence point to particular expressions of solidarity that emerge in everyday family life.

Attending to diverse and expansive understandings of family from global Catholic ethics, I propose an emphasis on justice in family relationships that can support not only marital bonds and parent-child relationships, but also relationships between siblings, extended family members, and chosen family. An emphasis on a diversity of family ties helps relativize the importance of biological kinship and encourages attention to the broader human relatedness captured in the Catholic understanding of solidarity. Recognizing justice as foundational to family relationships links the family's inward and outward vocations, calling not just those who are married, but all who participate in family relationships, to act justly within their particular families and within the whole human family.[3]

Solidarity in the Catholic Tradition

While a Catholic understanding of solidarity has been developed in particular contexts to foster commitments to political solidarity that align with the concept articulated in chapter 1 of this volume, solidarity in Catholic social thought refers more broadly to the recognition of the interconnectedness of all of humanity and the moral obligations binding individuals and collectives identified as following from that truth.[4] Namely, it stipulates that each person, along with social institutions, ought to make choices not merely out of self-interest, but in light of the common good with a commitment to responsibility for all persons.[5] Solidarity is understood in tandem with related concepts in Catholic social teaching, including the preferential option for the poor and vulnerable and the dignity of the person. The latter concept expresses the conviction that human life is sacred and possesses equal and inalienable value; the former asserts that the needs and perspectives of the poor ought to be considered in a special or primary way in both moral and social analysis and the development of theology.[6]

The Catholic tradition has long emphasized the family as a site through which the person learns to live in solidarity with others because family life facilitates the development of virtues needed for positive social participation. *Lumen gentium*, the Second Vatican Council's "Dogmatic Constitution on the Church," defines the family as the "domestic church" "in which new citizens of human society are born, who by the grace of the Holy Spirit received in baptism are made children of God, thus perpetuating the people of God through the centuries."[7] In *Familiaris consortio*, John Paul II's 1981 apostolic exhortation "On the Role of the Christian Family in the Modern World," the family is said to be "the first and fundamental school of social living . . . it is from the family that citizens come to birth and it is within the family that they find the first school of the social virtues that are the animating principle of the existence and development of society itself."[8] Echoing the Second Vatican Council, Pope Francis describes the family as "the fundamental cell of society, where we learn to live with others despite our differences and to belong to one another."[9]

John Paul II suggests that because of the changes brought by globalization, the family's role in society involves "cooperating for a new international order" via "worldwide solidarity" to address "issues of world justice, the freedom of peoples and the peace of humanity."[10] Pope Benedict XVI, like his predecessors, links the family, global solidarity, and the common good by appealing to the concept of the "human family," or the "community of peoples and nations," which as "an earthly city in unity and peace" anticipates the full unity of the "undivided city of God."[11] More recently, Pope Francis has developed a connection between the family, solidarity, and care for the earth.

In his apostolic exhortation *Amoris Laetitia*, he suggests that in the family "we can rethink our habits of consumption and join in caring for the environment as our common home."[12] Thus, both Francis and John Paul II assign the family a central role in society and in the moral development of Christians, preparing persons for social life on local, global, and planetary levels.

Papal teaching that establishes and reiterates the social mission of the family tends to frame the Church's teaching on marriage and the family as a consistent and unchanging source of insight that can challenge social dynamics that the hierarchy sees as threats to family life. Closely entangled with social inequities related to poverty, political conflict, and environmental degradation are concerns about same-sex marriage and abortion. In *Familiaris consortio*, John Paul II names the Church's "special mission" as "guarding and protecting the lofty dignity of marriage and the most serious responsibility of the transmission of human life" and laments trends of divorce and rejection of Church teaching on marriage and sexuality.[13] Benedict XVI, responding to declining birth rates in developed nations, finds that upholding marriage and the family "is thus becoming a social and even economic necessity."[14] He calls on states to "enact policies promoting the centrality and the integrity of the family founded on marriage between a man and a woman, the primary vital cell of society, and to assume responsibility for its economic and fiscal needs, while respecting its essentially relational character."[15] Describing concerns about secularization, individualism, globalization, and consumerism, Pope Francis states that "the family is experiencing a profound cultural crisis," and he laments the reduction of marriage to "a form of mere emotional satisfaction that can be constructed in any way or modified at will."[16]

Papal laments about threats to family life and the role of the Church in defending the family help elaborate the promise and pitfalls of the Church's teaching on the family. On the one hand, these documents point to pressing social ills that impede the flourishing of families, and they invite people of goodwill to help enact political and social change in solidarity with families on the margins. On the other hand, they clearly embrace heterosexual marriage and biological childbearing as the sequence of actions that produce the ideal family, with little recognition of other family configurations and no acknowledgment of the social context out of which Catholic teaching that prizes the nuclear family emerged.[17] In the following sections, I draw on intersectional methods in Catholic moral theology to scrutinize the narrow focus on the nuclear family often implied in official Church teaching. I find that the Church's overwhelming focus on promoting heterosexual marriage and biological childbearing impairs the conceptual development of solidarity in family life, as official teaching prioritizes the defense of a particular family structure—and pastoral sympathy for those who do not meet the nuclear standard—over consideration of the witness to solidarity that varying family configurations might offer. Drawing on a criterion of justice linked to Gospel-based challenges to social hierarchies reinforced via family systems, I argue that the Church's reliance on the nuclear family norm limits its own solidarity with families in their concrete realities and its capacity to recognize families' creative contributions that build up the common good.

Introducing an Intersectional, Feminist Methodology

Intersectional feminist methodologies help us assess and critique the normative account of the family put forward in official Church teaching by encouraging attentiveness to contexts in which theologies take shape, the diversity of human experiences, especially of people on the margins, and the shaping influences of sin and oppressive forces.[18] Meghan J. Clark, Anna Kasafi Perkins, and Emily Reimer-Barry draw on feminist and womanist insights to develop intersectional methods for Catholic ethics, linking the justice orientation of Catholic social teaching and liberation theologies to an analysis of unjust social structures that hinder human flourishing. Intersectional analysis recognizes how intersecting oppressions shape the contexts and experiences of people in a variety of ways. Clark, Perkins, and Reimer-Barry observe, "Because of people's shifting domains and locations, they can hold and wield power differently in different contexts, experiencing oppression and empowerment simultaneously in various aspects of their multiple identities."[19] In the realm of theology, "[i]ntersectional thinking invites critical analysis of ahistorical claims, demands contextual analysis of historical figures/theologians/popes, and reminds us that there is no perspective-free location from which anyone engages in the task of theological ethics."[20]

The following section draws on this intersectional methodology, linking it to Jesus's challenge to social hierarchies entrenched in family structures and conducting a justice-oriented assessment of the Church's reliance on the nuclear family model (made up of father, mother, and biologically related children). I define justice using Catholic social ethicist Lisa Sowle Cahill's characterization:

> Justice consists in establishing social relations which are conducive to the flourishing of all human persons. Justice goes beyond the assertion of their personal rights, by encouraging and supporting each person's participative contribution to all the conditions of social living which further the common good, including fulfillment of duties to other individuals and to the community as a whole.[21]

Emphasizing how an implicit endorsement of the nuclear family afflicted modern Catholic teaching on the family from the start, I surface how these dominant ideals and structures of marriage have primarily served wealthier, white people and contributed to the oppression of Black people, immigrants, and women in the US context. Underscoring how marriage and childbearing have been used socially and politically to entrench racist ideals, anti-immigrant sentiments, and gender inequalities, this history implicates the nuclear family in social injustices that harm the common good. I argue that the Church's almost exclusive emphasis on the ideal of the nuclear family weakens the Church's social witness by allowing, and at times encouraging, exclusion of families that do not align with this narrow ideal—both in parishes and more broadly in society. An emphasis on adherence to this particular family structure hinders the Church's capacity to call itself and its members into solidarity with families both locally and globally and to recognize the solidaristic witness of diverse Catholic families. Drawing from original qualitative research conducted with Catholic women contending with infertility, I illustrate how Church teaching on the family functions to reinforce dominant cultural ideals that idealize heterosexual marriage and biological childbearing, which excludes families who exist outside of that ideal from parish life.[22] Turning to international

Catholic sources, I argue that an emphasis on the nuclear family does not adequately recognize cultural diversity in family formation for Catholics across the globe, especially those on the margins. I advocate for a more wholehearted advancement of the Church's teaching on the social mission of the family, proposing that an emphasis on commitments to solidarity and justice in the family serve as a more inclusive foundation to support a diversity of Catholic families and a diversity of family relationships, including spousal and parent-child bonds, but also relationships between siblings, extended family, and chosen family.[23]

Evaluating the Nuclear Family

As Lisa Sowle Cahill notes, the family ideal of the first-century Mediterranean world out of which Christianity emerged "is decidedly not the nuclear family of today."[24] Rather than a unit consisting of parents and children, family was understood more expansively under the framework of a "household" or *domus*, which extended beyond biological family members to include all those living within a property.[25] In Greco-Roman culture, families catered to the concerns of fathers and sons and, entangled in commerce, landholding, and local politics, helped preserve the wealth of the elite and kept the poor from gaining power.[26] Israelite families differed in structure and organization somewhat, yet they too served to preserve social inequalities, as wealth passed from fathers to sons.[27] In both cases, families in the ancient Mediterranean world reinforced male power, with women relegated to reproduction to build the family and pass down wealth.[28] While the Gospels indicate that early Christians formed communities of spiritual kinship that challenged household-based models of family, and that Jesus's own teaching linked discipleship with rejection of one's family, Jesus also explicitly rejects divorce. To reconcile this seeming contradiction in the evaluation of family life, Cahill argues that Jesus's anti-divorce stance, like his challenging of kin ties, constitutes resistance to social hierarchies of domination. Divorce functioned to secure male interests, just as family structures at the time tended to, so Jesus's resistance to both indicates not a rejection of family in and of itself, but instead of family structures that reinforce and magnify injustice.[29] On Cahill's reading, then, the Gospels prompt us to remain alert to how cultural instantiations of family reinforce unjust social hierarchies; yet they also encourage transformation of these hierarchies through expansive formations of family committed to justice and equality.

Returning to modern papal teaching on the family, we observe a motivation to preserve and promote family ideals that serve the white, European upper class. Jacob M. Kohlhaas explains how Pope Leo XIII's *Arcanum divinae sapientiae* (1880), the "founding document" of modern Catholic teaching on the family, styles itself as universal while responding only to changes in European family laws and to the social and cultural context of the white, European upper class. The document ignores both "the newfound freedoms of formerly enslaved populations" to marry and form families and also the "ascendency of women's social rights."[30] Instead, it reiterates Victorian and Romantic linkages between gender and virtue popular at the time that contributed to the framing of the domestic sphere as "feminine" and the public, economic sphere as masculine.[31] Not only did Leo XIII neglect to contextualize these ideals within their geographic, temporal, social, and class contexts, but subsequent popes have reiterated these Victorian ideals as well, further developing emphases on women's maternal vocation, gender complementarity, and the importance of procreation.[32]

While papal teaching after the Second Vatican Council generally evinced more openness to the experiences of laypeople, this openness proved limited: official teaching on the family "has not generally received deviations from the structural norm of the family as theologically significant. Instead, structural diversities in family systems are treated as results of unfortunate circumstances, misguided ideological or moral deviation, or simply as affronts to magisterial authority itself."[33] More recent papal documents strain to both reiterate this ideal family structure while also integrating contemporary considerations related to gender equality and challenges plaguing families.[34]

Documents from Pope Francis's papacy reflect this tension. In the working document from the 2014 Synod on the Family, the Synod of Bishops worried about "critical situations" in families that "do not coincide with the idea of a traditional nuclear family, i.e., mother, father and children," identifying single parenthood and same-sex unions as threats to family unity.[35] While the document emphasizes the need for pastoral accompaniment for families in these circumstances, it clearly identifies them as outside the ideal family, categorizing them as challenges alongside family conflict, violence, abuse, and addiction.[36] In Francis's apostolic exhortation on the family, *Amoris Laetitia*, he laments the Church's theology of marriage that is "far removed from the concrete situations and practical possibilities of real families,"[37] and he recognizes extended family relationships beyond the nuclear family.[38] Nevertheless, he continues to sketch a vision of the family that assumes (partnered) mothers and fathers to be at the center.[39] Later in the same document, he seems to insist that heterosexual marriages that produce biological children make more important and fundamental social contributions than other families:

> There is a failure to realize that only the exclusive and indissoluble union between a man and a woman has a plenary role to play in society as a stable commitment that bears fruit in new life. We need to acknowledge the great variety of family situations that can offer a certain stability, but de facto or same-sex unions, for example, may not simply be equated with marriage. No union that is temporary or closed to the transmission of life can ensure the future of society.[40]

The Vatican's more recent decision to permit same-sex couples and couples in "irregular situations" to ask for a blessing of their union from the Church demonstrates the ongoing difficulty of retaining a narrow ideal of the family while attempting to be open to alternatives. Blessings for those in "irregular situations" and same-sex unions carry stipulations that distinguish them from heterosexual marriages, with the stated purpose being to "avoid any form of confusion or scandal."[41] Although the decision evinces an openness to recognizing LGBTQIA+ persons and their relationships, the stipulations accompanying the blessings underscore that they are set apart from heterosexual marriages, which ultimately accentuates that official Church teaching sees same-sex unions as falling short of the heterosexual marital ideal.[42] While Francis has helped foster greater openness to diverse family configurations and their concrete realities on the pastoral level, this openness remains limited by an attachment to a theology of marriage predicated on heterosexual marriage, intercourse, and biological childbearing.

An intersectional method prompts us to consider whether the nuclear family structure promoted in Catholic teaching has, as these documents indicate, consistently contributed to the common good and the development of society. I argue that the contemporary nuclear family, like the family in the ancient world, brings a troubling legacy. While family structures support the functioning of society, the nuclear family has propped up unjust social relations and therefore deserves scrutiny. As Linn Marie Tonstad has noted in a queer critique of the nuclear family, the Christian endorsement of the nuclear family is entangled with capitalist aims.[43] While a social vision of marriage packages it as involving "the highest fulfillment and love of two individuals in relation to each other" and "self-sacrificial, unselfish love of children," economic motivations of producing workers and accumulating private property are the concealed functions of marriage.[44] Tonstad emphasizes that religious meanings ascribed to marriage and the nuclear family help conceal the economic motivations behind these structures, casting "an aura of holiness, divine will, and ethical responsibility" to marriage, childbearing, and motherhood.[45]

A brief examination of historical operations of marriage in the US context makes it clear that marriage as an institution has been entangled not only in capitalism, but also in patterns of sexism, racism, classism, anti-immigrant bias, and homophobia. Before the Civil War, enslaved persons were not legally allowed to consent to marriage. After the Civil War, states banned interracial marriage: the penalty for marriage between a Black person and a white person in Mississippi was a life sentence.[46] By contrast, white opposite-sex couples were encouraged to marry. Even working-class couples, who often lacked money for marriage, were able to have informal marriages recognized as valid by the court system.[47]

In the early twentieth century, marriages between Chinese immigrant women and white American men were deemed a "threat" to the "purity" of the American body politic and were thus discouraged, while other state laws were meant to encourage marriage between white people.[48] The US government's effort to forcibly sterilize Black women, Latina women, people with disabilities, and incarcerated people reveals how eugenic ideas shaped policies not only around marriage but also around childbearing.[49] Heterosexual marriage was entangled with racism, legacies of slavery, and anti-immigrant sentiment well into the twentieth century. Sexual activity between persons of the same sex was illegal in every state until 1961, and same-sex marriage only became legal in every state and US territory in 2015.[50] Although heterosexual marriages were incentivized via new social security and income tax policies in the twentieth century, the policies assumed that fathers would function as financial providers for their dependent wives and children.[51] On the societal level, it is evident that heterosexual marriage (and biological childbearing within it) has been used to further entrench unjust social relations that marginalize people based on gender, ability, race, and sexual orientation.

The Nuclear Family Norm in Catholic Parish Life

Nuclear family norms also tend to dominate ecclesial settings, hindering inclusivity of parishes for those who fall outside the norm. Here, I explore how pastoral ministry developed to cater to the nuclear family and draw on qualitative research to underscore how this contributes to inadvertent exclusion of childless couples and furthers the intentional exclusion of same-sex couples. In US Catholic congregations, official Catholic teaching that links heterosexual marriage and sex with biological childbearing helps reinforce cultural ideals of the nuclear family, what some refer to as the "Standard North American Family"—meaning two married, heterosexual parents with multiple biological, genetically related children.[52] The convergence of religious and cultural ideals of the family took shape in the mid-twentieth-century development of parish ministry: Penny Edgell describes how US congregations in the mid-twentieth century developed family ministries to support mothers who stayed home with their children and often endorsed a gendered separation of domestic and economic spheres.[53] Her study conducted with Christian congregations in the United States in the 1990s and early 2000s found that the organizational structure of family ministries has changed little; they continue to be oriented around "the traditional gender and life-stage categories targeted to the needs of two-parent families with children."[54]

Recent surveys indicate that cultural privileging of the nuclear family among Catholics continues today. In 2015, Pew Research found that

90 percent of Catholics surveyed identified children being raised by a "married mother and father" as ideal.[55] Importantly, 48 percent and 43 percent of those surveyed responded that "unmarried parents living together" and "a gay or lesbian couple," respectively, would be as good as other family configurations, yet significant minorities of those surveyed expressed a preference for a heterosexual married couple over unmarried parents or a gay or lesbian couple.[56] Forty-one percent of US Catholics identified openness to having children as "essential" to being Catholic; another 41 percent identified it as "important but not essential."[57] As the ensuing discussion of the experiences of Catholic women with infertility will help demonstrate, cultural ideals about what constitutes the "good family" have power because they shape expectations about family formation and parenting and influence which families are welcomed and encouraged and which may be overlooked or found lacking.[58] Although official Catholic teaching on the outward-facing family can challenge this nuclear family ideal, parish settings tend to replicate it through ministry offerings, through cultural assumptions unearthed in social interactions, and through marriage preparation courses.

Through in-depth interviews that I conducted as part of a larger project on US Catholic women's experiences with infertility, I found that women in US parishes still encounter parish ministry offerings that cater to nuclear family structures.[59] For instance, Paola and her husband, who struggled to conceive, were active participants in their parish, yet they found it challenging to participate in ministry activities because the offerings were geared toward younger, single adults or parents of children.[60] After five years of participating in the young adult group, she concluded, "we're still with the single people. . . . It's like, okay . . . but we're married, where do we fit?" Kelly and her husband, who married in 2016 and began trying to have children right away, found their parish in the northeastern US isolating as they struggled with infertility. Although they continued attending mass, she did not feel welcome: "The parish is for families or it's for the elderly . . . so you really feel like this isn't for me . . . I don't have this feeling like I want to go there because it's not for us." After the pandemic occasioned a break from regular mass attendance, she expressed reluctance to go back. Taylor and her husband struggled to conceive and decided to foster a daughter, who was eventually placed with them permanently. Taylor recalled that parish priests found the arrangement perplexing. When she happened to mention having an eighteen-year-old daughter, one priest remarked, "Oh, you don't look old enough to have [an eighteen-year-old]." She did not take the comment as intentionally insensitive or exclusionary, but instead saw it as an indication that priests are unfamiliar with infertility and with foster families.

Maureen and her husband, who live in the Midwest, also actively participate in their parish. She has noticed that her parish tends to recognize large Catholic families and overlook couples without children, even though they volunteer frequently in the parish: "The families that get recognized as family of the year are large families. The families that are held up as good, they are good because all their kids are so involved in ministry. . . . I get that large families are cool to a point, but it does suggest that that is the way to be Catholic." She lamented that "two older childless couples" who "are awesome" and frequently volunteer were never "recognized . . . in more than a decade of attending there." She concluded, "I think that is telling."

Rose, who has been married for fifteen years and has undergone treatment in Catholic clinics for infertility, described her parish priest's "1950s view of the family," an ideal she sees as more "in our heads" than as a historical reality. She found that her priest seemed uncomfortable interacting with her because she did not reflect that "happy ideal" of the nuclear family: "It was like, he didn't know what to do with me . . . they don't know how to relate to me as an adult woman versus, 'oh, she's a mom, so I can put her in that box and understand and relate to her that way.'" Rose's experience helps illustrate how a narrow theology of marriage and family life can hamper pastoral support for people who fall outside the dominant ideal of the family. Rose not only lost out on the chance to receive support from her parish priest as she dealt with infertility, but she also left these interactions feeling overlooked: "It made me feel like, you do not see me as a person."

A sense of exclusion from consideration or irrelevance of parish offerings to one's life circumstances also occurred for many women I interviewed in their marriage preparation courses. Catholic couples preparing for marriage in the Church typically attend a series of classes, often called "pre-Cana," that are meant to prepare them for marriage. Overlooking overwhelming statistical data about Catholics' sexual behavior that indicates that most Catholics usually have sex before marriage and use contraception, pre-Cana curricula typically assume that couples have not had sex and will use Natural Family Planning methods to help avoid or achieve pregnancy.[61] Catholic marriage ministries exclude same-sex couples altogether, but in more subtle ways, they also exclude those who do not follow Church teaching regarding contraception, those who face various reproductive difficulties, and those who have discerned that they want to adopt children or to remain childless.

Vivian and her husband, who married before the pandemic began in 2020, now have a child after undergoing *in vitro* fertilization. Prior to getting married, when she and her husband went through pre-Cana, she already anticipated that she might struggle to conceive because she had been diagnosed with endometriosis. She felt that her pre-Cana course minimized the burden of infertility by encouraging couples to "just be very spiritually fruitful" if they could not have biological children. Describing the experience as "brutal," she concluded, "If I had had any delusions that there were going to be any resources for me, that right there would've killed the notion."

Maureen emphasized how encounters with ideals of motherhood and biological childbearing in parish settings reflected broader cultural ideals in the United States: "the Catholic Church reflects a larger problem of childless women . . . the world does not know what to do with us." Her conclusion helps illustrate how the emphasis on marriage, motherhood, and biological childbearing in Church teaching shapes parish structures and cultures, such that they intensify the cultural stigma associated with childlessness, rather than helping to challenge it. Reinforcing, rather than indicting and transforming, structural exclusion of childless couples neglects the Gospels' summons to counter social hierarchies found in culturally dominant family forms.

Family Founded on Justice

Beyond reinforcing stigma against varied family configurations in parishes, Church teaching that assumes a nuclear family norm and continues to privilege Eurocentric family models also misses the insights and challenges of contextual expressions of family life across the globe. A brief review of US Latinx family dynamics, challenges facing migrant families, and developing understanding of family in Africa helps illustrate the inadequacy of the nuclear family ideal. These examples gesture toward the promise of more expansive understanding of family, yet also point us to the need for justice and solidarity to promote the flourishing of families everywhere. Recognizing that an intersectional method invites "plurality, ambiguity, and context-dependent normative claims," this section embraces more expansive understandings of the family and argues for more flexible family norms founded on justice.[62]

Nichole M. Flores describes how Latinx families often prize extended family relationships and community relationships beyond what is legally or biologically considered "family." This more expansive way of identifying who is family encourages care for those outside of one's household, allowing for the building of communal networks of resource distribution and cultivation of "a community of response and resistance to social, economic, and political injustices facing Latinx communities today."[63] Kristin E. Heyer emphasizes that many Latin American families who have migrated to the United States "encounter a shocking dissonance between the ideal nuclear family understood as including mother, father, children (and dog!)" and the expansive and flexible understanding of family that Flores describes.[64] While the dominant nuclear family model can diminish broader familial networks that support physical and emotional well-being for migrants,[65] migrant families with undocumented members can draw on the flexibility of familial boundaries found in *familismo* to enact solidarity for *compadres* and *comadres* (godfathers and godmothers) who live "under the weight of illegality."[66] Gemma Tulud Cruz similarly describes how communities of migrant women in Hong Kong function as families who look after each other, brought together not by blood ties but by shared geographies and labor.[67]

Léocadie Lushombo describes how African understandings of the family developed to emphasize communal ties: the ancient Egyptian concept of "kemet," which understood the extended family as a "village section, not a nuclear cell" contributes to the understanding of the African family as "simultaneously nuclear and extended."[68] She critiques Benedict XVI's 2011 postsynodal apostolic exhortation *Africae Munus* for relying on "traditional

Western patriarchal family values" to suggest that fathers heading up families ought to protect and provide, overlooking women's economic contributions across the globe and traditions of women's family leadership and lineage in Africa in particular.[69] A model that idealizes a two-parent family headed by a father figure remains distant from the realities of many African mothers who take on parenting responsibilities on their own, often due to regional conflict, economic changes, sexual violence, and forced migration.[70]

It is important not to romanticize these various conceptualizations of family: ideals regarding motherhood and family alongside structural injustices can shape family relationships such that they become a site for gender injustice and the oppression of women.[71] These diverse configurations point to the potential inherent in defining family more expansively, yet they also remind us of the need to emphasize just social relations in families given the pernicious influence of sexism and other social sins. Indeed, Lushombo discusses the example of women victims of rape raising their children borne from these traumas. Highlighting the particular challenges of shame, abandonment, and alienation that come from sexual dehumanization and caregiving responsibilities linked to sexual trauma, she argues that women need both solidarity as well as "resistant virtuous anger" from people of faith to respond to the injustices of sexual violence amid armed conflict.[72]

Justice and Christian Discipleship within and beyond the Family

To balance acceptance of a diversity of family configurations with a normative understanding of the Christian family, Cahill proposes a focus on "function" over form. On this view, the fundamental duty of the Christian family is to live out "gospel-informed commitments" rather than to conform to a particular structure. An emphasis on justice can retain a recognition of families linked via marriage and kinship as a common "working concept of family" for many, but it allows for more varieties of family to be accepted.[73] Margaret Farley similarly advocates that we focus less on "preferences for, or idealization of, a 'best' model" of a family and instead emphasize "justice and love that a model makes possible."[74] Farley suggests that for families to support the flourishing of their members, "their structures need to be just."[75] A justice criterion not only facilitates scrutiny of cultural ideals that promote the authority of husbands and fathers and servility of mothers, but it also helps us consider what good and just relationships look like between siblings and extended family members.[76] The demands of justice include obligations to family members, and facilitate critique of relationships that involve abuse, exploitation, and other injustices, yet they also obligate families to work in solidarity with those on the margins to promote justice in society more broadly. As Pope Francis affirms the conclusions of the Synod on the Family, "the family is an agent of pastoral activity" committed to "the promotion of the common good and the transformation of unjust social structures."[77]

Emphasizing justice-seeking as a distinctive orientation for the Christian family supports the cultivation of solidarity in families, helps challenge dominant cultural assumptions of the family as private, and connects to the Gospels' challenge to hierarchy-reinforcing family structures. Julie Hanlon Rubio connects this outward duty of the Christian family to Christian discipleship, arguing that marriage and parenthood are "dual" vocations in that they are concerned with both the welfare of family members and the welfare of society, through hospitality, political participation, and solidarity with the poor and marginalized.[78] Locating the family as a place to live out Christian discipleship, "the primary ethical imperative asked of all Christians," helps preserve the centrality of family in an expansive and flexible way.[79] It makes room for a diversity of family configurations and challenges families to cultivate concern for the common good in addition to care for family members.

Witnessing Solidarity in Catholic Family Contexts

Examples drawn from recent research on the concrete realities of Catholic families demonstrate how an emphasis on justice can allow the Church to stand in solidarity with a diversity of families, both to call them to promote the common good and to recognize how they already serve as witnesses to solidarity. Prioritizing the family's social mission remains connected to the anthropological understanding of the interconnectedness and interdependence of the whole human family found in official Church teaching.[80] Duties of care for one another may include childcare for biological or adopted children; care for ailing parents, neighbors, and friends; education of community members; outreach to the unhoused and undocumented; and hospitality to those excluded. Situating families as witnesses to human interdependence and the solidarity asked of us helps to contextualize kinship ties amid a broader landscape of human relatedness.

First, I return to insights from two interviewees. Margaret, who was in the midst of infertility treatment, shared about her grandmother's efforts to transform gender inequalities and challenge expectations of childbearing that had left her without access to formal education in India. Margaret elaborates:

> In the early fifties and late forties when she was a young woman, especially in India, women weren't treated very well. I think she felt that dehumanization every day of her life . . . she didn't know how to read and write. . . . Because of that, she was actually marginalized quite a long time in my life. . . . So, what she did instead was ensure that her daughter, her daughter-in-law, and her granddaughters were educated, were women who could be independent. And it's so amazing because both my aunts are educators, my mom was a teacher herself. And my grandmother ensured that we had the sense of independence . . . that we are more than just incubators for babies, that traditional role. . . . She went to church and was active, but it was never that she found her worth in the church. . . . I know the church never gives women that, especially in those days. Even though the Church expects [childbearing] out of women, I think my grandmother . . . instilled that sense of work in her family, and I'm really thankful for that.

Margaret's grandmother's efforts not only changed what was materially possible for her daughter and granddaughter, but it also encouraged Margaret to critically evaluate the Church's emphasis on women as mothers and childbearers, which changed how Margaret experienced infertility. Margaret's own choice to have biological children helps illustrate that an emphasis on justice does not discount the value of childbearing and parenting; rather, it shifts the focus beyond this particular family structure, recognizing its contributions without asserting its primacy. Margaret's grandmother's work to challenge gender injustices also illustrates the private and public aspects of a justice-oriented Christian family. In seeking what is good and just for her family, Margaret's grandmother also contributes to the common good, helping to challenge cultural and religious understandings of motherhood that impede the flourishing of women.

Another interviewee, Lois, recalled challenges in conceiving and uncertainty about whether to adopt. She and her husband ultimately discerned that the youth-oriented social justice theater organization that they founded in their Midwestern city was "where we were supposed to be." For Lois, community theater became a way to work with children and adults "in the most challenged situations, whether they were refugees or in jail or homeless," to "find a way for their voices to be heard and for them to have agency and power in creating the story of their life." Recognizing that she and her husband found this work "really meaningful, really necessary, [and] really powerful," they discerned that community theater "was where our creative energy and our life force was to be spent." Dedication to their theater work allowed Lois and her husband to cultivate solidarity with those in need in their community, to facilitate their empowerment, and to recognize their dignity.

Their example resonates with Bridget Burke Ravizza's description of "outward-facing Christian marriage" among same-sex Catholic couples whom she interviewed. While many couples adopted or had children with the help of reproductive technologies, many chose other ways to extend care and concern to their extended families and communities. For instance, Michael and Brian decided to put their parenting aspirations on hold so that they could support their extended family members who were grieving and needed caregiving help. Brian has been able to help shepherd his late brother's sons through challenging teen years.[81] Another couple, Tom and Mark, choose to live more simply so that they can afford to share resources with those who need them. When Tom learned that a local college student, Phillip, who had aged out of the foster system, did not have a home to return to, Tom gave him a room in his home and a key. Although Phillip decided to join the Marines, he still has his room in Tom's house: "He has a key and a home to which he can (and does) return. He has a family, with no conditions attached."[82]

A more expansive vision of the family thus allows for marriage and childbearing to stand alongside other life paths as legitimate and holy responses to the common Christian call of discipleship. It welcomes diversity in living out this call and makes space to honor differing ways of forming a family and caring for the common good. A final set of examples helps emphasize how populations often marginalized in Church teaching have, by virtue of being excluded, often been first to form families beyond marital and biological ties, pointing the way toward solidarity for the whole human family. LGBTQ Catholics have come together to form communities in the face of rejection from biological family and from the Church. During the height of the AIDS epidemic, the Catholic LGBTQ organization DignityUSA established a ministry of care for those dying of AIDS, providing spiritual care, sacraments, and financial assistance. Jason Steidl Jack describes the ministry as a "spiritual family for the dying," emphasizing how many had faced rejection from their own families.[83] More recently, members of the "Out at St. Paul" group for LGBTQ Catholics at St. Paul the Apostle in New York City became a kind of "chosen family" for members who faced isolation, loneliness, and exclusion as Catholics and as transplants to the city.[84] These examples underscore how a justice orientation in family life recognizes the distinctive rewards and challenges of spousal and parent-child relationships but equally considers the importance of familial relationships beyond marriage, including extended family and "chosen family."

Each relationship within a family becomes an occasion to care for the other, cultivate solidarity, promote justice, and care for the common good. And each familial relationship can face scrutiny as a site where sin and injustice can take root. From mothers who have survived sexual violence to the companionship of *compadres* crossing the border, from couples empowering the unhoused and the incarcerated in their communities to queer activists and advocates forging new family ties, Catholics in context bear witness to a renewed understanding of the family that embraces a diversity of ways to live out a commitment to solidarity.

Notes

1 For further discussion of the Church's natural law approach as it relates to contemporary questions around gender identity and sexual orientation, see Craig A. Ford Jr., "Transgender Bodies, Catholic Schools, and a Queer Natural Law Theology of Exploration," *Journal of Moral Theology* 7, no. 1 (2018): 70–98.

2 See Mary M. Doyle Roche, *Schools of Solidarity: Families and Catholic Social Teaching* (Collegeville, MN: Liturgical Press, 2015).

3 Portions of the research and argument developed here stem from my dissertation: Emma Louise McDonald, "Forming Agents, Forming Families: Moral Agency in the Context of Procreation" (PhD diss., Boston College, 2023).

4 For further analysis on solidarity in the Catholic tradition, see Gerald J. Beyer, "The Meaning of Solidarity in Catholic Social Teaching," *Political Theology* 15, no. 1 (2014): 7–25.

5 See Conor M. Kelly, "Everyday Solidarity: A Framework for Integrating Theological Ethics and Ordinary Life," *Theological Studies* 81, no. 2 (2020), 416.

6 See Pontifical Council for Justice and Peace, *Compendium of the Social Doctrine of the Church* (Washington, DC: U.S. Conference of Catholic Bishops, 2004).

7 Second Vatican Council, "Dogmatic Constitution on the Church, *Lumen Gentium*, November 21, 1964," in *Vatican Council II: The Conciliar and Post Conciliar Documents*, ed. Austin Flannery (Collegeville, MN: Liturgical Press, 1975), §11.

8 Pope John Paul II, *Familiaris consortio* (November 22, 1981), §37, 42, https://www.vatican.va/content/john-paul-ii/en/apost_exhortations/documents/hf_jp-ii_exh_19811122_familiaris-consortio.html (accessed July 2, 2024).

9 Pope Francis, *Evangelii Gaudium* (November 24, 2013), §66, https://www.vatican.va/content/francesco/en/apost_exhortations/documents/papa-francesco_esortazione-ap_20131124_evangelii-gaudium.html. See also Second Vatican Ecumenical Council, *Apostolicam Actuositatem*, "Decree on the Apostolate of Lay People (November 10, 1965)," §11, https://www.vatican.va/archive/hist_councils/ii_vatican_council/documents/vat-ii_decree_19651118_apostolicam-actuositatem_en.html.

10 John Paul II, *Familiaris consortio*, §48.

11 Pope Benedict XVI, *Caritas in Veritate* (June 29, 2009), §7, https://www.vatican.va/content/benedict-xvi/en/encyclicals/documents/hf_ben-xvi_enc_20090629_caritas-in-veritate.html. For further elaboration on Benedict XVI's treatment

of family in his final encyclical, see Wilhelmina Uhai Tunu, LSOSF, "*Caritas in Veritate* and Cultural Development," in *Modern Catholic Family Teaching: Commentaries and Interpretations*, ed. Jacob M. Kohlhaas and Mary M. Doyle Roche (Washington, DC: Georgetown University Press, 2024), 201–9.

12 Pope Francis, *Amoris Laetitia* [On Love in the Family] (March 19, 2016), §277, http://www.vatican.va/content/dam/francesco/pdf/apost_exhortations/documents/papa-francesco_esortazione-ap_20160319_amoris-laetitia_en.pdf.

13 John Paul II, *Familiaris consortio*, §29, 7.

14 Benedict XVI, *Caritas in veritate*, §44.

15 Benedict XVI, *Caritas in veritate*, §44.

16 Francis, *Evangelii Gaudium*, §66.

17 For elaboration on the way in which this understanding of the family connects to a particular understanding of natural law, see Craig A. Ford Jr., "Natural Law in Catholic Family Teaching," in *Modern Catholic Family Teaching: Commentaries and Interpretations*, 20–28.

18 Meghan J. Clark, Anna Kasafi Perkins, and Emily Reimer-Barry, "Special Issue on Intersectional Methods and Moral Theology: Introduction," *Journal of Moral Theology* 12, no. 1 (2023), 11. This proposal resonates with Linn Marie Tonstad's desire for a queer theology that "needs to take the messy realities and complexities of people's lives seriously; it needs to stand against the distortive powers of capitalism and colonialism; it needs to express and honor human bodily being; it needs to get beyond the search for identity, fixity, and finality; and it needs to be about God's presence in, identification with, and love for the body, the way God calls us to bring love, lust, and justice together"; see *Queer Theology: Beyond Apologetics* (Eugene, OR: Wipf and Stock, 2018), 103.

19 Clark, Perkins, and Reimer-Barry, "Special Issue on Intersectional Methods and Moral Theology: Introduction," 9.

20 Clark, Perkins, and Reimer-Barry, "Special Issue on Intersectional Methods and Moral Theology: Introduction," 13.

21 Lisa Sowle Cahill, *Sex, Gender, and Christian Ethics* (Cambridge, UK: Cambridge University Press, 1996), 51.

22 Between 2020 and 2023, I conducted sixty-three in-depth interviews via Zoom with Catholic women contending with infertility and Catholic physicians who treat infertility. The interviews were coded using ATLAS.ti software. This research was conducted with the approval and oversight of the Boston College

Institutional Review Board (IRB protocol #21.185.01e). Participants reviewed a consent form before being interviewed, interview data was securely stored in accordance with IRB requirements, and all names used here are pseudonyms to protect participant confidentiality.

23 Surfacing an overreliance on the nuclear family ideal is not meant to critique heterosexual marriage and biological childbearing *per se*. As a later section will indicate, a solidarity-focused, justice-seeking orientation aims to include spousal and biological parent-child relationships, among others.

24 Lisa Sowle Cahill, *Family: A Christian Social Perspective* (Minneapolis, MN: Fortress Press, 2000), 19.

25 Cahill, *Family*, 19.

26 Cahill, *Family*, 23.

27 Cahill, *Family*, 24.

28 Cahill, *Family*, 26.

29 Cahill, *Family*, 32–33.

30 Jacob M. Kohlhaas, "Racial Memory and Catholic Family Teaching," in *Modern Catholic Family Teaching: Commentaries and Interpretations*, 48–49.

31 Kohlhaas, "Racial Memory and Catholic Family Teaching," 49.

32 Kohlhaas, "Racial Memory and Catholic Family Teaching," 49. See, for example, John Paul II's praise of (heterosexual) married couples for reflecting the divinely ordained plan for family life on earth (*Familiaris Consortio*, §14–16). While Church teaching explicitly endorses heterosexual marriage, it rarely states an outright preference for biological childbearing. Occasionally it even relativizes the importance of biological linkage between parent and child through references to spiritual kinship. Yet the insistence in official teaching that heterosexual marriage is the appropriate place for intercourse and that childbearing is one of the chief goods of marriage sets up a framework in which biological childbearing is the assumed norm. As Darlene Fozard Weaver makes clear, "The overwhelming majority of Catholic tradition assumes biologically intact families"; see Weaver, "Adoption, Social Justice, and Catholic Tradition," *Journal of Catholic Social Thought* 13, no. 2 (2016), 205.

33 Kohlhaas, "Racial Memory and Catholic Family Teaching," 48.

34 Jacob Kohlhaas, "Constructing Parenthood: Catholic Social Teaching 1880 to the Present," *Theological Studies* 79, no. 3 (2018), 630.

35 Synod of Bishops, "*Instrumentum Laboris* [The Pastoral Challenges of the Family in the Context of Evangelization]," 2014, §65, https://www.vatican.va/roman_

curia/synod/documents/rc_synod_doc_20140626_instrumentum-laboris-familia_en.html (June 25, 2024).

36 See *Instrumentum Laboris*, §64–69.

37 Francis, *Amoris Laetitia*, §36.

38 Francis, *Amoris Laetitia*, §187, 197.

39 Francis, *Amoris Laetitia*, §9. See Gemma Tulud Cruz, "It Takes a Global Village: Families in the Age of Migration," in *Sex, Love, and Families: Lived Christianity in Context*, ed. Jason King and Julie Hanlon Rubio (Collegeville, MN: Liturgical Press, 2020), 192, for an analysis of Francis's discussion of family structure in *Amoris Laetitia*.

40 Francis, *Amoris Laetitia*, §52.

41 Dicastery for the Doctrine of the Faith, *Fiducia supplicans* [On the Pastoral Meanings of Blessings], December 18, 2023, §31, 39.

42 See also Ish Ruiz, "Queer Theology and a Synodal Catholic Church," *Feminist Theology* 32, no. 3 (2024), 298–99.

43 Tonstad, *Queer Theology*, 80–82.

44 Tonstad, *Queer Theology*, 80–81.

45 Tonstad, *Queer Theology*, 82.

46 Nancy F. Cott, *Public Vows: A History of Marriage and the Nation* (Cambridge, MA: Harvard University Press, 2002), 41.

47 See Cott, *Public Vows*, 39.

48 Cott, *Public Vows*, 136–55.

49 See Dorothy E. Roberts, *Killing the Black Body: Race, Reproduction, and the Meaning of Liberty* (New York: Vintage, 1999). For further discussion of the role of "blood" ties in furthering racial divisions, see Camisha A. Russell, *The Assisted Reproduction of Race* (Bloomington: Indiana University Press, 2018), 109–15.

50 See Richard Weinmeyer, "The Decriminalization of Sodomy in the United States," *AMA Journal of Ethics* 16, no. 11 (2014), 917. See also William N. Eskridge Jr., *Dishonorable Passions: Sodomy Laws in America, 1861–2003* (New York: Viking, 2008).

51 See Cott, *Public Vows*, 173–77.

52 Bethany L. Letiecq, "Surfacing Family Privilege and Supremacy in Family Science: Toward Justice for All," *Journal of Family Theory and Review* (2019): 400.

53 Penny Edgell, *Religion and Family in a Changing Society* (Princeton, NJ: Princeton University Press, 2006), 15.

54 Edgell, *Religion and Family in a Changing Society*, 138.

55 Pew Research Center, "U.S. Catholics Open to Non-Traditional Families," September 2, 2015, https://www.pewresearch.org/religion/wp-content/uploads/sites/7/2015/09/Catholics-and-Family-Life-09-01-2015.pdf, 3.

56 Pew Research Center, "U.S. Catholics Open to Non-Traditional Families," 3.

57 Pew Research Center, "U.S. Catholics Open to Non-Traditional Families," 116.

58 Edgell, *Religion and Family in a Changing Society*, 146–47.

59 Between 2020 and 2023, I conducted sixty-three in-depth interviews: fifty-seven with women in the United States who identify as Catholic and who have dealt with infertility, and six with Catholic physicians in the United States who treat infertility.

60 All names referred to here are pseudonyms.

61 See Pew Research Center, "Few Catholics See Contraceptive Use as Morally Wrong," February 27, 2012, https://www.pewresearch.org/short-reads/2012/02/27/few-catholics-see-contraceptive-use-as-morally-wrong/.

62 Clark, Perkins, and Reimer-Barry, "Special Issue on Intersectional Methods and Moral Theology: Introduction," 14.

63 Nichole M. Flores, "'Our Sister, Mother Earth': Solidarity and Familial Ecology in *Laudato Si'*," *Journal of Religious Ethics* 46, no. 3 (2018): 466.

64 Kristin E. Heyer, *Kinship across Borders: A Christian Ethic of Immigration* (Washington, DC: Georgetown University Press, 2012), 81.

65 Heyer, *Kinship across Borders*, 82.

66 Victor Carmona, "Mixed-Status Families, Solidarity, and *Lo Cotidiano*," in *Sex, Love, and Families: Lived Christianity in Context*, 209.

67 Tulud Cruz, "It Takes a Global Village," 212.

68 Léocadie Lushombo, i.t., "*Caritas in Veritate* and *Africae Munus*," in *Modern Catholic Family Teaching: Commentaries and Interpretations*, 214.

69 Lushombo, "*Caritas in Veritate* and *Africae Munus*," 215.

70 Lushombo, "*Caritas in Veritate* and *Africae Munus*," 216.

71 See Heyer, *Kinship across Borders*, 82; Léocadie W. Lushombo, *A Christian and African Ethic of Women's Political Participation Living as Risen Beings* (Lanham, MD: Lexington, 2023); Flores, "Our Sister, Mother Earth," 466. See also Carmona, "Mixed-Status Families, Solidarity, and *Lo Cotidiano*," 208–9, for a discussion of citizenship status, power dynamics, and *familismo*.

72 Lushombo, *A Christian and African Ethic of Women's Political Participation*, 158.

73 Cahill, *Family*, xi.

74   Margaret A. Farley, *Just Love: A Framework for Christian Sexual Ethics* (New York: Bloomsbury Academic, 2008), 262.

75   Farley, *Just Love*, 263.

76   Farley, *Just Love*, 263.

77   Francis, *Amoris Laetitia*, §290, quoting *Relatio Finalis* (2015), §93.

78   Julie Hanlon Rubio, *A Christian Theology of Marriage and Family* (Mahwah, NJ: Paulist Press, 2003), 106–7.

79   Rubio, *A Christian Theology of Marriage and Family*, 98.

80   See also Sandra Sullivan-Dunbar, *Human Dependency and Christian Ethics* (Cambridge, UK: Cambridge University Press, 2017).

81   Bridget Burke Ravizza, *The Sacrament of Same-Sex Marriage: An Inclusive Vision for the Catholic Church* (New York: Sheed & Ward, 2024), 43–44.

82   Burke Ravizza, *The Sacrament of Same-Sex Marriage*, 48.

83   Jason Steidl, *LGBTQ Catholic Ministry: Past and Present* (Mahwah, NJ: Paulist Press, 2022), 55.

84   Steidl, *LGBTQ Catholic Ministry*, 158.

References

Benedict XVI. *Caritas in Veritate* [On Integral Human Development in Charity and Truth]. June 29, 2009. https://www.vatican.va/content/benedict-xvi/en/encyclicals/documents/hf_ben-xvi_enc_20090629_caritas-in-veritate.html.

Beyer, Gerald J. "The Meaning of Solidarity in Catholic Social Teaching." *Political Theology* 15, no. 1 (2014): 7–25.

Cahill, Lisa Sowle. *Family: A Christian Social Perspective*. Minneapolis, MN: Fortress Press, 2000.

———. *Sex, Gender, and Christian Ethics*. Cambridge, UK: Cambridge University Press, 1996.

Carmona, Victor. "Mixed-Status Families, Solidarity, and Lo Cotidiano." In *Sex, Love, and Families: Lived Christianity in Context*, edited by Jason King and Julie Hanlon Rubio, 199–210. Collegeville, MN: Liturgical Press, 2020.

Clark, Meghan J., Anna Kasafi Perkins, and Emily Reimer-Barry. "Special Issue on Intersectional Methods and Moral Theology: Introduction." *Journal of Moral Theology* 12, no. 1 (2023): 1–18.

Cott, Nancy F. *Public Vows: A History of Marriage and the Nation*. Cambridge, MA: Harvard University Press, 2002.

Cruz, Gemma Tulud. "It Takes a Global Village: Families in the Age of Migration." In *Sex, Love, and Families: Lived Christianity in Context*, edited by Jason King and Julie Hanlon Rubio, 211–221. Collegeville, MN: Liturgical Press, 2020.

Dicastery for the Doctrine of the Faith, *Fiducia supplicans* [On the Pastoral Meanings of Blessings], December 18, 2023.

Edgell, Penny. *Religion and Family in a Changing Society*. Princeton, NJ: Princeton University Press, 2006.

Farley, Margaret A. *Just Love: A Framework for Christian Sexual Ethics*. New York: Bloomsbury Academic, 2008.

Flores, Nichole M. "'Our Sister, Mother Earth': Solidarity and Familial Ecology in Laudato Si." *Journal of Religious Ethics* 46, no. 3 (2018): 463–78.

Ford Jr., Craig A. "Natural Law in Catholic Family Teaching." In *Modern Catholic Family Teaching: Commentaries and Interpretations*, edited by Jacob M. Kohlhaas and Mary M. Doyle Roche, 20–28. Washington, DC: Georgetown University Press, 2024.

———. "Transgender Bodies, Catholic Schools, and a Queer Natural Law Theology of Exploration." *Journal of Moral Theology* 7, no. 1 (2018): 70–98.

Francis, *Amoris Laetitia* [on Love in the Family]. March 19, 2016. http://www.vatican .va/content/dam/francesco/pdf/apost_exhortations/documents/papa-francesco _esortazione-ap_20160319_amoris-laetitia_en.pdf.

———. *Evangelii Gaudium* [On the Proclamation of the Gospel in Today's World] (November 24, 2013). https://www.vatican.va/content/francesco/en/apost _exhortations/documents/papa-francesco_esortazione-ap_20131124_evangelii -gaudium.html .

Heyer, Kristin E. *Kinship Across Borders: A Christian Ethic of Immigration*. Washington, DC: Georgetown University Press, 2012.

John Paul II. *Familiaris Consortio* [on the Role of the Christian Family in the Modern World]. November 22, 1981. https://www.vatican.va/content/john-paul-ii/en/ apost_exhortations/documents/hf_jp-ii_exh_19811122_familiaris-consortio.html.

Kelly, Conor M. "Everyday Solidarity: A Framework for Integrating Theological Ethics and Ordinary Life." *Theological Studies* 81, no. 2 (2020): 414–37.

Kohlhaas, Jacob. "Constructing Parenthood: Catholic Social Teaching 1880 to the Present." *Theological Studies* 79, no. 3 (2018): 610–33.

———. "Racial Memory and Catholic Family Teaching." In *Modern Catholic Family Teaching: Commentaries and Interpretations*, edited by Jacob M. Kohlhaas and

Mary M. Doyle Roche, 47–54. Washington, DC: Georgetown University Press, 2024.

Letiecq, Bethany L. "Surfacing Family Privilege and Supremacy in Family Science: Toward Justice for All." *Journal of Family Theory and Review* (2019): 398–411.

Lushombo, Léocadie W. "*Caritas in Veritate* and *Africae Munus*." In *Modern Catholic Family Teaching: Commentaries and Interpretations*, edited by Jacob M. Kohlhaas and Mary M. Doyle Roche, 210–19. Washington, DC: Georgetown University Press, 2024.

———. *A Christian and African Ethic of Women's Political Participation: Living as Risen Beings*. Lanham, MD: Lexington Books, 2022.

McDonald, Emma Louise. "Forming Agents, Forming Families: Moral Agency in the Context of Procreation." PhD diss., Boston College, 2023.

Pew Research Center. "Few Catholics See Contraceptive Use as Morally Wrong." https://www.pewresearch.org/short-reads/2012/02/27/few-catholics-see -contraceptive-use-as-morally-wrong/ (accessed July 1, 2024).

———. "U.S. Catholics Open to Non-Traditional Families." https://www.pewresearch .org/religion/wp-content/uploads/sites/7/2015/09/Catholics-and-Family-Life-09 -01-2015.pdf (accessed July 1, 2024).

Ravizza, Bridget Burke. *The Sacrament of Same-Sex Marriage: An Inclusive Vision for the Catholic Church*. New York: Sheed & Ward, 2024.

Roberts, Dorothy E. *Killing the Black Body: Race, Reproduction, and the Meaning of Liberty*. New York: Vintage, 1999.

Roche, Mary M. Doyle. *Schools of Solidarity: Families and Catholic Social Teaching*. Collegeville, MN: Liturgical Press, 2015.

Rubio, Julie Hanlon. *A Christian Theology of Marriage and Family*. Mahwah, NJ: Paulist Press, 2003.

Ruiz, Ish. "Queer Theology and a Synodal Catholic Church." *Feminist Theology* 32, no. 3 (2024): 283–304.

Russell, Camisha A. *The Assisted Reproduction of Race*. Bloomington: Indiana University Press, 2018.

Second Vatican Council. *Apostolicam Actuositatem* [Decree on the Apostolate of Lay People] (November 10, 1965). https://www.vatican.va/archive/hist_councils/ ii_vatican_council/documents/vat-ii_decree_19651118_apostolicam-actuositatem _en.html.

———. "Dogmatic Constitution on the Church, *Lumen Gentium*, November 21, 1964." In *Vatican Council II: The Conciliar and Post Conciliar Documents*, edited by Austin Flannery. Collegeville, MN: Liturgical Press, 1975.

Steidl, Jason. *LGBTQ Catholic Ministry: Past and Present.* Mahwah, NJ: Paulist Press, 2022.

Sullivan-Dunbar, Sandra. *Human Dependency and Christian Ethics.* Cambridge: Cambridge University Press, 2017.

Synod of Bishops. *Instrumentum Laboris* [The Pastoral Challenges of the Family in the Context of Evangelization.] 2014. https://www.vatican.va/roman_curia/synod/documents/rc_synod_doc_20140626_instrumentum-laboris-familia_en.html (accessed June 25, 2024).

Tonstad, Linn Marie. *Queer Theology: Beyond Apologetics.* Eugene, OR: Wipf and Stock Publishers, 2018.

Weaver, Darlene Fozard. "Adoption, Social Justice, and Catholic Tradition." *Journal of Catholic Social Thought* 13, no. 2 (2016): 197–213.

Weinmeyer, Richard. "The Decriminalization of Sodomy in the United States." *AMA Journal of Ethics* 16, no. 11 (2014): 916–22.

12

Feminist Solidarity and Trans Inclusion

Kori Pacyniak

"How do you define feminism?" I ask my introduction to gender and sexuality students on the first day of class since the term will undergird much of our learning together. After coaxing suggestions out of the students, we collectively sort through various definitions from feminist theory and occasionally some from opponents of feminism. Many students tend to be drawn to bell hooks's simple yet profound definition of feminism as "a movement to end sexism."[1] Easy enough to understand and capable of garnering consensus among the students, hooks's definition provides an accessible entry point to a topic that has become increasingly controversial in our polarized political landscape. Similarly, I begin this chapter with hooks's definition because of its fertile potential for a feminism that affirms and celebrates transness. If we understand sexism to be discrimination on the basis of sex or gender, then the logical conclusion would appear to be that feminism, as a movement to end sexism, would include affirming and protecting transgender people as part of that goal due to their increased discrimination on the basis of their gender. Too often, however, rigid, colonial-based systems of gender continue to haunt feminism and society at large, causing transgender concerns to become a divisive point of contention rather than a point of seemingly obvious solidarity.[2] Centuries after Western European empires sought to colonize and Christianize much of the world, the legacy of the binary gender system they imposed upon indigenous communities remains. Centering feminist ethics in embodied solidarity and justice rather than in fear-based trans-exclusionary rhetoric, I argue that intersectional feminism requires solidarity with queer and trans communities, who often find themselves working against multiple forms of oppression.

In 2014, *Time* magazine declared a "Transgender Tipping Point" with Laverne Cox, a Black trans activist and actor, gracing the magazine cover.[3] Trans people had been gaining greater public visibility in the early 2000s and 2010s and it seemed, at least to *Time*'s editors, that the cultural tide in the United States was shifting toward trans acceptance and affirmation, perhaps as the next logical step after marriage equality. Various states had passed nondiscrimination laws explicitly protecting transgender people, businesses and universities were striving to create greater safety in spaces of work and study, and health insurance was beginning to cover transition-related medical procedures.[4] In the decade since that *Time* magazine article, the pendulum has swung, bringing with it a continued rise in anti-trans legislation and anti-trans violence along with an increase in "gender-critical" feminism, with Catholic leaders and institutions among those advocating for anti-trans policies.[5] In reflecting on the *Time* "Trans Tipping Point" cover, pioneering trans studies scholar Susan Stryker says,

> I think in hindsight those years were indeed a tipping point, but not the one being imagined by *Time*'s editors. That's when the backlash to the gains of the previous quarter-century set in with a vengeance. There's been a really significant reaction that has set in since then. We're on the cusp, right now, of a very different historical period, one that I don't think is going to be good.[6]

Stryker is referring to the steep rise of anti-trans legislation throughout the country. In 2023 alone, the United States saw the introduction of six hundred anti-trans bills across forty-nine states, eighty-seven of which passed into law.[7] A recent Williams Institute survey of transgender youth revealed that 93 percent of transgender youth in the United States live in states that have passed or proposed anti-trans legislation.[8] Many of these laws employ the rhetoric of "protecting women and girls" as they legislate and restrict access to restrooms, limit participation in sports, and, in some cases, prohibit or criminalize access to gender-affirming healthcare or the changing of sex markers on legal documents.

These laws, and the campaigns for them, lead to trans people being othered and vilified, with accusations of child abuse, grooming, and sexual perversion. Judith Butler describes how, in the United States, gender "has become a phantasm with destructive powers, one way of collecting and escalating multiple panics," with the brunt of this panic being directed at transgender individuals.[9] Apart from these ideological and legislative attacks, research shows that trans people are often at higher risk of attempted suicide, nearly four times more likely to live in extreme poverty than cisgender people, and are battling employment discrimination and anti-trans violence at overwhelming rates, particularly when transphobia mixes with racism and misogyny.[10] I share these statistics not to provoke pity but to illumine the realities of trans existence.

Feminist theology and ethics have played pivotal roles in critiquing patriarchal structures, advocating for gender equality, and fostering solidarity among marginalized groups. However, the question of transgender inclusion within feminist discourse has provoked complex discussions surrounding identity, embodiment, and solidarity. For feminist theologians and religious ethicists committed to resisting and ending patriarchy and sexism, what is the obligation—or perhaps invitation—to solidarity with our trans siblings? As a trans, genderqueer, nonbinary scholar priest who comes out of a women's college and is ordained through the Roman Catholic Woman Priest movement, I have spent decades navigating feminist, and particularly Catholic feminist, theological, and spiritual spaces with various degrees of inclusion and welcome. Often, my nonbinary existence has been erased or ignored or, at best, treated like woman-lite, regardless of my gender presentation.

Many of these feminist Catholic spaces that I have spent time in are ones that emerged out of post–Vatican II church reform movements and are organized around social justice causes such as women's ordination and reproductive justice. Heavily influenced by the women's movement of the 1960s and 1970s, images of the divine feminine abound in these women-centered (though not exclusively women-only) spaces. Feminist theologians such as Mary Daly, Rosemary Radford Reuther, Elizabeth Johnson, and Joan Chittister have influenced the beliefs and priorities of these spaces, which lift women's voices and experiences in their commitment to end sexism and patriarchy within Catholicism. On more than one occasion, I have heard students and teachers of feminist theology within these spaces comment on how influential Daly in particular was to their understanding of feminism, Catholicism, and theology.[11]

While Daly has had an undeniable influence on feminist theology, as a trans feminist Catholic, I cannot think of Daly without thinking of her anti-trans views. Daly, and her student Janice Raymond, whose work Daly often cites, deny the realities of trans experience and refer to trans women as male-to-constructed-female, but still male.[12] Daly's treatment of trans people relies heavily on Raymond's *The Transsexual Empire* in positioning the existence of trans people, particularly trans women, as being contrary to the aims of feminist theology.[13] Trans women are seen as infiltrators in feminist and women's spaces, as invaders and deceivers. As Siobhan Kelly points out, this logic does not remain ensconced in the writings of the 1970s; rather, it is the same logic used in anti-trans legislation around bathrooms and locker rooms.[14] The aim is to protect feminist and women's spaces from the threat of trans women (and transness in general).[15]

When I have raised concerns about Mary Daly's anti-trans views, most responses have fallen somewhere between defensiveness and suggestions that I was misinterpreting Daly's writings.[16] It is a rare occasion when someone will reconsider their view of Daly when Daly's anti-trans views are pointed out. In feminist Catholic spaces that champion women's voices and resist the patriarchal aspects of the church, there is often a similar desire to protect the sacred feminist space that has been created. Most such spaces welcome male allies and supporters of the cause, but the question of trans and nonbinary inclusion is often unspoken, with many groups refraining from explicitly clarifying their positions, requiring trans Catholics to discreetly ask before entering what could be a potentially hostile space. Some organizations, including Catholics for Choice and Women's Ordination Conference, have explicitly adopted trans-inclusive language and include gender equity for trans, nonbinary, and gender nonconforming individuals as one of their priorities.[17] Others, like FemCatholic, have hosted book clubs around Abigail Favale's *The Genesis of Gender: A Christian Theory*, which states, "A woman is the kind of human being whose body is organized around the potential to gestate new life," excluding trans women and intersex women.[18] There is also the case of the Catholic women's college St. Mary's, in South Bend, Indiana, which in

November 2023 planned to allow admittance to trans women. Within a month of loud public outcry, St. Mary's reversed course, with several alumnae and donors even calling for the ousting of the college's president, claiming that trust had been broken.[19]

Given the diversity of Catholic feminist experiences, one would not expect all Catholic and feminist spaces to have the same policy. Without an explicit welcome, however, trans people have no way of knowing whether they will be welcomed, barely tolerated, ignored, or explicitly made to feel unwelcome. These are individuals who were often formed by the same feminist values, yet when they uncovered and lived into their trans identities, they sometimes found themselves unwelcome in feminist spaces. Many trans masculine individuals describe their trans identities as being intertwined with feminist commitments that were influential in their development, yet they often feel unwelcome in feminist spaces.[20] If trans women are, as Daly and Raymond suggest, invaders and deceivers, then trans men have betrayed their sex and gender. Transness itself becomes the threat, reflecting how the legacy of anti-trans feminist theology and theory has lingered, making feminist spaces risky to hostile for trans people to enter.

It is not all doom and gloom for trans people within feminist spaces. According to a 2023 Public Religion Research Institute survey, the majority of self-identified feminists would be comfortable with having a trans friend or using a trans person's correct pronouns.[21] The National Organization for Women has loudly come out in support of trans people, stating that transphobia is: "a feminist issue on two levels. First, like racism and homophobia, transphobia grows out of and helps perpetuate the same patriarchal ideology that dictates women's subordination as second-class citizens. Second, transphobia disproportionately harms women."[22] However, loud voices like those of J. K. Rowling and other so-called gender-critical feminists in the United Kingdom have actively campaigned against trans rights.[23] In the United States, Abigail Shrier's column in the *Wall Street Journal* calling the Equality Act a "Transgender War on Women" and Pamela Paul's columns in the *New York Times* suggest that transgender activists, academics, medical professionals, and others are trying to deny women their humanity through advancing trans rights.[24]

This language of war and erasure stokes the mentality that trans-inclusive feminism or an embrace of nonbinary identities somehow erases women's experiences and identities. It also runs counter to Catholic feminist ideals of radical welcome and equity and liberation theology's preferential option for the poor and most marginalized. Catholic musician and singer-songwriter Jessica Gerhardt found herself wrestling with this very question of trans inclusion and liberation. In an op-ed for *National Catholic Reporter*, she recounts how she was "wrestling with my theological and philosophical ideas about transgender people" with her partner who then shared they had experienced gender dysphoria.[25] Now in a queer relationship, questions Gerhardt had thought of in generalities were suddenly incredibly personal. Gerhardt suggests that trans-exclusionary thinking comes from fear associated with believing one's own gender identity is under attack and from a lack of faith in God's abundance. According to Gerhardt,

> A scarcity mindset is contrary to a kingdom mindset: one in which every person, exactly as they are, has a seat at the table. Without faith in God's abundance, a dualistic/all-or-nothing mindset leads the institutional church to cling to gender essentialism, and therefore to uphold a male-only priesthood, prohibit same-sex marriage and invalidate transgender identities.[26]

Intersectional feminism emphasizes that there is not one universal experience of womanhood. In *Transgender History*, Susan Stryker writes,

> To understand the oppression of any particular woman or group of women means taking into account all of the things that intersect with their being women, such as race, class, nationality, religion, disability, sexuality, citizenship status, and myriad other circumstances that marginalize or privilege them—including having transgender or gender-nonconforming feelings or identities.[27]

If our feminism claims to be intersectional and committed to solidarity with those who are marginalized, then the question is not whether feminism should be trans-inclusive, but how we might live out that solidarity through affirming trans experiences. Such feminist solidarity goes beyond mere tolerance of trans individuals; it embraces explicit welcome, inclusion, and affirmation, which may include reexamining language and practices that are rooted in cis-sexism. It also requires at least an acknowledgment of anti-trans strains within feminism;[28] ideally, it would include a response and rejection of such movements. Last, it draws on intersectional feminism, the trans-inclusive roots of radical feminism, and trans feminisms to fully embrace and live into practices of trans inclusion, affirmation, and solidarity.

Solidarity

Solidarity can be defined and interpreted in a myriad of ways. My understanding of solidarity is an embodied, relational, active commitment to collective liberation and resistance to oppression. It holds space for communion across differences and coalition-building. Solidarity, for me, is incarnational and interpersonal, calling us into an embodied lived experience of witness and justice-making. This understanding emerges from stories and lessons taught at the kitchen table by my parents and grandparents who insisted that "as long as you can help someone else, you ought to"—an understanding passed down among generations that to be Polish and Catholic meant viewing solidarity as that thing which linked humanity, regardless of ethnicity and background.

As the child of Polish immigrants enmeshed in the Polish diasporic community and the grandchild of Poles who fought in the resistance during World War II, the values of justice and resistance to oppression were interwoven with my faith and cultural formation. I grew up on stories of my grandparents' actions as part of the resistance during World War II and of my uncle smuggling newspapers, printing materials, and money to the anti-communist *Solidarność* (Solidarity) movement in Poland, resulting in his imprisonment under martial law. There was an intergenerational tradition of helping where one could that went beyond charity and reflected an understanding that my family's own freedom—their escape from the Nazi and Soviet armies and from communism—was bound up in the liberation of others.[29]

This understanding of solidarity draws on several cultural touchstones, including life in a partitioned Poland, a strong religious patriotism and resistance, and the influence of the *Solidarność* movement both in Poland and among Polish diasporic communities.[30] Originating within labor unions, the *Solidarność* movement in Poland was influential in bringing about the end of communism in Poland, and its leaders worked across borders in Eastern Europe to aid other resistance movements.[31] In the summer of 1980, against the backdrop of an oppressive communist regime, the *Solidarność* movement gathered millions of followers, inspired in their resistance by the visit of Pope John Paul II the prior year. Faith and justice were linked in the movement against communism.[32] The Solidarity movement unified not only residents of Poland but the Polish diaspora—many of whom recalled living under foreign rule during the partitions.[33]

Building upon these foundations, I stress the incarnational and interpersonal dimensions of solidarity, recognizing that our shared humanity invites us to stand with those who are oppressed. My understanding reflects, in part, what Brenda Lyshaug refers to as a need for enlarged sympathy to build solidarities, a concept on which I will expand below. This is the solidarity that I saw in Occupy Boston when seminarians from the schools of the Boston Theological Institute joined the encampments to serve as chaplains; it is the solidarity of protesters and activists in a cross-national, ecumenical Way of the Cross and Eucharistic Liturgy that begins yearly in Los Angeles and winds down to Friendship Park on the San Diego–Tijuana border where those who have the privilege to navigate the border crossing do so, bridging the constructed boundaries; it is the solidarity of those protesters with legal status and privilege who place themselves on the front lines of an immigration protest, facing down federal law enforcement armed with tear gas because they know they will not face deportation if arrested.[34] Each of these actions sought to highlight interconnectedness and interdependence. Solidarity can also look like the ally with "Free Mom Hugs" t-shirt at a pride march, activists forming a human chain outside Planned Parenthood to protect patients from hateful protesters, or parents attending school board meetings to protest book bans. Solidarity should not require shared oppression, but rather recognition that an injustice faced by one person calls out and invites us to accompany, to walk with, to stand with them, and, when possible, to use our privilege.

This is not to say that such a relational, embodied solidarity is not without limits. Any movement for solidarity asks the question, solidarity with whom?

And to what end? Such questions have often been fraught for members of marginalized communities. What are the limitations of communion across differences? At what point can a common opposition to injustice no longer unite two groups? This is a question I often find myself asking in ecumenical work as a trans and nonbinary person. Can I engage in activist work or participate in coalitions with groups or individuals who espouse and support anti-trans movements? When asked about solidarity, Susan Stryker responded, "You create solidarity from a diversity of positions and a diversity of stakes and concerns around which you're willing to work out differences and find common cause. . . . It's hard to find solidarity with people who are basically saying you don't exist, or you shouldn't exist."[35] It is the denial of trans people's humanity and rights that makes discussion of solidarity difficult, if not impossible, in some situations.

The question of trans inclusion and affirmation in feminist spaces as a matter of solidarity raises several points. First, it is important to distinguish between feminist spaces and women's spaces. While the former may be predominantly women, ideals, and commitments are the defining boundaries rather than gender. The inclusion of trans women in women's spaces is an extension of feminist solidarity; however, my primary concern is broader trans inclusion in feminist spaces. As Rosemary Kellison notes in chapter 1, many intersectional feminists have argued that because there is no one, singular experience of "womanhood," feminism is better served by a commitment-based solidarity rather than an identity-based one. Here we might return to bell hooks's definition of feminism as a shared commitment shared by both women and trans people. The question of trans inclusion as an application of feminist solidarity is not that simple, however, because we cannot ignore the fact that feminists have, at times, been culpable of gender-based exclusion of trans folks, often viewing trans women as a threat to cis women and denying that they are women. At the same time, trans men and trans masculine identities are invalidated or erased and trans men are seen as rejecting feminism and lesbianism.[36] To focus simply on a shared commitment-based model of solidarity risks ignoring the legacy of anti-trans harm within some strains of feminism. To counter this history requires that feminist solidarity reckon with the trans-exclusionary strains within its communities and highlight what

Cristan Williams sees as the inherently trans-inclusionary nature of radical feminism.[37]

Leaning into trans-feminist scholarship is certainly one method of doing this. To go beyond tolerance and mere inclusion to affirmation calls for a critical self-examination and leaning into the potential destabilizing and renegotiating of categories and boundaries. Solidarity is not meant to be comfortable. It carries risk. There are physical risks associated with actions of embodied solidarity through participating in protests and human shields. There is also the risk that in acknowledging or leveraging one's privilege to be in solidarity with others, one may lose that privilege. In an era where much is documented on social media and the internet, a statement or act of solidarity can lead to public outcry, accusations of wokeness, and sometimes even the loss of friendships, relationships, or job opportunities. To engage and embrace solidarity, we cannot ignore these risks. Instead, they should be acknowledged and each person must make their own assessment of when something is worth the potential cost.

The Uncomfortable Ambiguity of Solidarity

When I lead "Trans 101" trainings at hospitals, churches, and nonprofits, the sense of discomfort is often palatable. I can reach out and pet the elephant in the room. There is an anxiety that in embracing trans liberation, in shifting to an expansive understanding of sex and gender, some aspect of one's self will be lost. Self-revelation often appears dangerous and risky.[38] For those who have fought to make space for women in all-male spaces, to shift language from being all-male to including women, the potential undoing of those changes feels personal. What members of these feminist communities don't necessarily realize is that there is often a cis and binary privilege embedded in many aspects of the community—from language used to the bathrooms in a physical space. The lack of trans inclusion is not always based on malice. However, a shift from "women and men" focused language that reinforces the binary to "people of all genders" that makes room for nonbinary, agender, and third-gender individuals can be painful and destabilizing for members of the community, perceived as a threat to their identity. Most of our identities rely on distinguishing "us" from "them," and in doing so often attempt to force a spectrum of diverse identities into rigid boundaries. To move away, or past, these rigid boundaries, to renegotiate them, to change our understanding of gender, may indeed bring with it the loss of unquestioned gender identity. It can become, however, an act of solidarity, a way to experience a fragment of the gender journey that trans people often find themselves on. It asks the nontrans inhabitants of feminist spaces to let go of the security and privilege of previously held ideas around gender to be in solidarity with trans people.

In "Solidarity without Sisterhood," Brenda Lyshaug points out that coalition-building often requires giving up aspects of identity that bring us security for some greater purpose or reaching out to those who might make us uncomfortable. Similarly, relying too much on sisterhood or shared identity tends to erase differences. Instead, Lyshaug suggests a solidarity based on what she calls "enlarged sympathy," a mutual recognition and reciprocity that "imaginatively introjecting others' differences into oneself in order to claim a kind of kinship."[39] Preserving both similarities and differences between parties, this enlarged sympathy provides a method of building more equitable bonds of kinship and solidarity through self-awareness and greater flexibility around identities. Ideally, Lyshaug argues, this increased flexibility counters the knee-jerk defensive reaction to the "incursions" into feminist spaces by outsiders and facilitates critical self-reflection of privilege. "If feminist coalitions are to serve the needs of trans individuals, then non-trans feminists must learn to recognize and relinquish the privilege that accrues to those whose gender steadily 'matches' the sexed body they inhabit."[40]

The recognition of cis-privilege is often a struggle, especially among Christian feminist communities formed by second-wave feminism that pushed back against male-dominant spaces to claim leadership roles for women and push for reform. The view of the sexism they've had to combat is almost always rooted in a binary, cis-focused understanding of gender as mentioned earlier. The welcoming of trans individuals into these spaces can be seen as a destabilizing threat or as something that will be tolerated as long as it doesn't shift the focus or take away from the "feminist" goals and commitments. I suggest, however, that the "trans agenda" of protecting trans youth and trans rights lines up with feminist goals and commitments. A feminist solidarity of trans inclusion and affirmation is not rejecting gender altogether or erasing differences. It makes room for both cis and trans; male, female, and nonbinary; for a variety of genders (and none). It can even recognize the colonial legacy of the binary gender system without viewing that as a threat.

The Haunting of Colonial Gender

In recent years, conservative mainstream US media outlets and Catholic church officials have maligned even the very idea of "gender" as a harbinger of liberal wokeness and ideological colonization.[41] What such takes often ignore, however, is that the binary sex and gender system that much of the global north subscribes to is a remnant of colonialism. In "Extermination of the Joyas," Deborah Miranda demonstrates how Christian colonization led to the erasure of gender variance in indigenous communities in what is now California and Mexico. Miranda describes how Spanish colonizers "believed that American Indians were intellectually, physiologically, and spiritually immature, if not actual animals," a belief shared by other European powers who viewed indigenous peoples as without gender—thus lesser in stature than white Europeans—a view that allowed for the enslavement of indigenous peoples.[42] In present-day California, Spanish colonial policies led to the decimation of a local indigenous population from one million to a mere ten thousand in one hundred years due to what Miranda names "gendercide," something more than just homophobia or transphobia, but a systematic, active, conscious, violent, extermination of third gender individuals.[43]

What happened in California is not an anomaly within European colonial conquests. As María Lugones writes, "neither Indigenous people nor people kidnapped from the African continent and enslaved were considered and treated as gendered."[44] Denying indigenous and African people their gender, regardless of whether it aligned with the categories of male and female or not, was a way of further dehumanizing them and asserting European, and in this case Catholic, superiority, laying the foundations for linking contemporary society's understanding with notions of race. The intrinsically racist, colonial legacy of the binary gender system makes it even more necessary for feminists to critically wrestle with it and its implications, particularly for trans people and people of color.

Often, it is those who have been marginalized and oppressed who bear the burden of making space for themselves, of sacrificing parts of themselves in coalition-building. As Jules Gil-Peterson writes, "The demand placed on trans people for consistency and commitment . . . has the opposite of its intended effect in the outcome. Would-be allies think they are showing that they take trans people's identities seriously by intensely conforming to contemporary conventions, but what they are really saying is *I need you to be legible, clear, and easy for me to understand. I need your gender to make me comfortable.*"[45] In looking at the hauntings and legacies of colonialism, Melissa Pagán describes how subjectivity, how *being*, within a Catholic framework relies on the anthropology of a binary gender system.[46] Those who fall outside that binary, who are *illegible* according to Jules Gil-Peterson, become what Pagán calls *les indocumentadxs*, the undocumented. They occupy a space of (non)being. In the maintenance of this colonial binary gender system by our societies, those who do not conform are increasingly excluded and harmed.

Conclusion

As our world has become more polarized politically and as our climate crisis continues to grow, it is not entirely surprising that fear has unduly influenced our theology and ethical framework. In feminist spaces, fear of losing hard-won political and social victories and the erasure of gendered identities has at times led to the exclusion of trans individuals. As Alox Vaid-Menon asserts in *Beyond the Gender Binary*, "This is not about erasing men and women but rather acknowledging that man and woman are two of many—stars in a constellation that do not compete but amplify one another's shine."[47] Rather than give in to the fear of what might be lost, I suggest leaning into the potential of what might be gained by embracing the ambiguity and uncertainty that may come by standing in solidarity with trans people and affirming their place within feminist spaces. It may be messy. It may cause questioning of identity on both sides. However, confronting such fear and discomfort is but one of the growing edges of living into a more inclusive solidarity.

Rather than be consumed by fear or focus on differences and rigid identity boundaries, solidarity invites us to practice compassion and empathy, walking with those whose situation might be different from ours. It is an embodiment of liberation theology's preferential option for the poor and the marginalized. Rather than virtue signaling, it recognizes the dignity of all parties and empowers those who have been marginalized.[48] Solidarity, particularly solidarity across difference, does not mean that we agree on everything. It does not mean we are the same. Based on our shared humanity, solidarity invites us to stand alongside each other, to create interdependent relationships, to recognize that our liberation—now and in the future—is tied up in the liberation of our siblings. To put it in a Christian theological framework, it is the recognition that each person is created in *imago Dei* that is enough to call us into solidarity.

We do not need to cling to rigid, binary, biologically essentialist definitions of sex and gender that were inherited from Christian colonial powers. Nor should we be held captive by them. The trans individuals are not trying to invade feminist spaces to erase gender and difference. The trans agenda, in this case, is for a broadening of how we understand gender, a recognition that fighting transphobia is a feminist commitment because anti-trans rhetoric and legislation, like sexism and the patriarchy, harms trans and non-trans people alike. What might it look like, then, to step beyond the understanding of gender we inherited or discovered?

Such a move leads us to recognize, as Jessica Gerhardt did, that cis women's liberation is tied up with the liberation of trans and nonbinary people and that Catholicism invites us into a theology of abundance, not fear and scarcity.[49] Women's Ordination Conference and Catholics for Choice are two feminist organizations that have embraced the sometimes-challenging conversations around trans inclusion among their intergenerational membership. We can also draw inspiration from the Catholic social justice tradition that includes organizations such as Pax Christi, Call to Action, and Network's Nuns on the Bus, all of which reflect a commitment to embodied solidarity as inspiration for moving beyond trans inclusion in feminist spaces and into a broader civic and political activism for trans rights.[50]

By embracing principles of radical welcome, enlarged sympathy, and embodied solidarity, we can move beyond the colonial hauntings of an exclusionary binary gender system and adopt a trans-inclusive and affirming Catholic feminist tradition. We can acknowledge that feminist Catholic theology has anti-trans parts in its history *and* that it has been influential in advocating for gender equality. We can recognize that women have been erased and undervalued while understanding that there is room for trans and nonbinary people without losing the gains of feminist theology. To affirm trans and nonbinary people in feminist spaces is not to suggest that sexism is over and there is no need for feminism. Rather, it is a chance to lift up and stand with our trans and nonbinary siblings, united in our battle against sexism. If we recognize that feminist and trans agendas align in their aims to combat sexism, and that an embodied solidarity is inherently risky, then we can lean into a trans-affirming solidarity that carries with it the potential for greater coalition-building and transformative justice.

Notes

1 bell hooks, *Feminism Is for Everybody: Passionate Politics* (Cambridge, MA: South End Press, 2000), 3.

2 For further discussion of the effects of colonial gender systems, see María Lugones, "Methodological Notes toward a Decolonial Feminism," in *Decolonizing Epistemologies: Latina/o Theology and Philosophy* (New York: Fordham University Press, 2012), and Melissa Pagán, "Les Indocumentadxs: The Coloniality of Gender, Complementarity, and Rethinking Border Being/s," *Journal of Feminist Studies in Religion* 38, no. 1 (2022): 167–84.

3 Throughout this piece, I use trans and transgender interchangeably to denote anyone whose gender does not align 100 percent with the gender they were assigned at birth (i.e., anyone who is not cisgender), including nonbinary, genderqueer, agender, and other gender nonconforming individuals.

4 National Center for Transgender Equality, "Victory! Federal Government Modernizes Health Insurance," *Advancing Transgender Equality* blog, https:// transgenderequality.wordpress.com/2014/06/13/victory-federal-government -modernizes-health-insurance/ (accessed December 18, 2024).

5　In July 2021, the Diocese of Marquette (WI) issued a policy that pastors should deny trans, gay, and nonbinary Catholics the sacraments "unless the person has repented" signed by Bishop John Doerfler. In January 2022, the Diocese of Milwaukee issued a policy that bars church personnel from using trans people's preferred/lived pronouns and insisting that Catholic institutions and organizations "are to recognize only a person's biological sex." See David Crary, "Rejection or Welcome: Transgender Catholics Encounter Both," ABC News, February 26, 2022, https://abcnews.go.com/US/wireStory/rejection-transgender-catholics-encounter-83128201.

6　Ella Ben Hagai and Lily House-Peters, "Susan Stryker on Solidarity: An Interview for the *Journal of Lesbian Studies*," *Journal of Lesbian Studies* 28, no. 1 (2024): 189–204.

7　"2023 Anti-Trans Legislation," *Trans Legislation Tracker*, https://translegislation.com/bills/2023 (accessed March 1, 2024).

8　Elana Redfield, Kerith J. Conron, and Christy Mallory, "The Impact of 2024 Anti-Transgender Legislation on Youth," Williams Institute, UCLA School of Law, 2024, https://williamsinstitute.law.ucla.edu/publications/2024-anti-trans-legislation/ (April 26, 2024).

9　Judith Butler, *Who's Afraid of Gender?* (New York: Farrar, Straus and Giroux, 2024), 5.

10　Jaime Grant, Lisa Mottet, Justin Tanis, and D. Min, "Injustice at Every Turn: A Report of the National Transgender Discrimination Survey," National Center for Transgender Equality and National Gay and Lesbian Task Force, 2011, http://www.thetaskforce.org/static_html/downloads/reports/reports/ntds_full.pdf.

11　While Mary Daly renounced Catholicism as incompatible with feminism, her writing remains influential on feminist, particularly Catholic, theology. Daly was notably called out for racism by Audre Lorde in an open letter that was later reprinted in *Sister Outsider: Essays and Speeches* (Berkeley, CA: Crossing, 1984), 66–72.

12　Mary Daly, *Beyond God the Father: Towards a Philosophy of Women's Liberation* (Boston: Beacon Press, 1973), xvii–xviiiv. Raymond refers to transsexuality as an attempt to "colonize feminist identification, culture, politics and sexuality" and says, "All transsexuals rape women's bodies by reducing the real female form to an artifact, appropriating this body for themselves. . . . Transsexuals merely cut off the most obvious means of invading women, so that they seem non-invasive"; see

Janice Raymond, *The Transsexual Empire: The Making of the She-Male* (Boston: Beacon Press, 1979), 104.

13 For a more extensive trans reading of Mary Daly see Max Strassfeld, "Transing Religious Studies," *Journal of Feminist Studies in Religion* 34, no. 1 (2018): 37, which discusses the legacy of Mary Daly on feminist theology and trans rights and lays the groundwork for trans feminist theology; Siobhan Kelly, "Feminist Transphobia, Feminist Rhetoric: From Trans-Exclusive Radical Feminism to HB2," *Feminist Studies in Religion Blog*, August 30, 2016, http://www.fsrinc.org/feminist-transphobia-rhetoric/, which highlights how personal the harm of anti-trans writings in feminist theology can be and how this legacy has led to feminist opposition to trans rights in the form of bathroom access; and Cameron Partridge, "'Scotch-Taped Together': Anti-'Androgyny' Rhetoric, Transmisogyny, and the Transing of Religious Studies," *Journal of Feminist Studies in Religion* 34, no. 1 (2018): 68, which discusses how Daly's treatment of the androgyne and connections to transmisogyny.

14 Kelly, "Feminist Transphobia, Feminist Rhetoric."

15 Julia Serrano has written much about the exclusion of trans women from women's spaces. See "On 'Male Socialization' and the 'Trans Masc Versus Trans Fem' Discourse™" in *Medium*, November 28, 2023, https://juliaserano.medium.com/on-male-socialization-and-the-trans-masc-versus-trans-fem-discourse-14bccb196a63; *Excluded: Making Feminist and Queer Movements More Inclusive* (Berkeley, CA: Seal Press, 2013); and *Sexed Up: How Society Sexualizes Us, and How We Can Fight Back* (Berkeley, CA: Seal Press, 2022).

16 Mary Daly, *Gyn/Ecology: The Metaethics of Radical Feminism* (Boston: Beacon Press, 1990), 68.

17 In particular, see Women's Ordination Conference description of the Lucille Murray Durkin scholarship for women and non-binary people discerning ordination (https://www.womensordination.org/programs/scholarship/) and the insertion of gender equity into their mission statement: "The uncompromising feminist voice for women's ordination and gender equity in the Roman Catholic Church since 1975," https://www.womensordination.org/ (December 18, 2024). Catholics for Choice now lists gender equity as one of their main issues and includes several trans-affirming FAQs about transnesss and Catholicism, https://www.catholicsforchoice.org/issues/gender-equity/ (July 15, 2024).

18 Abigail Favale, *The Genesis of Gender: A Christian Theory* (San Francisco, CA: Ignatius Press, 2022), 120.

19 Jonathan Leidl, "'Trust Has Been Broken': After Trans Policy Fallout, Controversy Still Simmers at St. Mary's College," *National Catholic Register*, February 5, 2024, https://www.ncregister.com/news/trust-has-been-broken-after-trans -policy-fallout-controversy-still-simmers-at-st-mary-s-college; Heidi Schlumpf, "Catholic Women's College Opens to Trans Students, Drawing Bishop's Rebuke," *National Catholic Reporter*, December 6, 2023, https://www.ncronline.org/news /catholic-womens-college-opens-trans-students-drawing-bishops-rebuke. It is worth noting, per Schlumpf and CampusPride.org, that there are other Catholic women's colleges that do admit trans women; see https://www.campuspride.org/ tpc/womens-colleges/ (July 19, 2024).

20 Miriam J. Abelson, "Trans Men Engaging, Reforming, and Resisting Feminisms," *TSQ: Transgender Studies Quarterly* 3, no. 1–2 (May 1, 2016): 16.

21 Kelsy Burke, "'Identity Politics' and Transgender Equality," Public Religion Research Institute, https://www.prri.org/spotlight/identity-politics-and -transgender-equality/ (accessed July 8, 2024).

22 Terry O'Neill, "Why Transphobia Is a Feminist Issue," *National Organization for Women*, 2014, https://now.org/blog/why-transphobia-is-a-feminist-issue/ (accessed June 30, 2024).

23 For a thorough chronology of J.K. Rowling's anti-trans statements, see Aja Romano, "Is J.K. Rowling Transphobic? Let's Let Her Speak for Herself," *Vox*, May 14, 2024, https://www.vox.com/culture/23622610/jk-rowling-transphobic -statements-timeline-history-controversy. See also Fran Amery's "'Gender Critical' Feminism as Biopolitical Project," *Sexualities*, 0(0) (2024): 1–15 for a discussion the anti-trans actions of "gender critical" feminism in the United Kingdom.

24 Abigail Shrier, "The Transgender War on Women," *Wall Street Journal*, March 26, 2019, https://www.wsj.com/articles/the-transgender-war-on-women -11553640683; Pamela Paul, "The Far Right and Far Left Agree on One Thing: Women Don't Count," *New York Times*, July 3, 2022, https://www.nytimes.com /2022/07/03/opinion/the-far-right-and-far-left-agree-on-one-thing-women-dont -count.html.

25 Jessica Gerhardt, "How Trans-Inclusive Feminism Is Compatible with Catholicism," *National Catholic Reporter*, September 9, 2022, https://www .ncronline.org/opinion/guest-voices/how-trans-inclusive-feminism-compatible -catholicism.

26 Gerhardt, "How Trans-Inclusive Feminism Is Compatible with Catholicism."

27 Susan Stryker, *Transgender History: The Roots of Today's Revolution* (New York: Seal Press, 2017), 5.

28 See Kelly, "Feminist Transphobia, Feminist Rhetoric," for the importance of acknowledging the anti-trans legacy of feminist theology.

29 "If you have come to help me you are wasting your time. If you have come because your liberation is bound up with mine, then let us work together." Though this quotation is often attributed to Dr. Lilla Watson, a Gangulu woman, she prefers that it be attributed to Aboriginal activists group, Queensland, 1970s.

30 It is worth noting that the Solidarity union in Poland has shifted over the last forty years and is now closely aligned with Poland's nationalist governing party, Law and Justice, lobbying actively against LGBTQ persons and anyone else it views as "insufficiently respectful of the Polish nation and its traditional values." Andrew Higgins, "Poles Tussle Over an Icon of Their Past, With an Eye on the Future," *New York Times*, July 28, 2021, https://www.nytimes.com/2021/07/28/world/europe/poland-solidarity-lech-walesa.html/.

31 For more on the trans-national aspects of the Polish Solidarity movement, see Padraic Kenney, "Borders Breached: The Transnational in Eastern Europe since Solidarity," *Journal of Modern European History* 8, no. 2 (September 2010): 179–95.

32 See Bogdan Szajkowski, *Next to God-Poland: Politics and Religion in Contemporary Poland* (London: F. Pinter, 1983).

33 The three partitions of Poland between 1772 and 1795 by Prussia, Russia, and Austria resulted in the disappearance of Poland from the map. Although conditions varied by partition, there was a concerted effort to safeguard the Polish language (often intertwined with religion) among ethnic Poles. Poland would not reappear on the map until the end of World War I in 1918. During this time, patriotism took on a religious fervor as a form of cultural self-preservation. Norman Davies explains

> All "normal" manifestations of patriotism were officially repressed, and driven underground. As a result, Polish patriotism became the object of an intense, secret, and highly developed mysticism. It possessed its Scriptures, in the writings of the Romantics; its "Fathers of the Church," in the great poets; its Martyrs, in the victims of the Risings; its theologians, in the messianic philosophers and literary critics; its priesthood, in the intelligentsia; and a large number of Faithful. It was based on a system of irrational beliefs whose acceptance demanded an act of Faith; and its beliefs were intended as a guide to everyday living in a hostile, and equally irrational world.

Davies, *Heart of Europe: The Past in Poland's Present* (Oxford: Oxford University Press, 2001), 236–37.

34 See Joshua Eaton, "Faith and Spirituality at Occupy Boston," 2001, https://www.occupyboston.org/2011/10/24/faith-spirituality-occupy-boston/; Pat McCaughan, "Via Crucis: No Walls Can Separate Us from God's Grace," Episcopal Diocese of Los Angeles, 2012, https://diocesela.org/uncategorized/via-crucis-no-walls-can-separate-us-from-gods-grace/#LeavingJesus, a stations of the cross that begins in Los Angeles and ends at the San Diego/Tijuana border occurring annually since 2012 for immigration reform (June 27, 2024).

35 In Ben Hagai and House-Peters, "Susan Stryker on Solidarity," 199.

36 See C. Jacob Hale, "Consuming the Living, Dis(re)membering the Dead in the Butch/FTM Borderlands," *GLQ: A Journal of Lesbian and Gay Studies* 4 (1998): 311–28; Becky Walker, "Imagining the Future of Lesbian Community: The Case of Online Lesbian Communities and the Issue of Trans," *Journal of Media & Cultural Studies* 6 (2009): 921–35; Jennifer Earles, "The 'Penis Police': Lesbian and Feminist Spaces, Trans Women, and the Maintenance of the Sex/Gender/Sexuality System," *Journal of Lesbian Studies*, 23, no. 2 (2019): 243–56; Meredith G. F. Worthen, "This Is My TERF! Lesbian Feminists and the Stigmatization of Trans Women," *Sexuality and Culture*, 26 (2022): 1782–803.

37 Cristan Williams, "Radical Inclusion: Recounting the Trans Inclusive History of Radical Feminism," *TSQ: Transgender Studies Quarterly* 3, no. 1–2 (May 1, 2016): 254–58.

38 "The transformation of silence into language and action is an act of self-revelation, and that always seems fraught with danger." Audre Lorde, "The Transformation of Silence into Language and Action," in *Sister Outsider* (Berkeley, CA: Crossing Press, 1984), 42.

39 Brenda Lyshaug, "Solidarity without 'Sisterhood'? Feminism and the Ethics of Coalition Building," *Politics and Gender* 2, no. 1 (March 2006): 90.

40 Lyshaug, "Solidarity without 'Sisterhood'?" 94.

41 Throughout his papacy, Pope Francis has referred to "gender ideology" or gender theory as ideological colonization, comparing it to nuclear war and claiming that it has the potential to erase intrinsic differences between men and women. See Pope Francis's comments in *San Giovanni Paolo Magno* (2020) as well as *Dignitas Infinita* (2024) and Courtney Mares, "Pope Francis: Gender Ideology Is 'One of the Most Dangerous Ideological Colonizations' Today," *Catholic News Agency*, March 11, 2023, https://www.catholicnewsagency.com/news/253845/pope-francis-gender-ideology-is-one-of-the-most-dangerous-ideological-colonizations-today.

See also GLAAD's open letter to the *New York Times*, which details many of the *Times'* anti-trans articles, https://glaad.org/new-york-times-sign-on-letter-from -lgtbq-allied-leaders-and-organizations/.

42 Deborah A. Miranda, "Extermination of the *Joyas*," *GLQ: A Journal of Lesbian and Gay Studies* 16, no. 1–2 (April 1, 2010): 256.

43 Miranda, "Extermination of the *Joyas*," 256.

44 María Lugones, "Gender and Universality in Colonial Methodology," *Critical Philosophy of Race* 8, no. 1–2 (January 1, 2020): 26.

45 Jules Gil-Peterson, "My Undead Name," *Legacy: A Journal of American Women Writers*, September 21, 2020, https://legacywomenwriters.org/2020/09/21/my-undead -name/ (emphasis original).

46 Melissa Pagán, "Les Indocumentadxs: The Coloniality of Gender, Complementarity, and Rethinking Border Being/s."

47 Alok Vaid-Menon, *Beyond the Gender Binary* (New York: Penguin Random House, 2020), 60.

48 I am indebted to Nichole Flores's discussion of dignity and solidarity in *The Aesthetics of Solidarity* and in personal conversations.

49 Gerhardt, "How Trans-Inclusive Feminism Is Compatible with Catholicism."

50 Pax Christi is an international Catholic peace organization known for its work to end the death penalty and nuclear arms. The US branch is known for its protests against School of the Americas. https://paxchristiusa.org/about/ our-history/ (accessed July 23, 2024); Call to Action is a progressive Catholic organization founded in 1976 "challenging Catholics to act for justice and build inclusive communities, https://www.cta-usa.org/whoweare (accessed July 23, 2024); Network is a group of Catholic sisters who voted to create a nationwide "network" of women religious who would engage in political activism at the federal level for social justice in 1971. Between 2012 and 2018 they arranged yearly "Nuns on the Bus" tours focused on political action around social justice issues, https://networklobby.org/nunsonthebus/ (accessed July 23, 2024).

References

"2023 Anti-Trans Legislation." *Trans Legislation Tracker*. https://translegislation.com/ bills/2023 (March 1, 2024).

Abelson, Miriam J. "Trans Men Engaging, Reforming, and Resisting Feminisms."
    TSQ: Transgender Studies Quarterly 3, no. 1–2 (2016): 15–21.
Amery, Fran. "'Gender Critical' Feminism as Biopolitical Project." *Sexualities* 0, no. 0
    (2024): 1–15.
Ben Hagai, Ella, and Lily House-Peters. "Susan Stryker on Solidarity: An Interview
    for the *Journal of Lesbian Studies*." *Journal of Lesbian Studies* 28, no. 1 (2024):
    189–204.
Burke, Kelsy. "'Identity Politics' and Transgender Equality." Public Religion Research
    Institute, 2023. https://www.prri.org/spotlight/identity-politics-and-transgender
    -equality/ (July 8, 2024).
Butler, Judith. *Who's Afraid of Gender?* New York: Farrar, Straus and Giroux, 2024.
Catholics for Choice. "Gender Equity." https://www.catholicsforchoice.org/issues/
    gender-equity/ (December 18, 2024).
Crary, David. "Rejection or Welcome: Transgender Catholics Encounter Both."
    ABC News, February 26, 2022. https://abcnews.go.com/US/wireStory/rejection
    -transgender-catholics-encounter-83128201.
Daly, Mary. *Beyond God the Father: Towards a Philosophy of Women's Liberation.*
    Boston: Beacon Press, 1973.
———. *Gyn/Ecology: The Metaethics of Radical Feminism.* Boston: Beacon Press,
    1990.
Davies, Norman. *Heart of Europe: The Past in Poland's Present.* Oxford: Oxford
    University Press, 2001.
Earles, Jennifer. "The 'Penis Police': Lesbian and Feminist Spaces, Trans Women, and
    the Maintenance of the Sex/Gender/Sexuality System." *Journal of Lesbian Studies,*
    23, no. 2 (2019): 243–56.
Eaton, Joshua. "Faith and Spirituality at Occupy Boston." Occupy Boston, 2011.
    https://www.occupyboston.org/2011/10/24/faith-spirituality-occupy-boston/.
Favale, Abigail. *The Genesis of Gender: A Christian Theory.* San Francisco, CA:
    Ignatius Press, 2022.
Flores, Nichole. *The Aesthetics of Solidarity: Our Lady of Guadalupe and American
    Democracy.* Washington, DC: Georgetown University Press, 2021.
Francis. *Dignitas Infinita* 2024.
———. *San Giovanni Paolo Magno.* 2020.
Gerhardt, Jessica. "How Trans-Inclusive Feminism Is Compatible with Catholicism."
    National Catholic Reporter, September 9, 2022. https://www.ncronline.org/opinion
    /guest-voices/how-trans-inclusive-feminism-compatible-catholicism.

Gil-Peterson, Jules. "My Undead Name." *Legacy: A Journal of American Women Writers*, September 21, 2020. https://legacywomenwriters.org/2020/09/21/my-undead-name/.

Grant, Jaime, Lisa Mottet, Justin Tanis, and D. Min. "Injustice at Every Turn: A Report of the National Transgender Discrimination Survey." National Center for Transgender Equality and National Gay and Lesbian Task Force, 2011. http://www.thetaskforce.org/downloads/reports/reports/ntds_full.pdf.

Hale, C. Jacob. "Consuming the Living, Dis(re)membering the Dead in the Butch/FTM Borderlands." *GLQ: A Journal of Lesbian and Gay Studies* 4 (1998): 311–28.

Higgins, Andrew. "Poles Tussle Over an Icon of Their Past, With an Eye on the Future." *New York Times*, July 28, 2021. https://www.nytimes.com/2021/07/28/world/europe/poland-solidarity-lech-walesa.html/.

hooks, bell. *Feminism Is for Everybody: Passionate Politics.* Cambridge, MA: South End Press, 2000.

Kelly, Siobhan. "Feminist Transphobia, Feminist Rhetoric: From Trans-Exclusive Radical Feminism to HB2." *Feminist Studies in Religion Blog*, August 30, 2016. http://www.fsrinc.org/feminist-transphobia-rhetoric/.

Kenney, Padraic. "Borders Breached: The Transnational in Eastern Europe since Solidarity." *Journal of Modern European History* 8, no. 2 (2010): 179–95.

Leidl, Jonathan. "'Trust Has Been Broken': After Trans Policy Fallout, Controversy Still Simmers at St. Mary's College." *National Catholic Register*, February 5, 2024. https://www.ncregister.com/news/trust-has-been-broken-after-trans-policy-fallout-controversy-still-simmers-at-st-mary-s-college.

Lorde, Audrey. *Sister Outsider: Essays and Speeches.* Berkeley, CA: Crossing, 1984.

Lugones, María. "Gender and Universality in Colonial Methodology." *Critical Philosophy of Race* 8, no. 1–2 (2020): 25–47.

———. "Methodological Notes toward a Decolonial Feminism." In *Decolonizing Epistemologies: Latina/o Theology and Philosophy.* New York: Fordham University Press, 2012.

Lyshaug, Brenda. "Solidarity without 'Sisterhood'? Feminism and the Ethics of Coalition Building." *Politics and Gender* 2, no. 1 (2006): 77–100.

Mares, Courtney. "Pope Francis: Gender Ideology Is 'One of the Most Dangerous Ideological Colonizations' Today." *Catholic News Agency*, March 11, 2023. https://www.catholicnewsagency.com/news/253845/pope-francis-gender-ideology-is-one-of-the-most-dangerous-ideological-colonizations-today.

McCaughan, Pat. "Via Crucis: No Walls Can Separate Us from God's Grace." Episcopal Diocese of Los Angeles, 2012. https://diocesela.org/uncategorized/via-crucis-no-walls-can-separate-us-from-gods-grace/#LeavingJesus.

Miranda, Deborah A. "Extermination of the *Joyas*." *GLQ: A Journal of Lesbian and Gay Studies* 16, no. 1–2 (2010): 253–84.

National Center for Transgender Equality. "Victory! Federal Government Modernizes Health Insurance." *Advancing Transgender Equality* Blog. https://transgenderequality.wordpress.com/2014/06/13/victory-federal-government-modernizes-health-insurance/. (accessed December 18, 2024).

"New York Times Sign On Letter." GLAAD, 2023. https://glaad.org/new-york-times-sign-on-letter-from-lgtbq-allied-leaders-and-organizations.

O'Neill, Terry. "Why Transphobia Is a Feminist Issue." *National Organization for Women*, 2014. https://now.org/blog/why-transphobia-is-a-feminist-issue/.

Pagán, Melissa. "Les Indocumentadxs: The Coloniality of Gender, Complementarity, and Rethinking Border Being/s." *Journal of Feminist Studies in Religion* 38, no. 1 (2022): 167–84.

Partridge, Cameron. "'Scotch-Taped Together': Anti-'Androgyny' Rhetoric, Transmisogyny, and the Transing of Religious Studies." *Journal of Feminist Studies in Religion* 34, no. 1 (2018): 68–75.

Paul, Pamela. "The Far Right and Far Left Agree on One Thing: Women Don't Count." *New York Times*, July 3, 2022. https://www.nytimes.com/2022/07/03/opinion/the-far-right-and-far-left-agree-on-one-thing-women-dont-count.html.

Raymond, Janice. *The Transsexual Empire: The Making of the She-Male.* Boston: Beacon Press, 1979.

Redfield, Elana, Kerith J. Conron, and Christy Mallory. "The Impact of 2024 Anti-Transgender Legislation on Youth." Williams Institute, UCLA School of Law, 2024. https://williamsinstitute.law.ucla.edu/publications/2024-anti-trans-legislation.

Romano, Aja. "Is J.K. Rowling Transphobic? Let's Let Her Speak for Herself." *Vox*, May 14, 2024. https://www.vox.com/culture/23622610/jk-rowling-transphobic-statements-timeline-history-controversy.

Schlumpf, Heidi. "Catholic Women's College Opens to Trans Students, Drawing Bishop's Rebuke." *National Catholic Reporter*, December 6, 2023. https://www.ncronline.org/news/catholic-womens-college-opens-trans-students-drawing-bishops-rebuke.

Serrano, Julie. *Excluded: Making Feminist and Queer Movements More Inclusive.* Berkeley, CA: Seal Press, 2013.

———. "On 'Male Socialization' and the 'Trans Masc Versus Trans Fem' Discourse™." *Medium*, November 28, 2023. https://juliaserano.medium.com

/on-male-socialization-and-the-trans-masc-versus-trans-fem-discourse -14bccb196a63.

———. *Sexed Up: How Society Sexualizes Us, and How We Can Fight Back.* Berkeley, CA: Seal Press, 2022.

Shrier, Abigail. "The Transgender War on Women." *Wall Street Journal*, March 26, 2019. https://www.wsj.com/articles/the-transgender-war-on-women -11553640683.

Strassfeld, Max. "Transing Religious Studies." *Journal of Feminist Studies in Religion* 34, no. 1 (2018): 37–53.

Stryker, Susan. *Transgender History: The Roots of Today's Revolution.* New York: Seal Press, 2017.

Szajkowski, Bogdan. *Next to God-Poland: Politics and Religion in Contemporary Poland.* London: F. Pinter, 1983.

Vaid-Menon, Alok. *Beyond the Gender Binary.* New York: Penguin Random House, 2020.

Walker, Becky. "Imagining the Future of Lesbian Community: The Case of Online Lesbian Communities and the Issue of Trans." *Journal of Media & Cultural Studies* 6 (2009): 921–35.

Williams, Cristan. "Radical Inclusion: Recounting the Trans Inclusive History of Radical Feminism." *TSQ: Transgender Studies Quarterly* 3, no. 1–2 (May 1, 2016): 254–58.

Women's Ordination Conference. https://www.womensordination.org (December 18, 2024).

Worthen, Meredith G. F. "This Is My TERF! Lesbian Feminists and the Stigmatization of Trans Women." *Sexuality and Culture*, 26 (2022): 1782–1803.

Conclusion

Shannon Dunn and Rosemary Kellison

Solidarity as a practice promises connection, political recognition, and collaboration on a common goal. We will highlight and briefly elaborate on three broad themes advanced by feminist solidarity ethics that are woven throughout the volume. First, solidarity is deeply connected to justice and the critical evaluation of unjust social structures. Second, solidarity takes a view of moral agents as socially inscribed subjects who are also characterized by the capacity for ethical freedom. Third, feminist ethicists account for the role that unjust suffering and historical grief play in political solidarity.

What kinds of relationships and practices constitute authentic expressions of political solidarity? In the womanist and feminist contributions to this volume, solidarity is fundamentally connected to justice. There is a shared sense that any meaningful movement toward justice must be collective and fundamentally relational, considering differences in power and social status. In many of these chapters, solidarity represents an expression of human relationality in politics, to be achieved through making visible differences of identity and experience while not allowing differences to forestall necessary conversations about justice.[1]

In *The Aesthetics of Solidarity*, Nichole Flores argues that solidarity rooted in and committed to justice is virtuous, distinguishing it from sociopolitical movements that perpetuate violence and oppression. One example of the latter is the "Unite the Right" rally in Charlottesville, Virginia, in 2017.[2] This instance highlights how the desire for social and political connection in the modern political sphere can result in the dangerous phenomenon of the mob. If alienation from others, or a kind of deep social unmooring, is an omnipresent threat to modern political life, the response of the Charlottesville protesters represents a vicious reaction to it. And yet their racist rants reveal an all-too-common reaction: a response to the pain of alienation by adopting in-group and out-group thinking and submitting to racist distortions of reality. False solidarity upholds the fiction of sameness, is not capable of addressing social inequality, and thwarts the enactment of justice.[3]

The next theme in feminist solidarity is a view of moral agents who are deeply shaped by historical and social contexts and yet capable of influencing, through their collective efforts, the development of social norms, and narratives. There is recognition that we are inheritors of a social system disordered by manifold injustices and bolstered by myths of individualism, white supremacy, and patriarchy. With this knowledge, many feminist religious ethicists approach religious traditions as resources for fighting against these injustices. For traditions to be useful in this regard, however, there must be a conscious decoupling of religious symbols and communities from narratives, ideals, and structures of domination. There must also be an awareness of our global interdependency,[4] which informs our approach to religious traditions. This work necessarily assumes a critical posture toward power, including that of the state and of religious institutions and actors. It also entails redirecting our attention to alternate narratives, rituals, and other collective actions that permit us to imagine, practice, and sustain solidarity. These chapters, through storytelling, analysis, and consciousness-raising, bring greater awareness to experiences that might be widely invisible due to structural injustices and shift our sense of what is possible.

Finally, working for political solidarity in feminist ethics requires confronting histories characterized by unresolved pain and suffering related to racism and other forms of structural injustices, such as colonialism, for which there are no simple resolutions. This history demands creative and responsible approaches to broken systems and relationships. Practices of solidarity may allow for the transformation of a marginalized group's unjust suffering, with the goal of the eventual eradication of suffering. Several chapters address how suffering can be sublimated into a powerful collective political response, often through public protest and other forms of activism. But we note that alienation persists, due to the legacies of modern capitalism and colonialism and the distortive effects of these systems on human relationships and institutions. Contemporary political life is replete with symbols and other markers of these exploitative systems. Even the democratic institutions we imbue with legitimacy are products of exploitation or have intertwined histories with slavery and colonialism. Thus, the status of these institutions and their meanings will be matters of public contestation. How do we relate to each other, and to these things, given this reality?

In *The Ethics of Tainted Legacies*, Karen Guth highlights how womanist thinking, particularly the work of Emilie Townes, Delores Williams, and Renita Weems, offers a necessary methodological intervention for dealing with contested symbols in the United States, such as Confederate statues.[5] Guth attends to the importance of truth-telling about violence involving structural racism and views contests over public symbols like statues as embedded in larger narratives of white supremacy. Indeed, addressing the past truthfully and conscientiously is a foundational part of political solidarity work, as it is in the repair of all relationships.

A central, if obvious, political danger that threatens the possibility of solidarity—including the foundational work of truth-telling—is the embrace of ideological purity and political polarization. As Hannah Arendt warns, we should be wary of absolutist political movements that require party loyalty over individual conscience.[6] The operating logic of such movements is to make people impermeable to experience and/or argument: "identification with the movement and total conformism seem to have destroyed the very capacity for experience."[7] Arendt's observation from the mid-twentieth century presents a picture of the intertwined perils of political alienation, the human predilection for falling prey to powerful interests, and the corresponding inability to listen to the experiences of others, as well as to acknowledge how our own experiences shape our understanding of the ethical-political world. She also illuminates our susceptibility to social pressures and false information, which is now intensified by the nature of communicating in online spaces (with their omnipresent reach), the confusion of news with entertainment content, the rapid growth of artificial intelligence, and the manipulation of information by internet trolls. Thus, the opportunities for engaging in solidarity work are plentiful, and arguably the work has never been more necessary. Feminist and womanist religious ethicists remind us of the importance of being in community and holding one another accountable for the words we speak and the actions we undertake, in the spirit of working toward a more just society.

Notes

1 This idea resonates with Jodi Dean's description of reflective solidarity. See Dean, *The Solidarity of Strangers: Feminism after Identity Politics* (Berkeley: University of California Press, 1996).

2 Nichole M. Flores, *The Aesthetics of Solidarity: Our Lady of Guadalupe and American Democracy* (Washington, DC: Georgetown University Press, 2021), 5.

3 According to Arendt, the logic of tribal nationalism "claims its people to be unique, individual, incompatible with all others, and denies theoretically the very possibility of a common mankind [sic] long before it is used to destroy the humanity of man [sic]." Hannah Arendt, *The Origins of Totalitarianism* (Cleveland, OH: World Publishing Company, 1958), 227.

4 See Judith Butler, *Frames of War: When Is Life Grievable?* (London: Verso, 2010), chap. 1.

5 Karen V. Guth, *The Ethics of Tainted Legacies: Human Flourishing after Traumatic Pasts* (Cambridge: Cambridge University, 2022).

6 Arendt, *The Origins of Totalitarianism*, 249.

7 Arendt, *The Origins of Totalitarianism*, 308.

References

Arendt, Hannah. *The Origins of Totalitarianism*. Cleveland, OH: World Publishing Company, 1958.

Butler, Judith. *Frames of War: When Is Life Grievable?* London: Verso, 2010.

Dean, Jodi. *The Solidarity of Strangers: Feminism after Identity Politics*. Berkeley: University of California Press, 1996.

Flores, Nichole M. *The Aesthetics of Solidarity: Our Lady of Guadalupe and American Democracy*. Washington, DC: Georgetown University Press, 2021.

Guth, Karen V. *The Ethics of Tainted Legacies: Human Flourishing after Traumatic Pasts*. Cambridge: Cambridge University Press, 2022.

Index

Jewishness, 246, 250, 252, 255, 260, 270

Jewish solidarity, with Palestine, 9–10

Jewish Voice for Peace, 189n1

Jews for Racial and Economic Justice (JFREJ), 175–77, 180, 187

Jim Crow, 121, 130

John Paul II (Pope), 281, 282, 301n32, 316

Johnson, Elizabeth, 311

Jordan, Candace, xiii

Jordan, June, 94

Jordan River, 259

Journal of Feminist Studies in Religion, 15

Journal of Religious Ethics, 14, 15

Judaism, 176–77, 187–88, 236, 245–48, 256–68; antisemitism, x, 226, 250, 251, 254; ethics, 246–47, 253, 254, 257, 267, 269–70; INN and, 249–54; Jewishness, 246, 250, 252, 255, 260, 270; Mishnaic, 264; Mizrahi, 246, 257–60, 262–65, 267; solidarity with Palestine, 9–10

"judicial coup," in Israel, 262

justice: *adalah*, 225, 235; criminal justice system, 127–28, 138; in family, 294–95; family founded on, 292–94; juvenile justice system, 133; legality compared to, 121; political solidarity and, 182; reproductive justice movement, xiii, 186–89, 200, 311; restorative, 138–40; shared commitment to, xii; social, 220; transformative, 140. *See also* injustice

justice-seeking, 295

just laws, 123

"just wars," 28n67

juvenile justice system, 133

Kaba, Mariame, 229, 233

Kamitsuka, Margaret, 16

karamah (dignity), 197

KARAMAH: Muslim Women Lawyers for Human Rights, 194, 201, 203, 209n8

karuna (compassion), 107

Kavanaugh, Brett, 158–60, 168n28

Kellison, Rosemary, xi, 94, 317

Kelly, Siobhan, 312

kemet, 293

Kennedy, Emma McDonald, xv

Kennedy School of Government, 248

Kertzer, David, 182

Khezri, Haidar, 151

khilafah (individual moral agency before God), 197, 206

King, Martin Luther, Jr., 120–23, 153

kinship, 49, 294, 319; biological, 280; spiritual, 285

Klee, Paul, 253

Kohlhaas, Jacob M., 286

Kusuma, Bhikkhunī, 73–74, 76

Kwok Pui-Lan, 47, 52n2

Laidlaw, James, 14

Lam, Raymond, 62

Lama, Alfred, 144n2

Laos, 70–71

larger community, alienation from, 157

Las Casas, Bartolomé de, 38–39

late capitalist modernity, 41

Latinx communities, 293

law: Abolition Womanism and, 120–23; just, 123; natural law theory, 52n12, 120, 121, 299n1; privilege and, 121; secular, 198–99; segregation, 121, 122–23; Shari'a, 135–36, 199, 205. *See also* Supreme Court; *specific laws*

lawbreaking, 119–20, 125–26, 134–36

LBGTQIA+, 166, 199, 200, 210n21, 261, 269, 298; Black lesbian feminists, 5, 15; gay men, 158; homophobia and, 93, 106, 288, 320; same-sex marriage, 287, 289, 297. *See also* trans people

"Learning from the Sixties" (Lorde), 101

legality: justice compared to, 121; morality compared to, 122

legal positivism, 122

Leitz, Lisa, 164

Leo XIII (Pope), 286

lesbians, Black feminist, 5, 15

Letter from a Birmingham Jail (King), 122–23

letter writing, 164

Levinas, Emmanuel, 46, 49

Levitt, Laura, 55n39

Lewis, Thomas, 13

liberal individualism, 46

liberalism, 44

About the Editors and Contributors

EDITORS

Shannon Dunn is department chair and professor of religious studies at Gonzaga University.

Rosemary Kellison, associate professor of religion at Florida State University, is the author of *Expanding Responsibility for the Just War: A Feminist Critique* (2019).

CONTRIBUTORS

Molly Farneth is associate professor in the Religion Department at Haverford College. She is the author of *Hegel's Social Ethics: Religion, Conflict, and Rituals of Reconciliation* (2017) and *The Politics of Ritual* (2023).

Juliane Hammer (she/her) is professor of religious studies at the University of North Carolina at Chapel Hill. She is the author of three monographs: *Peaceful Families: American Muslim Efforts against Domestic Violence* (2019); *American Muslim Women, Religious Authority, and Activism: More Than a Prayer* (2012), and *Palestinians Born in Exile: Diaspora and the Search for a Homeland* (2005).

Candace Jordan is an Advancing Future Faculty Diversity Postdoctoral Scholar in the Religion, Culture & Society Department at Lehigh University. Her current book project *The Beauty of Anger: Anger as Acknowledgement of Injustice* illuminates the epistemic and noninstrumental value of anger, especially as a resource for those suffering gender and racial oppression.

Emma McDonald Kennedy is assistant professor of Christian ethics at Villanova University. She recently published the article "Finding the Maternal Divine in Contextual Realities of Motherhood" in the *Journal of Feminist Studies in Religion* (2023).

Atalia Omer is a Religion, Conflict, and Peace Studies Professor at the Kroc Institute for International Peace Studies and the Keough School of Global Affairs at the University of Notre Dame. Omer was awarded an Andrew Carnegie Fellowship in 2017, resulting in *Decolonizing Religion and Peacebuilding* (2023). Omer is the author of *When Peace Is Not Enough: How the Israeli Peace Camp Thinks about Religion, Nationalism, and Justice* (2015) and *Days of Awe: Reimagining Jewishness in Solidarity with Palestinians* (2019).

Kori Pacyniak is a PhD candidate at the University of California, Riverside, and 2024 Charlotte W. Newcombe Dissertation Fellow. Their dissertation "Sacred Bodies, Sacred Lives: Trans Catholic Joy, Resistance, and Liberation" examines the lived religious experiences of transgender Catholics through ritual, ethics, and the construction of identity.

Darcie Price-Wallace is a Visiting Scholar at Northwestern University and part-time faculty at DePaul University and Loyola University in Chicago. She is currently working on a monograph about Tibetan Buddhist Nuns in India and finishing a translation of a Tibetan scholar's manuscript on issues concerning ordination for Tibetan Buddhist nuns. She has published articles in *Religions* and the *Journal of Global Buddhism*.

Nikia Smith Robert is assistant professor of Religious Ethics and Social Justice at the University of Kansas. She is also the Founder and Executive Director of Abolitionist Sanctuary. Her work can be found in the *Journal of the Society of Christian Ethics*.

Maria Tedesco is associate teaching professor of Islam at Seattle University. Her work has been published in the *Journal of Political Theology* and in edited collections.

Rima Vesely-Flad is the founding director of the Initiative for Black Buddhist Studies and a Visiting Fellow at Princeton University's Center for Culture, Society, and Religion. She is the author of *Black Buddhists and the Black Radical Tradition: The Practice of Stillness in the Movement for Liberation* (2022) and *Racial Purity and Dangerous Bodies: Moral Pollution, Black Lives, and the Struggle for Justice* (2017). She is currently at work on *The Fire Within: The Dharma of James Baldwin and Audre Lorde* (forthcoming).